STATE BUILDING

AND

MILITARY POWER

IN

RUSSIA

AND THE

NEW STATES OF EURASIA

THE INTERNATIONAL POLITICS OF EURASIA

Editors:
Karen Dawisha and Bruce Parrott

This ambitious ten-volume series develops a comprehensive analysis of the evolving world role of the post-Soviet successor states. Each volume considers a different factor influencing the relationship between internal politics and international relations in Russia and in the western and southern tiers of newly independent states. The contributors were chosen not only for their recognized expertise but also to ensure a stimulating diversity of perspectives and a dynamic mix of approaches.

THE INTERNATIONAL POLITICS OF EURASIA

Volume 5

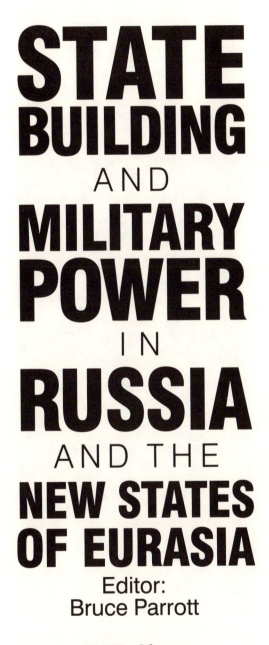

STATE BUILDING
AND
MILITARY
POWER
IN
RUSSIA
AND THE
NEW STATES
OF EURASIA

Editor:
Bruce Parrott

M.E. Sharpe
Armonk, New York
London, England

Library of Congress Cataloging-in-Publication Data

State building and military power in Russia and the new
states of Eurasia / edited by Bruce Parrott
p. cm.—(The International politics of Eurasia: v. 5)
"This book is an outgrowth of a conference jointly conducted by
the Russian Littoral Project, the Department of War Studies at
King's College, London, and the International Institute for
Strategic Studies"—CIP pref.
Includes bibliographical references and index.
ISBN 1-56324-360-1 (alk. paper).
ISBN 1-56324-361-X (pbk. : alk. paper).
1. Former Soviet republics—Politics and government.
2. National security—Former Soviet republics.
3. Former Soviet republics—Military policy.
I. Parrott, Bruce, 1945– . II. Series.
DK293.S73 1995
322′.5′0947—dc20   95-13179
CIP

Printed in the United States of America

Contents

About the Editors and Contributors

Karen Dawisha is professor of government at the University of Maryland, College Park. She graduated with degrees in Russian and politics from the University of Lancaster in England and received her Ph.D. from the London School of Economics. She has served as an advisor to the British House of Commons Foreign Affairs Committee and was a member of the policy planning staff of the U.S. State Department. She has received fellowships from the Rockefeller Foundation, the Council on Foreign Relations, and the MacArthur Foundation. She is a member of the Royal Institute of International Affairs and the Council on Foreign Relations. Her publications include *Russia and the New States of Eurasia: The Politics of Upheaval* (coauthored with Bruce Parrott, 1994), *Eastern Europe, Gorbachev, and Reform: The Great Challenge* (1989, 2d ed. 1990), *The Kremlin and the Prague Spring* (1984), *The Soviet Union in the Middle East: Politics and Perspectives* (1982), *Soviet–East European Dilemmas: Coercion, Competition, and Consent* (1981), and *Soviet Foreign Policy Toward Egypt* (1979).

Bruce Parrott is professor and director of Russian Area and East European Studies at The Johns Hopkins University School of Advanced International Studies, where he has taught for twenty years. He received his B.A. in religious studies from Pomona College in 1966, and his Ph.D. in political science in 1976 from Columbia University, where he was assistant director of the Russian Institute. His publications include *Russia and the New States of Eurasia: The Politics of Upheaval* (coauthored with Karen Dawisha, 1994), *The Dynamics of Soviet Defense Policy* (1990), *The Soviet Union and Ballistic Missile Defense* (1987), *Trade, Technology, and Soviet-American Relations* (1985), and *Politics and Technology in the Soviet Union* (1983).

Jonathan Aves is lecturer in twentieth-century Russian studies at Sussex University in England. Previously Dr. Aves was at the Centre for Defence Studies, King's College, in London. He received his Ph.D. in Russian history from the

School of Slavonic and East European Studies, University of London, in 1989. He is a frequent visitor to and writer on the Transcaucasus.

Bess A. Brown is researcher at the Radio Free Europe/Radio Liberty Research Institute in Munich. She received her M.A. and Ph.D. from Indiana University in Uralic and Altaic Studies, specializing in contemporary Central Asia and the development of national and ethnic consciousness in nineteenth-century Hungary. Dr. Brown has been writing on developments in Central Asia since 1979.

Julian Cooper is professor and chair of Russian Economic Studies, and director of the Centre for Russian and East European Studies at the University of Birmingham. He received his Ph.D. in 1975 from the University of Birmingham. Dr. Cooper's research has been focused on the former Soviet economy, industry, and science and technology policy. His most recent research is on the restructuring on the defense industrial base of Russia and the other former Soviet states.

Raymond L. Garthoff is senior fellow at the Brookings Institution and a retired U.S. Ambassador. A graduate of Princeton University, he holds a Ph.D. from Yale University. He is author of many works on Russian and Soviet political and military affairs and international security issues, including *The Great Transition: American-Soviet Relations at the End of the Cold War* (1994).

Elaine M. Holoboff is lecturer in the Department of War Studies, Kings College, and director of the department's Programme on Post-Communist Security Studies (PPCSS). She received her M.A. from York University in Toronto and her Ph.D. from King's College. Dr. Holoboff has written extensively on national security, military, peacekeeping, conflict zones, and energy issues in Russia and the former Soviet Union.

Major General Nicholas S. H. Krawciw is president of The Dupuy Institute and a consultant on matters pertaining to Ukraine in the Department for Defense of the United States. General Krawciw was advisor on defense matters to the Ukrainian Ministry of Defense in 1992 and 1993. Previously he was military assistant to the deputy secretary of defense and the executive officer to the supreme allied commander at SHAPE in NATO. Just prior to his retirement from the Army in 1990, General Krawciw was the director for NATO Policy in the International Security Policy Office of the secretary of defense in Washington.

Taras Kuzio is editor of *Ukraine Business Review*, research fellow at the Centre for Russian and East European Studies, University of Birmingham, consultant to the Ukraine Business Agency, and honorary research fellow at the School of Slavonic and East European Studies, University of London. He received his

M.A. in Soviet Studies from the University of London. Mr. Kuzio was previously a research associate at the International Institute for Strategic Studies.

Craig Nation is resident associate professor and coordinator of Russian Area and East European Studies at the Bologna Center of The Johns Hopkins University's School of Advanced International Studies. He received his Ph.D. in Soviet Studies and Contemporary History from Duke University. Dr. Nation previously taught at Duke University, Cornell University, and the University of Southern California.

Anatolii Rozanov is professor of international security studies in the Department of International Relations at Belarusian State University. He received his Candidate of History degree from Belarusian State University in 1982 and his Doctor of History in 1991 from the Academy of Sciences in Moscow. Dr. Rozanov was most recently a Fulbright Scholar at Tufts University. His major research interests include the new European security structure, Belarusian security policy, and strategic studies.

Tatiana Shakleina is senior researcher at the Institute of USA and Canada Studies in Moscow and assistant professor of Russian-American relations at the Russian State Humanities University. She received her Ph.D. in international relations and history in 1984 from the Institute of USA and Canada Studies. She has recently been involved in joint Russian-American projects on ethnic relations in the former Soviet Union. Dr. Shakleina is vice-chair of the association "Women in Global Security." Her research is devoted to Russian foreign policy, Russian-American relations, and ethnic conflicts.

Mikhail Tsypkin is associate professor in the Department of National Security Studies at the Naval Post-Graduate School in Monterey. He received his Ph.D. from Harvard University in 1985. Dr. Tsypkin is coordinator of Russian and Eurasian Studies in Monterey. Before joining the Naval Post-Graduate School in 1987, he was the Salvatori Fellow in Soviet Studies at The Heritage Foundation, and senior associate scholar at the National Institute for Public Policy.

Preface

This book is the fifth in a projected series of ten volumes produced by the Russian Littoral Project, which is sponsored jointly by the University of Maryland at College Park and the Paul H. Nitze School of Advanced International Studies of The Johns Hopkins University. As directors of the project, we share the conviction that the transformation of the former Soviet republics into independent states demands systematic analysis of the determinants of the domestic and foreign policies of the new countries. This series of volumes is intended to provide a basis for comprehensive scholarly study of these issues.

The collapse of the Soviet Union has demolished the international political order of the past half-century and created a host of new states whose security policies must be devised even as their political and national structures are being built. This book analyzes the interplay between state-building and military power in the post-Soviet states. Focusing on conventional military forces, this volume aims to clarify the diverse influences shaping conceptions of national security and military policies in each country. These influences include, inter alia, shifting national identities, political and economic upheaval, and a volatile external environment. Like the Russian Littoral Project as a whole, this book aims to avoid an excessive preoccupation with Russia by paying close attention to political-military developments in the other post-Soviet states as well as in Russia.

This book is an outgrowth of a conference jointly conducted by the Russian Littoral Project, the Department of War Studies at King's College, London, and the International Institute for Strategic Studies. We owe a special debt of gratitude to Lawrence Freedman of King's College and to Gerald Segal of IISS for their intellectual contributions to the conference and their willingness to cosponsor the enterprise.

We wish to thank the contributors to this volume for their help in making this phase of the Russian Littoral Project a success and for revising their papers in a timely fashion. We are also grateful to the numerous conference discussants—

particularly Roy Allison—whose comments and suggestions substantially improved the quality of the final papers. Special thanks are due to Janine Ludlam and Florence Rotz for their skillful handling of the preconference logistics and their unstinting labor on the book manuscript. We also wish to express our appreciation to Fiona Paton and Kjetil Ribe for their able support in administering the conference, and to Michael Turner and Stephen Guenther, who provided essential assistance in the preparation of the final manuscript.

The Russian Littoral Project

The objective of the Russian Littoral Project is to foster an exchange of research and information in fields of study pertaining to the international politics of Eurasia. The internal development and external relations of the new states are being studied in a series of workshops taking place in Washington, DC, London, Odessa, and other locations between 1993 and 1996. Scholars from the new states, North America, and Europe are invited to present papers at the workshops.

Focusing on the interaction between the internal affairs and the foreign relations of the new states, the project workshops examine the impact of the following factors: history, national identity and ethnicity, religion, political culture and civil society, economics, foreign policy priorities and decision making, military issues, and the nuclear question. Each of these topics is examined in a set of three workshops focusing in turn on Russia, the western belt of new states extending from Estonia to Ukraine, and the southern tier of new states extending from Georgia to Kyrgyzstan.

The Russian Littoral Project could not have been launched without the generous and timely contributions of the project's Coordinating Committee. We wish to thank the committee members for providing invaluable advice and expertise concerning the organization and intellectual substance of the project. The members of the Coordinating Committee are Dr. Adeed Dawisha (George Mason University); Dr. Bartek Kaminski (University of Maryland and the World Bank); Dr. Catherine Kelleher (The Brookings Institution); Ms. Judith Kipper (The Brookings Institution); Dr. Nancy Lubin (Carnegie Mellon University); Dr. Michael Mandelbaum (The School of Advanced International Studies); Dr. James Millar (The George Washington University); Dr. Peter Murrell (University of Maryland); Dr. Martha Brill Olcott (Colgate University); Dr. Ilya Prizel (The School of Advanced International Studies); Dr. George Quester (University of Maryland); Dr. Alvin Z. Rubinstein (University of Pennsylvania); Dr. Blair Ruble (The Kennan Institute); Dr. S. Frederick Starr (The Aspen Institute); Dr. Roman Szporluk (Harvard University); and Dr. Vladimir Tismaneanu (University of Maryland).

We are grateful to the John D. and Catherine T. MacArthur Foundation and the Ford Foundation for funding the conference from which this book is derived; we are especially grateful to Kennette Benedict of the MacArthur Foundation for her firm support of the whole project from the beginning, and to Geoffrey Wiseman of the Ford Foundation.

We also wish to thank President William Kirwan of the University of Maryland at College Park and President William C. Richardson of The Johns Hopkins University, who have given indispensable support to the project. Thanks are also due to Dean Irwin Goldstein, Associate Dean Stewart Edelstein, Director of the Office of International Affairs Marcus Franda, and Department of Government and Politics Chair Jonathan Wilkenfeld at the University of Maryland at College Park; to Provost Joseph Cooper and Vice-Provost for Academic Planning and Budget Stephen M. McClain at The Johns Hopkins University; to Professor George Packard, who helped launch the project during his final year as dean of the School of Advanced International Studies, to SAIS Dean Paul D. Wolfowitz, and to SAIS Associate Dean of Academic Affairs Stephen Szabo.

Finally, we are grateful for the guidance and encouragement given by Patricia Kolb at M.E. Sharpe, Inc. Her faith in the idea of the project and in the publication series has been crucial to the success of the whole endeavor.

Karen Dawisha
University of Maryland
at College Park

Bruce Parrott
The Johns Hopkins University
School of Advanced International Studies

STATE
BUILDING
AND
MILITARY
POWER
IN
RUSSIA
AND THE
NEW STATES
OF EURASIA

1

Introduction

Bruce Parrott

The collapse of the Soviet Union has demolished the international political order of the past half-century and set in motion a global transformation whose long-term consequences are impossible to foretell. In the absence of a general war, one of the two geopolitical pillars of the international system has disintegrated into a host of new states. This upheaval, which has few if any parallels in twentieth-century history, has not only posed perplexing security dilemmas for the emerging post-Soviet governments but has also called into question the security policies of most of the world's major states. No longer is the international system dominated by two superpowers methodically pursuing goals and interests rooted in long-standing state structures and national traditions. A global system characterized by a large degree of stability—whatever its moral consequences—has dissolved into a fluid network of international alignments determined more often by shifting domestic political and economic tides than by larger geopolitical calculations.

This sweeping transformation requires fresh approaches to the study of military affairs in the lands of the former USSR. Due both to philosophical preconceptions and to the sheer intellectual difficulty of proceeding in any other fashion, many past Western studies of Soviet military policy were framed in rather narrow terms that took the domestic sociopolitical context of military policy making for granted.[1] However, this approach, always of doubtful validity, became increasingly untenable in the Gorbachev period and manifestly impossible after the disintegration of the USSR into fifteen independent states. Cohesive military institutions and fully developed military policies can exist only in a polity characterized by a substantial measure of agreement on the nation's vital interests and a solidly grounded state structure for promoting and protecting those interests. Yet neither of these general preconditions for normal military institutions and military policy making is present in Russia and the other new states of Eurasia.

Specialists on the former USSR thus find themselves in a situation bearing a certain resemblance to that of natural scientists facing revolutionary discoveries. In periods of unusual theoretical ferment and anomalous research findings, scientists are compelled to abandon the established paradigms of "normal science" in favor of fundamentally new paradigms generated by "revolutionary science."[2] Of course, this analogy is imperfect. Social scientists cannot reasonably aspire to build models of reality as rigorous as those devised by natural scientists, and the Soviet implosion has forced analysts of post-Soviet developments (unlike natural scientists adjusting to revolutionary discoveries) to abandon old paradigms before creating any adequate substitutes.[3] But the parallel is apt in one respect. The unprecedented upheaval in the lands of the former USSR requires students of post-Soviet military affairs to take account of a dizzying array of political and socioeconomic forces that previous analysts seldom felt obliged to incorporate into their field of view.

Regarded from a military standpoint, the post-Soviet period differs from the Soviet era in at least five fundamental ways. First, standard usage notwithstanding, fully institutionalized states do not yet exist in the territories of the former Soviet republics. The societies that have emerged from the wreckage of the Soviet system are states in name, but in fact they have just begun a protracted process of state-building. Although the challenge of building a durable new state is far more severe in some of the former republics than in others, none of the post-Soviet countries possesses a firmly established and time-tested political structure. Second, few if any of these countries have achieved a working consensus on the essential meaning of national security, both because of the fluidity of the external environment and because they are engaged in a difficult process of nation-building. Reaching basic agreement on national interests and security requirements is exceptionally difficult when the definition of the "nation" itself remains an object of vigorous public controversy and many citizens are living through a wrenching socioeconomic transition.[4] Third, the collapse of Moscow's dominion has transformed the territory of the former USSR into a new military-diplomatic arena. Relations between the new states in this arena and the established states beyond the boundaries of the former USSR have only begun to crystallize, and their strategic implications remain uncertain. Fourth, the demise of the Soviet "outer" empire in Eastern Europe and the "inner" empire of the non-Russian republics has generated strong centrifugal forces inside the North Atlantic and Pacific alliances, whose basic raison d'être was to contain Soviet military power. Finally, the problematic prospects of the Asian countries that still call themselves communist—particularly China, whose extraordinary economic dynamism serves only to underscore uncertainties about its future political structure and international role—cloud the picture further.

This book, one of a series published under the auspices of the Russian Littoral Project, aims to clarify the diverse forces shaping conceptions of national security and military policies in the post-Soviet states.* The focus is on conventional military forces; the nuclear aspects of post-Soviet security policies are treated in a companion volume.[5] Like the Russian Littoral Project as a whole, this book aims to avoid a "metrocentric" preoccupation with Russia by paying close attention to developments within the other new states located on the former Soviet "periphery."[6] Although the course of military and security policy in Russia is vitally important to the future of all the post-Soviet states, the events unfolding inside the former USSR cannot be adequately understood by examining them through Russia's eyes alone. It is equally important to scrutinize the security concerns and military policies of the other new states, both to understand their behavior and, in some instances, to grasp the real range of options available to Moscow in dealing with these countries. Hence, the following chapters examine security issues and policies not only in Russia but in the western belt of countries reaching from Estonia to Ukraine and the southern tier of countries extending from Georgia to Kyrgyzstan. This approach assumes that quite different military policies and patterns may emerge in particular post-Soviet states. For each non-Russian country these patterns are likely to depend not only on relations with Russia but on the country's internal dynamics and its relations with other states, including states outside the former USSR.

The flood of change since the late 1980s has posed a complex array of interrelated security issues for the leaders and citizens of each of the post-Soviet states. One challenge, entwined with debates over national identity, has been to conceptualize the country's national interests and rank the potential threats to those interests. The collapse of the old international system has created deep uncertainty about which other countries, if any, constitute significant security threats to the new governments. Even in cases where potential foreign threats can be identified, the unsettled nature of regional alignments and the erratic internal politics of other post-Soviet states have impeded the identification of potential allies—a matter scarcely less essential for prudent military planning than the correct diagnosis of threats, especially in periods of economic stringency. In many cases, efforts to devise effective security policies have also been shaped by a widespread sense that the country is threatened at least as much from within as from without. The analysis of debates over national interests and security threats figures prominently in the chapters by Mikhail Tsypkin, Tatiana Shakleina, Nicholas Krawciw, Taras Kuzio, and Elaine Holoboff. In examining these de-

---

*In this book, the term "post-Soviet states" is generally used to describe all fifteen former Soviet republics. From a legal standpoint, this term is more accurate than the term "Soviet successor states," which also has entered current usage, although the latter designation has much to commend it from a sociopolitical and economic standpoint. In the twilight of the Soviet era, the democratically elected governments of Estonia, Latvia, and Lithuania rejected the legality of their original annexation by Moscow, and the Soviet government recognized the independence of these countries a few months before the dissolution of the USSR.

bates, a number of the contributors explore various currents of opinion among national elites, along with the effects on security policy of differences between elite and mass attitudes.

A second challenge to the new states has been to determine an appropriate policy toward the Soviet conventional military forces situated on their territory at the time of the USSR's collapse. National leaders have had to decide whether these forces constitute a valuable asset that should be appropriated and used to counter potential security threats, or whether the forces themselves pose a major risk to the new state's security and should therefore be removed from the country or demobilized. In weighing these choices, the government of each new state has had to take account of its country's historical experience and national sentiments, as well as the post-independence situation inside and outside the country. Political leaders' decisions about these matters have had a major impact on their country's military potential, its sense of identity, and, in a number of cases, the evolution of the domestic political system. Raymond Garthoff's chapter provides an overview of the institutional fate of the various geographical components of the Soviet military establishment; the chapters by Taras Kuzio, Elaine Holoboff, Bess Brown, and Jonathan Aves illustrate the divergent outcomes that have occurred under varying national circumstances.

A third challenge has been to reconcile the ordinary requirements of security policy with the internal socioeconomic turmoil exacerbated by the Soviet breakup. Policy makers have often faced hard choices between ensuring a modicum of military-technical preparedness and shoring up their state's shaky domestic foundations. Calculations of military-technical preparedness have generally indicated a need to acquire new weapons, provide regular training and maintenance for the armed forces, and, in some instances, carry out costly military redeployments. Considerations of political stability, however, have counseled that military budgets should be slashed and that the lion's share of the remainder should be devoted to the material needs of restive officers and servicemen. Given these contradictory pressures, the authors of several chapters inquire whether the post-Soviet governments have managed to develop coherent military policies and whether these policies mesh with the actual military capabilities at the disposal of the state. This theme figures in the chapters of, inter alia, Raymond Garthoff, Julian Cooper, Nicholas Krawciw, and Anatolii Rozanov.

A fourth challenge to post-Soviet policy makers has been to maintain control of national military forces in the midst of internal upheavals that virtually invite military intervention in domestic politics. No less than other institutional survivors of the Soviet era, professional military forces have been buffeted by intense socioeconomic pressures and rent by deep internal tensions. In a number of countries, these forces have become important political actors able to destabilize or overthrow the new political regime, whether or not that regime has a democratic cast. Drastic cutbacks in military budgets and personnel, often coupled with controversies over the proper ethnic composition of the officer corps, have made civil-military relations a highly sensitive issue. A related matter concerns the impact of defense industrialists on domestic reform and security policy making. Civil-military relations have become especially volatile in those countries where elements of the professional military have become allied with contending civilian factions or where paramilitary groups have sprung up entirely outside the formal military chain of command. These issues receive close attention from Tsypkin, Cooper, Kuzio, and Aves.

A fifth challenge for policy makers and citizens in the new states has been to formulate effective security and military policies toward other countries. For Russia this has meant evaluating the relative geopolitical importance of the new countries of the so-called near abroad in comparison with major powers located outside the boundaries of the former USSR. Russian policy makers also have had to decide whether any of the post-Soviet states present a significant threat to their country's security and geographical integrity—or, alternatively, whether any of them present an attractive opportunity for the expansion of Russian influence or the reestablishment of Moscow's imperial control. Not least, Russian policymakers have had to consider the potential interaction between Russia's relations with the other new states and its relations with such major powers as the United States, Germany, and China. These topics are treated by several of the contributors, including Tsypkin, Garthoff, and Shakleina.

For their part, the non-Russian states have had to decide what mix of military competition and cooperation vis-à-vis Russia best serves their national interests and security needs. This decision has been colored not only by perceptions of Russia but by perceptions of other regional threats to the particular country's security. For each new state, the choice of policy toward Russia has been linked to the parallel issue of whether the country's security can be enhanced through cooperative military relationships with other governments. Although the candidates for such relationships include other post-Soviet states besides Russia, the principal focus of attention and decision has been the major powers outside the former USSR—above all, the members of NATO. Several chapters, particularly those by Holoboff, Krawciw, and Rozanov, touch on how the new states have addressed this issue.

The final part of this book sets military developments in the post-Soviet states in a broader interpretive context. The chapter by Craig Nation assesses the evolution of Western responses to the emergence of a new constellation of military forces in Eurasia. Nation also identifies the main Western responses that have been advocated and discusses the strengths and weaknesses of each approach. In the final chapter, I attempt to synthesize the book's empirical findings and discuss the question of whether Russia has embarked on a policy of neoimperialism. In the process, I also propose some indicators to help future observers sort out the prevailing trends in post-Soviet military affairs. Here, as elsewhere in the book, some policy judgments are offered, but the main emphasis is on analyzing events and identifying trends. In the current state of flux, wise Western policies presuppose a nuanced understanding of the complex realities with which policy makers must deal. The contributors to this book have concentrated on clarifying these realities.

Notes

1. This tendency paralleled the outlook of the dominant realist tradition in international relations theory. For a discussion of the theoretical issues, see Richard Rosecrance and Arthur A. Stein, "Beyond Realism: The Study of Grand Strategy," in *The Domestic Bases of Grand Strategy*, eds. Richard Rosecrance and Arthur A. Stein (Ithaca, NY: Cornell University Press, 1993), pp. 3–21. See also Matthew Evangelista, "Internal and External Constraints on Grand Strategy: The Soviet Case," in ibid., pp. 154–78; and Bruce Parrott, "The Soviet System, Military Power, and Diplomacy: From Brezhnev to Gorbachev," in *The Dynamics of Soviet Defense Policy*, ed. Bruce Parrott (Washington, DC: Wilson Center Press, 1990), pp. 7–40. Soviet civil-military relations became the subject of a substantial literature, but for the most part these works were not closely connected with the analysis of Soviet external policy. See, for example, Roman Kolkowicz, *The Soviet Military and the Communist Party* (Princeton: Princeton University Press, 1967); Timothy J. Colton, *Commissars, Commanders, and Civilian Authority: The Structure of Soviet Military Politics* (Cambridge, MA: Harvard University Press, 1979); and Timothy J. Colton and Thane Gustafson, eds., *Soldiers and the Soviet State: Civil-Military Relations from Brezhnev to Gorbachev* (Princeton: Princeton University Press, 1990).

2. See Thomas Kuhn, *The Structure of Scientific Revolutions* (Chicago: University of Chicago Press, 1962).

3. It is worth noting that the prevailing paradigms in Soviet studies were always the subject of considerable disagreement among scholars. This fact has been neglected in much of the post-1991 controversy over the intellectual lessons to be drawn from the Soviet collapse. For two unusually perceptive discussions of these issues, see George Breslauer, "In Defense of Sovietology," *Post-Soviet Affairs*, vol. 8, no. 3 (July–September 1992), pp. 197–238, and Raj Menon, "Post Mortem: The Causes and Consequences of the Soviet Collapse," *The Harriman Review*, vol. 7, nos. 10–12 (19 November 1994), pp. 1–10. See also "The Strange Death of Soviet Communism: An Autopsy," *The National Interest*, special issue, no. 31 (spring 1993).

4. See Roman Szporluk, ed., *National Identity and Ethnicity in Russia and the New States of Eurasia* (Armonk, NY: M.E. Sharpe, 1994); and Karen Dawisha and Adeed Dawisha, eds., *The Making of Foreign Policy Priorities in Russia and the New States of Eurasia* (Armonk, NY: M.E. Sharpe, 1995).

5. *The Nuclear Challenge in Russia and the New States of Eurasia*, George Quester, ed. (Armonk, NY: M.E. Sharpe, forthcoming).

6. For an illuminating discussion of the analytical limitations of the metrocentric approach in the study of empires, see Michael Doyle, *Empires* (Ithaca, NY: Cornell University Press, 1986).

I

State-Building and
Military Power in Russia

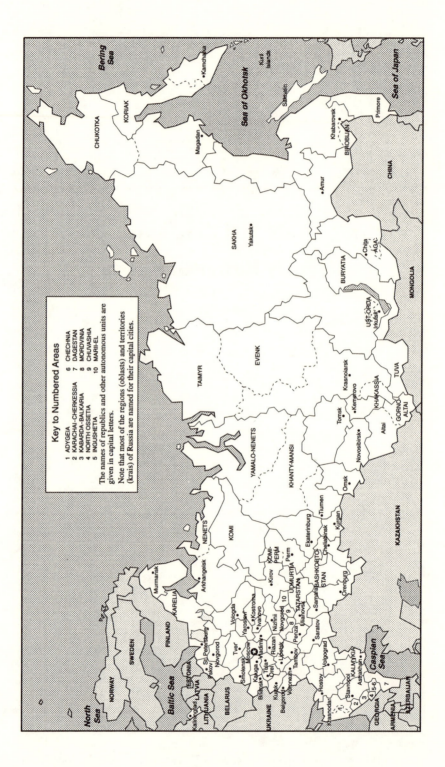

Key to Numbered Areas

1	ADYGEIA	6	CHECHNIA
2	KARACHAI-CHERKESSIA	7	DAGESTAN
3	KABARDA-BALKARIA	8	MORDVINIA
4	NORTH OSSETIA	9	CHUVASHIA
5	INGUSHETIA	10	MARII-EL

The names of republics and other autonomous units are given in capital letters.

Note that most of the regions (oblasts) and territories (krais) of Russia are named for their capital cities.

2

The Politics of Russian Security Policy

Mikhail Tsypkin

Sergei Yushenkov, the chairman of the Committee on Defense in the State Duma, expressed his hope soon after the Duma was convened in January 1994 that the work of his committee would not be marred by political differences, because Russian security matters are too important to become "excessively politicized."[1] Reaching a significant and lasting political consensus over national security policy[2] is difficult even for an exceptionally well institutionalized two-party democracy like the United States. Today's Russia has difficulty developing and implementing a policy in any area without bitter political rancor. Can Russia's security policy be an exception?

Barely one year after the disintegration of the Soviet Union, Western analysts began to speak about a shift of Russian national security policy toward greater assertiveness, and even imperial designs on the former Soviet republics, buttressed by a new willingness to use military force throughout the non-Russian periphery of the former Soviet empire.[3] Russian observers also agreed that, already by the end of 1992, Russian security policy had begun to shift decisively from a preoccupation with cooperation with the West toward pursuit of a Russian agenda along its periphery.[4] In the spring and fall of 1993, President Boris Yeltsin adopted an "assertive" foreign policy concept and a military doctrine that appeared to define Russia's periphery not only as the zone of Russian vital national interests but also as the possible area for Russian unilateral military interventions.[5] The electoral success of communists (who advocate, at least verbally, the restoration of the USSR) and Vladimir Zhirinovsky's misnamed Liberal Democratic Party (which skillfully played the card of Russian imperial nationalism) and the Kremlin's subsequent turn toward a national security policy that appeared to incorporate at least some of Yeltsin's antireformist opponents' views have left Western and even some Russian observers seriously concerned. Zbigniew Brzezinski spoke about the new "ominous" military doctrine "establishing a preponderant security interest" throughout the former Soviet empire.[6]

The *New York Times* warned against the danger of Russian "democrats" succumbing to the imperialist temptation, while its correspondent in Moscow wrote
about a growing "nostalgia for the Soviet empire."[7] A Moscow-based centrist-
liberal public organization, the Council on Defense and Foreign Policy, while
approving the new, more "realist" security policy for Russia, warned in May
1994 about Russia's growing hubris regarding the Kremlin's ability to dominate
the former Soviet republics.[8]

Thus the new national security policy appears to have done away with the
reliance (in the spirit of the "new thinking") on multilateral international organizations in favor of a Russian unilateral approach in providing security. The
search for security has currently focused on the weak (compared to Russia)
former Soviet republics and former Soviet satellites in Eastern Europe.[9] Among
Russia's goals in the region are the exclusion of other powers (for example,
preventing the "enlargement" of NATO into East-Central Europe); the assertion
of Russia's strategic interests (such as control over the early-warning radar facilities in the former Soviet republics); and the prevention of threats to Russian
security arising from the former Soviet republics (for instance, ensuring that
Ukraine does not become a nuclear power or that fighting in Transcaucasia does
not flood Russia with refugees). The means to implement this security policy
appear to include military, economic, and diplomatic instruments, all areas in
which Russia is superior to its neighbors. Military and diplomatic instruments
were used in Georgia, where Russia discreetly threw its military support behind
the Abkhazian separatists, then, after making a deal with Georgia's leader
Eduard Shevardnadze on creating Russian military bases in Georgia, began to
give military support to Tbilisi, and finally negotiated itself into the role of
peacekeeper. Diplomatic and economic instruments have been used vis-à-vis
Ukraine: Russia diplomatically isolated Ukraine over the issue of nuclear weapons, while demonstrating Ukraine's dependence on Russian energy supplies.

Is there a consensus about Russian national security among the Russian elites
and the public? As one analyst put it, "Some observers believe that a muscular
foreign and defense policy in the 'near abroad' is now embraced by Russia's
entire political spectrum, from Vladimir Zhirinovsky to Foreign Minister Andrei
Kozyrev."[10] This new consensus is often attributed to the emergence of Russian
nationalism as the ideology most appealing to the major sectors of Russian
society, an ideology inevitably gravitating toward imperialism.[11] Others see the
new security policy as a product of the reformist forces' defeat. According to this
interpretation, lacking a concept of Russian national interests, the Foreign Ministry under Andrei Kozyrev caved in to the pressure of a military eager to establish
Russian dominance in the "near abroad," and President Yeltsin has to tread a
"precarious line" in Russian security policy in order to "accommodate the
change in the mood in some sectors of the Russian population."[12] The first
interpretation implies that consensus is a long-term phenomenon, because it is
driven by some innate characteristic of the Russian polity (such as the allegedly

imperial character of Russian nationalism). The second interpretation implies that, on the contrary, the current security policy masks serious political conflicts, and therefore can be a temporary phenomenon.

If consensus over security policy has indeed been achieved in Russia, it must be rooted in a certain degree of institutional cohesion. Government institutions should have a clear division of powers regarding security policy. When dealing with security policy, these institutions should be able and inclined to address the substance of such policy issues, in addition to using the policy process as an instrument to compete for political turf. The institutions involved in security policy making should be reasonably cohesive internally. The elites should have well-developed interests in national security. The policy process leading to a consensual policy should be informed by a set of ideas regarding the means and ends of national security policy that do not fundamentally contradict each other. Last, but not least, public opinion should support not only the general ends of a national security policy but also the specific means required to implement it.

Thus, this chapter will address the politics[13] of Russian security policy. The political process in today's Russia is highly complex and volatile and reflects the interaction of nascent and highly diversified political actors: political parties, economic pressure groups, government bureaucracies, regional interests, and so forth.[14] I will discuss only the most important actors with influence over security policy, the institutional arrangements associated with these actors, the most widely accepted ideological influences these actors are exposed to, and public opinion regarding national security.

The Soviet Heritage

The Soviet heritage of security policy making (which includes elements of the prerevolutionary Russian heritage preserved and magnified by the Soviet regime) has been well studied in the West, although, in the absence of thorough archival research, it is not yet equally well understood. Russian studies of the subject have been similarly handicapped and additionally hampered by the understandable concentration of Russian scholars on current policy. Nevertheless, we can speak quite confidently of several fundamental characteristics of Soviet security policy making.

The Soviet institutional heritage included strict centralization, domination by civilian politicians over the military, and a tendency toward bureaucratic conflict. Various analysts in the past described the state of civil-military relations in the Soviet Union as either adversarial control of the military by the Communist Party,[15] cooperation between Communist functionaries and soldiers,[16] or a relationship blending cooperative and adversarial elements.[17] Former Soviet General Secretary and President Mikhail Gorbachev's ability to introduce policies highly unpopular among the military (arms control agreements, unilateral troop reductions, and withdrawal from Eastern Europe) indicates that the Communist Party leadership indeed had the power to dominate the military. Possessing such power was not synonymous with actually using it. Leonid Brezhnev's regime, for instance, with its tendency "to chart a middle course between divergent views and interests,"[18] preferred to accommodate the military in matters pertaining to defense policy, the latter constituting "the formulation and implementation of adequate measures for protection against foreign enemies."[19] The military's influence on defense policy was strengthened by its monopoly on expertise in security issues, a monopoly it shared only with the military-industrial complex. During the Brezhnev era, attempts to create a cadre of academic specialists in national security were halfhearted at best.[20] But, during Mikhail Gorbachev's years in power, this monopoly was broken by civilian analysts from the "think tanks" of the Academy of Sciences, whose recommendations had considerable weight during the heyday of the "new thinking."

The Soviet military appears to have had little or no influence in matters concerning societal issues (economic, technological, and sociocultural issues "loosely related to military security"), and certainly at no point did it contest the sovereign power in an attempt to displace the ruling civilian politicians.[21] The Communist Party dominated security policy making due to its unquestioned control of economic resources and personnel matters. This, however, did not prevent fierce bureaucratic conflict over various aspects of security policy. Such conflicts did not necessarily involve controversies among various branches of the bureaucracy (e.g., the military against the Ministry of Foreign Affairs), but in some cases they pitted individual branches of an agency against each other. For instance, the conflict over the decision of whether to build aircraft carriers created conflicts within the military establishment as a whole, as well as within the Soviet navy itself.[22] The Soviet military and the defense industry were traditionally prone to conflict.[23] The tense relations between the defense industry and the military were best exemplified by the acrimonious debate between the shipbuilders and the navy over blame for the MIKE submarine disaster in 1990.[24]

The Communist Party was able to exercise such a centralized authority due also to its ability to impose a rigid all-encompassing ideological framework on any security policy debate. This ideology postulated, in a deterministic fashion, the necessity of international conflict on a global scale, named the opposing sides, and predicted the outcome of this zero-sum game. Such an ideology provided for considerable harmony in civil-military relations; the civilian politicians' insistence on a security policy predicated on a fatalistic anticipation of global confrontation practically guaranteed extravagantly large defense spending, extraordinary secrecy enveloping the activities of the military, especially its high command, and considerable privileges for the officer corps.

Institutions and Elites

Executive and Legislative Branches

Security policy making in Russia is fragmented today both vertically and horizontally. Vertically, there are two major independent policy-making actors: the executive branch, headed by the president, and the legislative branch (the Federal Assembly, which consists of the upper chamber, the Federation Council, and the lower chamber, the State Duma). The executive-legislative relationship has been riddled with conflict; such conflicts are supposed to be regulated by the Constitutional Court (newly established after the new constitution was adopted in December 1993). Given the traditional lack of an impartial judiciary in Russian-Soviet tradition, it is likely that in a crisis any Constitutional Court will quickly abandon the neutral refereeing process in favor of political interference, something it did quite blatantly during the confrontation between the president and the legislature in October 1993. A new draft law on the Constitutional Court, adopted by the State Duma, weakens the Constitutional Court by, among other things, increasing the number of judges, shortening their terms of service, and making them subject to dismissal.[25] It is doubtful, however, that simply weakening the new Constitutional Court will by itself significantly harmonize the two branches of government.

The letter of the constitution and the reality of policy making can be strikingly far apart. Before the September 1993 dissolution of the Supreme Soviet, President Yeltsin's powers, including those in security policy, vis-à-vis the legislature were quite limited, but he was prepared to confront the Supreme Soviet head-on. The new constitution, custom-tailored for Yeltsin, gives him very considerable powers, including those in security policy. The president, according to the constitution, is the commander in chief of the armed forces and can hire and fire government ministers (the minister of defense included) without the parliament's agreement; the president, on his own, promotes high-ranking officers, appoints members of the Security Council and serves as its head, approves military doctrine, and introduces martial law (with a notification to the legislature). In contrast, the legislature's powers in this sphere are quite limited; the Federation Council can vote on the introduction of martial law and on the use of Russian troops outside Russia, while the Federal Assembly as a whole controls the budget.[26]

Inexperience in writing constitutional documents may have created a future loophole for parliamentary opponents of the president's security policy. According to the constitution, the president "determines the main directions of the domestic and foreign policies of the state in accordance with the constitution and federal laws."[27] The State Duma has already approved a draft law requiring Russia not to take part in the international sanctions against the rump Yugoslavia, a step against Yeltsin's policy. The opposition hopes that once the draft becomes law, Yeltsin would face the choice of either complying or being accused of violating the constitution. Even if adopted, however, the law has to survive a vote of the Federation Council, where pro-Serbian sympathies have so far been less pronounced than in the Duma, and then face the possibility of a presidential veto.[28]

After the double shock of the October 1993 fighting in Moscow and Yeltsin's supporters' poor showing in the December 1993 elections, the president, despite his very considerable formal powers, is demonstrating caution in dealing with the legislature, including in matters of security policy. After complaints about the planned joint Russian-American peacekeeping exercise, Yeltsin suggested the whole issue be reviewed again. The clamor in the parliament against NATO air strikes against the Serbs has been accompanied by Yeltsin and Kozyrev's criticism of NATO operations. Similarly, after parliamentary criticism, Yeltsin delayed for several months Russia's entrance into NATO's Partnership for Peace program. President Yeltsin also invited Ivan Rybkin, the speaker of the State Duma (and a member of the Agrarian Party, which opposed joint U.S.-Russian exercises), to join the Security Council alongside the speaker of the Federation Council, Vladimir Shumeiko. (In fact, both joined the Security Council only during the war in Chechnia.) In none of the above cases, however, has the executive branch decisively reversed its previous policy in order to mend fences with the legislature. The legislature, in turn, lacking the direct constitutional means to redirect the president's security policy, has so far been satisfied with the superficial impact of its criticisms.

But what about the legislature's role in the defense budget process? The legislature, of course, has control of the purse strings, which very fundamentally affects the security policy of Russia; during the summer 1994 debates on defense spending, the State Duma passed a budget of 40.6 trillion rubles, much below the "minimum" 55 trillion rubles demanded by the Ministry of Defense. This will certainly result in a severe decline in defense production; salaries and benefits to the military, which now constitute about 65 percent of the defense budget, will have to be paid at the expense of research and development programs, weapons acquisition, and construction, which will decline to one quarter of what was originally planned.[29] (A curious reversal of priorities has taken place: in 1989, research and development and weapons acquisition took up 62 percent of the defense budget.)[30] As a result, 1.2 million workers in the defense industry may possibly be laid off.[31]

The impact of the legislature on security policy is evident, but it is hardly tantamount to a policy-making role. The Duma significantly curtailed the president's freedom of security policy making but did not advance any coherent security policy of its own. This budgetary process was a case of struggle for power, not an attempt to redefine Yeltsin's security policy. The legislature, according to a well-informed source, has no access to a detailed military budget that shows clearly how much is to be spent on which program.[32] Without such information, no serious attempt at security policy making is possible. Indeed, the budget debate of 1994 did not touch upon the programmatic detail of Russian security policy, but rather was framed by general references to the need to reduce the budget deficit or, conversely, to save the military from destruction.

One can conclude that the relationship between the executive and legislative branches of the Russian government does not provide a foundation for a lasting consensus on security policy. The executive branch has tried to monopolize, as much as possible, the formulation of security policy. The legislature has no means to seriously develop security policy, but it does have the requisite instruments to destroy the president's policy in this area, thus scoring a point in a power struggle between the two branches of the government.[33]

Conflicts Within the Executive Branch

The executive branch itself is hardly a model of unity when it comes to security policy making. It is divided into the government (*pravitel'stvo*) and the presidential administration (*administratsiia prezidenta*). While the Cabinet of Ministers (part of the government) includes all ministers in charge of security policy (defense, foreign and internal affairs, intelligence and counterintelligence, and emergencies), their activities in the field of security appear to be coordinated outside the cabinet, within the framework of the Security Council under the direction of the president.[34] The Security Council, chaired by the president (who appoints its members) and run by his longtime political ally Oleg Lobov (who serves as the secretary of the Security Council), includes the prime minister, the speakers of both chambers of the Federal Assembly, the ministers of defense, foreign and internal affairs, and emergency situations, the heads of the intelligence and counterintelligence agencies, and the commander of the border guards. The Security Council plays an advisory role to the president. Its primary importance lies in staff work preparing decisions for consideration by the president as the chairman of the Security Council.[35]

While the Security Council was initially created in March 1992 as a relatively small body providing direct support for presidential security decision making, its staff and missions have grown considerably.[36] In addition to the Security Council staff (*apparat*) proper, which prepares the paperwork for the meetings of that body, provides analyses, and controls implementation of presidential decisions, the Security Council also includes ten interagency commissions (on foreign policy, defense, interregional affairs of Russia, public security, informational security, scientific and technological aspects of the defense industry, environment, economy, health, and crime). The interagency commissions help establish priorities for policy making; in this task they are aided by the Research Council of the Security Council, a group of scholars and scientists permanently employed outside the Security Council, which is chaired by retired Admiral Vladimir Pirumov.[37]

The Security Council is a relatively large and complex bureaucratic mechanism, where heads of the most powerful government agencies are represented. Can the Security Council synthesize a security policy for Russia and make various agencies stick to its implementation? While some participants in the decision-making process insist that policy synthesis does occur in the Security Council,[38] the Council on Foreign and Defense Policy, a public organization, maintains that the Security Council cannot coordinate policy effectively and that government agencies continue to pursue their own policy agendas.[39] It is difficult to certify either of these claims because the operations of the Security Council are largely secret. There are, however, examples of the Security Council acting in contradiction to the interests of some of its powerful members. For instance, it was reported that the Security Council opposed the joint Russian-American peacekeeping exercise, a venture supported by the defense minister, in a gesture calculated to humiliate General Grachev.[40] The overall picture of the decision-making process suggests, however, that the Security Council cannot be the fulcrum of security policy making because it lacks a gatekeeping mechanism to control its most powerful members' access to the president.

The secretary of the Security Council has direct access to the president, but so do most members of the council, who can plead their cases to Yeltsin, bypassing the council's interagency commissions. In addition, the president's national security advisor, Iurii Baturin, who had previously served as Yeltsin's legal advisor, has even better access to the president of Russia.[41] The post of national security advisor was established in January 1994; Baturin's responsibilities include supervision of all "power structures" (*silovye struktury*), such as the military, intelligence and counterintelligence, the Ministry of Internal Affairs (MVD), and the border guards.[42] This new appointment, with responsibilities duplicating the original mission of the Security Council, suggests Boris Yeltsin's disappointment with the council.

The emergence of the office of national security advisor is also a result of a power struggle between the head of the presidential administration (of which the Security Council is a part), Sergei Filatov, and the president's first aide (in effect, the chief of the presidential chancellery), Vladimir Iliushin, who directly supervises Baturin.[43] The national security advisor works with a small staff in physical proximity to the president in the Kremlin, while the overgrown Security Council is located several crucial blocks away in the former Communist Party headquarters. Lobov naturally views Baturin as dangerous competition and has made attempts (unsuccessful, so far) to absorb the office of the national security advisor.[44] Thus the decision-making structures working immediately for the president are exceedingly complex, and prone to duplication and competition— conditions not likely to foster consensus on security policy.

There is a sharp competition for scarce resources between the military and other power structures. Chief of General Staff Mikhail Kolesnikov said that "Russia now has five militaries, since apart from the armed forces, which consist of 2.3 million men, other government institutions, such as the Federal Counterintelligence Service, the Ministry of Emergency Situations, the Federal Agency of Government Communications, and the Presidential Guard have created their own military formations."[45] To this list, one should add the border guards, whose strength is about 200,000; the troops of the MVD (350,000 strong); the railroad troops, the troops of the Firefighting Service of the MVD, and other smaller services. According to some sources, the strength of military and militarized formations outside the armed forces may be approaching one million men and women.[46]

Minister of Defense Grachev has been trying to subordinate the border guards to his ministry, but he has not succeeded. The commander of the border guards, Colonel General Andrei Nikolaev (formerly deputy chief of the General Staff) argued sharply against Grachev at a meeting of the Security Council (of which both are members) and later attacked in print the new military doctrine, produced under Grachev's supervision, for failing to provide guidance for the armed forces.[47] A turf war has quickly escalated to a clash over the general direction of Russian security policy.

The impact of the budget competition on the salaries of officers in the military and in other military and militarized services (as of mid-1994) is indicative of the current priorities of Russian security policy. The salaries of military officers compare very unfavorably (1.5 to 2 times lower) to those of the officers of the Federal Counterintelligence Service, the Foreign Intelligence Service, the Federal Agency of Government Communications, the Security Service of the President, and the MVD.[48] While preferential treatment (compared to the military) of intelligence, counterintelligence, and security agencies—all heirs to the privileged KGB—is hardly a novelty, the better position of the previously underprivileged MVD must be an indication of its increased political clout. So is the growth in the number of the troops of the MVD, which is said by some Russian sources (in mid-1994) to include close to half a million troops, just about half the strength of the ground forces, an assessment that differs sharply from the 120,000 MVD troops given in *The Military Balance 1993–1994*.[49] This growth (whatever the exact numbers may be) results from the growing role of the MVD's mobile forces (the Dzerzhinskii Division, the Twenty-seventh Brigade, and possibly others) in increasingly important law and order projection operations inside Russia.[50] The military is planning mobile forces, but they will be quite expensive (and therefore, their future existence is in doubt); moreover, the use of internal security troops inside Russia is more acceptable—both to the public and to the troops themselves—than the use of military units. It appears that internal security missions are assigned a higher priority than the more traditional external security missions for which the military is primarily trained and equipped.

The Fragmentation of the Military

The military itself is hardly unified. At the very top, there is an ongoing conflict between the General Staff, headed by General Mikhail Kolesnikov, and the minister of defense. According to Pavel Fel'gengauer, one of the most respected military correspondents in Russia, the General Staff officers tend to view General Grachev with considerable skepticism, and may be amenable to replacing him with his civilian deputy, Andrei Kokoshin, which would incidentally leave General Kolesnikov the highest-ranking military officer in Russia.[51] It is difficult to separate personality issues from the policy ones in this conflict. General Kolesnikov is a classic Soviet General Staff officer, with extensive experience in ground forces command, while General Grachev is a bit of a rank-skipper, lacking the experience traditionally expected in a military officer appointed minister of defense in the Soviet Union (of course, in the Soviet past civilians occupied this post without the military's resistance; the Communist Party's domination insured that). As far as policy issues are concerned, General Kolesnikov has been rumored to be much less enthusiastic about the planned mobile forces than General Grachev, a difference not surprising in view of the latter's exclusively paratroop background and the former's skepticism (understandable in a ground forces officer) about an expensive scheme that gives a great deal of power over the Russian military to the airborne forces command.

On the horizontal level, the military is also fragmented. In a process parallel to the devolution of political power to the regional authorities, the Ministry of Defense is engaged in transforming the system of command in the military districts. In the past, the commanders of the military districts had to share their authority with the services' commander in chief in Moscow. Now they are supposed to receive much greater control over practically all the troops in their districts (this naturally excludes the elements of strategic nuclear forces). This new command structure is to be tested in the North Caucasus Military District.[52] At the same time, moves are being made to decentralize the system of military supply in favor of a greater logistical dependence of military forces on regional, rather than central, sources.[53] Such a move, at a time when Russian regional authorities are challenging the power of the central government in Moscow, may have grave implications for the cohesion of the Russian military if it results in an emergence of regional warlords.

The potential for horizontal fragmentation of the military has been demonstrated by a May 1994 episode in the Far East. While the government in Moscow is continuing a policy of improved relations with China, the local civilian authorities are disturbed by what some believe to be "peaceful expansion" and "infiltration" into the Far East and Siberia by the Chinese.[54] Indeed, the degree of growing Chinese influence in the area is well illustrated by the following fact: Birobidzhan, the tiny Jewish Autonomous Region in the Far East, with little industry and an underdeveloped infrastructure, in 1993 attracted 5.9 percent (!) of all foreign investment in Russia (compared, for instance, with the leader in that area, Moscow, with 26.2 percent), mostly due to Chinese investment.[55]

On 1 May 1994, according to Russian sources, five Chinese naval craft were stopped by Russian border guards from crossing the Russian border on the Amur near Khabarovsk. The order to the Russian forces to stop the Chinese intrusion was apparently given not by Moscow, but by the civilian head of administration of Khabarovsk Krai, Viktor Ishaev, who demanded that Moscow renounce the 1991 Sino-Soviet treaty regarding the border between the two countries. One of the issues unresolved by the treaty is the Bol'shoi Ussuriiskii island in the Amur; Ishaev stated that China was trying to seize the island and threatened that "the people of Khabarovsk Krai will defend their island by all means."[56] While the border guards, in accordance with a presidential decree of 30 December 1994, are subordinated formally to the president of Russia,[57] and not to the Ministry of Defense, in border military districts they can be operationally tied into the local military chain of command. (Indeed, a joint exercise involving both border guards and the military, as well as MVD troops and forces of the Federal Counterintelligence Service and other agencies, was reported to have been held in the Far East in September 1994.)[58] If a head of a regional administration today can give orders to the border guards without concern for Moscow's policies, tomorrow he could begin to issue commands to the military.

Other factors contributing to the fragmentation of the military are the use of some of its units for internal security missions, great disparities in social conditions and economic prospects among different groups of officers, and differences between enlisted volunteers and conscripts. Units used for security missions (such as the troops that took part in the fighting in Moscow in October 1993) are treated by the government as elite units, with appropriate material rewards for the officers serving in them.[59] The officer corps lacks common aspirations, writes a Russian military sociologist. The junior officers (lieutenants and captains) tend to be primarily concerned with avoiding service in an area where fighting is taking place; with some luck, they hope to make money out of their military connections and leave the service. The "lucky" ones (and here is another fault line in the officer corps) are those who can enrich themselves from sales of excess military property, as happened on a mass scale in the Western Group of Forces in Germany. The middle-ranking officers (from major to major general) usually see no prospects for themselves in civilian life and are committed to their service and to traditions in general; they are critical of the reforms begun by Gorbachev and continued by Yeltsin. The top officers who serve in the General Staff and Ministry of Defense in Moscow have learned to profit from closely following the twists and turns of Kremlin politics; a wide gulf separates them from those serving in the "provinces." Finally, mixing the enlisted volunteers, former reservists who serve in order to make a living, with eighteen-year-old conscripts, 50 percent of whom do not want to serve, is bound to produce another conflict.[60]

Despite all these tensions, the military has remained a reasonably disciplined and obedient instrument of the government—so far. The nature of the relationship between the military, on the one hand, and the civilian government and political forces, on the other, is crucial in preventing or fomenting a breakdown of military centralization and discipline.

Civil-Military Relations

Can the weak and fragmented Russian civilian government effectively control the military? Both the August 1991 and October 1993 crises demonstrated graphically the crucial importance of the military in Russian politics, a perception strongly confirmed by Boris Yeltsin's personal accounts of both events.[61] In August 1991, the hardline plotters, including Minister of Defense Marshal Dmitrii Yazov and Commander of the Ground Forces General Valentin Varennikov, were defeated when the military refused to serve as an instrument for political repression. Once the troops had been brought out into the Moscow streets, it became apparent to the whole chain of command that they were not reliable as a police instrument, at which point the coup collapsed. In October 1993, Yeltsin called in the military to crush an armed uprising by the supporters of the Supreme Soviet (dissolved by the Russian president in September 1993) once it turned out that the forces of the MVD were not up to the task. The military followed the orders, initially reluctantly, but once the fight was joined, decisively; the Supreme Soviet building, which served as the headquarters of the rebels, was shelled by tanks, and the anti-Yeltsin forces were on the run several hours after the first shots had been fired by the military.

Given the military's central role in these crucial events, how much and what kind of power does the Russian military have? Timothy Colton has distinguished between three types of power that the military can have: first, power over the defense policy; second, a somewhat broader power over various "economic, technological and sociocultural . . . issues . . . loosely related to military security as such;" and, third, "sovereign power," the power to decide "whether soldiers or statesmen are to be supreme in the state."[62] Since the moment the Russian military was officially established in May 1992, it has certainly striven to increase its power over the formulation and execution of defense policy.

Compared to Gorbachev's years, the military has managed to reduce the influence of civilian analysts in defense matters.[63] Gorbachev used his immense powers as the Communist Party leader to translate into defense policy a number of ideas, especially regarding arms control and military cuts, popular among academic civilian analysts and very unpopular among the Soviet high command. Weakening of civilian authority naturally resulted in the military's improved ability to resist such interventions into its professional matters. Moreover, the inadequacy of Gorbachev's "new thinking," associated with academic civilian analysts, in dealing with problems of the disintegrated Soviet Union has emboldened the military to resist recommendations that run too much against its taste.[64] The military has found, after initial resistance, some of the concepts advanced by civilian analysts to be acceptable, especially in view of the miserable economic situation: effective abandonment of the pursuit of conventional parity with the United States, intrusive verification of arms control agreements, and desirability of deep cuts in the offensive strategic arsenals of Russia and the

United States. Other ideas, derided by the military as unworkable and "unmilitary" from the very beginning, have been successfully rejected: the prime example is the much-touted (under Gorbachev) concept of "defensive defense," something the Russian military now finds impossible.[65]

The military has learned a lesson from its early failures in debates with civilian analysts better prepared for open discussions. It has begun cultivating its "own" civilian analysts. Here the military has benefited from the massive retirements of highly qualified officers from education and research institutions of the Ministry of Defense, officers whose voices previously could not be heard because of excessive secrecy. One example is the work of the Section of Geopolitics and Security of the Russian Academy of Natural Sciences,[66] which is composed mostly of retired military officers; this section serves as an important research contractor on defense matters for the Security Council of the Russian Federation.[67] Another outlet for the work of retired military specialists is the Committee of Scientists for Global Security.[68] The availability of retired military scholars has had an obvious impact on the work on a "national doctrine for Russia" carried out by the RAU Corporation under contract to a private concern, MOST Ltd.; a very large section of the project report deals with military threats to Russian interests at the expense of such issues popular with the "new thinkers" as the role of international organizations in providing for Russia's security, economic reform, democracy building, and so on.[69]

Since Gorbachev's glasnost, Soviet and Russian generals have been making, from time to time, political pronouncements suggesting that they have been seeking not only power over various "economic, technological and sociocultural . . . issues . . . loosely related to military security as such," but perhaps even political power as well. Especially during the last two years of Gorbachev's regime, some high-ranking and even middle-ranking military officers exerted direct and public pressure on the government to reverse the course of reforms.[70]

Throughout 1994, Lieutenant General Aleksandr Lebed', an outspoken paratrooper in command of the Fourteenth Army based in the Trans-Dniestria region of Moldova, openly criticized both the minister of defense and President Yeltsin and asserted his right to become involved in politics because of the civilian politicians' incompetence.[71] Subsequent to his criticisms, an attempt to remove Lebed' from his command, apparently organized by General Grachev, failed when General Lebed' received support from Boris Yeltsin himself.[72] When threatened with the loss of his command, General Lebed''s counterthreat was not a military rebellion, but rather his entry into civilian politics with a rumored run for the Russian presidency. Thus, one of the major reasons, if not the reason, for Yeltsin's decision not to remove Lebed' was the concern that the very popular general would resign his commission and join politics; apparently, a disobedient general is viewed in the Kremlin as the lesser evil when compared to a charismatic political challenger to Yeltsin, who might be capable of uniting the fractured opposition forces. Only time will show whether Yeltsin and his advisors are right.

Has the military in effect conducted its own national security policy in the "near abroad"? There is a precedent for this in history: Russia's conquest of Central Asia in the second half of the nineteenth century was in part due to "the excessive ambition of unruly local commanders willing to gamble that euphoria over easy victories would expunge the consequences of insubordination," an ambition that ignored the warnings of the Foreign Ministry about the negative consequences of such conquests for Russia's national security.[73] There is no documentary evidence on the decision making for the recent peacekeeping operations of the Russian military in Tajikistan, Georgia, Moldova, and Nagorno-Karabagh; therefore, a definitive conclusion on whether the Russian forces there acted in compliance with or in contradiction to the orders of civilian authorities (ultimately, the commander in chief, President Boris Yeltsin) must wait. There is enough evidence, however, to suggest that the civilian control over these operations has been very weak at best. According to Emil' Pain, the director of interethnic relations and conflict forecast studies at the Analysis Center of the President of the Russian Federation, there is no "clear system of civilian control" over the "peacekeeping operations" of the Russian military. There is no legal foundation for Russia's peacekeeping operations in the "near abroad." "Under such conditions, decisions with political and even international implications are frequently taken by military commanders directly in the zone of hostilities." The military command does not report at all to the representative bodies.[74]

A contradiction is growing by each day regarding the relative importance of the military in Russia, due to the weakness of civilian institutions there, and the military's failure to exert more influence on crucial defense policy issues, such as the budget, let alone larger economic and sociocultural issues. The October 1993 events have not resulted in a drastic change in the military's position. Evidence indicates that it was reluctant to intervene by force; Boris Yeltsin, whose vantage point in October 1993 was very different from the one in August 1991, noted how slowly and inefficiently, as if to sabotage the civilian politicians' orders, the military deployed on both occasions. This conduct can be attributed, as Boris Yeltsin does, to the success of civilians' recent efforts to convince the military it should stay out of politics,[75] or to the Soviet tradition that punished the military (as it did any other group) for encroaching upon the province of politics reserved for the communist elite. The seeming paradox after the October crisis, when the military finally and reluctantly rescued Yeltsin's government, is that its political capital did not increase appreciably; some might say it has even decreased. Why?

The military is preoccupied with its sectional interests: social conditions for the officer corps, procurements, protection of defense policy making from civilian interference, and so forth. Despite its lukewarm support for Yeltsin's policies of reform, which has been most prominently manifested by a large proportion (up to 40 percent) of officers voting for the extremist Vladimir Zhirinovsky in the December 1993 election, the officer corps appears to have no desire to elbow out the civilian political elites.[76] Given the still vast economic needs of the Russian military (despite all the cutbacks), the exceptional complexity of Russia's economic problems, and the lack of a tradition of military rule, the Russian military is not likely to view the burden of political power as a panacea for its corporate ailments. The military's corporate interests can be better satisfied either when the civilian political elite views military power and attendant expansion as a domestic legitimizing tool for itself, as happened under the Soviet regime, or when civilian elites, striving to achieve or maintain political power, court the military, something President Yeltsin has done quite consistently.[77] Intervening on the side of Yeltsin to help him triumph over his political opponents has made the military temporarily less politically powerful. As a former Soviet general noticed regarding the October 1993 crisis, "Having ensured the victory of the politicians, the army itself suffered a defeat. In the long run it failed to establish itself in the status of the key guarantor of peace and stability. In fact, it became a hostage of the victorious side."[78]

Indeed, the events after the October crisis support this interpretation. In the immediate aftermath, the president thanked the military by adopting a version of military doctrine much to their tastes, but this doctrine is not worth the paper it is printed on without an appropriate fiscal foundation. In the crucial matter of the budget the military took a severe beating when Viktor Chernomyrdin's government initially allocated only 37 trillion rubles for the 1994–95 fiscal year against the 80 trillion requested by the military.[79] The State Duma, which General Grachev initially ignored or was unable to lobby, supported the low government request, to the shock and dismay of the military.[80] Even a subsequent massive public relations offensive by the military, now supported by the executive branch (both the president and the prime minister) and the leadership of the Federation Council,[81] did not result in a significant increase in the defense budget. The military turned out to have no significant and committed political allies. And this is despite the fact that the military continues to be, together with the Russian Orthodox Church, the most popular institution in Russia; in September 1993, 70 percent of respondents to an opinion survey had a great deal or a fair amount of confidence in the military, as compared to 69 percent for the church, and 28 percent for the Council of Ministers![82] These numbers suggest that the military does not have the capability to translate its institutional popularity into a political advantage, but they also confirm that it should by no means be written off as a political actor.

If the economic situation of the officer corps continues to deteriorate, it will feel increasingly betrayed by President Yeltsin and may very well turn toward extremist politics. "A survey of political views among Russian officers from all service branches ... finds growing support for authoritarian rule over society, restiveness in the ranks, and 'a trend toward secret organization.' Sixty-two percent of the overall sample subscribe to the view that Russia requires 'authoritarian rule' to solve its problems; less than half approve of the government's introduction of market reforms and private ownership; and 80 percent aspire to 'Russia's restoration as a great power respected in the entire world.' Some individual officers acknowledged participating in the proceedings of secret, self-styled 'courts' that passed symbolic death sentences on the commanders of the October 1993 operation that crushed Yeltsin's adversaries. Absolute majorities of the respondents 'do not want Yeltsin as president' or Pavel Grachev as defense minister. The . . . pollsters contrasted the politicization of the officer corps with the political apathy of the civilian population."[83] Replacing civilian politicians as the supreme power in the state is an extreme measure for a disgruntled military with no tradition of doing so. A less extreme and therefore more feasible approach for the Russian military would be to throw its weight behind civilian contenders for the supreme power who seem likely to be more sympathetic to the military's corporate interests.

Alliance Between the Military and Russian Hypernationalists?

One of the most worrisome scenarios discussed in the West is the possibility of an alliance between the Russian military and the Russian hypernationalists.[84] Such an alliance would guarantee the military's support for or at least nonintervention in the hypernationalists' violent takeover of the democratic institutions of the Russian Federation. If such an alliance had existed in October 1993, Boris Yeltsin's government would have fallen to an attack by the Russian hypernationalist forces.

There are reasons to be seriously concerned about such a scenario: there is probably no other group in Russia whose status has experienced such a great relative decline in the last several years as the military. Indeed, large numbers of military officers voted for Zhirinovsky, some of whose campaign promises (increase in arms exports, restoration of Russia in the borders of the USSR, and mass transfer, instead of discharge, of military officers to internal security troops) were bound to appeal to the military, who had suffered more than any other corporate group from the loss of the Soviet position as a major international weapons merchant and from the disintegration of the empire.[85] A link between nationalism and maintenance of mass armies makes the military view political groups with nationalist appeal as natural allies.[86] Given that the rise of nationalism is likely to lead to increased tensions in areas such as Eastern Europe and the former USSR,[87] one can see how the military may want to cooperate with hypernationalists in order to improve its own declining fortunes.

Indeed, numerous attempts have been made, beginning in 1988, to establish an alliance between the military and Russian hypernationalists.[88] The latest and most concrete embodiment of such attempts has been the Union of Officers, led by retired Lieutenant Colonel Stanislav Terekhov, who is also a cochairman of the National Salvation Front, a "coalition of nationalist, communist and imperialist groups."[89] The Union of Officers played an active part in the October 1993 crisis, when it provided some militants to fight on the side of the Supreme Soviet, along with the openly fascist Russian National Unity, an organization that espouses the idea of a hypernationalist military dictatorship and has a substantial paramilitary wing.[90] In 1994, Terekhov and a number of members of the Union of Officers set up a new Great Power Party.[91] One of the leaders of the pro–Supreme Soviet forces in the October 1993 violence, retired General Al'bert Makashov, was a leader of the hypernationalist organization, Fatherland (Otechestvo).[92] When circumstances are favorable, the military acts in concert with Russian hypernationalist groups, as it did in Trans-Dniestria, where the Fourteenth Army in fact supported Russian separatists (it should be noted, however, that lately the Fourteenth Army commander, General Aleksandr Lebed', has been quarreling with the "government" of Trans-Dniestria, accusing it of dishonesty).[93]

Despite all the factors favoring a military-hypernationalist alliance, such an alliance has failed to emerge. Why? The hypernationalists have failed to coalesce into a political movement due to several factors: "amorphous ideology and lack of developed anti-crisis programs, . . . continuing ideological and political, and, even more important, personal conflicts among the [hyper-]nationalists, organizational and personnel weakness."[94] Indeed, in October 1993, Vladimir Zhirinovsky's party rendered no support to the hypernationalist enemies of President Yeltsin. Today, relations between Zhirinovsky's Liberal Democratic Party and the Russian National Unity are hostile.

The Russian/Soviet military's tradition has been to cast its lot with a faction ready to govern in order to best protect the military's corporate interests.[95] High on the list of such interests is the unity of the military; during the October crisis the anti-Yeltsin forces, with prominent participation of hypernationalists, threatened the unity of the armed forces by appointing their own "alternative" minister of defense, General Achalov (retired), an action that probably contributed to the Russian high command's eventual decision to storm the White House.[96] As long as the Russian hypernationalists are not a reasonably cohesive political movement capable of making a power grab without endangering the unity of the military, the latter's alliance with the former appears unlikely.

The New Business Elite

In a broad historical perspective, the most important thing happening in Russia today is the redistribution of huge state properties to private individuals, a process whose impact on society can be compared only to the "second" Soviet revolution of the late 1920s. A new class of entrepreneurs is emerging out of the crucible of the privatization and free market reforms, however imperfect the latter may be. This process is uneven but irreversible.[97] The new business elite will undoubtedly have an impact on Russia's security policy. It certainly already is having an impact on the political process, but the new Russian business class is so poorly studied, partially because it frequently has to operate in a legal no-man's-land, that it is simply impossible to form a clear picture of its influence in this area of policy making. Anecdotal evidence, usually centered on influence-buying operations between government officials and businesspeople, abounds.

How can the new business elite affect Russia's security policy?[98] In the most general sense, a pursuit of strongly protectionist policies prompted by the pressure of Russian businesspeople could contribute to Russia's isolation from industrial democracies. A more specific and immediate issue is the fate of the Russian defense industry, which constitutes about 80 percent of the former Soviet military-industrial complex.[99] "By the end of 1994 about 1,500 of the roughly 2,000 major defense plants in Russia are due to have been formally privatized."[100] Privatization in its initial phase does not mean, however, an immediate transfer of defense works to new entrepreneurs; it means rather that factories become joint-stock companies, with the majority of the shares held by workers and management.[101] Most of these newly privatized defense manufacturing complexes suffer from problems such as overstaffing and lack of marketing expertise; moreover, they are badly undercapitalized.[102] The rapid reduction of the defense budget will make it impossible for the defense industry to survive without an infusion of private capital.

So far the privatization of defense enterprises has been slow; by April 1994, only about one hundred of the total of seventeen hundred factories and five hundred research and development facilities were privatized. The capital, available mostly through commercial banks, has not been forthcoming because commercial banks have been wary of both the structural problems of the defense industry and the antimarket mentality of its managers.[103] This may change. Recently thirty to forty financial-industrial groups were established by commercial banks, defense enterprises, and trading and insurance companies, with the goal of producing "the most modern" weapons and returning Russia, in five to six years, to the position of a leading arms exporter on a global scale.[104] The exact composition of these groups, nicknamed "locomotives" (after the idea advanced some time ago by the first deputy minister of defense in charge of armaments policy, Andrei Kokoshin),[105] has been kept secret, but apparently they will include the top aerospace companies, such as Sukhoi, the Mikoian and Yakovlev design bureaus, and the Energiia scientific and production enterprise. A new Military-Industrial Export-Import Bank and a special insurance group are to make the new locomotives independent of the unreliable state budget.[106]

If this plan is implemented, the new businesspeople are likely to become a serious force in security policy making, with an influence over arms export and related policies. For example, the oil company Germes has bought the Zvezda marine diesel engine factory in St. Petersburg. (Zvezda has specialized in production of diesel engines for missile boats and patrol craft, as well as nonmagnetic diesel engines for submarines.) Zvezda has exported its diesels for decades. Now Germes has invested $1.5 million into international representation of

Zvezda and proposes to establish a worldwide network of repair facilities for its diesel engines in foreign countries whose navies already own such engines. Such networks, according to the president of Germes, "may become foci of an infrastructure that could supply and service Russian ships in long cruises."[107] In exchange, Germes would like to use the network of Russian military attachés to gather market information and lobby for Zvezda products and services. Germes also wants the military's support in order to lease the use of the vast military energy supply and communications infrastructure![108]

As private interests acquire an increasing stake in the Russian fuel and energy industry, the new businesspeople will inevitably play a role in the struggle for control of energy resources in the former Soviet republics. Such a struggle has been going on since 1992 regarding the issue of the Caspian Sea oil; here Russian interests have collided with those of Azerbaijan, Turkey, the United States, Great Britain, and France. The economy and security are very closely intertwined in this case, with Russia using the conflict between Armenia and Azerbaijan over the enclave of Nagorno-Karabagh to obtain a very favorable deal in the development of the Caspian Sea oil.[109]

Arms export control (or lack of such) is the most obvious area for the new private sector's pressure on the government's security policies. The soil here has been well prepared by complaints of defense industry managers, Russian nationalist politicians, and mass media about a Western plot to destroy Russia as an arms exporter by the two-pronged policy of cutting its links with traditional radical Third World customers (such as Libya) while keeping the traditional Western arms export markets closed to Russia. Needless to say, the struggle for arms markets, and especially demands for removal of arms export controls regarding what the West considers to be outlaw regimes, may substantially influence the attitudes of the new business class toward the West.

Russian arms exporters' interests may collide with the interests of the politicians, both at the regional and central levels. There can be very intriguing conflicts regarding arms exports to China, an activity that the Ministry of Defense and General Staff view positively, apparently as a way to save the Russian defense industry. Upon concluding his visit to China in April 1994, Chief of General Staff Mikhail Kolesnikov said that Russia has "a lot to share with China [regarding] supplies of various types of weapons."[110] While Russian authorities in the Far East warn about the Chinese encroachments, as mentioned earlier, the aviation factory in Komsomol'sk-na-Amure has a very different view of its southern neighbor, which is now the largest customer for the factory's main product, SU–27 jet fighters.[111] If and when this factory is privatized, the new owners will have to become involved in the conflict between Moscow and Khabarovsk regarding Russia's security policy toward China. Eventually, the Russian military itself may become concerned about arms exports to China, which will result in friction between the Ministry of Defense and companies exporting weapons to Russia's great neighbor.

Similar conflicts of interest are possible in other areas. For instance, in April 1994 the Russian Ministry of Defense signed an agreement on military-technical cooperation with its Turkish counterpart. Under the terms of the agreement, defense industries of both countries may coproduce weapon systems, with a view toward exporting them.[112] At the same time, Moscow views Turkey as a threat to Russian influence in Transcaucasia and Central Asia. Moscow also believes that Turkey's opposition is the main reason NATO has refused Russia's request to revise upward the limitations imposed by the Treaty on Conventional Forces in Europe in the so-called flank areas, which prevent Russia from deploying larger forces in the area of the North Caucasus and Transcaucasia.[113] Turkey, as mentioned earlier, is also seen as a competitor to the Russian energy industry in the Caspian Sea. Thus, we have a potential for an eventual conflict of interest between arms exporters and the military, as well as between the arms exporters and the oil producers, who may support the military in an anti-Turkish policy against the wishes of the arms exporters; the latter conflict would pit one sector of the new business elite against another.

Geopolitics and Public Opinion

The Russian culture requires, as mentioned earlier, a central idea for policy action. Two major factors impede the emergence of such a unifying idea for security policy. The first is the chaotic and fluid condition of Russian politics, with a multitude of poorly institutionalized actors at play. The second is the still unstable character of the new Russian statehood; the Russian borders with the new independent states are not certain, and such centrifugal forces as regionalism and ethnic nationalism of non-Russians in Russia are challenging the character of the Russian Federation.[114] Egor Gaidar pointed to this instability: "We must know, at last, in what country, with established borders, we live."[115] It is too early for a definitive central idea of Russian national security, but its general outline is emerging in the vibrant debate on geopolitics.

What Kind of Geopolitics?

Geopolitics is very fashionable in Russia today for several reasons. It is popular because Russians view geopolitics as a logical and all-encompassing science (*nauka*) "studying processes and principles of development of states, regions, and the world as a whole with consideration for the systemic influence of geographic, political, economic, military, ecological, and other factors."[116] This approach satisfies both the predilection of the Russian culture for a central idea and the ingrained habit (from decades of ideological domination by Marxism-Leninism) to look for a scientific view of the world, as well as the more traditional Russian preoccupation with history and geography.[117] Also, geopolitics, with its focus on geography, history, state boundaries, demographics, and the rise and fall of great powers, presents a very suitable intellectual tool for Russians, who have to deal with a sudden decline of their power status, new and unstable boundaries, various demographic problems, ethnic conflicts, and so forth.

This brand of geopolitics is closer to the more realistic and scholarly British-American discipline of Halford J. Mackinder and Nicholas Spykman than to the propagandistic and militaristic ideas of the pre–World War II German school of *Geopolitik*.[118] *Geopolitik*, however, holds considerable fascination for Russian hypernationalists; just as the Nationalist Socialists used, in the words of Colin Gray, its "pseudo-scientific rationales . . . for Germany's bid for world conquest,"[119] politicians of the Zhirinovsky type are using spurious geopolitical arguments to justify plans for imperial conquests.[120]

While just about any geopolitical discussion contains a call for Russia to preserve its great-power status, all nonextremist debate participants basically agree that

> the range of vital interests of Russia is objectively more narrow than that of the former USSR. In the past, the geopolitical space controlled by the USSR directly touched upon the geopolitical space where the leading roles were played by the United States and China. The confrontation with Washington and, to a lesser degree, with Beijing determined the essence of Soviet foreign policy. Under new conditions, Russia's neighbors are . . . an unstable conglomerate of states consisting, with the exception of Japan and China, for the most part of the former Soviet republics and adjacent states of the "distant abroad." It is obvious that the zone of Russia's vital interests will be limited to this area until the year 2010. To be more specific, we are talking about the territory of the former USSR and immediately adjacent regions.[121]

Nonextremist Russian attitudes toward major Western powers will be primarily determined by their perceived impact on this new and volatile "zone of Russia's vital interests." The most dramatic innovation in the Russian military doctrine has been the threat to use nuclear weapons against any state allied with nuclear powers if it attacks Russia—a reorientation of strategic deterrence from a direct bearing on NATO to a possible nexus between NATO and Ukraine.[122] The initial Russian reaction to the Partnership for Peace plan (a general inclination to join the partnership so as not to be shunned by Western powers, combined with a request for a special relationship to NATO, which would presumably give Russia a veto over NATO's actions in the zone of Russia's vital interests) clearly demonstrates the new "closer to home" orientation of Russian security policy. In the East, the situation with Japan and especially China, sharing the longest land border with Russia, is different. There are concerns, as mentioned above, especially among the politicians from the Russian Far East and those in Moscow banking on the "regional" agenda (such as Sergei Shakhrai), about Chinese encroachment on the Russian Far East.[123] Such concerns can be mitigated by a belief that China would be threatened by the disintegration of the Russian Federation and thus would assiduously avoid any steps fomenting separatism within Russia.[124]

The identification of the zone of vital interests as the belt of adjacent newly independent (and, to a certain point, former Warsaw Pact) states does not by itself provide a security strategy for dealing with this zone. Two perspectives on the zone can be found in Russia today. The Council on Defense and Foreign Policy has concluded that "[i]ntegration with many of the former USSR republics is almost inevitable, from a strategic perspective. There is simply no alternative. The only question concerns the 'forms and conditions.' The 'forms and conditions' are either 'hard' integration, complete with establishment of 'a new federate state,' or a 'soft' version, involving political independence [for the former republics] in exchange for unrestricted access to their markets of goods, services, and capital, establish[ment of] an effective defensive military-political bloc, and a common legal space for all ethnic minorities that would guarantee them full rights." The council clearly favors the "soft" integration.[125]

The second perspective is clearly associated with the *Geopolitik* of Russian hypernationalists and a hard integration: Zhirinovsky proposes re-creating the Russian Empire, where non-Russians would have no autonomy whatsoever, while the communist/hypernationalist opposition to Yeltsin (the Communist Party of the Russian Federation; former Vice President Aleksandr Rutskoi; former chairman of the USSR Supreme Soviet Anatolii Luk'ianov; former chairman of the Supreme Court Valerii Zorkin; and the generals Valentin Varennikov, Al'bert Makashov, and Vladislav Achalov) wants to put the old USSR together again, as the most "natural" form of Russian statehood.[126]

There are important similarities between the proponents of "hard" and "soft" integration: both view the former Soviet and Russian imperial possessions as predetermined to fall under the sway of Moscow. Both regard the new states that constitute the former imperial periphery as an area into which Russian power should expand, in a more or less benevolent fashion. The difference between these two perspectives is, however, more important. "Soft" integration requires minimum use of military instruments, and its proponents tend to balance any gains in the zone of vital interests against resulting deterioration of relations with the West. Thus, there are some inherent constraints on Russia's actions in the zone, and the West receives a certain leverage over Russian actions there. "Hard" integration is impossible without the use of military force, and its proponents view the inevitable collateral damage to Russia's relations with the West with equanimity. It is plausible that the hypernationalists and their communist allies would actually welcome a downturn in Russia's relations with the West over Russia's neoimperialism, because of their unrelenting hostility to the West and their desire to isolate Russia from Western influences. Therefore, hard integration leaves the West with little prospect of curbing Russia's use of force along its periphery and guarantees a sharp worsening of Russia's relations with the West, a development that may in its own turn strengthen the militaristic, authoritarian, and imperalist tendencies in Russia.

Use of Force: Constraints and Opportunities

When the outline of Russian military doctrine was published in November 1993, its provisions for use of military force in the zone of its vital interests reflected the operational realities of Russian security policy. By that time Russian troops were engaged in operations of various kinds in Central Asia, Transcaucasia, and Moldova. The plans for creation of substantial rapid deployment elements in the Russian armed forces, combined with the proclamation of the Russian right to intervene militarily in the "near abroad," are indicative of intentions to develop a capability for brushfire operations along Russia's periphery and on the territories of the newly independent states.[127]

The opportunities for use of military force in the zone of vital interests are abundant, primarily because of the weakness of the newly independent states, the proliferation of ethnic and civil conflicts there, the existence of the former Soviet military infrastructure there, and the resolute unwillingness of the international community to become involved. This can lead to a dangerous overextension. The Council on Defense and Foreign Policy warns:

> The weakening of the neighboring states arouses (on a par with the general growth of nationalism) the growth of a feeling of Russia's alleged omnipotence on the part of both the general public and political circles. This feeling is extremely dangerous. The result could be Russia's involvement in a number of conflicts for the purpose of maintaining stability or supporting integration processes. However, Russia has neither the social, military, nor economic potential for this. Russia itself is in a critical economic situation.[128]

The economic constraints on military action in the zone of vital interests are obvious; the defense budget is under so much pressure that some leaders of the privatized defense industry have been proposing that their companies pay for new weapons for Russian rapid deployment forces, naturally in exchange for preferential treatment from the government![129] While an increasing number of Russians believe that Russia is a true owner of parts of the former republics, less than half of them are in favor of the use of force to defend the Russians living there.[130] Opinion polls show that, despite somewhat increasing concerns over foreign threats, Russians continue to be preoccupied with domestic problems.[131] A bill to dispatch Russian troops for a peacekeeping mission in Georgia lost on the first vote in the Federation Council. Peacekeeping missions of Russian armed forces in Georgia, Tajikistan, and the Balkans have been greeted rather skeptically not only by the liberal press but also by the daily newspaper of the Ministry of Defense, a reaction that is not very surprising given the increased role of the Afghanistan War veterans in the high command.[132]

The new and unstable mechanism of Russian government is not conducive to a sustained military-imperial expansion. The fragility of political parties and interest groups and the coalitions between them, as well as the ill-defined nature of executive-legislative relations make coalition logrolling by expansionist groups quite difficult—so far.[133] Under this set of political and economic circumstances, the use of military force in Russia's zone of vital interests has been limited. Russia lacks a mechanism for mobilizing its resources; as one Russian analyst put it, "neither the Great Russian (*russkaia*) nor the All-Russian (*rossiiskaia*) nor the communist ideas work, and the central core of Russia—the metropolis—has been neglected, [so] we will have to rely not on military force, but on diplomacy" in relations with the "near abroad."[134]

Russian public opinion is quite ambiguous regarding use of force in the zone of vital interests. There is little doubt that most Russians regret the disintegration of the USSR; only 19.6 percent of those surveyed agreed that the end of the USSR was a good thing, while 71.6 disagreed, most of them strongly. In the same survey, 24.9 percent agreed with the opinion that "Russia is better off with the republics of the former USSR going their own way," while 59.5 agreed with the proposition of reuniting the former republics into a new union.[135] Similar sentiments of nostalgia were found by another survey, which also investigated Russians' attitudes toward military entanglements abroad: it turned out that, despite the nostalgia for the USSR, a majority of Russians are against maintaining military bases in the "near abroad"; 60 percent are against stationing Russian troops in Tajikistan, where they are involved in a civil war.[136] When asked direct and specific questions about interventionist policies in the zone of vital interests, the Russians are less likely to support such policies. For instance, when asked a general question regarding the possible use of military force to protect the "rights of fellow countrymen who live outside Russia's borders," 49.3 percent expressed support for such a policy, while 35.9 expressed their opposition.[137] One of the primary areas of concentration of Russians outside the Russian Federation is the Crimea in Ukraine; when asked if Russia should support a democratically approved secession of the Crimea from Ukraine with military force, 56 percent of Russian respondents were opposed to the use of force, while only 30 percent supported such a policy option.[138]

When the situation of ethnic Russians is not brought into play at all, the Russians are even more skeptical about military intervention in the former Soviet republics; only 6 percent of the respondents supported decisive use of Russian armed forces to stop interethnic conflicts in the newly independent states, while 47 percent were against it. Today Russian citizens feel little personal connection to life in the former Soviet republics; only 16.7 percent see a strong connection between their personal lives and other former republics, while 59.2 percent do not see such a connection at all.[139]

Opinion research suggests that preoccupation with Russia's international situation and external threats to it is characteristic primarily of the elites.[140] Opinion surveys indicate that the concern about external threats is declining among the Russians: in December 1991, 53 percent of the respondents saw the greatest threat to Russian security from within Russia, and 19 percent from outside; in May 1994, these numbers were, respectively, 68 and 13 percent. An issue that has lately preoccupied the Russian elites—Russia's supposed duty to protect the Serbs—has barely scratched the public's consciousness; despite considerable mass media coverage of the war in Yugoslavia that is frequently friendly to the Serbs, only 14 percent believed in May 1994 that Russia should support the Serbs, while 67 percent believed that Russia should be impartial in the conflict.[141]

The public mood briefly explored above is anti-interventionist, at least in the short term, but its inherent contradiction can be eventually exploited for interventionist policies. This contradiction is graphically illustrated by the views of the most prominent moderate Russian nationalist, Aleksandr Solzhenitsyn. In his article "The Russian Question by the End of the Twentieth Century," published to coincide with the writer's return to Russia after twenty years of exile, Solzhenitsyn puts the blame for many economic and political ills in the last three centuries of Russian and Soviet history on unnecessarily activist Russian/Soviet national security policies that exhausted the nation's economy and frayed its social fabric. Solzhenitsyn even breaks with his own intellectual tradition—that of the Russian Slavophiles—to condemn the Russian Pan-Slavism of the last quarter of the nineteenth century because it led to Russian involvement in the Balkan wars, an involvement seen then by much of the Russian public as an expression of commitment to the rights of brotherly Orthodox Christian Slavs trampled upon by the Ottoman Empire. In the next breath, however, Solzhenitsyn criticizes Yeltsin's government for "abandoning" "twenty-five million" ethnic Russians who now live in the newly independent states. Solzhenitsyn, true to his moderate views, eschews any calls for expanding Russian power into the former republics for the sake of protecting the ethnic Russians there. Nevertheless, his ideas on protecting these Russians' rights (a search for unification with Ukraine, Belarus, and Kazakhstan and demands for local autonomy of areas with Russian majorities in the newly independent states) can lead to growing tensions between Russia and some of the newly independent states and someday may be used to justify the use of military force by Russia.[142]

Russia's use of force against its neighbors may acquire a more consistent and decisive character if some of the internal constraints are removed. For instance, this will happen if nascent pluralism is replaced by authoritarianism, or if Russia's political agenda is hijacked by a coalition of interest groups with an expansionist agenda, in combination with growing hypernationalism.[143] Increased opportunities (growing chaos in the "near abroad" and Western indifference to the situation there) are likely to have a similar impact on Russia's tendency to use force in its zone of vital interests.

Conclusions

Russia lacks a consensus on its national security policy. Security policy making in Russia is in as much turmoil as the Russian political system itself. While the executive branch controls the most important levers of security policy, it is cautious about implementing policies that come under strong and persistent criticism from the legislature. Despite its hardline rhetoric regarding the use of military force, the parliament has neither the ability nor real inclination to shape Russia's national security policy. Instead, the legislature uses its control over the defense budget to engage in turf battles with the executive branch.

The executive branch suffers from a lack of cohesion and discipline. The Security Council has failed to become the fulcrum of national security decision making; its overgrown staff now has to compete with the influence of the separate office of the national security advisor to the president of the Russian Federation. There are increasing policy and budgetary conflicts between the armed forces and the military and militarized formations of various security agencies. The armed forces are themselves quite badly fragmented, and the worst is yet to come, as the budget shortfalls of 1994 will be compounded by the anticipated lack of funds in 1995.

Civil-military relations are characterized by a contradiction between the military's crucial political importance (because of the weakness of the civilian institutions) and its lack of power in deciding major issues of the defense policy, such as the budget. Perhaps mindful of the potentially dangerous nature of this contradiction, President Yeltsin has been trying to increase the power of various militarized security formations in order to reduce his dependence on the military (so painfully demonstrated in October 1993) and create a counterweight to its might—a delicate balancing act without a safety net. At the same time, the military in effect runs Moscow's security policy in the hot spots of the "near abroad" without much control by the civilian authorities. The military continues to lack independent political ambitions, but a pursuit of its corporate interests could lead it into an alliance with the Russian hypernationalist forces—once these forces can build a strong political movement, something they have been unable to do so far. Despite its high institutional popularity in the eyes of the public, the military's political clout has been further weakened by its internal fragmentation and poor morale. Thus, the institutional cohesion necessary for a stable consensus on Russian security policy is lacking.

There is a somewhat greater cohesion regarding the set of ideas that form the foundation of security policy. Russia is so weakened politically, economically, socially, and militarily that despite all the proclamations of its great-power status, its security policy cannot help but be focused on the former Soviet republics, and on former Warsaw Pact allies insofar as their situation (for instance, the prospect of their NATO membership) has an impact on the "near abroad," now renamed the zone of vital interests. The basic consensus on Russia's role as an "overseer" of this zone of vital interests has emerged among the liberal and centrist forces now in power.[144] This consensus overlaps, but only partially, with the views of the Russian hypernationalists, like Vladimir Zhirinovsky, and nationalist communists, like Aleksandr Rutskoi, who want to forcibly integrate the zone of vital interests back into a reborn Russian Empire, something the centrists and liberals, content to expand Russian influence into the "near abroad," are not willing to do. The liberals and centrists would avoid using military force against the "near abroad" as much as possible and are sensitive to the negative impact of Russian actions in the zone upon Moscow's relations with the West. The hypernationalists and their ilk would be much more inclined to use force in the zone of vital interests, while being less sensitive to the damage to Russia's relations with the West. The emergence of the new business elite, whose interests in security policy are just now taking shape, makes a stable consensus over security issues even less feasible. Thus, there is no wide-ranging consensus among the elites over the means and the ends of Russian security policy.

The Russian public in general offers an even less cohesive picture when it comes to views of national security. Opinion polls show a gap between what may look like a general neoimperialist mood of the public and isolationist responses to specific policies of expanding Russian power into the zone of vital interests that might cost in blood and treasure.

Russia lacks the conditions necessary for a stable consensus on security policy. The agreement on the rather obvious importance of the "near abroad" does not translate into a wide-ranging consensus (that is, one enjoying support outside the circle of President Yeltsin's advisors) over precisely what policies should be implemented there and by what means. The implications of this go well beyond the newly independent states, because Russia's perception of other major powers will be shaped to a considerable degree by their actions regarding the zone of vital interests, which will be determined, in their own turn, primarily by the unstable, contradictory, and fluctuating Russian security policy.

Notes

The views and opinions expressed in this chapter are the author's solely and are not meant to reflect the views and opinions of the Department of the Navy or any agency of the U.S. government. The author would like to express his appreciation to John Arquilla, Amy Corning, Jacob Kipp, and Tim Thomas for directing his attention to some valuable research materials.

1. Oleg Odnokolenko and Sergei Iushenkov, "Oborona ne dolzhna byt' ob''ektom politicheskikh razdorov," *Krasnaia zvezda*, 2 February 1994.

2. I will define national security as a set of policies pursued by a nation in order to "protect itself against the possibility of external attack." Michael Mandelbaum, *The Fate of Nations* (Cambridge: Cambridge University Press, 1988), p. 1.

3. John Lough, "The Place of the 'Near Abroad' in Russian Foreign Policy," *RFE/RL Research Report*, vol. 2, no. 11 (12 March 1993), pp. 21–29; Suzanne Crow, "Russia

Seeks Leadership in Regional Peacekeeeping," *RFE/RL Research Report*, vol. 2, no. 15 (9 April 1993); John Lough, "Defining Russia's Relations with Neighboring States," *RFE/RL Research Report*, vol. 2, no. 20 (14 May 1993), pp. 53–60.

4. Sovet po oboronnoi i vneshnei politike, "Strategiia dlia Rossii (2)," *Nezavisimaia gazeta*, 27 May 1994.

5. Suzanne Crow, "Why Has Russian Foreign Policy Changed?" *RFE/RL Research Report*, vol. 3, no. 18 (6 May 1994), p. 3; "Osnovnye polozheniia voennoi doktriny Rossiiskoi Federatsii (izlozhenie)," *Voennaia mysl'*, November 1993, special issue, pp. 6, 7.

6. Zbigniew Brzezinski, "A Bigger—and Safer—Europe," *New York Times*, 1 December 1993.

7. Karl E. Meyer, "The Great Game, Again?" *New York Times*, 2 January 1994; Celestine Bohlen, "Nationalist Vote Toughens Russian Foreign Policy," *New York Times*, 25 January 1994.

8. Sovet po oboronnoi i vneshnei politike, "Strategiia dlia Rossii (2)."

9. Crow, "Why Has Russian Foreign Policy Changed?" p. 1.

10. Paula J. Dobriansky, "Ukraine: A Question of Survival," *The National Interest*, no. 36 (summer 1994), p. 66.

11. Suzanne Crow, "Russia Asserts Its Strategic Agenda," *RFE/RL Research Report*, vol. 2, no. 50 (17 December 1993), p. 7; Crow, "Why Has Russian Foreign Policy Changed?" pp. 5, 6; Zbigniew Brzezinski, "The Premature Partnership," *Foreign Affairs*, vol. 73, no. 2 (March/April 1994), p. 72.

12. Lough, "The Place of the 'Near Abroad' in Russian Foreign Policy," p. 29. Also see Vera Tolz, "The Burden of the Imperial Legacy," *RFE/RL Research Report*, vol. 2, no. 20 (14 May 1993), pp. 44, 45.

13. I will use the following definition of politics: any persistent pattern of human relationships that involves, to a significant extent, control, influence, power, or authority. Robert A. Dahl, *Modern Political Analysis* (Englewood Cliffs, NJ: Prentice-Hall, 1991), p. 4.

14. Iurii Levada, "Obshchestvennoe mnenie v god krizisnogo pereloma: Smena paradigmy," *Segodnia*, 17 May 1994.

15. See Roman Kolkowicz, *The Soviet Military and the Communist Party* (Princeton: Princeton University Press, 1967), p. 11.

16. See William Odom, "The 'Militarization' of the Soviet Society," *Problems of Communism*, vol. 25 (September–October 1976), pp. 34–51.

17. See Timothy J. Colton, *Commissars, Commanders and Civilian Authority: The Structure of Soviet Military Politics* (Cambridge, MA: Harvard University Press, 1979). For an overview of these three approaches to the issue, see Timothy J. Colton, "Perspectives on Civil-Military Relations in the Soviet Union," in *Soldiers and the Soviet State*, eds. Timothy J. Colton and Thane Gustafson (Princeton: Princeton University Press, 1990), pp. 12–14.

18. Bruce Parrott, "Political Change and Civil-Military Relations," in Colton and Gustafson, eds., *Soldiers and the Soviet State*, p. 55.

19. Colton, "Perspectives on Civil-Military Relations," p. 7.

20. Parrott, "Political Change and Civil-Military Relations," p. 55.

21. Ibid.

22. L. Khudiakov, "O kontseptsiiakh po voprosu sozdaniia otechestvennykh avianesushchikh kreiserov," *Morskoi sbornik*, no. 12 (December 1991), pp. 6–12; V. Kuzin, "Avianesushchie kreisera: My znali, chto delali," *Morskoi sbornik*, no. 2 (February 1992), pp. 34–38.

23. See Peter Almquist, *Red Forge: Soviet Military Industry Since 1965* (New York: Columbia University Press, 1990), pp. 126–31.

24. Aleksandr Emel'ianenkov, "Argumenty admirala Chernova," *Sobesednik*, no. 30

(July 1990); idem, "Podvodnye techeniia," *Komsomol'skaia pravda*, 8 February 1990; S. Bystrov, "Gibel' atomokhoda," *Krasnaia zvezda*, 15 March 1990.

25. *Komsomol'skaia pravda*, 13 May 1994, translated in *WPS News*, 16 May 1994.

26. "Konstitutsiia Rossiiskoi Federatsii," *Izvestiia*, 10 November 1993.

27. Ibid.

28. Sergei Parkhomenko, "Parlamentskoe partnerstvo vo imia voiny," *Segodnia*, 14 May 1994.

29. Pavel Fel'gengauer, "Chernyi peredel biudzheta: VPK protiv armii," *Segodnia*, 7 July 1994. Similar figures have been given by Stepan Sulakshin, chairman of the State Duma Subcommittee on the Military-Industrial Complex; see Stepan Sulakshin, "Dva kvartala na golodnom paike," *Krasnaia zvezda*, 28 May 1994.

30. Aleksei Arbatov, "Bol'she—ne vsegda luchshe," *Obshchaia gazeta*, 24–30 June 1994.

31. Sulakshin, "Dva kvartala na golodnom paike."

32. Colonel Ivanov, "Chto segodnia nuzhno dlia oborony Rossii?" *Nezavisimaia gazeta*, 28 May 1994.

33. "Komu prinadlezhit vlast' v Rossii?" *Izvestiia*, 9 July 1994.

34. Vladimir Berezovskii, "Dva politicheskikh lageria federal'noi elity Rossii," *Svobodnaia mysl'*, no. 9 (September 1994), p. 83.

35. See Liudmila Telen', "Sovet bezopasnosti bez grifa 'sekretno,'" *Moskovskie novosti*, 5–12 June 1994; Aleksandr Pel'ts, "Vysshii kriterii—blago Rossii," *Krasnaia zvezda*, 28 June 1994.

36. Vladimir Mironov, "Poslednii sovet strany sovetov," *Vek*, 16–22 September 1994.

37. Telen', "Sovet bezopasnosti"; Pel'ts, "Vysshii kriterii—blago Rossii"; Vladimir Pirumov, interview by author, Moscow, 14 July 1994.

38. Pirumov, interview.

39. Sovet po oboronnoi i vneshnei politike, "Strategiia dlia Rossii (2)."

40. I. Bulavinov, "Tough Summer for Gen. Grachev," *Kommersant Daily*, 5 May 1994, p. 13, translated in *WPS Defense and Security*, 11 May 1994.

41. Valerii Vyzhutovich, "Dispetcher," *Moskovskie novosti*, 17 July 1994.

42. Leonid Nikitinskii, "Samyi bezopasnyi iz pomoshchnikov prezidenta?" *Izvestiia*, 11 January 1994.

43. Berezovskii, "Dva politicheskikh lageria," p. 71.

44. Interview by author with a Russian government official who requested anonymity, Moscow, July 1994.

45. *RFE/RL Daily Report*, 25 May 1994.

46. Oleg Falichev, "Liudi v pogonakh," *Krasnaia zvezda*, 2 August 1994; Pavel Fel'gengauer, "Kakova zhe chislennost' armii?" *Segodnia*, 17 June 1994.

47. Iurii Golotiuk, "Grachev khotel by podchinit' sebe 'zelenye furazhki,'" *Segodnia*, 14 July 1994; Colonel General Andrei Nikolaev, "Pogranichnye voiska v sisteme bezopasnosti gosudarstva," *Rossiiskie vesti*, 4 August 1994.

48. Falichev, "Liudi v pogonakh"; "Komu prinadlezhit vlast' v Rossii?"

49. Falichev, "Liudi v pogonakh"; *The Military Balance 1993–1994* (London: International Institute for Strategic Studies, 1993), pp. 99, 106.

50. See discussion of Aleksandr Belkin, "The Building of the Russian Armed Forces," paper prepared for a conference on Post-Soviet Military Policies: Russia, Ukraine and Others, at the Naval Postgraduate School, Monterey, CA, 15 and 16 November 1993.

51. Steven Erlanger, "Russia's Military in Need of New Goals," *New York Times*, 23 May 1994.

52. Communication from Pavel Fel'gengauer, 15 September 1994.

53. Aleksandr Oliinik, "Problemy tyla segodnia—eto vyzhivanie armii i flota zavtra," *Krasnaia zvezda*, 3 November 1993.

54. V. Mal'tseva, "The Problems of Novosibirsk," *Sovetskaia Sibir'*, 27 April 1994, p. 2, translated in *Provincial Press: WPS Weekly Supplement*, 25 May 1994.

55. Mikhail Deliagin, "Inostrannye investitsii idut v neeffektivnye otrasli," *Finansovye izvestiia*, 14–20 April 1994, p. 1.

56. "Predotvrashchen proryv voennykh korablei KNR cherez granitsu," *Segodnia*, 7 May 1994.

57. *RFE/RL Daily Report*, 4 January 1994.

58. Iurii Golotiuk, "Pavel Grachev utverzhdaet, chto ego liudi ne uchastvovali v 'Vostoke–94,'" *Segodnia*, 17 September 1994.

59. Iurii Deriugin, "Trevozhnye tendentsii v rossiiskoi armii," *Nezavisimaia gazeta*, 24 August 1994.

60. Ibid.

61. Boris Yeltsin, *The Struggle for Russia* (New York: Times Books, 1994), pp. 80, 87–89, 273–78.

62. Colton, "Perspectives on Civil-Military Relations," p. 7.

63. On civilian analysts under Gorbachev, see Benjamin S. Lambeth, "A Generation Too Late: Civilian Analysis and Soviet Military Thinking," in *Soviet Strategy and the New Military Thinking*, eds. Derek Leebaert and Timothy Dickinson (New York: Cambridge University Press, 1992), pp. 217–47.

64. On the rise and decline of the "new thinking," see Mikhail Tsypkin, "Military Power in Russian National Security Policy," in *The Soviet Empire Reconsidered: Essays in Honor of Adam B. Ulam*, eds. Sanford Lieberman, David Powell, Carol Saivetz, and Sarah Terry (Boulder, CO: Westview Press, 1994), pp. 189–97.

65. The published military doctrine of Russia addresses the need to prepare the troops for "both defensive and offensive actions." "Osnovnye polozheniia voennoi doktriny Rossiiskoi Federatsii," p. 18.

66. Not to be confused with the much more prestigious and established Russian Academy of Sciences, the heir to the USSR Academy and the Russian Imperial Academy.

67. Konstantin Sorokin, interview by author, Moscow, 10 April 1994; communication from Jacob Kipp, 26 May 1994.

68. Meeting with the delegation of the Committee of Scientists for Global Security in Monterey, CA, 23 May 1994.

69. "Natsional'naia doktrina Rossii (problemy i prioritety)," *Obozrevatel'*, 1994, nos. 5–8, special issue.

70. See Mikhail Tsypkin, "Will the Military Rule Russia?" *Security Studies*, vol. 2, no. 1 (autumn 1992), p. 42.

71. Svetlana Gamova, "Aleksandr Lebed': Sama zhizn' zastavliaet generalov zanimat'sia politikoi," *Izvestiia*, 20 July 1994.

72. Gleb Cherkasov, "General Lebed' ne budet poslushnym ispolnitelem prikaza," *Segodnia*, 16 August 1994; Natal'ia Prikhod'ko, "Reorganizatsiia 14-i armii zamorozhena," *Nezavisimaia gazeta*, 16 August 1994; Viktor Litovkin, "Prezident Rossii zashchishchaet generala Lebedia," *Izvestiia*, 16 August 1994.

73. William C. Fuller Jr., *Strategy and Power in Russia 1600–1914* (New York: Free Press, 1992), pp. 289, 290.

74. Emil' Pain, "Mirotvorchestvo Rossii—ne imperskaia politika, a instrument uregulirovaniia konfliktov," *Rossiiskie vesti*, 20 September 1994.

75. Yeltsin, *Struggle for Russia*, p. 277.

76. Tsypkin, "Will the Military Rule Russia?" pp. 45, 46; V. Dudnik, "The Army Can't Stay Out of Politics," *Rossiiskaia gazeta*, 17 May 1994, pp. 1–2, translated in *WPS Defense and Security*, 23 May 1994.

77. Adam Ulam pointed out that "the [Soviet] regime believes that its internal security

is inextricably bound up with the advance of its external power and authority. . . . [W]ith the country's mounting social and economic problems, with the ideology itself having become discredited in the minds of the mass of the Soviet people, the regime tries to demonstrate its viability and dynamism through foreign expansion." Adam B. Ulam, *Dangerous Relations* (New York: Oxford University Press, 1983), pp. 311, 312. On Yeltsin's relations with the military, see Tsypkin, "Will the Military Rule Russia?" pp. 51–54; M. Berger, "The Mercedes Attack," *Izvestiia*, 12 May 1994, translated in *WPS Defense and Security*, 16 May 1994.

78. Dudnik, "The Army Can't Stay Out of Politics."

79. Berger, "The Mercedes Attack."

80. I. Bulavinov, "Minister as Lobbyist," *Kommersant Daily*, 14 May 1994, p. 3, translated in *WPS Defense and Security*, 16 May 1994.

81. *Nezavisimaia gazeta*, 24 May 1994, p. 1, translated in *WPS Defense and Security*, 27 May 1994.

82. "Russia Prepares for New Elections Amidst Strong Public Doubts," *Opinion Research Memorandum* (Washington, DC: U.S. Information Agency, Office of Research), 29 September 1993, p. 3.

83. *RFE/RL Daily Report,* 9 September 1994.

84. Hypernationalism is "the belief that other nations or nation-states are both inferior and threatening and must therefore be dealt with harshly." John J. Mearsheimer, "Back to the Future: Instability in Europe After the Cold War," *International Security*, vol. 15, no. 1 (summer 1990), p. 21.

85. Vladimir Zhirinovsky, "LDPR znaet, chto delat'," *Krasnaia zvezda*, 10 December 1993.

86. See Barry R. Posen, "Nationalism, the Mass Army, and Military Power," *International Security*, vol. 18, no. 2 (fall 1993), pp. 120–22.

87. See Stephen van Evera, "Hypotheses on Nationalism and War," *International Security*, vol. 18, no. 4 (spring 1994), p. 34.

88. Tsypkin, "Will the Military Rule Russia?" pp. 58–62.

89. Vladimir Pribylovsky, "A Survey of Radical Right-Wing Groups in Russia," *RFE/RL Research Report,* vol. 3, no. 16 (22 April 1994), p. 36.

90. Ibid., p. 34; Wendy Slater, "Russia," *RFE/RL Research Report*, vol. 3, no. 16 (22 April 1994), p. 26.

91. Pribylovsky, "Survey of Radical Right-Wing Groups," p. 29.

92. Tsypkin, "Will the Military Rule Russia?" p. 62.

93. Aleksei Chelnokov, "General Lebed': Takaia eto rabota . . . " *Izvestiia*, 3 February 1994.

94. V.D. Solovei, "Evoliutsiia sovremennogo russkogo natsionalizma," in *Russkii narod: Istoricheskaia sud'ba v XX veke* (Moscow: ANKO, 1993), p. 304.

95. Tsypkin, "Will the Military Rule Russia?" pp. 43–45.

96. Stephen Foye, "Civilian and Military Leaders in Russia's 'New' Political Arena," *RFE/RL Research Report*, vol. 3, no. 15 (15 April 1994), p. 3.

97. Evgenii Vasil'chuk, "Vremia aktivnoi promyshlennoi politiki eshche ne prishlo," *Finansovye izvestiia*, 3–9 February 1994.

98. I will speak of an "elite," although obviously this "elite" can be divided into various groups for reasons of geography, business interests, and so forth.

99. Keith Bush, "Conversion and Privatization of Defense Enterprises in Russia," *RFE/RL Research Report*, vol. 3, no. 17 (29 April 1994), p. 22.

100. Ibid., p. 21.

101. Ibid., p. 20.

102. Ibid., p. 21.

103. "Trudnyi al'ians s 'oboronkoi,' " *Finansovye izvestiia*, 19 April 1994.

104. Ibid.

105. Adam N. Stulberg, "The High Politics of Arming Russia," *RFE/RL Research Report*, vol. 2, no. 49 (10 December 1993), p. 5.

106. "Trudnyi al'ians s 'oboronkoi.' "

107. Aleksandr Vorob'ev, "Nas vporu prichislit' k VPK," *Krasnaia zvezda*, 25 January 1994.

108. Ibid.

109. Stephen J. Blank, *Energy and Security in Transcaucasia* (Carlisle Barracks, PA: Strategic Studies Institute, U.S. Army War College, 1994).

110. "Nam est' chem podelit'sia s Kitaem," *Krasnaia zvezda*, 15 April 1994.

111. Aleksandr Andriushkov, "My delaem luchshii v mire perekhvatchik," *Krasnaia zvezda*, 13 January 1994.

112. Pavel Fel'gengauer, "Brosok na iug sostoialsia," *Segodnia*, 22 April 1994.

113. Ibid.

114. Jessica Eve Stern, "Moscow Meltdown: Can Russia Survive?" *International Security*, vol. 18, no. 4 (spring 1994), pp. 40–65.

115. Egor Gaidar, "Novyi kurs," *Izvestiia*, 10 February 1994.

116. V.S. Pirumov, "Nekotorye aspekty metodologii issledovaniia problem natsional'noi bezopasnosti Rossii v sovremennykh usloviiakh," *Geopolitika i bezopasnost'*, 1993, no. 1, p. 7.

117. For a groundbreaking discussion of the impact of geographical and historical factors on the prerevolutionary Russian security policy, see Fuller, *Strategy and Power in Russia*.

118. On the difference between *Geopolitik* and geopolitics, see Colin S. Gray, *The Geopolitics of the Nuclear Era: Heartland, Rimlands, and the Technological Revolution* (New York: Crane Russak, 1977), pp. 19–21, 29, 30.

119. Ibid., p. 19.

120. V.V. Zhirinovskii, *Poslednii brosok na iug* (Moscow: Rait, 1993), pp. 35–45; V.V. Zhirinovskii, *S moei tochki zreniia* (Moscow: Rait, 1993), pp. 5, 14, 34; Jacob W. Kipp, "The Zhirinovsky Threat," *Foreign Affairs*, vol. 73, no. 3 (May/June 1994), pp. 77, 78.

121. Pirumov, "Nekotorye aspekty," p. 10.

122. "Osnovnye polozheniia voennoi doktriny Rossiiskoi Federatsii," p. 5.

123. Sergei Shakhrai, "Strategy Needed for Relationship with China," *Izvestiia*, 20 May 1994, translated in *FBIS Daily Report—Central Eurasia*, 20 May 1994.

124. A. Iakovlev, "Rossiisko-kitaiskii uzel v mirovoi politike," *Obozrevatel'*, 1993, no. 22, p. 84.

125. Sovet po oboronnoi i vneshnei politike, "Strategiia dlia Rossii (2)."

126. Zhirinovskii, *S moei tochki zreniia*, p. 31; *RFE/RL Daily Report*, 15 September 1994; Nikita Gololobov, "We Should Find a Common Language," *Nezavisimaia gazeta*, 23 September 1994, translated in *WPS News*, 26 September 1994.

127. On planned mobile forces, see John W.R. Lepingwell, "Restructuring the Russian Military," *RFE/RL Research Report*, vol. 2, no. 25 (18 June 1994), pp. 20–22. Also see "Osnovnye polozheniia voennoi doktriny Rossiiskoi Federatsii," p. 18.

128. Sovet po oboronnoi i vneshnei politike, "Strategiia dlia Rossii (2)."

129. Valentin Rudenko, "Budushchee—za finansovo-promyshlennymi gruppami," *Krasnaia zvezda*, 5 March 1994.

130. *The Russians Rethink Democracy: Pulse of Europe II* (n.p.: Times Mirror Center for People and the Press, 1993), pp. 18, 20.

131. "Russian Security Concerns on the Rise," *Opinion Research Memorandum* (Washington, DC: U.S. Information Agency, Office of Research), 31 March 1993, p. 1.

132. Aleksandr Gol'ts, "V kavkazskom melovom kruge," *Krasnaia zvezda*, 5 February 1994; idem, "Bosniiskii uzel i politika Moskvy," *Krasnaia zvezda*, 12 February 1994; Leonid Mlechin, "Za osobuiu rol' Rossii v Tadzhikistane prikhoditsia platit' slishkom doroguiu tsenu," *Izvestiia*, 12 February 1994; Pavel Fel'gengauer, "Balkanizatsiia istorii," *Segodnia*, 19 April 1994.

133. On coalition logrolling and its role in imperialist expansionism, see Jack Snyder, *Myths of Empire* (Ithaca, NY: Cornell University Press, 1991), pp. 17–19.

134. V.A. Artamonov, "Geopolitika Rossii i 'blizhnee zarubezh'e,' " *Geopolitika*, 1993, no. 1, p. 88.

135. *Survey Commissioned by the Media and Opinion Research Department of the RFE/RL Research Institute*, conducted by ROMIR.

136. Richard B. Dobson, "Russians Desire Cooperation with the West, Are Wary of Entanglements in the 'Near Abroad,' " *Opinion Research Memorandum* (Washington, DC: Office of Research, U.S. Information Agency), 3 August 1994, pp. 15–18.

137. *Survey Commissioned by the Media and Opinion Research Department.*

138. Dobson, "Russians Desire Cooperation," p. 20.

139. Emil' Pain, "Konsolidatsiia Rossii ili vosstanovlenie Soiuza," *Segodnia*, 22 July 1994.

140. Ibid.

141. Dobson, "Russians Desire Cooperation," pp. 9, 21.

142. A. Solzhenitsyn, " 'Russkii vopros' k kontsu XX veka," *Novyi mir*, no. 7 (July 1994), pp. 135–48, 150–52, 156, 157, 169–71.

143. Snyder, *Myths of Empire*, p. 17.

144. Artamonov, "Geopolitika Rossii," p. 88.

3

Russian Military Doctrine
and Deployments

Raymond L. Garthoff

Russian military planners today, as in the spring of 1992, when the Russian Ministry of Defense, General Staff, and armed forces were reconstituted after seventy years, face truly formidable tasks. Although inheriting many of the assets of the Soviet armed forces, they also inherited many of its encumbrances, as well as new difficulties created by the changed post-Soviet situation. Not only is the external environment suddenly, drastically changed, so too is the internal foundation of the armed forces and of the state itself. Not only is there a need for identification and definition of possible external threats, there is also a new need for identification and definition of the Russian state and its interests. Even the dividing line between what is "internal" and "external" is blurred and in flux. The Union of Soviet Socialist Republics was gone in a flash, but what succeeded it? It was succeeded by the Russian Federation and eleven other republics, as well as a Commonwealth of Independent States (CIS)—which initially had extensive if vague and, as it turned out, largely ephemeral responsibilities for the armed forces.

CIS authority over the armed forces was initially stipulated as extending to "strategic forces" (although the definition of such forces was interpreted diversely by member states) and such other forces as the republics placed under its command. CIS authority was, however, soon supplanted with respect to most forces. By necessity rather than by preference, Russia, among the last of the republics to do so, had no practical recourse other than to create its own armed forces in April–May 1992. Russia followed the lead of Ukraine and most other republics in nationalizing military forces on its own territory (initially excepting strategic forces under commonwealth control), but unlike the others it also assumed authority over the large, formerly Soviet armed forces contingents still stationed in other countries (mainly Germany, Poland, and the three Baltic states) or stationed in other former Soviet republics not claimed or controlled by those states (mainly in Transcaucasia and Central Asia, but some in Moldova), a few where claims clashed (most notably the Black Sea fleet, claimed also by Ukraine, which became a major issue; and some units in Belarus later resolved without great difficulty).

On the whole, however, the devolution of the former Soviet armed forces to control of the successor republics, while somewhat more protracted, was almost as smooth as the devolution of the Soviet Union to the newly independent successor republics.[1] Just as no one challenged the Russian claim to be the successor "continuing state" inheriting the Soviet Union's seat on the United Nations Security Council and its membership as a nuclear-weapons state in the Nuclear Nonproliferation Treaty, so too no one chose to challenge Russian authority over the Soviet armies in Germany, Poland, Lithuania, Latvia, Estonia, and Moldova (or many units in all the other republics except Ukraine).

The initial transition had been unnerving for the General Staff and many others in Moscow (as well as many forces in the field) who were, from the end of December 1991 until April–May 1992, not sure whether they were serving Russia or a commonwealth, or still a Soviet Union that had expired in all its other manifestations. This transition was made without serious difficulties. But the formal constitution of new successor states and their authority over elements of the armed forces was but the starting point for reevaluation.

From Soviet to Russian Military Doctrine

Military doctrine and strategy are based on a balance of a number of factors, and changes in any of these can be disruptive until a modified or new doctrine responsive to the change can be developed. To take the most central example, a significant change in political relationships with other relevant external countries will lead to important changes in military doctrine, strategy, and force structure and deployment. The United States, its NATO allies, and the former members of the defunct Warsaw Pact are all still making sometimes not easy decisions about changes in doctrine, strategy, force structure, and deployments as a result of the end of the Cold War. That event, of course, involved a momentous change. There are, however, great differences in the problems of adjustment faced by the Western countries and those of the East, which have also experienced a nearly simultaneous change in state ideology and policy, major transformations in their economic systems, and the sudden collapse of their alliance. Russia not only bears the greatest burden of adjustment to that change but in addition faces the need to deal with the consequences of the dissolution of the Soviet Union as well. Moreover, these major internal and external transformations, and the necessary transitions they entail, are overlapping but not identical in their timing and effects.

Russian military doctrine is the successor to Soviet military doctrine, but that was a doctrine that itself had recently undergone significant modifications and was still in the throes of further revision.

Soviet military doctrine in the late 1970s and early 1980s had been undergoing a difficult readjustment to meet the implications of the "new military-technological revolution" in weaponry. Pressed by Marshal Nikolai Ogarkov in particular, and against opposition not only from more conservative military leaders but also elements of the military-industrial complex, an effort was being made to shift from the traditional Soviet reliance on massed firepower to more effective modern precision-guided munitions and application of advanced technology to means of command, control, communications, and intelligence (C^3I). In strategy, this included a modification of traditional massed attacks to more mobile forces and greater reliance on maneuver, combining elements of deep advance, defense, and withdrawal within a continuing offensive.

From 1986 through 1988, there was an important conceptual change in Soviet military doctrine: the application of "new thinking," which entailed not only a criterion of "reasonable sufficiency" instead of maximum insurance in meeting military requirements but also the redefinition of requirements to provide "defensive defense" instead of "offensive defense." Underlying both was a replacement of the strategic objective. While Soviet *policy* had always been to prevent war, the aim of Soviet military *strategy* had been to prepare to "win" if war should come (hollow though the very conception of victory was recognized to be in the case of general nuclear war). That strategy was seen as both the best deterrent to enemy attack and the natural military response if deterrence should fail. Under Gorbachev's revolution in military doctrine, however, the aim not only of state policy but also of military strategy was set as prevention of war. Moreover, if war should come, the military objective was no longer to win by taking the offense, but the more modest aims of preventing the attacking enemy from winning by defense and terminating hostilities as quickly as possible. Although the abandonment of a strategy of taking the offensive with a major thrust in Europe toward the English Channel in case NATO launched a war (the only recognized contingency for major war in Europe) was not welcomed by some Soviet military planners and commanders, the new doctrine was adopted in 1987.[2]

The second stage of the new Soviet military doctrine was implemented over the years 1989 through 1991 (and was still under way when the Soviet Union collapsed). The change in doctrine was applied to strategy and force structure. Initiated by the unilateral reduction of Soviet forces in Central Europe and concentrating on reduction of armored strike forces, it was extended further by a Soviet agreement in the Conventional Forces in Europe (CFE) Treaty to drastically reduce Soviet (and other Warsaw Pact) forces in order to establish an agreed-to balance between NATO and Warsaw Pact forces in Central Europe. This major change in policy was only feasible after Moscow had decided to give up its preponderance of forces long maintained under a strategy of offensive action in case of war. Midway through this process, even before the CFE Treaty could be completed and signed, the Warsaw Pact dissolved in the wake of a rapid revolutionary movement overthrowing communist rule in all of Eastern Europe.

Soviet military planners by 1990–91 thus faced a situation drastically altered even from the recently accepted change from Soviet/Warsaw Pact predominance to equality in forces. Now, the Soviet Union, shorn of its six Warsaw Pact allies and the defensive glacis on the ground (and for air defense), stood as in 1941 on its own borders, and with forces permitted under the CFE Treaty that were far inferior in numbers to those of NATO. (Moreover, the forces of its former allies not only could not be counted upon, they were indeed likely to be on the opposing side if a war came.) The saving grace, of course, was that with the end of the division of Europe the Cold War was over. The danger of a NATO-Soviet war, while much more militarily daunting for the Soviet Union than at any previous time, was also now recognized to be extremely unlikely. (Although Soviet military planners recognized that fact, some worried that the favorable political situation might sometime change, while the adverse military situation would not.)

Although far less important, it should also be noted that during those last years the Soviet Union was also slashing its other commitments abroad. Soviet military involvements (except supply of arms and, to a lesser extent, advisors) had always been minimal, other than the intervention in neighboring Afghanistan, from which the Soviet Union had now withdrawn. The four-division force stationed in Mongolia was now withdrawn. Naval presence in distant areas was sharply cut in 1989–91, even in the nearby Mediterranean. The last Soviet token military presence in Cuba and Vietnam was ending. Distant force projection had never been a major Soviet military requirement; now it was no longer even a factor.

To sum up, the Soviet military doctrine inherited by the Russian military command and planners in early 1992 had accepted a major change of threat assessment that discounted deeply the likelihood of war with the United States and the NATO alliance and reluctantly also had accepted the loss of its alliance and glacis in East-Central Europe. In addition, the successful American-led offensive in the Persian Gulf in 1991 had proven the advantage of advanced technology over massed conventional forces, calling for major organizational, operational, and military-technological changes. The fluidity of political developments south of the Soviet Union also left open some questions of threat assessment.

Meanwhile, developments within the Soviet Union itself had begun to have serious effects on Soviet military doctrine. In the first place, the declining role of the Communist Party of the Soviet Union in 1990 and 1991, even before August, had raised questions of the role of the traditional institutions of party control within the armed forces. Even more disturbing, the involvement of armed forces in reestablishing order in cases of civil unrest (above all in Tbilisi in April 1989 and Baku in January 1990) had caused serious concern both within the armed forces and in the society at large. Another issue raised was the use of the military in even more questionable cases, in which civil unrest had been provoked and then quelled for political intimidation (in Vilnius, Lithuania, and Riga, Latvia, in January and February 1991). The internal role of the armed forces was becoming a political (as well as doctrinal) issue. The involvement of the minister of defense and several of his deputies in the August 1991 attempted coup, and the near confrontation of troops and populace near the Russian parliament building in Moscow, posed the issue of political-military relations still more acutely. Thus the question was sharply posed as to what, if any, *internal* security role the armed forces should play (particularly since there existed a separate body of internal security troops under the Ministry of the Interior [MVD], and yet other armed security forces under the Committee of State Security [KGB], including the border guards and three elite divisions; these MVD and KGB forces had been juridically removed from "the armed forces" in 1989).

In less dramatic and less obvious ways other internal developments also had come to affect the Soviet military establishment and the resource component of military doctrine and strategy. In particular, the economic system was changing, although reform moved slowly. Not only was military procurement cut substantially from 1989 through 1991, but relations between the military establishment and various economic and civil authorities were changing. A shortage of apartments for families of military officers began to assume a serious scale, and local authorities would or could no longer simply act to provide housing. New rules of military accounting and arrangements for local procurement (for provisions other than weapons) became necessary. Draft evasion began to assume a larger scale, especially in some outlying republics. Civic pride in military service was low and so was the attractiveness of a military career. The military was, indeed, part of society, but as the traditional workings of Soviet society began to falter in 1990–91, so too did this affect the military.

Russian Military Forces, 1992

With the breakup of the Soviet Union, Russian military planners now faced a doubly disadvantageous consequence of this sudden change. First, the Russian Federation was not returned to 1939 or 1917 borders; rather, with the loss of the territories of Ukraine, Belarus, and Kazakhstan in particular, Russia was back roughly to the borders of the seventeenth century. Second, the largest, best-equipped, and best-trained forces had been deployed in regions along the western borders—the old borders—above all the thirty divisions in Ukraine and Belarus. The Moscow military district suddenly had become a border district—but almost without troops. It had only the two elite "parade" divisions (the Second Guards Taman Motorized Rifle Division and the Fourth Guards Kantemirov Tank Division); the 106th Guards Airborne Division at Tula and Naro-Fominsk; the ex-KGB First Special Purpose (formerly Dzherzhinskii) Division; the Twenty-seventh Separate Motorized Rifle Brigade; and the Second Special Purpose (Spetsnaz) Brigade.[3]

In all, Russia was left with about eighty-five divisions, most abroad or beyond the Urals, as contrasted with a Soviet total of over two hundred (of varying strength) only a few years earlier. Gorbachev had eliminated about seventy divisions, many of them largely paper mobilization base divisions, in 1989–91. Other divisions located in the other republics at the end of 1991 were for the most part either being nationalized or disbanded. (These comprised twenty in Ukraine, ten in Belarus, eleven in the Transcaucasian republics, and eleven in the Central Asian republics.)[4] Even that was an inflated and not sustainable force level. But before discussing force structure and deployments, my purpose in citing these figures is only to illustrate the drastically changed nature of the military forces.[5]

Even more important than the shrunken size of the Russian armed forces was the problem of determining how they could be refashioned to meet the requirements of the new state and the constraints on its available resources. The Soviet navy, for example, with the exception of the challenge and dispute from Ukraine with respect to the Black Sea fleet, was intact—but in trouble. It was already in need of attention, and the lack of resources and facilities to maintain it posed a growing problem that was compounded by the approaching mass obsolescence of many ships, including large numbers of unserviceable nuclear-powered submarines (over one hundred) that presented difficult and costly problems of disposal.

Two other necessarily priority problems were the need to fulfill international agreements on the restationing of the remaining forces (over 250,000 military men plus nearly as many dependents) still in Germany and Poland and meeting local (and to some extent international) pressures to remove the 140,000 troops in the three Baltic states. In addition, while most forces in Transcaucasia and Central Asia could in time be phased into national units or disbanded, and a few withdrawn and redeployed, local conflicts and disorders made Russian military outposts and weapons stocks in Transcaucasia attractive targets for lawless raiders seeking arms.

The repatriation of Russian forces stationed beyond the borders of the Russian Federation thus constituted a priority requirement. Theoretically, but in practice only to a limited extent, the return of such forces could help to meet such problems as the absence of forces deployed in the western borderlands of Russia. But the problems and costs of moving and especially resettling such units with their equipment and personnel were often too great. If units were disbanded, the equipment could be spread around to other units in need, or stored, or scrapped; the enlisted conscript personnel could be released, although the problem of resettling officers and their families remained—even if they were discharged from service.

During 1992, the Russian political and military leadership had to sharply cut back its expectations for security arrangements under the CIS, but it did not abandon them. Negotiations were conducted with individual republics concerning military forces on their territory; agreements were reached recognizing either Russian or local authority over them; and arrangements were made for stationing, withdrawing, or disbanding units and disposing of weapons and equipment. In May 1992, just as national armed forces and ministries of defense were being reconstituted, about half the members of the commonwealth signed a Treaty on Collective Security (Russia, Armenia, Kazakhstan, and the other Central Asian members except Turkmenistan). This grouping was later joined by Belarus, Georgia, and Azerbaijan, but not Ukraine or Moldova. It provides a coalition alliance of CIS members in addition to bilateral military cooperation agreements. This collective security undertaking by most CIS members did not lead to a closely integrated alliance, but it does provide a framework within which various bilateral or other groupings of CIS members can provide further coordinated or even collective defense arrangements.

Thus, notwithstanding that in June 1993 the post of Supreme Command of the Armed Forces of the CIS was abolished and plans for "Joint Armed Forces" abandoned, more limited but effective arrangements were gradually reached. In August 1993, the original six members (and later some others) agreed on coordination of air and missile defenses, helping to fill a large gap created by the breakup of the former united Soviet defense establishment. Similarly, although most republics initially moved to establish independent border guard forces (as Russia did in June 1992), several for practical reasons allowed Russian-controlled border guards (Armenia, Georgia, Kyrgyzstan, and Tajikistan), and Ukraine and all others (except Moldova) later agreed to coordination. Finally, "peacekeeping" was discussed at CIS summit meetings beginning in February 1992, and in September 1992, the CIS Treaty on Collective Security signatories agreed to include peacekeeping in the sphere of its activities.

Nonetheless, the armed forces and military structure of the former Soviet Union had been shattered with the breakup of the Soviet Union.

Ukraine was most adamant on maintaining control over virtually all forces on its territory, except (initially) for acceptance of CIS (and de facto Russian) control over strategic nuclear forces, and settling the dispute over the Black Sea fleet, which continued to remain under Moscow's control. But the conventional forces—twenty ground force divisions and extensive air and air defense forces, in all over seven hundred thousand men—were subordinated to Kiev. Belarus agreed that in addition to the mobile ICBMs under CIS/Russian control, Russia would have control over most of the medium bomber forces and some other units on its territory, but it too took over the ten ground force divisions (including the elite 103rd Guards Airborne Division at Vitebsk, despite Russian protests) and most air force fighter and fighter-bomber units. In Moldova, a civil war erupted between the Trans-Dniester area (which had been part of Russia and then the Soviet Union for over a century) and the remainder of the country (which had been part of Romania until 1940). The local Soviet Fourteenth Army headquarters and one subordinate division in Tiraspol (the Fifty-ninth Motorized Rifle Division) were placed under nominal Russian control, but they played a largely independent role. Other units in Moldova were either withdrawn to Russia (including a paratroop regiment) or taken over by Moldova with Russian agreement (including a MiG–29 regiment).

In Transcaucasia, the eleven ground force divisions and most other units were taken under Moscow's control, although Azerbaijan sought to nationalize forces on its territory and above all to obtain their weapons. In Georgia as well as Azerbaijan, irregular local forces succeeded in taking many stocks of arms by force. Russia disbanded seven of the army divisions in Transcaucasia and the Nineteenth Air Defense Division and turned over most of the armaments and equipment to the three governments. (The exceptions were the 104th Guards Airborne Division in Gandja, Azerbaijan, taken under Russian control and in 1993 repatriated to central Russia; one Russian division remaining in Armenia by agreement; and two Russian divisions remaining in Georgia near the Turkish border, codified later by agreement with Georgia.)

In Central Asia, most of the eleven army ground force divisions were gradually placed under dual or local authority, although with seconded Russian officers (the 201st Motorized Rifle Division in Tajikistan, however, remained as a Russian unit later assigned a peacekeeping role, and an air assault brigade in Uzbekistan and air defense units in Turkmenistan also were taken under Russian control).[6]

The Russian forces in the three Baltic states were acknowledged as such by the three governments. The problem there was different; while not claiming the units or their weapons, the local governments pressed for their immediate withdrawal to Russia. In addition to six ground force divisions and tactical aviation, there were major bases of the Baltic fleet in all three states. Russia agreed to withdraw its forces, but argued that it could not do so quickly and that terms of temporary presence and withdrawal must be negotiated.

In addition to the problems of sorting out what parts of the Soviet military forces beyond the border of the Russian Federation were to be part of the Russian armed forces, the new Russian Ministry of Defense faced intensifying problems in maintaining even the forces within Russia itself. One partial solution was to reduce the size of the forces. In all, Russia had inherited armed forces totaling about three million men. During the first year, the intention was to reduce the overall size by about 500,000 to 700,000 men to about 2.5 million men overall, and later to reduce forces further to about 2 million, and ultimately to 1.5 million or even less. While it was relatively easy to reduce the size of the conscript-enlisted complement (indeed, the problem soon was to find conscripts), it was far less easy to reduce the large officer corps. In many respects it proved more costly to reduce than to maintain the officer corps, numbering about one million. Pensions and severance pay, housing (which had to be provided for each officer retired or released, as well as for those on duty), remaining problems of management of a rapidly shrinking military infrastructure, and other things all cost a great deal.

Officers and conscripts had come from all over the Soviet Union into one army, and their assignments and locations at the time the union dissolved were fortuitous. Young conscripts (most serving two years) would in a year or two complete their service and could simply return home, wherever that was. But for officers and their families, there were more difficult questions of nationality, preferences, living quarters, retirement, and in some cases (above all in Ukraine) pressures to assume a new allegiance. Most officers stayed where they were as units were "nationalized." For personnel in the new Russian army, the change was not great: the Russian Federation and its army, as with their Soviet counterparts, were multinational. Moreover, Russia did not institute a new oath of allegiance. For those serving in Russia who identified with one of the other newly independent states there was the option to leave and serve in that state, but no pressure to do so. For Russians, particularly officers, serving in Ukraine or in one of the units nationalized in other republics, there was more of a problem. Ukraine required an oath, a commitment. Nonetheless, the overwhelming majority of officers of all nationalities stayed wherever they were.

The rapid decline of the overall Russian economy, the new and often chaotic situation caused by privatization of enterprises, and the disbanding of central economic controls all magnified the problems of maintenance and operation of all facets of the armed forces.

Russian Military Doctrine, 1992

It may seem unusual to have begun a discussion of Russian military doctrine by reviewing briefly some of the major problems of defining and holding together the new Russian armed forces. Yet that is the situation that the Russian military authorities faced. These questions could not simply be put aside to wait for a balanced review of doctrine and assessment of requirements.

Military doctrine *was* being intensively reviewed and developed at the same time. But there remained a disjunction between the measured theoretical analysis by the General Staff and the ineluctably ad hoc government dealings with the crisis of the day.

Even before the dissolution of the USSR, a new formal statement of military doctrine had been in draft since 1990, and during the final four months of 1991, after the attempted coup, modifications of Soviet military doctrine and reform of the military institution were being considered to meet the changing nature of the then expected new, looser, probably confederative union of sovereign states. This concerned particularly the anticipated need to adapt to a situation in which part of the armed forces might be controlled and deployed only in individual republics, with only part of the forces available for service in other republics.[7] Other changes in doctrine and organization were, however, also under way, including the announced establishment of a united "strategic nuclear forces" incorporating intercontinental missile, bomber, and submarine-launched missile forces and including some strategic defenses, at least space, early warning, and ABM components. This reflected the reciprocal unilateral American and

Soviet steps in the fall of 1991 to remove nuclear weapons from all naval units except submarine-launched ballistic missiles (SLBMs) on nuclear submarines (SSBNs), tactical army missiles and artillery, and most tactical air forces. This was particularly important because it facilitated steps taken in 1991 to remove all nuclear weapons from most republics (except tactical and strategic warheads in Ukraine and Belarus, and strategic warheads in Kazakhstan). This made easier the removal of all remaining tactical (including medium bomber) nuclear weapons from Belarus and Ukraine (and naval nuclear weapons from Ukraine) in the first four months of 1992. (Strategic bomber nuclear warheads were also quietly removed from Kazakhstan; Ukraine would not permit their removal from that country.)

Based on continuing work in the General Staff (and at the General Staff Academy), the new Russian Ministry of Defense was able almost immediately to publish a draft "Basic Fundamentals of the Military Doctrine of Russia" in May 1992.[8] This was not, however, offered as more than a draft and interim document, a hasty adaptation to an unforeseen changed situation. It was challenged both by professional military criticisms offered at a conference on the "Military Security of Russia" held at the General Staff Academy in late May 1992,[9] and by a competitive draft "Statement on the Priorities of the Military Policy of the Russian Federation" issued by the Presidium of the Supreme Soviet under a resolution signed by Ruslan Khasbulatov, in a challenge to both President Yeltsin and his Ministry of Defense by the legislature.[10] Russian military doctrine and policy thus quickly became a subject of not only professional debate but also political controversy, as is discussed later.

The most prominent feature of the General Staff's draft doctrine was its conclusion that the threat of nuclear world war had been "significantly reduced." Not all possibility of large-scale conventional or even nuclear war, however, had been eliminated. Large armies and nuclear arsenals remained. But the likelihood that an enemy (NATO or the United States had of course been the putative enemy) would deliberately launch a major war was now regarded as minimal. The chief reliance for keeping that possibility minimal was placed on a continuing strategic nuclear deterrent.

There did, nonetheless, remain one clear if implicit remnant of Cold War thinking in the General Staff document. A source of continuing danger of war was said to remain in "the political aspirations and actual military capabilities" of some (unnamed) "states or coalitions of states" desiring "to dominate the world community or certain regions" and displaying a readiness "to settle disputable issues by military means." This could only be a veiled reference to NATO, and a decidedly anachronistic Cold War interpretation of Western aims.

"A conventional large-scale war," the doctrine held, "may begin as a result of escalation of local wars and armed conflicts directed against Russia, against allied [CIS] states, or in regions contiguous to its borders." The fact that a deliberate large-scale attack or invasion, conventional or nuclear, was virtually ruled out meant that the means to deter or to deal with these more limited attacks or local wars were quite different from the old scenarios of the Warsaw Pact versus NATO. No longer was there a requirement for very large standing armies poised either to launch a major offensive if the enemy started a war (the pre-1987 Soviet/Warsaw Pact strategy) or to defend in place against any attempted invasion (the post-1987 strategy). Rather, what was now seen as the requirement under the new strategic situation was a force posture and strategy designed to deter or repulse an attack, counter an invasion, restore the Russian (CIS) borders, and "frustrate further attempts to renew the aggression." In terms of force posture and strategy, this was translated in the new Russian doctrine into a defense in all directions (adopting the French term "defense on all azimuths") comprising three components: (1) army, navy, and air force units "limited in strength but kept in constant readiness for action, deployed in Theaters of Operations (along axes) designed to repel a local aggression"; (2) "mobile reserves or a rapid reaction force capable of maneuver (with air or sea lift) within the shortest time possible to any region, and in conjunction with the deployed constant readiness forces capable of defeating a medium-sized aggression"; and (3) "strategic reserves, mobilized in a prewar situation or during a war, designed to conduct large-scale operations." These three elements would be echeloned in time and space to engage up to whatever level was required to defeat the aggression.

Somewhat at variance with the conclusion that a large-scale conventional war would arise through escalation from a local war (perhaps one even waged against a different adversary), the view of large-scale conventional war depicted was a major enemy offensive, possibly initially only by air and naval forces, relying on precision-guided munitions and electronic warfare—in short, a war on the model of Desert Storm (of the year before). A major land offensive could, however, follow in a second phase. Also a substantial period of tension and buildup of forces was likely to precede such a war (again, as in Desert Storm).

Although the strategic purpose of the armed forces would be for defense, and the limited forces maintained in forward deployment and in combat readiness would clearly limit initial offensive capabilities, the 1992 doctrine abandoned the "defensive defense" of the Gorbachev 1987–91 doctrine. Without returning to the earlier offensive defense, the new doctrine left open whatever combination of defensive and offensive maneuvers would be required to defeat the aggression. Although not positing a large-scale counteroffensive onto enemy territory to defeat an aggressor's armies, the doctrine pointedly left open that possibility. Training of the armed forces would be carried out both for "defense and offense . . . to perform [whatever] missions are required on the battlefield," including "seizure of the strategic initiative and defeating the enemy." Thus the professional military theoreticians and planners discarded the aspect of the Gorbachev-imposed operational doctrine that they had found most constraining.

The two other principal hallmarks of the Gorbachev-era Soviet military doctrine were, however, retained: "defensive sufficiency" as a criterion for forces and "prevention of war" as the strategic objective.

Defensive sufficiency for strategic forces was defined as quantitative and qualitative capability sufficient for deterrence and retaliation—not to "prevail." For general-purpose forces, sufficiency was identified as a capability "to provide reliable defense of Russia," while remaining sufficiently limited "to preclude surprise attack by its own forces and large-scale offensive operations without additional buildup."

Prevention of war includes national and international political-military measures, including curbing the arms race, establishing confidence-, security-, and stability-building measures, and developing a "comprehensive collective system of international security." Russia would pursue these objectives through its national policies, in the CIS, with the CSCE, NATO, and the United States. In terms of military strategy and operations, the prevention of war would include deterrence and collective security (in particular of the CIS), and in case of war "repulsing the aggression, defeating the enemy, and producing the conditions for the earliest termination of hostilities and restoration of a just and lasting peace." Again, this is open to varying applications, and because of the conditions cited would appear to be less of a commitment to earliest termination of hostilities. On the other hand, it is difficult to compare, inasmuch as the 1987 doctrine was focused on a possible Warsaw Pact–NATO war, and the 1992 doctrine on a possible large-scale war escalating from a local war.

The 1992 doctrine reaffirmed the long-standing Soviet pledge on no first use of nuclear weapons. There was, however, one interesting modification introduced. An aggressor's deliberate attempt to disrupt the functioning of Russian strategic nuclear forces through precision conventional attacks or deliberate attacks on nuclear power plants or similar hazardous (e.g., chemical) installations would be "regarded as the beginning of the use of weapons of mass destruction," permitting in response the use of nuclear weapons. Thus under some conditions nuclear first use was now sanctioned.

The 1992 doctrine for the first time was explicitly keyed to Russian "national security." It also explicitly identified the objectives of a war launched against Russia as attempting to compel Russia to yield to economic, political, or other demands or attempting to annex part of Russian territory. In case of war, the principal goal would be "to secure the sovereignty and territorial integrity of its own and allied states of the commonwealth." Possible conflicts *within* the commonwealth or even within the Russian Federation were acknowledged: "In the event a military conflict is triggered between some states of the commonwealth or subjects of the federation, Russia regards as its highest objective to achieve a cessation of hostilities and settlement of the conflict by political and diplomatic means. In exceptional cases, when all means have been exhausted and have failed to bring about positive results, Russia regards as legitimate the use of military force to restore and maintain the peace." For peacemaking or peacekeeping actions within the commonwealth, however, a consensus of the CIS states was said to be necessary. For this reason, there is (as of mid-1994) no CIS or Russian peacekeeping presence in the Nagorno-Karabagh region of Azerbaijan—Azerbaijan, Armenia, and the authorities in Nagorno-Karabagh have been unable to agree on terms for a cease-fire.

The main professional military criticisms of the new doctrine focused on three aspects. One was a view held by many military theoreticians that while the probability of a nuclear world war was admittedly greatly reduced, the political-military situation could change again and the nature of a possible all-out world war required hedging preparations. In particular, the possibility of an all-out *nuclear* war, with the whole array of advanced military technologies, including space components (necessarily a war launched by the United States, although that political aspect was not featured), posed quite different requirements for the armed forces. The requirements to meet that threat would indeed bring back the full burden of requirements seen at the late peak of the Cold War. As can be seen from the discussions in *Voennaia mysl'*, this criticism by military theorists received relatively less support from military planners, and virtually none from anyone else.

The second military criticism found wider resonance. While supporting the change from the Gorbachev-era "defensive defense," Colonel General Igor Rodionov of the General Staff Academy and others felt the change had not gone far enough. They wished to revive a more offensive-minded operational doctrine. The proponents of this view, however, could not pose a realistic alternative in terms of envisaging a sustainable Russian force posture.

The third main military criticism was in a sense the obverse of the other two. If, as indeed was the case, Russia was in no condition at least for a long time to restore a force posture capable of waging a large-scale modern conventional war, it must depend more on nuclear deterrence—on extended nuclear deterrence—not only to help defend its CIS allies but to defend Russia from a conceivable (even if remote) threat of a major conventional attack. Hence there was a new criticism of the nuclear no-first-use doctrine. Again, this criticism was sounded by General Rodionov, but also by many others. Even if, in practice, an American, NATO, Chinese, or Islamic conventional invasion threat was low, so long as it was conceivable, why not meet it with a strategic declaratory response that required only doctrinal modification?

The political challenge was more diffuse and related less to doctrine than to the executive-legislative tug-of-war over military reform plans and political power in general. The Supreme Soviet did in 1992 mandate a ceiling of only 1.5 million men for the armed forces after 1995. Similarly, the START II Treaty signed in January 1993 became the subject of much debate centered on criticism of Yeltsin for agreeing to an American proposal that reduced areas of greatest Russian strength (large counterforce-capable land-based ICBMs) while leaving to the United States its greatest strength (in modern, counterforce-capable

SLBMs), which it would be costly for Russia to emulate. Eventually the issue receded from attention as the strategic arms issue was shelved pending resolution of the START I impasse created by Ukrainian (and for a time Kazakh) delays in agreeing to nonnuclear status.

Doctrine and Forces, 1993–94

From the fall of 1992 to October 1993, the formulation of military doctrine was stymied as a by-product of the standoff in the executive-legislative political struggle between President Yeltsin and the Supreme Soviet and Congress of People's Deputies. Immediately following the dissolution of the legislature, the Ministry of Defense's draft "Basic Provisions of the Military Doctrine of the Russian Federation" (one of at least three competing drafts) was approved by the Security Council of the Russian Federation on 2 November 1993, and on the same date was promulgated by decree of the president.[11]

In several important respects the 1993 official statement of Russian military doctrine differed from the mid-1992 draft. For one thing, it went further in abandoning Cold War thinking about a potential adversary and thinking in terms of a possible major conventional or nuclear war. At the same time, it gave greater attention to possible local wars and the need to prepare for them. Thus, instead of vague allusions to "certain states or coalitions" with pretensions to world or regional domination that might lead them to start a war, the danger of outbreak of war is attributed to "social, political, territorial, religious, national ethnic and other conflicts and the desire of a number of states to want to resolve them by means of armed conflict." Similarly, among "the basic existing and potential sources of external military danger for the Russian Federation" depicted were territorial claims on Russia or its allies; spillover from "existing or potential local wars and armed conflicts, particularly those in the immediate vicinity of the Russian border"; nuclear proliferation; and several other categories.

The new doctrine also incorporated as a source of external military danger "the suppression of the rights, freedoms, and legitimate interests of citizens of the Russian Federation in foreign states." This indirect assertion of Russian state interest in the rights of its citizens abroad was not given as a justification for intervention, but that seemed to be implied by its listing a category of acts that could create "an external military danger." While this inclusion was responsive to widely and strongly held Russian feeling of responsibility for compatriots living abroad, and perhaps even reflected foreign policy interests, it seemed out of place in military doctrine. On the other hand, by narrowing the reference to "citizens" rather than Russians or Russian-speakers, the revised doctrine reduced the potential scope of application and the concerns of other new states.

Another potential source of military danger was identified as "expansion of military blocs or alliances to the detriment of the interests of the military security of the Russian Federation." This category raises a potential issue over any future eastward expansion of NATO.

While these were all warning flags of situations that Russia might see as creating a military danger, five other situations were identified as possibly "transforming a military danger into an immediate threat": (1) a buildup of (indigenous) military forces on the Russian border that could disrupt the prevailing correlation of forces; (2) the introduction of foreign troops into the territory of neighboring countries; (3) the training of armed groups on the territory of other countries for introduction into the territory of Russia or its allies; (4) attacks on border installations of Russia and its allies to create border conflicts or provocations; and (5) actions to interfere with the functioning of Russian systems for the support of its strategic nuclear forces and of state and military command and control, above all the space component.

A number of internal sources of military threats were also identified, of which the main one was "illegal activity by nationalist, separatist, or other organizations aimed at destabilizing the situation in the Russian Federation or violating its territorial integrity and which is carried out using armed violence."

The main strategic missions of the armed forces remained basically unchanged: the strategic nuclear forces are designed for deterrence; general purpose forces are for defense and the repelling of aggression on a local or regional scale. Less is said about the nature of the operational plan for defense, but other authoritative military statements continued to speak of the roles of forces in place, mobile and rapid reaction forces, and strategic reserves. The nuclear deterrent role was bolstered by abandoning the unilateral no-first-use pledge of the past, in order to more fully provide for a "flexible response" posture.

Although discarding a no-first-use policy is not an indication of any Russian desire or even inclination to use nuclear weapons if war should come, it is not without significance. The change was widely discounted in Western commentary on the grounds that the earlier Soviet pledge had only been rhetorical. That was a serious misreading of what had been a significant Soviet strategic policy to keep any hostilities nonnuclear if at all possible. What has changed is not the desire to avoid nuclear war, but a Russian belief that its weakened strategic situation may no longer give it the option of keeping a war nonnuclear, thus placing the burden for such a decision on the other side, and that deterrence requires making a pledge to resort, if necessary, to first use of nuclear weapons if conventional defense does not suffice.

The general focus of military strategic preparation, however, had shifted further to conclude that "the main danger" was now posed by local wars and armed conflicts, the likelihood of which in some regions was said to be growing.

War termination, as a complement to war prevention, was also highlighted. Thus, "the main objective of the use of the armed forces of the Russian Federation and other troops [e.g., border troops] in armed conflicts and local wars is to localize a seat of tension and terminate military operations at the earliest possible stage in the interests of creating preconditions for the settlement of the conflict by peaceful means under conditions that accord with the interests of the Russian Federation."

Finally, the new military doctrine was explicitly described as intended to serve for a transition period, albeit probably an extended one. Also, the doctrine acknowledged that its implementation must take into account the real economic and technological constraints of the country's capacity.

In the period since the issuance of the "Basic Provisions" in November 1993, there has been little discussion of military doctrine (although professional attention of course continues). Spirited debates among military professionals continues on many subjects, such as whether aircraft carriers are needed, subjects that are without current relevance if only because of the lack of resources and realistic choices. In the longer run, however, these may become relevant.

A CIS "concept of military security" was also issued in October 1993, although it elicited little attention.[12] It contained many of the same general provisions as the Russian military doctrine (including the aim of prevention of war and an offensive-defensive operational doctrine). Emphasis was, appropriately, placed on the benefits of collaborative efforts in collective defense. It was, however, completely dependent on political decisions by the CIS member states on concrete military commitments, preparations, and actions.

In general, military doctrine again moved out of the limelight, with debates in Russia focused on the military budget, which was severely reduced in mid-1994.

During 1992 and 1993, as earlier noted, the CIS also elaborated agreements on establishing peacekeeping forces, and this element is reflected in both the Russian and CIS doctrinal documents. Indeed, it has become an important element in the new Russian military doctrine. Russia has earmarked several units for peacekeeping roles (in particular the Twenty-seventh Motorized Rifle Division in the Volga military district and the Forty-fifth Motorized Rifle Division in the Leningrad military district, and several airborne regiments), as well as participating in the UN peacekeeping effort in Bosnia.[13]

By late 1993, when soldiers conscripted for service in the Soviet army had completed their tour of duty, the Russian armed forces were seriously undermanned. Russia had a population of 150 million, instead of the nearly 300 million of the Soviet Union, and the demographic curve plus general health deficiencies combined to reduce sharply the available draft cohort. In addition, the Supreme Soviet had granted educational deferments to all students in higher educational institutions (vocational and technical, as well as universities). With reduced fear of authorities and much reduced discipline, many failed to show up when called into service, and the families of others bribed officials or doctors to get medical or other exemptions. In short, while the *structure* of the armed forces was reduced from about 3.7 million at the end of 1991 to about 2.5 million in 1992, to about 2.3 million by the end of 1993, and to 1.9 million by mid-1994, the real level of forces was down from about 3.0 million to about 1.5 million—

fully half of them officers. While educational deferments in the fall of 1993 were withdrawn for vocational schools and discipline on reporting for call-up improved, there remained a severe shortage of enlisted personnel. In 1992–93, some 120,000 volunteers at higher, but still low-pay were taken in on two- or three-year contracts (initially, not all of suitable quality), and about 40,000 more were added by mid-1994; it became too expensive, however, to expand on the scale desired and needed (250,000 are now authorized).

By 1993, with considerably reduced forces, it had become necessary to complete the withdrawal (from Germany, Poland, and the Baltics), disbanding (many from Germany and the Baltics, and most in Transcaucasia), or turnover to local authority (in Central Asia) of most divisional structures and field forces that were not in Russia (or had not come under Ukrainian or Belarusian authority in 1992). Bases, facilities, arms stocks, and residual officer complements were also withdrawn (from the Baltics) or taken over by local governments or freelancers (in Transcaucasia). Negotiations led to the withdrawal of all remaining forces from Lithuania by August 1993, and Latvia and Estonia by August 1994. The last of the Russian forces in eastern Germany also left by August 1994.

During 1993–94 there was a change of attitude by the military command in Moscow with respect to the residual military presence in the CIS countries. While during 1992 there had been a desire to withdraw units before they would disintegrate or be overrun (as happened in a number of cases in Azerbaijan and Georgia), by the end of 1993 there was new interest in retaining bases or a small presence in a number of areas in the CIS, leading in 1994 to a decree on Russian bases in the CIS. The actual deployments, partly to maintain garrisons on the southern border or radar facilities, partly in conjunction with CIS peacekeeping forces (Moldova, Georgia, Tajikistan, and putatively in Armenia and Azerbaijan if agreement could be reached on a cease-fire over Nagorno-Karabagh), were quite limited.

The new Russian military interest in strengthening CIS military ties and in a limited Russian forward deployment and involvement in the CIS clearly seems to stem more from defensive concerns than from expansive ambitions. The very nature of the specific forms of commitment support such a conclusion: enhancing air defense, outer CIS border controls, and even forward (CIS) and backup deployments in Russia in the North Caucasus area (even though the external threat from the south seems exaggerated to most observers in the West).

Thus by the fall of 1994 the situation had settled down to a new post-transitional situation. *No* Russian forces were stationed abroad beyond the CIS (except for manning one radar installation in Latvia until 1998). Beyond the borders of the Russian Federation were the following: (1) a set of cooperatively run ballistic missile early warning radars (Russian-run in Latvia, Belarus, Azerbaijan, and Kazakhstan; Ukrainian-run in Ukraine); (2) a major space range plus several air and missile defense and strategic missile test ranges (Russian-run in Kazakhstan); (3) defensive garrisons along the southern CIS border (border troops plus two army divisions in southern Georgia; one division in Armenia; border troops plus one division in Tajikistan; combined Russian-officered Turkmen and Uzbek border troops and three local divisions in Turkmenistan; border guards in Kazakhstan and Kyrgyzstan on the Chinese border; and three or four largely Russian-officered Kazakh army divisions and one Kyrgyz division); (4) peacekeeping contingents numbering sixteen thousand (Moldova—one airborne regiment; Georgia—one airborne regiment in Abkhazia, one battalion in South Ossetia, and one regiment on the Abkhazian-Georgian border [borrowed from a Russian garrison division in southern Georgia]; Tajikistan—one Russian division and border guards [double-committed as garrison forces]; and abroad in Bosnia—one regiment and one battalion); and (5) the Black Sea fleet, using several main bases in the Crimea.

Within the Russian Federation, the main area of buildup in redeployment of forces was not in the west, where the defense forces were thinnest, nor facing Ukraine, but in the south in the North Caucasus military district, to the north of Georgia, Armenia, and Azerbaijan. In part this reflected concerns over instability in this region of the Russian Federation itself (including breakaway Chechnia) and in Transcaucasia beyond—Abkhazia and South Ossetia, Georgia proper, the Armenian-Azerbaijan conflict over Nagorno-Karabagh, and general instability within Azerbaijan. It also reflected concerns over possible contingencies involving Turkey and Iran, particularly in conjunction with possible developments in Armenia and Azerbaijan, or (less likely) Georgia.

Although the buildup in this region is modest in scale (only a few new divisions and brigades), the focus on this region and the redeployments have posed to the Russian military command real concern over the flank constraints on numbers of tanks, armored vehicles, and artillery imposed by the CFE Treaty when it goes into effect on 1 January 1995. Russia (and Ukraine, which is also limited in what it can deploy in its southern areas, the former Odessa military district) has raised this matter officially repeatedly since 1992 (also in high-level consultations with the United States), but there is great resistance by most signatories to reopening any provisions of the treaty (as well as opposition by Turkey and by the Scandinavian and Baltic countries along the northern flank, which are indirectly affected under a paired and shared constraint on arms deployment on both flanks). Perhaps agreed interpretation can alleviate the problem (e.g., additional armored vehicles are allowed for internal security forces).

In the north, Russia will probably retain only modest forces in the far north and the St. Petersburg region (in the old Leningrad military district). The only sizable concentration of forces remaining has been the Kaliningrad exclave (in former German East Prussia). The Sixty-first Army is being reduced from six to probably two or three divisions. Baltiisk in the Kaliningrad enclave is now the principal base—apart from Leningrad and Kronstadt, the only remaining base—of the Russian Baltic fleet. (Both here and in the far north, there will probably be a brigade or division of the naval coastal defense forces, which have recently absorbed coastal missile artillery and the naval infantry or Russian marines.) A few divisions may be added to the few in the Moscow and Leningrad military districts, but no large addition is likely. The central Volga and Urals military districts are the main center for the strategic reserve forces. The airborne division (the 104th) formerly deployed in Azerbaijan, for example, was relocated to Ul'ianovsk on the central Volga. Another airborne division (the Seventh) from Lithuania was redeployed to the North Caucasus district. In all, by mid-1994, the ground forces in the Northern, Moscow, and North Caucasus districts of European Russia totaled fifteen divisions and thirteen brigades.

The Siberian, Transbaikal, and Far Eastern military districts and Pacific fleet have been the least affected by change, except for general reductions and neglect. For example, the Pacific fleet has lost both of its small aircraft carriers and several of its cruisers owing to lack of maintenance (including inability to return the carriers to their Black Sea shipyard in Ukraine for overhaul; the last two cruisers sent back there for refit in the late 1980s were never returned).

In all, the Russian army is likely to end up with something on the order of twenty active divisions in Europe and twenty in Asia—a fraction of the Soviet force of 1991, to say nothing of the peak force of 1988. The size of its air forces and navy are also being sharply cut by well over half, with an effort to maintain the newest aircraft and ships. For the future, however, deeper problems of maintaining research and development programs, production facilities, and existing equipment will continue to be strained by the severe overall resource constraints imposed by economic conditions in the country.

Future developments in Russian military doctrine and force development and deployment will depend on a multiplicity of factors, but above all on two complexes of questions: future political developments in the CIS states and the wider strategic environment beyond, and political-economic developments within Russia itself.

Notes

1. The best general review of developments involving former Soviet military forces in 1992–93 is Roy Allison, *Military Forces in the Soviet Successor States*, Adelphi Paper no. 280 (London: Brassey's for the International Institute for Strategic Studies, 1993).

2. See Raymond L. Garthoff, *Deterrence and the Revolution in Soviet Military Doctrine* (Washington, DC: Brookings Institution, 1990).

3. In June 1992 General Pavel Grachev, soon after being made minister of defense, urged the establishment of a new western "Smolensk military district." While logical, that action would have made sense only if it were accompanied by a redeployment of forces to that region, and that was regarded as too costly, strategically unnecessary, and politically provocative (toward Ukraine), so the idea was abandoned.

4. Very little official information is available on the reduction of division formations, in part because the Soviet (and later Russian) military establishments sought to make required reductions without sacrificing at least nominal "division" designations in order to justify larger numbers of general officers on the active duty rolls. Even in 1993–94 many

low-strength divisions remained, although the number was declining as the authorized strength levels of the armed forces were reduced.

During 1989–91, the Soviet army was reduced by at least thirty-seven tank and motorized rifle divisions, twenty-five in the European part of the USSR and twelve in Siberia and the Far East. This left, as of mid-1991, a total of 146 divisions, according to the U.S. Department of Defense, *Military Forces in Transition* (Washington, DC: Department of Defense, 1991, p. 12, and enclosed map of deployments.) There was no explanation for the discrepancy from the last previous reported total of 214 divisions as of December 1988. *Soviet Military Power, Prospects for Change, 1989* (Washington, DC: Department of Defense, 1989), p. 103.

The estimated eighty-five Russian divisions included twenty-three in Germany, the Baltic states, Moldova, and Mongolia, and only seventy-one in Russia itself, but about half of those abroad were disbanded rather than redeployed in Russia. A rather well-informed tally of divisions deployed at the end of 1991 was given in *Moskovskie novosti*, 29 December 1991, p. 9.

5. The Soviet army in 1991 was also beginning at least a partial changeover from the traditional organization of divisions subordinated to armies to smaller brigades grouped under corps. That change has tentatively been continued in Russia (and in Ukraine and Belarus), although a mix of brigades and divisions seems likely to continue. This factor also makes it more difficult to track force levels.

6. Eight of the eleven divisions were organized into the Fortieth Army in Kazakhstan and the Fifty-second Army in Turkmenistan; each of the other three republics had only one division deployed in each.

7. To cite but one important example, see "Politika, doktrina i strategiia v meniaushchemsia mire: General armii, Vladimir Lobov o voennoi reforme," *Krasnaia zvezda*, 23 October 1991, pp. 1–2.

8. "Osnovnye polozheniia voennoi doktriny Rossiiskoi Federatsii (proekt)," *Voennaia mysl'*, spetsial'nyi vypusk (May 1992), 16 pp.

9. Another special issue of *Voennaia mysl'* was devoted to the major presentations at the conference, of which the most important was that of the chief of the academy, Colonel General Igor Rodionov, "Nekotorye podkhody k razrabotke voennoi doktriny Rossiiskoi Federatsii," *Voennaia mysl'*, spetsial'nyi vypusk (July 1992), pp. 6–20.

10. "Zaiavlenie Prezidiuma verkhovnogo soveta rossiiskoi Federatsii o prioritetakh voennoi politiki Rossiiskoi Federatsii," 1 April 1992, *Krasnaia zvezda*, 15 April 1992, p. 2.

11. "Osnovnye polozheniia voennoi doktriny Rossiiskoi Federatsii (izlozhenie)," *Voennaia mysl'*, spetsial'nyi vypusk (November 1993), 23 pp. This is a slightly abridged version made public; the full text has not been published.

12. See "Kontseptsiia voennoi bezopasnosti gosudarstv uchastnikov Sodruzhestva Nezavisimykh Gosudarstv," *Voennaia mysl'*, spetsial'nyi vypusk (October 1993), pp. 1–16. This special issue also republished the then recently promulgated "Voennaia doktrina Ukrainy," pp. 17–24.

13. For example, the Twenty-seventh Division has rotated units to keep one regiment in Moldova along the cease-fire line on the Dniester River, and the Forty-fifth Division has kept one battalion in South Ossetia and another in Tajikistan. The 345th Separate Airborne Regiment has been in Abkhazia.

Personnel of these units are mixed professional contract and conscripted soldiers, but all sent on peacekeeping assignments are volunteers for such service and are paid extra salary for serving on dangerous peacetime duty.

Within the Russian Federation, rather than army forces, units of internal security troops have been stationed on the North Ossetian-Ingushetian disputed border area to maintain the peace.

4

Defense Industries in Russia and the Other Post-Soviet States

Julian Cooper

Russia and the other successor states inherited from the Soviet system a fateful legacy—a defense industry of a scale and character that threatened to obstruct efforts to create market economies and democratic polities. Soviet commentators in the years of former Soviet leader Mikhail Gorbachev began to use the term "military-industrial complex" (MIC) to characterize this hypertrophied defense industry, adopting a term hitherto reserved in Soviet ideology for the United States and other capitalist countries. The Soviet MIC began to be identified with political conservatism, or outright reaction, as a constellation of military, economic, and political forces determined at all costs to block reform and preserve the socialist system and the union. Whether this was ever an accurate characterization of the Soviet defense industry is debatable. As this author has argued elsewhere, the Soviet defense industry was not monolithic in behavior and attitude and did not necessarily share common interests with the uniformed military.[1] However, it is undeniable that some of the leaders of the abortive August 1991 coup represented a conservative "military-industrial" interest, and there is also no dispute that from the 1930s on the defense industry, with its associated governmental and party institutions, was one of the strongest pillars of the Soviet state.

For the post-Soviet nations, above all Russia, an important question is whether we can now identify a stable and coherent common interest uniting the uniformed military and the armaments industry such that we can speak in a strict sense of an MIC. (The Russian habit of using MIC [VPK] as a a purely descriptive term, in my view, is not one that should be copied by Western authors.) Perhaps a Russian MIC is in embryo, but at present the situation remains one of shifting, temporary alliances between far from united partners. It is precisely the absence of a truly united and strong military-industrial alliance with a coherent political platform that offers hope that the Russian defense industry, the heart of the former Soviet command-administrative economy, will prove not to be an insuperable obstacle to postcommunist economic and political transformation.

Much of the discussion of the former Soviet defense industry has focused on the issue of "conversion." The agenda of conversion was set by Gorbachev in 1988: defense industry enterprises and research establishments would switch to alternative work in such a way that a declining military burden would be accompanied by a simultaneous augmentation of civilian production. The success or failure of conversion has been identified widely as a crucial policy issue for the post-Soviet states. However, as will be argued here, the question of whether conversion can succeed is too narrow. The important issue for Russia, it neighbors, and the world at large is whether the Soviet defense industry legacy can be reduced in size and restructured to make it compatible with the country's true economic strength and new security requirements without provoking politically destabilizing social unrest with a potential to check or reverse the broader transformation policy. Some success has been achieved, but the process is far from complete. The same issue faces other post-Soviet states, particularly Ukraine, but not in such an acute form.

The Post-Soviet Legacy

Russia is the only state of the ex-USSR to have inherited something approximating a coherent defense industry able to meet most of the country's requirements for modern weaponry. The other newly independent states find themselves in possession of those random elements of the former Soviet defense industry that happen to be located on their territories as a result of Moscow-made decisions.[2] While the breakup of the USSR has created many problems for the Russian armaments industry, it has not in any fundamental sense threatened the country's ability to develop and manufacture most categories of weapons systems. The basic policy option facing Ukraine, Belarus, Kazakhstan, and the other states is of a different order: whether or not to attempt to restructure the inheritance to create national defense industries able to meet at least certain core requirements of their newly created armed forces.

The Ministerial Legacy

For better or worse, Russia inherited almost all the administrative structures of the Soviet defense industry, in particular the personnel and offices of the industrial ministries. These ministerial structures were profoundly "vertical" in character, horizontal coordination being provided by three organizations that have disappeared or been transformed radically since 1991: the Central Committee of the Communist Party of the Soviet Union, with its Defense Industry Department and secretary responsible for oversight of military production; the Military-Industrial Commission; and the State Planning Committee (Gosplan). Since 1991, administrative horizontal coordination has given way, in a halting and imperfect manner, to the market, but vertical management agencies have been retained in the shape of the State Committee for the Defense Industry (Goskomoboronprom), internally organized by departments representing scaled-down versions of the former ministries, and usually staffed by some of the same personnel. The only industrial ministry to survive the collapse of communism, the Ministry of Atomic Energy (Minatom), remains almost wholly intact and in many respects appears to operate as before, following the traditions of the former Ministry of Medium Machine Building, which in the USSR was almost a state within the state. This is a rare case in which continuity with the communist past provides some reassurance to the outside world. Parts of the old defense industrial ministries converted into semicommercial "unions," "associations," and "concerns." What has survived these changes in Moscow is "ministerial" allegiance, a form of "corporate" loyalty that still poses obstacles to the formation of a common defense industry interest.

Other administrative continuities from the Soviet period can also be found. The old defense industry department of the USSR Gosplan has been retained, with many of the same staff, as a department of the Ministry of the Economy, and as such maintains its involvement in defense ordering, preparation of the military budget, and mobilization planning. Within the apparatus of the Russian government there is a department for the defense industry, headed since October 1994 by Valerii Mikhailov, formerly first deputy economics minister, which fulfills some of the coordinating functions of the former Military-Industrial Commission.

Radical Downsizing

Since the beginning of 1992 the Russian defense industry has experienced a radical and traumatic downsizing. The Gaidar government's 68 percent cut in the procurement budget for 1992 served notice that the postcommunist regime was making a decisive break with the past. Simultaneously, price liberalization, although incomplete, began to reveal the true cost to a weak economy of the maintenance of a vast weapons industry with an across-the-board capability. Deprived of state orders, for a time enterprises attempted to keep up levels of production in expectation of export sales or a reversal of policy; but exports collapsed and the government stood its ground. The new low levels of procurement were retained in the 1993 budget in the context of a stable share of military expenditure in GDP.[3] To make matters worse, the demand for the traditional civilian goods of the defense industry, and even for some of the new "conversion" products of the Gorbachev years, began to decline, deepening the industry's crisis. As a result, in 1993 the total output of the defense complex (enterprises overseen by Goskomoboronprom) declined to barely 55 percent of its 1990 level, with a collapse of military output to a mere 30 percent and of civilian output to three-quarters of their 1990 levels. The civilian share of output rose dramatically, from 50 percent in 1990 to almost 80 percent in 1993, but this was hardly a product of successful "conversion." In the first half of 1994 the downward trend was maintained: in relation to the first six months of 1993, the military output of the defense branches of industry fell by 39 percent, the civilian by 36 percent.[4] In the face of foreign competition, the consumer goods production of the military sector has been hit severely: for enterprises of Goskomoboronprom, output in September 1994 was less than half the level of September 1993.[5] Having fared relatively well during 1992–93, Minatom also began to experience a downturn during the first half of 1994, its civilian production declining by 18 percent.[6]

Budget allocations to military research and development were also cut, but not to the same extent as for procurement, the reduction in the period 1990–92 being a claimed 26 percent.[7] However, allocations to the high technology civil R&D undertaken by the defense sector, which formerly accounted for a substantial share of total civil industrial research, diminished sharply, by 38 percent in 1992 alone, although the aviation and space industries had some success in making claims for a sizable proportion of the Ministry of Science's budget for state science and technology programs.[8] In short, the Russian defense industry has had no choice but to adapt to sharply reduced levels of state support. To make matters worse, for the few remaining orders undertaken for the Ministry of Defense, payment was invariably delayed, and when it came was substantially eroded by inflation. In these circumstances, it is not surprising that many defense sector enterprise managers began to question the desirability of staying in the arms production business.

Salvation Through Arms Exports?

From the outset in 1992, some within the defense industry had high expectations that military output could be maintained by resorting to an active export policy. The most vigorous advocate of this approach was Mikhail Malei, during much of the period Russian President Boris Yeltsin's advisor on conversion issues.[9] During 1992, military output would have exhibited an even sharper decline if it had not been for exaggerated expectations of export sales. In any event, hopes have been dashed. In 1992 and 1993, annual exports of arms and other military equipment have remained at the low level of approximately $2 billion.[10] There has also been a marked decline in exports of the defense industry's civil goods.[11]

In an attempt to improve the situation, a major reorganization of the structures for arms exports was implemented in late 1993, switching administrative authority from the Ministry of Foreign Economic Relations to the presidential apparatus. Rosvooruzhenie, the new state trading organization, has been energetically promoting Russian weaponry, but no radical change is expected. The target set by Rosvooruzhenie for 1994 is $3.4 billion and, notwithstanding the successful

MiG–29 deal with Malaysia and sales to China, Kuwait, and Brazil, may prove overoptimistic.[12] The obstacles to a rapid expansion of Russian arms exports are substantial, as many within the Russian defense sector now realize. However, provided that funding can be found to maintain core development programs, there would appear to be no reason why a modest increase should not be achieved over the next few years, providing some support for the Russian arms industry during its difficult transition. However, whereas the former Soviet Union (FSU) transferred a wide range of weapons systems to its allies and friends, often free of charge, Russia is likely to specialize to an increasing extent, focusing on certain sectors of the market where genuine competitive strength is apparent, for example, in combat aircraft, antimissile sytems, tanks, multiple rocket launchers, and other equipment for ground forces.

Costs of Contraction

The rapid contraction of military production has had a profound impact on the defense industry. Unfortunately, labor force statistics for the Russian defense sector remain profoundly inadequate. Very substantial losses of personnel from military production have been claimed, but these are often gross figures that do not take into account the transfer of the freed workers to civil work, usually at the same enterprise. According to the chairman of Goskomoboronprom, Viktor Glukhikh, between 1991 and 1993 the core industry overseen by the state committee lost 23 percent of its personnel.[13] In the first half of 1994, the rate of decline accelerated, with the fall in the number of industrial production personnel amounting to 15 percent in comparison to the same period of the preceding year.[14] By the end of the year, the decline in defense industry employment is likely to exceed two million since the collapse of the USSR. Wage levels have declined dramatically: in 1991, the average wage in the defense industry was 85 percent of the average for industry as a whole; by January 1994, it was only 59 percent.[15] In June 1994, the average wage in the electronics industry, the branch that has suffered the most severe contraction of output and employment, was a mere 43 percent of the national industrial average wage; but in the nuclear industry, which has contracted the least, the average wage was almost 30 percent above the national figure.[16]

The low wages, loss of status, and poor prospects have provoked voluntary exit from the industry on a substantial scale with, to date, a relatively modest scale of forced redundancies. In particular, young skilled workers, managers, and technical personnel have left to seek their fortunes in the new private sector. Many of those remaining in employment have experienced part-time work and extended holidays. Delayed wage payments have become a normal phenomenon, provoking occasional strikes and protest meetings, which the government has been able to contain by getting the Ministry of Finance to release money to settle debts on a selective basis. Many enterprise leaders have been reluctant to dismiss workers, recognizing that they are heavily dependent on the workplace-linked social facilities and housing. It is striking that the share of total defense industry investment for the development of so-called nonproductive facilities has risen during the past two years, from 38 percent in 1992 to 45 percent in 1993.[17] With privatization, however, enterprise managers are beginning to recognize that they can no longer afford to maintain the social infrastructure as they have in the past. Increasingly, new solutions are being sought, usually involving transfers to the local municipal authorities. Changes in the system of local taxation are probably required before this necessary process can develop on a wide scale.

It could be argued that the policies pursued by the government, intentionally or otherwise, have been remarkably successful in that they have already resulted in a substantial loss of labor from the defense industry, while the social impact of the cuts has been moderated by the partial retention of institutions and practices of the communist past. Valuable time has been gained for psychological adjustment to the new realities of a market economy. While further reductions in employment are inevitable as enterprise adjustment intensifies, it may be a mistake to assume that this will give rise to major social problems and unrest, although some mono-facility communities do clearly face major problems. In addition to the ten "closed" cities of the nuclear weapons industry, with a total population of approximately 750,000, there are some seventy towns of an average size of about 100,000 people that are built around defense plants, often factories of the conventional munitions industry.[18] It will probably be neccessary to strengthen the social safety net to meet the specific circumstances of these communities.

Privatizing the Defense Industry

In the Russian transformation process to date the most striking development in terms of its scale and social impact has been mass voucher privatization. While in most cases this has amounted to little more than a formal transfer of ownership, yet to be converted into effective property rights and corporate governance, it has undoubtedly helped to render the break with communism irreversible. Given the centrality of the defense industry to the country's economy and the prevalence of traditional modes of thinking about national security, it is not surprising that the privatization of facilities engaged in the development and manufacture of weapons has been controversial. Nevertheless, the change effected within the past two years has been striking. Many famous plants of the Russian military sector are now operating as joint-stock companies, including producers of end-product weapons.[19] Depending on their perceived importance for national security, the state has retained an ownership share of variable size, taking the form of a single "golden share" in many instances, in facilities directly involved in military production. A core set of especially sensitive facilities has been identified for retention in the state sector. According to a presidential order of 19 August 1993, subsequently modified by government decree, 474 facilities

(214 enterprises and 260 R&D organizations) under Goskomoboronprom were identified as candidates for state ownership.[20] Earlier in the year, in April, a similar order had identified almost sixty facilities of Minatom excluded from privatization.[21] For Goskomoboronprom, the intention is that approximately 20 percent of its enterprises and 40 percent of its R&D facilties will remain fully owned by the state. For those companies retaining a state share, the directors won a major concession: in many cases the rights of the state holding will be exercised by the board of directors itself. The measures adopted thus represent a major contraction of state involvement in the Russian defense industry.

It is apparent that many enterprise directors and managers have welcomed privatization and the opportunity it has presented to weaken the controlling hand of Moscow. For some it has opened the option of withdrawing completely from military work. Given the unsatisfactory financial terms and the chronic uncertainty of contracts from the Ministry of Defense, this can be an attractive prospect. Other companies, more firmly rooted in the military sector and possessing poor prospects for civilianization, have been content to remain in the state sector. It will be interesting to see whether a division in attitudes and behavior emerges in time between the state and private facilities of the defense industry. If a fair proportion of the latter demonstrate an ability to prosper in a market environment, we can expect some of the former to begin lobbying for a change of status. However, there is little doubt that the privatization process has begun already to weaken traditional ministerial-type allegiances and has reduced the prospect of any form of concerted action by the defense industry to change government policy.

The Regional Dimension

As Moscow's central control and ability to provide funding have diminished, so have the regional orientation and engagement of the organization of the defense industry strengthened. It is notable that in 1993 the scale of local budget funding of investment in the defense sector began to increase sharply, although in volume representing barely 1 percent of total investment during the year.[22] Now in a number of regions the local authorities are attempting to gain control over at least part of the state share of ownership of major defense plants located on their territories.[23] Many republics and regions now have their own conversion and restructuring programs, often with local sources of finance, providing for joint activities by defense industry facilities regardless of their "ministerial" affiliations. These developments are serving to weaken traditional loyalties and foster new alliances. From this perspective, it is not surprising that the creation of so-called financial-industrial groups (FIGs) is being being taken up most energetically at the local level. Hardly any such groups have been created to date because of inadequacies in the existing legislation, but the first to involve defense sector facilities has a republican focus—Ural'skie zavody in Udmurtiia.

Regional authorities are promoting them as vehicles for securing local economic revival. There is a distinct possibility that similar FIGs will mushroom in the coming period in other regions where the defense sector is strongly represented. However, this "territorial" version of the FIG is not the only one contending for support. The principal proponent of the financial-industrial group as the instrument for restructuring Russian industry according to the priorities of the state is the civilian first deputy defense minister, Andrei Kokoshin.

"Locomotives" or Brakes?

On taking office in April 1992, Kokoshin, responsible for the armaments and scientific-technical policy of the armed forces, began to use his position to promote a vision of the revitalization of the Russian economy based on a restructuring of the defense industrial base to create a high-technology sector equally capable of generating advanced weaponry and competitive dual-use goods.[24] His National Industrial Policy was unveiled in August 1992 and from the outset attracted influential support. Central to the realization of Kokoshin's plan is the creation of a limited number (thirty to forty) of FIGs on the basis of the leading production, research, and design facilities of the defense industry together with commercial banks, insurance companies, trading houses, and other commercial structures. Kokoshin is convinced that such a "corporatization" of the defense industry will secure the survival of an advanced military production capability at the same time it promotes the development of a competitive high-technology sector of Russian industry. He has also noted that the FIG has a potential role in the maintenance of the country's mobilization capability. In short, the FIGs will become "locomotives" (Kokoshin's term) of Russia's economic revival.

Notwithstanding Kokoshin's vigorous advocacy of defense sector FIGs and the influential support of such figures as the economist Sergei Glaz'ev (now chair of the Economic Policy Committee of the State Duma and one of the originators of the idea of creating these new corporate structures) and First Deputy Premier Oleg Soskovets, developments in practice have been modest. Legislative inadequacies have played a role, as has the manifest opposition of the privatization agency, the State Committee for the Management of State Property under Anatolii Chubais, which has been more concerned with breaking up existing conglomerates than creating new ones. Goskomoboronprom was initially wary of the idea, in part perhaps because of its military provenance, and defense sector organizations, many having just attained a new degree of independence as joint-stock companies, seem understandably reluctant to contemplate a new form of corporatization, especially one decreed from the Moscow center. In addition, commercial banks and other financial institutions have shown a marked lack of enthusiasm for the idea.[25] In September 1994, Goskomoboronprom decided to create eleven FIGs by the end of 1995 and appears to envisage a top-down approach to their formation.[26] But this planned rate of creation of FIGs within the defense sector hardly matches Kokoshin's ambitions.

There must be doubts as to the potential efficacy of the FIGs as conceived by Kokoshin. The very concept may be flawed. At present there is virtually no demand for high-technology civil or dual-use goods of the type envisaged, and it will take time to gain a foothold on world markets. Arms exports are problematic. There is also a danger that the defense sector FIGs will require state subsidies and that they will become brakes on the country's economic revival rather than locomotives.

Acquisition and Mobilization

Just as the military's vision of the future shape of the defense industrial base of Russia does not accord fully with views within the defense industry itself, so also do differences exist on two other central issues—the military's goal of switching to a U.S.-style acquisition system and its desire to retain a sizable mobilization capability. The proposed transformation of the acquisition system has provoked the leadership of Goskomoboronprom into open polemic with the Ministry of Defense. Iurii Glybin, the committee's first deputy chairman, has argued that a switch to a U.S.-style contract system is premature given the absence of appropriate institutional arrangements. In particular, Glybin notes that the Ministry of Defense lacks a suitable infrastructure of research organizations capable of providing the necessary expertise for fully informed procurement decisions, and there is little doubt that Goskomoboronprom fears that some of its own establishments may have to be transferred to the Defense Ministry in order to fill this gap. The title of Glybin's article said it all: "Our Ministry of Defense Is Not Yet the Pentagon."[27]

The Soviet Union had an extraordinarily elaborate system of mobilization preparedness that remained intact in Russia after 1991. Enterprises were expected to retain substantial reserve capacities and stockpiles of equipment, materials, and components, permitting a rapid buildup of production in the event of war or other national emergency. This system was funded through the state budget and treated as a matter of the highest level of secrecy. In 1992 and 1993, many defense sector enterprises were obliged to retain substantial capacities in reserve even though military orders had dried up. Some of the reserve stocks of materials, however, found their way, legally or illegally, onto export markets, and there is little doubt that the proceeds from such sales have helped cushion the shock of reduced military orders and have permitted accumulations of capital awaiting productive investment. The requirement to retain reserve capacities frustrated efforts to convert production facilities to civil purposes and, to make matters worse, the system of budget funding for the maintenance of such mobilization capacities broke down, with the result that many enterprises found themselves meeting the costs from their own inadequate resources.

The issue of reform of the system of mobilization preparedness was first raised in public discussion in 1991 by Vitalii Shlykov, then deputy chairman of the Russian State Committee for Defense.[28] However, the Russian Ministry of Defense was reluctant to act, even though many in the defense industry, especially at the enterprise level, favored radical reform. The Ministry of Defense's thinking on a new mobilization policy appeared to envisage the need to prepare in advance for the possibility that supplies currently obtained from other CIS countries would have to be substituted—a mode of thinking that favored the retention of a sizable mobilizational capability. A stalemate developed between the military and the defense industry that was resolved only by presidential action in July 1994. Yeltsin's order, On the Reduction of Mobilizational Capacities and Mobilizational Reserves, met most of the demands of the defense industrialists. The scale of the mobilization system is to be reduced substantially. Reserve capacities and stocks will be retained only at those enterprises heavily involved in military production. Enterprises released from mobilizational obligations are free to dispose of their reserve stocks and may convert or lease production facilities previously held in reserve.[29] This measure increases the independence of many enterprises of the military sector and offers new possibilities for restructuring; it has been widely welcomed within the defense industry, but is unlikely to have been appreciated by traditionalists within the armed forces.

New National Defense Industries?

Developments in Russia since 1991 have been matched by similar processes in other newly independent states. As noted above, for Ukraine, Belarus, Kazakhstan, and other post-Soviet states the tasks of restructuring are not as formidable as for Russia in terms of scale, but they have an additional dimension: should a national defense industry be created on the basis of the facilities inherited from the USSR?

After Russia, Ukraine has the largest and most highy diversified defense industrial base, capable of designing and building a range of end-product weapons, including strategic missiles and tanks. It also has shipyards capable of building naval vessels, including heavy surface ships, although most of the design and research facilities traditionally associated with the Ukrainian shipyards are located in Russia. A total of 344 enterprises and R&D organizations (of which 54 were responsible for 80 percent of military production) were formerly under the USSR defense industrial ministries and, following independence, were incorporated into a Ministry of Machine-Building, the Military-Industrial Complex, and Conversion.[30] As in Russia, military production fell sharply: as a share of the total output of the ministry, from 23 percent in 1991 to only 7 percent in 1993.[31] A conversion policy has been pursued with mixed results but it has not been helped by a very unfavorable macroeconomic environment during the first two years of independence. Privatization of defense industry enterprises has started but has been pursued much more cautiously than in Russia.

In Ukraine, policy for the military industrial base has gradually evolved, with evidence of growing interest in the formation of an embryonic national defense industry. The Kharkiv Malyshev plant, one of the principal centers of the Soviet tank industry, has developed a new model, the T–80UD, and efforts have been made to organize the domestic production of systems formerly obtained from Russia. Foreign customers are being sought for this product. The manufacture of new infantry weapons has been organized, and attempts are being made to consolidate a Ukrainian aviation industry on the basis of the Antonov design organization and mainframe and engine plants in Kiev, Kharkiv, and Zaporizhzhia. At the same time, there is Ukrainian interest in retaining collaborative links with facilities of the Russian defense industry. This is understandable; in 1993, Viktor Antonov, then minister for the industry, claimed that 80 percent of components needed by the Ukrainian defense industry were obtained from outside the country.[32] In Ukraine, work is under way on state programs for the development of weapons to the years 2000 and 2010. These programs have the aim of maximizing the autonomy of supply, but they also envisage a maintenance of supply links with Russia when that is unavoidable.[33] The Commission for Questions of Defense and State Security of the Supreme Council has called for the creation of a Ministry of the Defense Industry to consolidate the development of this embryonic domestic military industrial base, but this proposal has not been implemented.[34] However, the fact that the civilian defense minister, Valerii Shmarov, newly appointed in October 1994, will oversee the development of both the armed forces and the defense industry suggests that a Ukrainian military-industrial complex is in the process of formation.

Parallel processes have been under way in Belarus and Kazakhstan. Within the Soviet division of labor, the former did not build many end-product weapons systems but was an important supplier of systems—electronic, optical, and transport—incorporated into Russian-built armaments. Thus for Belarus the task of creating a national defense industry is more complex and may yet be considered a nonviable option. However, the new state has the potential to meet some of its military equipment requirements from domestic sources, and this appears to be official policy. There are even plans to create, with Russian assistance, a new Belarusian aviation industry with the potential to build for both civil and military requirements. The new draft program of armaments envisages a rising share of domestic supply of equipment for the forces, from a current low level of 3 percent up to 20 percent by the year 2000.[35] Supply links with Russia will be maintained. In the case of Belarus there has been a wide-ranging agreement for military-technical collaboration with Russia, and similar, but less ambitious, agreements have been concluded with other CIS members, including Uzbekistan.[36]

In the case of Kazakhstan, the defense industrial inheritance is mixed, embracing end-product weapons, systems, and materials. However, some of the weapons produced have little relevance to Kazakhstan's military requirements;

for example, the Moscow-determined union division of labor has left the new state with several facilities for the manufacture of naval armaments. There have been efforts to maintain links with Russian partners, but some of the facilities are being converted to civil work. However, in 1994 there were signs of a growing interest in the formation of a defense industry able to meet some of the requirements of the domestic armed forces. This culminated in October 1994 in the adoption of a presidential decree on the establishment of a defense industry committee under the Council of Ministers to oversee and coordinate the work of defense industry enterprises and to implement state policy for the development and production of military and dual-use products. The new committee is also charged with creating mobilizational capacities and reserves.[37]

An important factor pushing the newly independent states in the direction of creating their own defense industries is the aging of the stocks of weapons that fell to them as a result of the breakup of the Soviet military. As the Belarusian minister of defense, A. Kostenko, has made clear, shortages of spare parts and other supplies are now being experienced, and before long the new armed forces will require new equipment.[38] Implicit is the concern that it may not be possible to obtain these supplies from Russia: a certain minimum domestic capability is being created as an insurance policy. What cannot be ruled out is growing cooperation between Ukraine, Kazakhstan, and other states in the field of military production, but given the sensitivity of such a development for Russia, it is unlikely that collaboration of this type will receive much publicity.

These developments have potential implications for the Russian defense industry. There is mounting evidence of a concerted effort by Russia to substitute for strategically sensitive supplies hitherto obtained from the "near abroad," particularly from Ukraine, to such an extent that the author suspects that a special national program for military import substitution may exist. This import substitution activity is creating work for the Russian defense industry, and as it proceeds it will place limits on the extent to which traditional links will be restored in the event that some form of closer economic or political union is forged in the future.

With privatization in Russia and other states, a new possibility is beginning to emerge: the creation of transnational joint-stock companies, or investment by Russia in companies located in other states. There are already some modest examples, in particular the Vympel corporation, a Russian-Belarusian company developing and building over-the-horizon radar systems. Goskomoboronprom now intends to create a new interstate financial-industrial group, Mezhdunarodnye aviamotory, linking aeroengine plants in Perm', Samara, and Zaporizhzhia in Ukraine.[39]

As Ukraine, Belarus, and other states pursue reform strategies that bring their economies more into line with that of Russia, the possibilities for new forms of interstate collaboration are likely to expand. While the desire for normal interstate links is often heard, it is difficult to find evidence to support the view that within the defense industry there are strong "restorationist" sentiments with regard to the former Soviet union.

From Lobbies to a New Russian MIC?

Given the turmoil of the past three years, it is not surprising that a need has been felt for organizations to represent the interests of the defense industry. In Western discussion of the post-Soviet situation it has become something of a cliché to characterize the Russian Union of Industrialists and Entrepreneurs, led by Arkadii Vol'skii, as being the representative body of the military-industrial interest. While Vol'skii and his organization undoubtedly have had some standing in defense industrial circles, especially during the period 1991–92, and Vol'skii likes to boast of his close links with the military sector, in reality it is the League in Support of Defense Enterprises that has won the backing of the leading figures of the industry at the enterprise level.

Under the energetic leadership of Aleksei Shulunov, director of the radio industry's Central Research Radiotechnical Institute, the league has become an effective lobbying organization. Unlike Vol'skii and some of his associates, Shulunov has been careful to keep out of politics, and the league has become an apolitical business organization supported by directors of both state and privatized defense sector companies. At the national level, it is the only representative organization that truly cuts across the old ministerial barriers. However, the league is relatively small, with only a very modest formal structure—in essence it is little more than a nationwide information network with Shulunov at its center, in regular telephone contact with his fellow directors throughout the country.[40] And while it is regularly consulted by the government on policy issues and new legislation, its ability to shape events is relatively limited.

In recent months the labor unions of the defense industry sector have become more active in defense of their members' interests, but they have tended to focus on specific grievances, notably the nonpayment of wages, rather than take up fundamental issues of policy with respect to the industry. The trade unions are still organized on a traditional "ministerial" basis, which may limit their ability to forge a unified front. As noted above, it is only at the republican, oblast, and city levels that genuine collaborative relations are beginning to strengthen, often promoted by local government agencies. Thus, "ministerial" corporate consciousness is beginning to give way to "territorial" loyalty, but even this process has limits in circumstances in which every organization is above all concerned with its own survival.

On the military side, there is some evidence of a deliberate attempt to construct a united military-industrial interest. To the fore has been the newspaper *Krasnaia zvezda*, which has sought to speak for the industrial interest by running regular features on the arms industry and, from the spring of 1994, an occasional special supplement, *Russkoe oruzhie*. This provides a regular platform for

Shulunov and other industry leaders. Another recent innovation is the glossy bilingual publication, *Military Parade/Voennyi parad*, which, while principally concerned with the promotion of Russian weapons on export markets, also carries some material on policy for the defense industry.[41] But these modest efforts tend to confirm that at present there is no strong common interest; a true Russian "military-industrial complex" has yet to emerge. The present conditions, which put a premium on individual survival and leave many issues between the armed forces and the defense industry unresolved, may not be conducive to the forging of a strong common interest. Further evidence for this has been provided by budgetary politics in 1994.

The 1994 Budget Battle

The relative weakness of the combined armed forces–defense industry lobby in the present political conjuncture was revealed in the struggle over the 1994 military budget. In the aftermath of the storming of the White House, the military was quick to seize the opportunity and appeared to gain Yeltsin's backing for protection of allocations for military research and development and procurement in 1994. Yeltsin declared in favor of a 10 percent share for R&D in the defense budget (as opposed to the actual share of 6 percent in 1993), and in December, in the absence of the finance minister and other members of the government responsible for the economy, the Security Council approved an order for weapons and other military hardware for 1994 of no less than 28.3 trillion rubles.[42] This was a major victory for Kokoshin. On the basis of this decision, the Ministry of Defense drew up a budget request of 87.8 trillion rubles, but it later emerged that this was based on a pessimistic assumption that the rate of inflation would remain at the high level of 1993.[43] But the Ministry of Finance had other ideas: at the beginning of March it set a defense budget of 37.126 trillion rubles, maintaining the military expenditure share of GDP at the 1993 level. In the pages of *Krasnaia zvezda* and elsewhere, the armed forces counterattacked with a vigorous campaign designed to convince parliamentarians, the public, and, it appears, the president that the proposed budget would lead to the collapse of the defense industry, with a loss of four million jobs and a grave weakening of the country's defenses. This was a campaign led by Kokoshin and the military. Goskomoboronprom and the defense industry in general were less vocal, although Shulunov did back efforts to secure an increase in the budget.[44] In any event, notwithstanding the Federal Council's attempt to increase the budget to 55 trillion rubles, both houses accepted a final figure of 40.6 trillion rubles plus a vague promise that supplementary extrabudgetary funds would be found.[45] In the face of tough lobbying, the government and Yeltsin stood firm. The voting patterns on the budget were revealing: the Communist Party of the Russian Federation, the Agrarian Party, and even some supporters of Vladimir Zhirinovsky were not prepared to back a larger defense budget.

The military may yet pay a price for its somewhat hysterical campaign: it appears to have convinced the president of the need to step up efforts to scale down the armed forces. Shortly after the final vote on the budget Yeltsin called for more vigorous action to reduce the size of the forces and urged further reductions in spending on military equipment.[46] The prime minister, Viktor Chernomyrdin, has also expressed irritation with the demands of the military sector. At a meeting of the government in July 1994 he did not conceal his conviction that weapons were still being produced in excessive quantity, at times for no other reason than for maintaining workers in employment. He called for a further narrowing of the range of arms manufactured and a concentration of military production at a smaller number of enterprises.[47]

A grudging recognition that economic stabilization must have first priority now unites much of the mainstream political spectrum of Russia. The episode of the 1994 defense budget provides evidence that in Russia today there is no strong, united military-industrial complex able to extract endless concessions from the government and dictate the course of economic and political transformation. A new struggle over the size of the 1995 defense budget began in the autumn of 1994. The Ministry of Defense initially requested 115 trillion rubles; the draft budget of the Ministry of Finance set spending on national defense at 45.275 trillion rubles, representing a modest increase in the military share of total budget expenditure.[48] A struggle is likely to ensue, but this process is beginning to take on the appearance of an annual ritual of a kind not unknown in countries of the West.

Adaptation and Contraction

While battles rage over the budget and general economic transformation maintains its fitful progress, enterprises and R&D organizations of the defense industry strive to adapt to the new conditions. The responses are varied, but in many cases the energy and initiative being shown are striking. Privatization has provided an additional impulse for change. The first examples have appeared of the voting out of Soviet-era directors and their replacement by representatives of the new business class emerging rapidly in Russia. The most dramatic example in the defense sector is the replacement of the general director of the Permskie motory joint-stock company (an aeroengine plant employing thirty-five thousand workers) by a representative of a minority (5 percent) external shareholder, the Moscow-based Mikrodin private company.[49] In St. Petersburg, Nizhnii-Novgorod, and other reform-oriented regions, dynamic new joint-stock companies are appearing on the basis of breakouts from former state-owned associations.[50]

Some recently created joint-stock companies of the military sector have undertaken far-reaching restructuring resulting in increased activity and employment. A notable example is the Nizhnii-Novgorod Nitel company, a leading manufacturer of radar systems and televisions, which during four years has reduced the military share of its total output from 80 percent to 20 percent but maintained its overall level of output, achieving a 25 percent growth rate in 1993.[51] A famous arms plant producing infantry weapons, aviation guns, and other systems, the Tulamashzavod joint-stock company, has been so successful in expanding its civilian output, including dual-use items, and in winning export sales for its motor scooters, that it has been able to increase its provision of social infrastructure for the workforce.[52]

Examples of this type are becoming ever more frequent. A common theme emerges: enterprise directors now understand that they can no longer expect subsidies and cheap credits from the state; survival rests in their own hands. The strengthening of this understanding is the best guarantee that the Russian defense industry will adapt to the challenge of transformation.

As privatization and restructuring gather pace, attention is turning to policy for the remaining core defense industry. A consensus is emerging that a further contraction is required, concentrating military production at a smaller number of specialized facilities and with a reduction in the number of types of armaments retained in production. Such a policy has been advocated by the League in Support of Defense Enterprises, which has elaborated a set of proposals for a major structural transformation of the defense branches of industry. More than 60 percent of enterprises would be withdrawn from the military sector, freeing them to become independent private companies. For each branch of the defense industry a core set of lead enterprises and R&D organizations would be identified and provided with appropriate conditions for effective work for the development and manufacture of equipment required by the armed forces and for export.[53] The league's policy would appear to command wide support both within the defense industry and also within the Ministry of Defense. If implemented, it would mark a further step in the partial demilitarization of the Russian economy.

On a Path of "Normal" Development?

Over the past few years in Russia, and also to some extent in the West, there has been a tendency to demonize the former Soviet defense industry, seeing it as one of the principal bastions of conservatism, or even reaction. In Russia debate has often been unproductively polarized between patriots and opponents of the "VPK." Within the defense sector, those endeavoring to adapt to the changes, to find means of survival in the evolving market economy, increasingly resent this overpolitization. Notwithstanding all the forecasts to the contrary, the defense industry has not blocked market transformation and privatization and has not taken up the banner of ultranationalism or the restoration of the old order. As the radical processes of change take ever deeper root in Russian society, the possibility that a militant "military-industrial complex" could overturn the hard-won achievements of the postcommunist order appears to the present author as increasingly remote. By halting and painful steps, the Russian defense industry is beginning to embark on a "normal" path of development. In time it may become clear that this has been one of President Yeltsin's greatest achievements.

In other successor states the trajectory of development is somewhat different: new national defense industries are being formed on the basis of the Soviet inheritance. These industries will permit some of the new nations to supply at least a modest proportion of the needs of their armed forces and may offer possibilities for arms sales on a limited scale. The consolidation of domestic defense industries may serve an additional function insofar as it should assist in the process of state-building now under way in the newly independent states. Again, from the unfavorable legacy of the Soviet military-industrial complex, the "normal" is beginning to emerge.

Notes

1. See Julian Cooper, *The Soviet Defense Industry: Conversion and Reform* (London: Pinter/RIIA, 1991), chap. 6; and idem, "The Defense Industry and Civil-Military Relations," in *Soldiers and the Soviet State*, eds. T.J. Colton and T. Gustafson (Princeton: Princeton University Press, 1990), pp. 189–91.

2. See Julian Cooper, "The Soviet Union and the Successor Republics: Arms Industries Coming to Terms with Disunion," in *Arms Industry Limited*, ed. H. Wulf (Oxford: Oxford University Press/SIPRI, 1993), pp. 87–108.

3. In 1992, the defense budget amounted to only 4.3 percent of GDP; in 1994, 4.4 percent (not taking into account some military outlays under other budget headings). *Voprosy ekonomiki*, 1994, no. 5, pp. 49–50.

4. *Segodnia*, 30 September 1994.

5. *Krasnaia zvezda*, 22 October 1994.

6. *Segodnia*, 30 September 1994, and *Rossiiskie vesti*, 1 June 1994.

7. *Voprosy ekonomiki i konversii*, 1993, no. 1, p. 32.

8. *Konversiia v mashinostroenii*, 1994, no. 1, p. 8. In 1992 the space and civil aviation programs accounted for more than 70 percent of the Ministry of Science's expenditure on state scientific and technical programs; in 1993 more than 40 percent. *Razvitie nauki v Rossii*, L.E. Mindeli, ed., (Moscow: Tsentr issledovanii i statistiki nauki, 1993), pp. 411–14.

9. For an extended discussion see the chapter by Julian Cooper in *Cascade of Arms*, ed. A. Pierre (Washington, DC: Brookings Institution, 1994).

10. According to Russian statistics, arms exports amounted to $1.6 billion in 1992, rising to $1.8 billion in 1993. *Segodnia*, 24 August 1994.

11. From approximately $2 billion in 1990, to only $0.5 billion in 1993. *Segodnia*, 27 January 1994.

12. *Segodnia*, 3 June 1994. According to *Komsomol'skaia pravda*, 15 October 1994, there are expectations of arms exports valuing $5 billion in 1995.

13. RICA Information Agency, *Conversion Weekly*, 24 May 1994.

14. *Segodnia*, 30 September 1994.

15. *Krasnaia zvezda*, 13 March 1993; *Komsomol'skaia pravda*, 27 April 1994.

16. *Segodnia*, 30 September 1994.

17. *Rossiiskie vesti*, 1 June 1994.

18. See *Izvestiia*, 30 December 1993; and *Krasnaia zvezda*, 25 June 1994. In addition, there are two dozen closed towns of the Ministry of Defense. *Delovoi mir*, 22 July 1994.

19. By the beginning of November 1993, 433 facilities of Goskomoboronprom had been privatized, including 74 in the aviation industry, 32 in the missile-space industry, 66 in the armaments industry, 72 in the radio industry, and 42 shipbuilding plants. *Konferentsiia—"Problemy VPK"* (December 1993) (Moscow, 1994), p. 33. It has been claimed that by August 1994, almost one-half of the defense industry's approximately 2,300 enterprises and R&D organizations had been transformed into joint-stock companies. *Delovie liudi*, September 1994, p. 34.

20. Ukaz prezidenta RF, "Ob osobennostiakh privatizatsii i dopolnitel'nykh merakh gosudarstvennogo regulirovaniia deiatel'nosti predpriiatii oboronnykh otraslei promyshlennosti," 19 August 1993. The breakdown of facilities identified for retention in state hands has been derived from the appendix of this unpublished order.

21. *Rossiiskaia gazeta*, 25 May 1993.

22. *Rossiiskie vesti*, 1 June 1994.

23. For example, in view of its importance to the local economy, the property management fund of Iaroslavl' Oblast has taken over part of the state share of the vast Rybinsk aeroengine plant. Described as a "factory-town," the company funds 60 percent of the budget of Rybinsk. *Delovoi mir*, 2 July 1994; *Izvestiia*, 28 June 1994.

24. Kokoshin's ideas are discussed at length in Julian Cooper, "Transforming Russia's Defense Industrial Base," *Survival*, vol. 35, no. 4 (winter 1993–94), pp. 146–62.

25. See "Proizvodstvenniki tianutsia k bankam sil'nee, chem bankiry—k proizvodstvu," *Finansovye izvestiia*, 27 September 1994.

26. *Segodnia*, 15 September 1994. The first defense sector FIGs will be formed in the aerospace, optical, and shipbuilding industries.

27. I. Glybin, "Nashe Ministerstvo Oborony poka eshche ne Pentagon," *Nezavisimaia gazeta*, 9 July 1993.

28. See *Soiuz*, 1991, no. 5, p. 16, and no. 24, p. 11.

29. *Rossiiskaia gazeta*, 13 July 1994 (text of the order).

30. *Inzhenernaia gazeta*, 1992, nos. 129–30 (October).

31. I.S. Byk, "Innovatsionnaia politika v mashinostroitel'nom i voenno-promyshlennom komplekse v usloviiakh konversii" (unpublished paper, Kiev, 1994), p. 3.

32. *Golos Ukrainy*, 15 May 1994.

33. BBC, *Summary of World Broadcasts*, SU/2077 D/1, 18 August 1994. See *Golos Ukrainy*, 2 August 1994, for the strongly pro–defense industry views of the commission's chairman, Vladimir Mukhin.

34. BBC, *Summary of World Broadcasts*, SU/2131 G/2, 20 October 1994.

35. *Krasnaia zvezda*, 25 June 1994 and 26 August 1994.

36. *Krasnaia zvezda*, 16 September 1994.

37. *Finansovye izvestiia*, 30 June–6 July 1994.

38. *Krasnaia zvezda*, 25 June 1994; *Pravda vostoka*, 10 March 1994.

39. *Segodnia*, 15 September 1994.

40. This discussion of the league is informed by information supplied by my CREES colleagues Elena Denezhkina and Adrian Campbell, who interviewed Shulunov at length in September 1994.

41. See, for example, Andrei Kokoshin, "National Industrial Policy: A New System of Values and Ideas Behind Their Realization," *Military Parade*, May/June 1994, pp. 9–13.

42. *Izvestiia*, 11 December 1993; *Kommersant Daily*, 21 January 1994; *Novoe vremia*, 1994, no. 14, pp. 8–9; *Segodnia*, 10 March 1994.

43. *Rossiiskie vesti*, 1 June 1994; and *Segodnia*, 10 March 1994. Precise figure calculated from *Segodnia*, 10 March 1994, and *Konversiia*, 1994, no. 3, p. 27.

44. *Nezavisimaia gazeta*, 8 June 1994.

45. *Krasnaia zvezda*, 25 and 28 June 1994; *Segodnia*, 9 June 1994.

46. BBC, *Summary of World Broadcasts*, SU/2020 B/6, 13 June 1994.

47. *Rossiiskie vesti*, 19 July 1994; *Nezavisimaia gazeta*, 16 July 1994. According to the latter, Chernomyrdin challenged the military directly: "Why do we need howitzers? With whom are we going to fight?" According to *Izvestiia* (16 July 1994), "Chernomyrdin declared that the might of a state is determined not by the number of missile launches, but by the well-being of its citizens. At this moment Pavel Grachev . . . covered his face with his hands."

48. BBC, *Summary of World Broadcasts*, SU/2125 C5/6, 13 October 1994; *Rossiiskaia gazeta*, 29 October 1994.

49. *Kommersant Daily*, 10 August 1994.

50. Information supplied by Elena Denezhkina (CREES), based on study visits to St. Petersburg and Nizhnii-Novgorod, August–September 1994.

51. *Rabochaia tribuna*, 9 September 1994.

52. *Rossiiskaia gazeta*, 25 October 1994.

53. *Nezavisimaia gazeta*, 25 October 1994.

5

Russian Policy Toward Military Conflicts in the Former Soviet Union

Tatiana Shakleina

Conflict management and conflict resolution have quite recently become important issues on the Russian political agenda. To date they have not received adequate attention from either the former Soviet government or the new Russian leadership. The ignorance about the most urgent political issues demonstrated by the new Russian leaders, and their evident neglect in formulating a definitive foreign policy and military doctrine after the dissolution of the Soviet Union, has led to serious mistakes.

After the dissolution of the Soviet Union the Russian government, and especially the Russian Foreign Ministry, became the object of severe criticism from both the conservative and the liberal wings of the opposition. These groups' main criticism concerned the lack of a clearly formulated national Russian foreign policy strategy, which, they argued, resulted in serious damage to the international status of the Russian Federation. From their perspective, these policy ambiguities led to grave mistakes in relations with near abroad countries, encouraged the activities of certain nationalist leaders in the former Soviet republics, and contributed to the aggravation of ethnic tensions inside the Russian Federation and beyond its borders.

In fact, Russian Foreign Minister Andrei Kozyrev has articulated the assumption that Russian foreign policy should be reactive and responsive to particular situations Russia might have to face abroad. In April 1992, Kozyrev stated, "There can be no blueprint. What exists are reactions to a specific situation, and those reactions display Russia's national interests. No country has an official description of its national interest."[1] As for the near abroad, this area for some time was on the periphery of Russian foreign policy, which put its major emphasis on relations with the West in order to integrate Russia into the "community of civilized nations." The Russian approach to ethnic conflict management has also been under the influence of this general attitude.

The necessity of formulating national foreign policy and military doctrines has become even more urgent following the events of October 1993 and the December 1993 elections. The shattered position of the president and the government demanded a serious correction of foreign policy course in accordance with the new challenges Russia faced.

The main issues of Russian foreign and defense strategy are still at the center of governmental and academic debates. Among them, the question of Russia's management of conflicts is the most controversial.

Russia's approach toward military ethnic conflicts and its foreign policy strategy are closely interconnected. The position of the Russian government concerning its involvement in any conflict in the former Soviet republics is formulated with regard to a number of factors, including the national interests of the Russian Federation (among them, ensuring the political stability and integrity of the Russian Federation; retaining certain positions and functions of a global character inherited by Russia from the USSR; and preventing the emergence in Europe, South Asia, and the Far East of regional hegemonic states that might develop expansionist attitudes toward unstable regions of the former Soviet Union), changes in its geopolitical position, and challenges Russia faces in the new international order.

The general concept of Russia's role in peacekeeping and peace-building in the postcommunist world, particularly in neighboring states, is a matter of great debate in both Russia and the West. Of no less concern are such issues as the use of military force in conflict settlement, particularly North Atlantic Treaty Organization (NATO) forces, and the future role of the United Nations and other nonmilitary international organizations.[2]

The answer to these questions, as well as the course of Russia's foreign and defense policy, will be determined by the political group that becomes dominant. There are four main groups that can be listed in this context: liberal confederationists, isolationists, neoimperialists, and those who think that Russia's foreign policy strategy should be a combination of different approaches.

It is necessary to mention that the proposed classification, like any other classification, is to a certain extent arbitrary, especially when we use it for characterizing the unstable and constantly changing political situation in Russia. Representatives of different political groupings shift from one position to another, sometimes declaring views contrary to ones expressed a year ago. One example of such a dramatic change of orientation and political behavior was demonstrated by a group of Russian "liberals," or confederationists, who began expressing neoimperialist views in 1993–94.

Policy differences can also exist within one political grouping—for example, among those who express moderate nationalist or isolationist ideas. Although they share a common political and cultural orientation, and their policy positions do sometimes coincide, such subgroups often give divergent policy prescriptions.

If dramatic changes occur in Russia (for instance, as a result of presidential or parliamentary elections) the suggested classifications might help in understanding the new distribution of political power and the political background and orientation of the new political leaders.

Before proceeding with the description of these groups' different approaches to Russian military and nonmilitary involvement in existing conflicts, it is useful to examine the main issues within Russian foreign policy decision making. An analysis of the present Russian geopolitical position allows us to make certain observations and generalizations upon which there is consensus among representatives of different political groupings. As will become apparent, Russia's attitude toward military conflict resolution will continue to evolve according to its geopolitical and regional interests.

Russian Foreign Policy Strategy: From Global to Continental Aims

A central assumption shared by all political groups is that the global period of Russian history has come to an end. Russia does not have the resources to continue its former foreign policies. This does not mean that Russia should remove itself from active participation in world politics (a thesis that was very popular at the beginning of perestroika). Rather, Russia is in the process of changing its geopolitical priorities, rationally narrowing its sphere of activities, shifting to continental policies with a preference toward geopolitical pragmatism, and sustaining national integrity and stability. Many groups recognize that the essential prerequisites for the formulation of realistic political objectives and an effective strategy are the adequate understanding of international realities as well as the domestic and external limitations on the ability to reach desired foreign policy goals. Otherwise the policy will evolve by way of drift, rather than consistency, and will frequently produce results that are exactly the opposite of the genuine interests of the state.[3]

There are certain issues that are subordinate to the main foreign policy priorities and to a great extent determine Russia's transition to a continental policy. The following points of concern in the establishment of Russian foreign policy should be considered:

1. The instability and complexity of the political and economic situation in the Russian Federation, particularly the growth of separatism in the regions of Sakha, Tuva, Chechnia, Tatarstan, and Bashkortostan, and the potential danger of the reemergence of conflict in the Caucasus (Chechnia, Ossetia, Ingushetia, and so forth.);
2. Continuing disagreements with the Baltic states, Ukraine, Kazakhstan, Georgia, Chechnia, Sakha, Tuva, and others on economic, military, political, and ethnic issues and the possibility of emerging territorial disputes

between Russia and the former Soviet republics (Estonia-Russia, Russia-Ukraine, Kazakhstan-Russia) and inside the Russian Federation (Sakha, Tuva, Chechnia) that may pose a serious threat to Russia's integrity and regional stability in general;

3. The need to solve the problem of Russians living outside the Russian Federation;

4. The weakening (in some cases the complete destruction) of existing economic ties, because of the unwillingness of the Commonwealth of Independent States (CIS) and East European countries to cooperate effectively with Russia, and also because of their orientation to the West, with the result that Russia could be cut off from its Western partners;

5. The possible military threat coming from the southern regions of the former USSR, which might lead to the entanglement of Russia in local and regional conflicts similar to the one in Afghanistan;

6. The problem of building up a new alliance structure, following the collapse of the Warsaw Pact and the Soviet Union, in conformity with Russia's new geopolitical status and national interests.

One of the basic national priorities of Russian foreign policy is the stability and survival of the state. Issues of security, therefore, both domestic and international, will remain of primary concern for the Russian leadership. The problems of federal stability require a separate analysis. The focus here is on the issues of regional stability, or to be more exact, Russia's involvement in regional conflict management and its counterbalancing policy against possible regional hegemonies.

In Europe, Russia will play an active role in collective security policy. This attitude has been demonstrated by Russia's joining the Partnership for Peace initiative, after long debate among different political groups, and its decisive actions in the former Yugoslavia. Aleksei A. Arbatov, a prominent specialist on security problems and director of the Center for Geopolitical and Military Forecasts (Moscow), thinks that "whatever the name of the new security system in Europe, it is clear that is has to rely on three major pillars: EC/WEU [the European Community/Western European Union], the United States, and Russia. This trilateral balance of power is the most stable basis for a multilateral security system to guarantee stability, conflict resolution, suppression of internal and international violence, and security of smaller states in Central and Eastern Europe.[4]

Russia cannot play a substantial geopolitical role in Europe because of its present weakness and the fear among East European countries and former Soviet European republics of Russian expansionism; however, Russia is still interested in closer cooperation—especially economic cooperation—with these countries. Among the greatest concerns for Russia in Europe are the outlets to the Baltic and Black Seas and the threat of growing Turkish influence in the south. These fears have become stronger since Turkey introduced, on 1 July 1994, a new charter for ships passing through the Bosporus and the Dardanelles.[5]

At present, the balance of power in Europe is not favorable for Russia. It would be a mistake to state that the Russian Federation has serious enemies in Europe, but it must be admitted that Russia does not have good friends among its former allies either, except perhaps Belarus. Under these circumstances, especially in its relations with Ukraine, Moldova, and the Baltic states, Russia will have to use the old tactic of "carrot and stick" to pursue its goals.

The challenges Russia faces in Asia and the Caucasus are far more serious than those coming from Europe. The essential tasks of Russian foreign policy in these regions will be to contain separatism in the North Caucasus, which threatens to spread to Tatarstan and Bashkortostan; diminish the growth of Turkish and Iranian influence in the Central Asian states; prevent the formation of new, strong regional hegemonies; and play an active and leading role in collective peacekeeping activities in the emerging conflicts. Thus the geopolitical role of Russia can be more actively realized in the Eurasian south, where there exists a real threat to its security.

In this geopolitical context Russia will have to seek all possible ways of establishing friendly relations with all Central Asian countries. Only Kazakhstan, however, is a truly geopolitically important Russian ally. Both countries have common security concerns: the spread of military conflicts in Central Asia; the possible growth of extreme Muslim fundamentalism; and the expansion of China into Kazakhstan (China's economic expansion into the Far East has already started). Though Russia has declared its right to a privileged role as a peacekeeping force in the post-Soviet space, the success of this policy is envisaged through collective efforts, as through cooperation with Kazakhstan.

The question of Russia's allies in the post-Soviet period is a topic for a separate analysis.[6] Here it is only necessary to mention that the establishment of relations with Russia's neighbors will depend on the character of political power in the country.

The Influence of Political Groups on Russian Foreign Policy

The new multipolar world made it quite complicated for the Russian government to formulate a new concept of national and regional security. One of the main difficulties in the policy formulation process is the great diversity of views and approaches to the concept of Russian national policy. Therefore, one of the biggest dilemmas for the Russian leadership is to formulate a centrist strategy based on the views of leading academic and political experts that is at the same time palatable to a majority of the Russian population.

The character of the threats and challenges facing the Russian state changed after the dissolution of the Soviet Union. Among the greatest concerns are the military conflicts in the former Soviet space. To a great extent, the degree and character of Russian involvement abroad will be determined by the general strategy of Russian foreign and defense policy. The year 1994 can be characterized as a turning point in Russian foreign policy. The ideas of Russian revival and hopes for the restoration of its status as a great power are reemerging. As long as Russia remains a strong state, capable of effectively resisting or managing regional threats, the number and intensity of threats will diminish. Conversely, a weak and destabilized Russia will only encourage encroachments on its territory and contribute to the growth of instability, placing in question its very survival as a sovereign state.

Four domestic political groupings are exerting their influence on the Russian foreign policy decision-making process. Accordingly, within existing limits and constraints, Russia's foreign policy toward its closest neighbors may follow very different avenues. Russian foreign policy might contain varying degrees of prudence and adventurism, transparency and secrecy, liberalism and nationalism, and so on. Taking account of these alternatives and the range of options that they present is crucial, because some of the radical opposition political leaders, should they come to power, might try to ignore existing constraints on these options and attempt to redefine the acceptable range of policy choices. Hence, these leaders' views, no matter how utopian or unrealistic they appear today, cannot be overlooked for the future.

The Liberal View of Russian Foreign Policy

If we look back to 1991–92, there is much evidence to support the view that the official Russian position concerning conflicts in the former Soviet republics actually contributed to the emergence and further escalation of ethnic tensions.

Russian liberals, whose influence on foreign policy was crucial at that time, behaved more like "internationalists" than national leaders. They never tried to develop a liberal Russian national agenda and never attempted to develop a concept of the Russian national interest that would have informed such an agenda. The mere notion of nationalism was alien, and even carried a negative connotation for them.

During the Gorbachev era, liberal intellectuals were never much interested in defining the state interests of the USSR. For them the entire idea of the state was obsolete and irrelevant. Much more attention was paid to the concept of the new world order, UN reform projects, analyses of transnational trends in global politics, and so forth. In a sense, like their most ardent orthodox Marxist-Leninist opponents, liberal intellectuals were pure ideologues basing their concepts on values and beliefs rather than facts and interests.

After the Soviet collapse Russian liberals were suddenly faced with the prospect of living in a nation-state, and this prospect was not very appealing to them. They were therefore not ready, either intellectually or psychologically, to compete for political influence with Russian nationalists. Their ignorance of the necessity of formulating a Russian national policy not only made liberals the object of intense criticism, but given their ongoing influence over Russian policy, yielded certain immediate negative results in relations between Russia and the newly independent states. In particular, liberal approaches to interstate and ethnic conflicts aggravated tensions between Russia and the newly independent states, owing to the powerful liberals' inability to manage these new or reemerging conflicts.

At the highest political levels Russian foreign policy was conducted under the decisive influence of the secretary of state, Gennadii Burbulis, who, as many believe, was the mastermind behind the CIS idea and the Minsk and Almaty agreements. In the Foreign Ministry his views were strongly supported by Minister Andrei Kozyrev and his deputy on CIS affairs, Fedor Shelov-Kovediaev. A liberal faction in the Supreme Soviet was represented by Viktor Sheinis, Sergei Iushenkov, Vladimir Kuznetsov, Gleb Yakunin, and Galina Starovoitova. In the media the same positions were promoted by Evgenii Kiselev, Egor Iakovlev, Otto Latsis, Iurii Kariakin, and many others.

In the military sphere the position of Russian liberals in December 1991 was based on the assumption that, with the new commonwealth, it was possible to preserve a relatively stable post-Soviet "common defense space" embracing most, if not all, the territory of the former Soviet Union, with a common military doctrine for all the members of the CIS. The idea was that the defense postures of Russia and the other republics would be based on two parallel military doctrines: the doctrines of the individual republics, reflecting the specific defense needs of these new states, and a common interstate military doctrine of the commonwealth, worked out between member states.

Russia was perceived by most civilian strategists as the nucleus of the entire CIS security system, with its special responsibility for footing the bill for the lion's share of CIS defense expenditures, and with special rights that included a dominant decision-making role at the operational level. In many of its key elements, this military-political alliance was similar to what Gorbachev proposed in his last version of the Union Treaty in October 1991, with one important difference: Russia was to replace the Soviet center.

The Almaty agreements envisaged the preservation of a similar "common military-strategic space," but from the very beginning, Ukraine, Azerbaijan, and Moldova dropped out of this space, while Uzbekistan and Turkmenistan insisted on building their own national armies before agreeing to any military integration with other CIS members. In response, in May 1992 Russia announced that it would start its own national army, one that would be autonomous from the structures of the CIS Supreme Command. As a result, the idea of an integrated armed forces was put aside for the time being.

To be sure, a number of important documents in the security sphere were signed in 1992–93. Among them, an agreement on peacekeeping was signed by Armenia, Belarus, Kazakhstan, Kyrgyzstan, Moldova, Russia, Tajikistan, and Uzbekistan, and a Treaty on Collective Security was signed by Armenia, Kazakhstan, Kyrgyzstan, Russia, Tajikistan, and Uzbekistan. But neither these nor other agreements were implemented in practice.

The failure of Russian liberals, who sometimes are called confederationists (because of their preoccupation with the idea of a new confederation of states) to establish a stable commonwealth, the emergence and escalation of ethnic conflicts in the newly independent states, and the growing instability inside the Russian Federation required a new approach to Russian foreign and defense policy making. This new approach included a reevaluation of the role of Russian military forces in conflict resolution. No wonder Andrei Kozyrev, acting as a "Russian Shevardnadze" in 1992 when he used "new political thinking" slogans, was sharply criticized by the very same journalists and academics who had enthusiastically supported Eduard Shevardnadze between 1985 and 1990.

Russian liberals were mostly criticized for too deep an absorption in global problems, for their pro-Western orientation, and for the absence of a nationally oriented foreign policy strategy. Criticism was heard from both liberal and conservative camps. Sergei Karaganov, at that time the deputy director of the Institute of Europe, pointed out, "The sphere of Russia's international influence has narrowed dramatically. This fact dictates quite a new foreign policy agenda for the new Russian state. Its prosperity will be 90 percent dependent on Russia's ability to influence the policies of Ukraine, Belarus, Kazakhstan, and other former Soviet republics, and not on the relations with the United States and Europe, though they will remain extremely important too."[7]

Conservatives attacked liberal Russian leaders for their anti-Russia policy. One of the leaders of the Constitutional Democratic Party, Natal'ia Narochnitskaia, said, "Democratic Moscow, full of negativism toward Russia's history, restores the Trotskyist-Bolshevik interpretation of 'hated empire,' and destroys its own state." As a result of such a policy, she said, "Russia is thrown back in history to the time of the Levonic War in the northwest [the Baltic region], and in the south Russia is facing the danger of losing its Black Sea power status, as happened after the Crimea war." Narochnitskaia blamed Russian democrats for ignorance about Russia's historic geopolitical and civilizational interests, and for the loss of its historic mission and role in the world.[8]

The Russian leadership did not clearly formulate Russia's new foreign policy strategy, or outline its geopolitical and regional priorities, especially concerning Russian allies in the new international situation, or devote enough attention to the question of ethnic Russians in the other post-Soviet states. This approach had dramatic consequences for the evolution of ethnic relations in the former Soviet Union and contributed to the emergence of conflicts.

In the Baltic states the governments adopted discriminatory citizenship and language laws for the Russian population, thereby posing new obstacles for the improvement of interstate relations. Most tragically, the uncertain Russian position influenced the events in Moldova and Georgia.

At the meeting of the members of the Conference on Security and Cooperation in Europe (CSCE) on 25 March 1992, the foreign ministers of Russia, Ukraine, Moldova, and Romania made statements about the recognition of the territorial integrity of Moldova. A few days later, in his speech on 2 April 1992, Russian Vice President Aleksandr Rutskoi, during his visit to the Trans-Dniester

Republic, advocated the idea of the republic's independence. In Moscow, the Congress of People's Deputies adopted a special resolution on Moldova, particularly stressing the necessity to safeguard human rights in the Trans-Dniester Republic.[9]

Meanwhile, the Russian Fourteenth Army, awaiting directions from Moscow, continued to endure severe criticism by the Moldovan parliament and came under attack by Moldovan citizens. The people of Trans-Dniestria were demanding protection from the Russian military. General Ia. Netkachev, the commander of the Fourteenth Army, declared in May 1992 that if the shooting at the positions of the army did not stop, the army would go beyond Moscow's control and act according to the circumstances.[10]

While in Russia nationalist aspirations in defense of Russians and the Russian-speaking population in Moldova and other former republics were growing, in Moldova extreme forces, supporting the idea of unification with Romania, were also on the rise. This idea was strongly supported by certain political groups in Romania, which contributed to a further aggravation of the political situation in Moldova. In a television interview President Mircea Snegur accused Rutskoi of heating up separatist aspirations in the Trans-Dniester region and, in fact, trying to legitimate the occupation of the region by the Russian Fourteenth Army.[11] Later, in a speech before the Moldovan parliament, he declared that Russia was merely seeking to play the role of a gendarme in the CIS.[12]

In the fighting that followed this political battle between 21 June and 6 July 1992, hundreds of people were killed during the offensive of the Moldovan army in Bendery, Tiraspol, and nearby villages (according to some sources, seven hundred people were killed and four thousand wounded).[13] The Fourteenth Army, which by then had a new commander, General Aleksandr Lebed', also came under attack by the Moldovan army and air force. With its commander standing firm and the Fourteenth Army actively supporting the population of the Trans-Dniester Republic, the bloody fighting soon ceased.

That phase of the hostilities finished when peacekeeping forces from Russia, Ukraine, and Moldova were brought into the conflict zone. The Fourteenth Army remained in the Trans-Dniester Republic; the question of its status and withdrawal had not been solved as of the summer of 1994. Many facts about the real situation in the republic and about the role of the Fourteenth Army before and after the military conflict still remain secret. But the known facts show us how dramatic the consequences of political ambitions and uncertainty can be.

In August 1994, President Snegur declared the government's decision to recognize the autonomy of the Trans-Dniester region and Gagauziia.

These events and the course of Russian-Moldovan relations in 1994 testified to the fact that serious changes had taken place in the approach of the Russian leadership to Russia's foreign policy strategy and its role in conflict resolution in the former Soviet Union. The position of the Moldovan leadership also underwent a dramatic change. These new shifts in Russian-Moldovan relations demonstrated the practicality of realistic attitudes among Moldovan political leaders after the defeat of extreme nationalist forces during the elections in 1993, and the necessity of establishing constructive, friendly relations with the former Soviet republics, especially Russia. By this time, the idea of Moldovan and Romanian unification lost its appeal among both Moldovans and Romanians. The leaders and population of both countries understood that the problem did not have a simple solution, given the economic and political crises in the countries, existing ethnic problems, and the border issue.

By mid-1992, liberal Russian leaders and their interpretation of Russia's future role in the world and its foreign policy had become unpopular and had lost much of their initial appeal in Russia. The conflict in Moldova, the discrimination against Russians in the Baltic states, and Russia's passive position in the Yugoslavian conflict gave rise to even more severe criticism of Russian liberals. Nationalist leaders blamed them for betraying Russia, and their democratic colleagues did not approve of the reactive character of Russian foreign policy and its retreat from vitally important regions on Russia's borders.

Revival of Great Russia?

The analysis of Russian nationalist groups is a special topic, and the constraints of this chapter do not allow us to proceed with detailed chracteristics, as Russian nationalists have never coalesced into any cohesive political grouping.[14]

The most radical versions of neoimperialist policies were vigorously rejected by the Russian executive leadership and moderates in the Supreme Soviet. Different degrees of moderate neoimperialism were personified by Russian Vice President Aleksandr Rutskoi; the chairman of the Supreme Soviet, Ruslan Khasbulatov; the chairman of the Russian Democratic Party, Nikolai Travkin; the head of Russia's Industrial Union, Arkadii Vol'skii; and the head of the parliamentary Constitutional Committee and the Social-Democratic Party, Oleg Rumiantsev.

Within the executive branch, the positions of the moderates were espoused by the leaders of the military-industrial complex and the leaders of various sectoral ministries, especially energy and transportation. The chief of the Security Council, Iurii Skokov, and the vice premiers Oleg Lobov and Mikhail Malei also implicitly or explicitly backed the moderate neoimperialist vision of relations between Russia and the near abroad. Among the intellectual proponents of this position were Sergei Karaganov, Andrei Zubov, Sergei Stankevich, Andranik Migranian, and Aleksandr Tsipko.

One of the manifestations of the moderate neoimperialist position can be found in a report entitled "A Strategy for Russia," which was developed in the summer of 1992 by the Moscow-based Council on Foreign and Defense Policy. The council includes influential politicians, academics, generals, and businesspeople. The report calls for Russia to pursue an "enlightened postimperial integrationist course" in relations with the former Soviet republics. It assumes that Russia is the only player capable of maintaining stability in the region and calls for "an active and, if possible, internationally sanctioned Russian role in preventing and ending conflicts." The council also subscribes to the use of military force to this end and advocates the prevention of extensive human rights violations.[15]

These positions reflect not only an increasingly popular conception of the Russian national interest but also the institutional interests of the Russian military. Liberal intellectuals have continually accused the military of wasting national resources and have demanded drastic reductions of the Russian armed forces irrespective of the possible social and political consequences of such rapid change. In all, as a result, liberals have attempted to deprive the army of a voice in foreign policy decision making. For liberals the Russian military presence in the near abroad was, in most cases, a negative, rather than positive, factor, raising suspicions about Russian intentions and thereby slowing down the process of natural political integration.

By contrast, moderate neoimperialists have held that a rapid withdrawal of the Russian military forces from the near abroad might be dangerous and short-sighted. The military establishment in Moscow expressed concern that if Russia politically and militarily abandoned the near abroad, the resulting vacuum would be filled by other countries to the detriment of long-term Russian interests. The moderate neoimperialists have therefore tried to justify a relatively high Russian military presence abroad, giving the army a new sense of mission.[16]

After moderate nationalist views made their way into the thinking of members of the Russian foreign policy establishment, Foreign Minister Andrei Kozyrev, in his January 1994 statement at a meeting with ambassadors from the CIS and Baltic states, emphasized the need to preserve the Russian military presence on the territory of the former Soviet Union. He argued that proposals to withdraw militarily were "extremist" because, if Russia were to leave the near abroad, the security vacuum there "would inevitably be filled by other powers not always friendly, and in many cases hostile to Russian interests."[17]

One can note that moderate neoimperialists would like to get the best of both worlds: securing the Russian Federation's right to intervene in the former Soviet republics while, at the same time, gaining international political and financial support for Russian actions in the near abroad. This apparent contradiction does not look like one at all in the eyes of moderate neoimperialists. From their perspective, Russian attempts to bring law and order to the highly explosive regions of Eurasia satisfy not only Russian national interests but also the strategic interests of the entire global community. In this view Russia is the bulwark of the West, capable of absorbing destabilizing impulses coming from the Caucasus, Central Asia, and other regions of the former Soviet Union. Therefore Russia is entitled not only to Western recognition of its special role but also to substantial Western support in this role.

At least at the rhetorical level, this position has been accepted by both the Russian government and President Boris Yeltsin. In a February 1993 speech to the Civic Union, Yeltsin stated that "Russia continues to have a vital interest in the cessation of all armed conflicts in the territory of the former USSR. Moreover, the world community is increasingly coming to realize our country's special responsibility in this difficult matter. I believe the time has come for authoritative international organizations, including the UN, to grant Russia special powers as guarantor of peace and stability in this region."[18] Later the Foreign Ministry officially approached the UN and the CSCE and requested that these institutions grant Russia special peacekeeping rights and responsibilities in the near abroad.

Since the initial reaction of the international community to these claims was, at best, ambiguous (most of the near abroad countries were very emphatic in their rejection of Yeltsin's idea), the Russian leadership tried to modify the initial formula, placing most of the emphasis on the multilateral CIS peacekeeping aspect of this approach.[19]

In light of the growing pressure in Russia from radical neoimperialists, it is not clear whether Yeltsin is in a position to fine-tune his moderate approach to the near abroad. After the December 1993 parliamentary elections, this pressure intensified. The newly elected State Duma might well turn into the stronghold of neoimperialist forces. The Liberal Democratic Party (of Vladimir Zhirinovsky) gained control over the newly formed Committee on Geopolitics, now chaired by Viktor Ustinov, and the Communists gained control over the Committee on Security, chaired by Viktor Iliukhin.

The Committee on International Affairs, led by Vladimir Lukin from the Yabloko bloc, promises to be more moderate than the other two committees. Nevertheless, Lukin has more than once criticized Foreign Minister Andrei Kozyrev for his alleged pro-Western and pro-American policies. The only way that Yeltsin can hope to withstand the pressure of the State Duma (if, of course, Yeltsin cares about the legislature at all) is to exploit the inevitable differences and conflicts between deputies of radical and moderate nationalist orientation.

The disagreements among neoimperialists in the parliament and in the government, and the change of command by various influential groups over the decision-making process, affected quite visibly Russia's approach to the Georgia-Abkhazia conflict in 1992–93. The indigenous roots of this conflict go back deep into history. The resumption of the conflict in the post-Soviet period occurred for many reasons, among them, the growth of separatism in Abkhazia, the development in Tbilisi of a hypernationalist commitment to the Georgianization of the country's minorities, the severe political struggle for power in Georgia, and the unwillingness of the Georgian and Abkhazian governments to make some concessions at the most critical moments of the conflict.

Russia also bears a certain amount of responsibility for the aggravation of the conflict after 1992, but the conflict was also fueled by strong antagonisms within the region itself. The shift toward a neoimperialist Russian foreign policy in mid-1992 soured relations between Russia and Georgia and intensified the Georgia-Abkhazia struggle. The foreign policy shift was shaped by a number of factors: the Russian nationalists' growing campaign in support of Abkhazia, the bitter political battles between the Russian government and the Russian Supreme Soviet, the policy controversies inside the military establishment, and the attendant growth of political instability in Moscow. A resolution on the Georgian-Abkhazian conflict adopted in a closed session of the Russian parliament on 25 September 1992 exemplified the new neoimperialist tendency. In this document the deputies condemned the policy of the Georgian government and recommended that the Russian government abstain from signing any economic agreement with Georgia providing it with Russian arms and military equipment. A special point about the territorial integrity of Georgia and Russia's respect for this state integrity was obliterated.[20]

The next crisis happened in the spring of 1993, after the attempt of the Abkhazian army to capture Sukhumi on 15–16 March 1993. At that time, articles appeared in the Georgian and Russian mass media about the direct Russian military support of Abkhazia. Eduard Shevardnadze stated in the Georgian parliament on 26 March 1993, "We have to admit the beginning of an open Russian-Georgian conflict."[21]

Despite the political struggle in the Russian leadership, the Russian executive branch still managed to pursue a strategy that was designed to reach a settlement of the conflict in Georgia and that was based on the assumption that Russia would perform the peacekeeping mission together with the UN and the CSCE. The result of these efforts was the signing of the agreement in Sochi on 27 July 1993 by Russia, Georgia, and Abkhazia on the regulation of the conflict in Abkhazia.

The prevalence of neoimperialist aspirations among the military, however, and its growing influence on the decision-making process, showed itself in the autumn of 1993. As the Russian Minister of Defense Pavel Grachev acknowledged in February 1994, after Russia and Georgia signed the agreement on friendship and cooperation, "Eduard Shevardnadze declined Russia's suggestion of bringing Russian peacekeeping forces into Georgia in September 1993. It was a strategic mistake on the part of Georgia."[22] This "mistake" and the hardline position of Russia at that time caused another crisis in Georgian-Russian relations and the resumption of military actions in Abkhazia. Abkhazian forces broke peace agreements and at the beginning of September started a wide-scale offensive that resulted in the fall of Sochi.

On 3 February 1994, in Tbilisi, Boris Yeltsin and Eduard Shevardnadze signed an agreement on friendship and cooperation between the two countries. During the negotiations twenty-five documents were signed. In the military sphere Georgia and Russia signed a special protocol that includes the following issues: the enlargement of Russian military bases in Georgia; the status of Russian border troops in Georgia; cooperation in protecting the borders; and the Russian peacekeeping mission in Abkhazia.

The leader of the Russian military delegation in Tbilisi, Lieutenant General A. Galkin, stated that the "presence of Russian troops in the region is in the strategic interests of both Russia and Georgia, and it guarantees security in the Caucasus and North Caucasus regions. Russian troops will play a stabilizing role in Georgia, will protect the Russian-speaking population, and will give assistance in the formation of a Georgian national army."[23]

The bilateral Russian-Georgian agreement was a certain victory for the neoimperialist grouping in the government. However, some criticism was heard from the supporters of a more hardline Russian policy toward Georgia after Russia and Georgia signed the bilateral agreement in February 1994. During a closed session of the State Duma Committee on the CIS, Andranik Migranian warned that Russian assistance in creating the Georgian army would inevitably make the situation in the region more complicated. Vladimir Lukin, from the Yabloko bloc, characterized this agreement as delusive because none of the countries could implement its provisions.[24]

The chairman of the State Duma Committee on the CIS, Konstantin Zatulin, summed up the results of the discussion at the closed session in his speech before the members of the Duma: "The agreement is beneficial only for the present Georgian government. After its implementation the Russian military presence in Georgia will decrease, while Russia must have a much higher military status in this region as a guarantor of peace and security." He also pointed out that the agreement might be ratified only after Georgia implemented its obligations concerning Abkhazia and South Ossetia.[25]

The neoimperialist approach in Russian foreign policy, especially when it concerned Russian peacekeeping and peace-building strategy, has been the most decisive in the decision-making process. There is, however, an opposition to this course that consists of those who advocate a more moderate and more pragmatic approach. The criticism comes from Russian isolationists and from the proponents of a selective approach.

Russian Isolationism

Russian isolationism is not an entirely new phenomenon. It existed during most of the Soviet period as a reaction to the alleged economic, political, and cultural discrimination against Russia within the Soviet state. The slogan "Russia first" was actively and very successfully used by Boris Yeltsin in his power struggle against Mikhail Gorbachev in the late 1980s. After the Soviet disintegration, isolationist sentiments became more acceptable, especially in the wake of Russia's constant failure to achieve any meaningful level of economic, political, and military integration within CIS structures, and because of the widespread perception that Russia was not being treated fairly by its neighbors, who were draining its resources while ignoring its legitimate interests and concerns.

Isolationist ideas became popular for three reasons. First, an unprecedented negative campaign against Russian history, culture, and national character was being conducted by the Soviet and Russian mass media in the late 1980s at the behest of Russian democrats. Second, a passive, reactive foreign policy was being pursued by Soviet and Russian leaders, including the rapid retreat of Russia from active participation in world affairs, leading to the loss of Russia's international status. And, third, these same leaders were neglecting the fate of ethnic Russians despite the infringement on human rights of Russians living in the former Soviet republics and even in the government units of the Russian Federation formally designated as belonging to non-Russian ethnic groups.[26]

The theme of isolationism was very popular in 1992. In the debate over Russian foreign policy between liberals and conservatives, Russian democrats considered isolationism an uneasy but necessary step in the direction of a true, mutually beneficial integration. As for Russian conservatives, they exploited isolationist ideas more actively and with different accents.

Some nationalist leaders who supported the idea of the restoration of the USSR or Russian Empire looked at the near abroad countries as highly artificial creations that were unable to sustain themselves politically, economically, or militarily upon gaining independence. From this perspective the only reason these newly independent states did not collapse overnight was that they continued to receive open or covert Russian subsidies. For the nationalists the withdrawal of economic subsidies and political and military support would lead to the bankruptcy of these quasi states, leading in turn to their absorption into the Russian Federation.

During the December 1993 parliamentary election campaign, isolationist ideas were expressed by Vladimir Zhirinovsky. He threatened to cut all economic ties with the near abroad countries to make them join Russia as separate administrative units or *gubernii*. In one of his preelection speeches on the Ostankino channel, Zhirinovsky repeated his assertion that states such as Ukraine, Belarus, Kazakhstan, Latvia, and Estonia never existed, adding that their reintegration into the Russian Empire was only a matter of time (or, to be more exact, a matter of his accession to power).[27]

In 1992–93, isolationist ideas became the centerpiece of debates on the theme of Eurasian resistance to Eurasian union, and Atlantacism. The future of the Russian state, as well as the prospects of its possible integration with the former Soviet republics, was also discussed. At that time some moderate nationalists from the conservative camp supported isolationist ideas and strongly opposed the idea of creating a Eurasian union. Their main postulate was that "Russia was a unique civilization that could not be compared to Europe or Asia," that "Russia's membership in the CIS [or any other union] was not profitable for Russia and damaged its interests." One of the most ardent advocates of Russia's unique status, K. Mialo, stated, "The unprecedented campaign of Russophobia in 'the friendly republics' gives Russia moral freedom from any obligations it has taken before. To suffer an undisguised direct insult of Russian history and national character is too great a price that Russia doesn't have the right to pay for any kind of union."[28]

The idea of Russian isolation from Western influence was also popular among Russian conservatives. In their publications S. Kurginian, K. Mialo, S. Fomin, N. Lysenko, and others pointed out that "Russia does not need either an Anglo-Saxon or an Islamic nucleus, or a Teutonic one either. It must have its own nucleus, determined by God and national history. It should be the nucleus of Russian national culture, one of the most universal in the world."[29]

In 1992, isolationist sentiments were limited to economic relations between Russia and the near abroad countries; cultural and historic issues, mainly the revival of Russian traditions and culture; and the issue of preserving Russians as a nation. Yet some signs of an isolationist mood could be traced in other spheres as well.

One of the earliest symptoms of political and military isolationism that gained ground in Russia was the almost unanimous disapproval by both the Democratic Russia movement and the Russian Supreme Soviet of Yeltsin's decision to use military force to handle the Chechnia drive to independence in November 1991. Facing strong opposition to this policy, Yeltsin had to reverse himself quickly.

The president also had to face mounting opposition to the Russian military presence in Nagorno-Karabagh, which led to inevitable human and material losses. Despite his intention to maintain Russian influence in this part of the former Soviet Union, in the spring of 1992 Yeltsin was forced to order the Russian (at that point, CIS) troops to withdraw from Nagorno-Karabagh and to request simultaneously the deployment of NATO troops as a peacekeeping force in the region. Furthermore, Russia actually encouraged Turkey and Iran to mediate the Armenian-Azerbaijani conflict.

If the isolationist mood prevailed in the Karabagh case, the Russian approach to the conflict in Tajikistan evolved under the growing influence of those in the Russian Defense Ministry and the Russian government who advocated the idea of "Russia's unique mission" as a peacekeeper in the former Soviet Union. Some people in the Defense Ministry suggested that Russia should pursue a more cautious and reserved policy in Central Asia. These aspirations cannot be characterized as strictly isolationist, but in 1993 it was too early to speak about the emergence of a new selective approach. The Russian deputy defense minister, General Boris Gromov, was among those who did not approve of the deep involvement of Russian military forces in Tajikistan. He had a strong feeling born of his Afghanistan experience and tried from the very beginning to secure a multilateral character for this operation so as to make it truly a CIS enterprise.[30]

Isolationist criticism of the Russian foreign and defense policies, however, was not decisive during the preparation of the deployment of Russian military forces along Tajikistan's southern border. More sharp and detailed criticism of the Russian strategy in Central Asia was initiated by the proponents of a selective approach, whose arguments are discussed below.

In 1994 the deputies in the State Duma of the new Russian parliament started to express some isolationist views in opposition to the government policy. As Sergei Shakhrai stated on 14 June 1994, during a roundtable on the problems of a Eurasian confederation, in the Russian government there are two opposing groups. One is strongly against any kind of cooperation with the former republics and stresses the necessity of concentrating on domestic problems. The other is promoting the idea of reintegration.[31]

The tendency to take an isolationist position on conflict resolution can be found in the ideas expressed by the chairman of the State Duma, Ivan Rybkin, in an interview in *Nezavisimaia gazeta* in June 1994. The speaker stated that there was a decisive majority bloc in the State Duma (about 60 percent) that could influence the decision-making process. He mentioned that despite existing disagreements among the deputies, prudence and constructiveness had prevailed. Rybkin assumed that this majority bloc was strong enough to withstand extreme nationalists like Vladimir Zhirinovsky.

The chairman's reserved position toward a Russian role in conflict resolution is also quite clear. Alluding to the traumas experienced by the young Soviet soldiers who fought in Afghanistan, he demonstrated his attitude by stating: "My task is to let no Russian soldier fight outside the Russian Federation." He said that any declarations about sending Russian battalions to the south, to Bosnia or the Persian Gulf, would never get support in the Duma or among the Russian people.[32]

The attitudes of the Russian deputies and the Russian public allow us to predict that when Russian troops start to suffer losses in conflict zones or when the economic costs of Russian involvement climb higher, isolationists will not miss their chance to highlight the government's responsibility for these costs.

Isolationist aspirations were, and still are, more widespread on a mass level. The people of the Russian Federation strongly object to the deployment of Russian military forces in Central Asia. The fear of Muslim revenge can be explained by the fact that a number of terrorist acts in the Caucasus—such as the capture of airplanes by Chechen terrorists and the murders of several Russian officers and soldiers, and even of one Russian priest—also had parallels in Tajikistan.

The post-Afghan syndrome was vividly reflected in public opinion surveys. They showed that the majority of the population of the Russian Federation (60 percent) did not support the stationing of Russian troops in Tajikistan; 67 percent thought that Russia should adopt an impartial stance toward the fate of the Serbs in the Yugoslav civil war; a majority said that Russia should not maintain military bases or station troops in the Baltic states; and half said the same about Moldova and the Transcaucasus.[33]

Isolationist arguments concerning Russia's approach to conflict resolution in the near abroad can be summed up as follows. First, no Russian government, no matter how powerful or popular, will be able to maintain stable public support for a large-scale military involvement in the near abroad. The public still remembers Afghanistan and will resolutely oppose any actions that can potentially lead to another Afghan war.

Second, the Russian army is not ready to engage in peacekeeping and peacebuilding operations in the near abroad. To perform such functions, the armed forces would have to be retrained and reequipped, a process that would inevitably take time and money.

Third, Russian diplomacy is not mature enough to mediate in near abroad conflicts: it tends to take sides and miscalculate. Moreover, given past experience, even if the Russians acted as "honest brokers" in these conflicts, they would be looked upon with suspicion and distrust, at least by some parties to the conflicts.

Fourth, instead of providing for greater security, such an involvement would likely create more insecurity for Russia. There are fears that those opposed to a Russian peacekeeping mission, in the case of Tajikistan and other Central Asian states, might commit acts of terrorism or rouse anti-Russian sentiments among Muslims living in the Russian Federation, thereby reinforcing secessionist trends in autonomous republics.

Finally, as isolationists from the liberal camp suggest, a considerable military involvement abroad cannot help but undermine democratic values and institutions in the country, thereby making renewed dictatorship more likely.

Isolationism in its different forms is likely to be a long-term factor in Russian political life. Domestic isolationism will tame some of the most aggressive manifestations of Russian neo-imperialism. Isolationist ideas have also become part of a new, selective approach to Russian foreign and defense policy that is advocated by many political analysts and members of the Russian leadership.

A Selective Approach to Conflicts in the Former USSR

A "selective engagement" strategy of the Russian Federation in the territory of the former Soviet Union is now in the process of being forged. To a large extent, it borrows from the ideas and concepts of the three approaches analyzed above: liberal, neoimperialist, and isolationist.

The basic assumption behind the selective engagement strategy, however, is distinctly different from the other three approaches. To be "selective" means to apply different rules and different patterns to various situations, thereby abstaining from any universal approaches, blueprints, or guidelines. Advocates of selective engagement start from the premise that Russian resources are scarce, and that it is simply impossible to muster sufficient power and domestic political support to restore the Russian Empire or build a reliable collective security system in the territory of the former USSR. On the other hand, Russia cannot afford an isolationist policy either. The selective engagement strategy as applied to the Russian near abroad suggests, first and foremost, that instead of applying one set of political, economic, or military rules within the territory of the former USSR, policy makers must envision very different regional and subregional accommodations, with varying levels of Russian participation.

The selective involvement approach further maintains that for Russian foreign, economic, and defense policies, it is important to avoid mutually exclusive obligations in different regions, and it is unwise to pay disproportionate attention to any one of them at the expense of others. At the same time, in this view,

Russia should develop a clear set of regional and subregional priorities to save scarce resources and avoid imperial overextension. By participating in different multilateral and bilateral alliances and unions, Russia could coordinate the economic development and security interests of all the former subjects of the USSR in such a way as to simultaneously protect its own interests and promote overall Eurasian stability.

In 1994, in a number of publications, the advocates of the selective approach spelled out their ideas on future Russian foreign policy, with special attention paid to the role of Russian military forces in conflict resolution in the countries of the near abroad. The main assumptions of the selective strategy have been discussed in the articles of A. Arbatov, A. Voskresenskii, E. Pain, A. Kortunov, A. Umnov, and others. There are many supporters of the selective approach among the members of the Russian prime minister's team, including Viktor Chernomyrdin himself. Some scholars of moderate nationalist orientation, like Sergei Karaganov, are also very close in their views to this theory.[34]

The question of Russia's role in conflict resolution in the post-Soviet space to a great extent depends on the form and degree of integration between the former Soviet republics. It is no accident that the advocates of the selective approach became more active in promoting their ideas in the summer of 1994. At that time President Nursultan Nazarbaev of Kazakhstan put forward the project of a Eurasian Union, and the debate on the possible ways Russia could integrate with the former Soviet republics started.[35] The variants of a Eurasian Union, or confederation, and the benefits and disadvantages of the integration process for the Russian Federation have once again become the centerpiece of debates in Russian political circles. The outcome of this discussion, the practical application of the ideas of confederation, will be a crucial factor for the future geopolitical and regional role of Russia.

In the view of the proponents of a selective approach, the declarations about Russia's integration with other former Soviet republics and its readiness to be the principal mediator in conflicts in Central Asia and the Caucasus lack clear strategic and political pragmatism. They think that integration might be constructive only on condition that the level of economic development of the integrating states is very close, their political and social systems are compatible, and they have a common historic and cultural heritage. Otherwise the new integration structure would be too similar to that of a colonial or neocolonial empire, with an unstable structure because of the emerging conflicts. This instability is an inevitable outcome of the rise of nationalism in the post–Cold War era. Under such circumstances Russia might become too deeply involved in conflicts with its neighbors, an entanglement that could only damage its economic prosperity and political stability.

According to this theory, only several former Soviet republics can become important allies for Russia. They are Armenia, Belarus, Georgia, Kazakhstan, Ukraine, and possibly Kyrgyzstan. But although Georgia is acknowledged to be an important Russian ally in the Caucasus, there are disagreements between the neoimperialist and selective involvement groups on the tactics and methods for achieving geopolitical goals in the region. Moreover, the proponents of a selective strategy do not support neoimperialist ambitions about the dominant role of Russia in conflict resolution in the former Soviet Union.

A member of the Presidential Council, E. Pain, disputing the criticism expressed by the opponents of a forceful diplomacy in Georgia, in an exclusive interview to the correspondent of ITAR-TASS, characterized the Georgian-Russian agreement as one "giving evident pragmatic benefits to Russia." He also aimed his remarks at radical deputies in the Duma who were dissatisfied with the agreement; according to Pain, any criticism of this achievement of Russian foreign policy cannot be justified. Referring to the critics in the State Duma, he asserted that it was not correct to condition the signing of interstate agreements on the settlement of domestic conflicts.[36]

The Russian policy in Central Asia has been seriously criticized by the proponents of a selective involvement strategy. They argued that the decision to protect the Tajik-Afghan border was taken in the absence of any military or political doctrine. Neither Russia's national interest, nor the means to defend these interests had been properly articulated and analyzed. As a result, Russia was in the process of being drawn into a military conflict with lengthy and unreliable communication lines, an absence of powerful local allies, strong hostility from parts of the Tajik population, and very limited economic, military, and diplomatic resources available.

Selectivists pointed out that Russian involvement in this conflict was very difficult to justify on economic grounds; Tajikistan lacks marketable resources and cannot be said to represent any economic value for Russia even in the long term. Nevertheless, the republic was readily incorporated into the ruble zone and promised large-scale credits. Furthermore, the need to protect the Russian minority in Tajikistan was not a very convincing justification for intervention; given current migration rates, there will be no Russians in this country by 1996.

According to the opinion of scholars supporting a selective strategy, Central Asia is the least important subregion in the former Soviet geopolitical space. This is the main angle from which they view the events in Tajikistan. They think that Russia has to be extremely selective in its military actions in the region, and in most cases restrict itself to economic and political influence. Kazakhstan is considered the closest partner of Russia. Any military actions should be based on multilateral operations of Central Asian republics and always conditioned on approval by Kazakhstan.[37]

These assumptions have already proved to be quite true concerning the war in Tajikistan. Practically all other CIS members showed absolutely no inclination to help Russia in its peacekeeping efforts. Not only Ukraine and Moldova, but also Russia's closest ally, Belarus, resolutely refused to get involved. Belarus even slowed down its military cooperation with Russia in the fall of 1992 in order to avoid any commitments in Tajikistan.

The commander of the Collective Peacekeeping Forces (CPF), General Valerii Patrikeev, stated in July 1994 that the CPF in Tajikistan consisted of the Russian 201st Division, a motorized battalion from Uzbekistan, and a company from Kyrgyzstan.[38] Kazakhstan sent a battalion to reinforce the Russian border troops in Tajikistan after Russia, Kazakhstan, Kyrgyzstan, Tajikistan, Turkmenistan, and Uzbekistan signed a "Memorandum on Cooperation in Protection of the External State Borders" on 24 December 1993.[39]

Some advocates of selective engagement have suggested that Russian military involvement in conflict zones such as Tajikistan should not be open-ended but limited to a certain deadline (say, two years). In the meantime the local regime should be obliged to search for accommodation with the opposition, and Russia could arrange and equip the defense of its new perimeter, preferably along the southern border of Kazakhstan, upon agreement between Moscow and Almaty. Such an arrangement would provide the time to move about two million ethnic Russians from Central Asia back to Russia and Kazakhstan, if they should desire to immigrate.

Some of the proponents of the selective policy among military and academic scholars see as a possible solution to the Central Asian dilemma the establishment of a NATO-type multilateral alliance with Russia playing the role of the United States and its Central Asian partners that of Western Europe. Russia would provide its allies with a nuclear umbrella against any aggression from the south and cover a part of their defense needs as the United States did during the Cold War in Europe. The advocates of this proposition stress that in this case the alliance would not imply any automatic Russian involvement in a conventional conflict or any Russian obligations to mediate in "domestic" disputes and clashes.[40]

The NATO-type alliance, however, does not look as promising for the settlement of conflicts in the Caucasus. The "Lebanonization" of the region is already a fait accompli, and one should not expect any political or military stability in the region in the near future. The conflicts tearing apart the Caucasus—the Nagorno-Karabagh conflict, the Armenian-Azerbaijani border war, the South Ossetian–Georgian war, the Georgian-Abkhazian war—are deeply embedded in history, and have no evident solutions. They were suppressed for almost two centuries, but the genie is now out of the bottle again.

According to the selective involvement strategy, Russia should prevent geographical escalation of these conflicts toward its borders. That is, Russia has to stop all arms trade and prevent republics like Georgia and Azerbaijan from interfering politically or militarily in the region to the north of the Caucasus Mountains. To limit the risks to Russia, Russian policy makers should follow clear geopolitical priorities. In the case of Georgia, for example, they should pursue a diplomatic strategy designed to encourage international organizations, such as the United Nations and the CSCE, to help deal with the conflict. Similarly, Iran and Turkey should be invited to cooperate in mediating the Armenian-Azerbaijani conflict. Aleksei Arbatov believes that forcible methods, as in the case of Georgia, should not be used. He thinks that any agreement signed with the objective "of pushing the opponent into the corner" will not last, and will not contribute to the establishment of stable relations and coalitions.[41]

In 1994 the Russian neoimperialist group won certain victories in Georgia and Tajikistan. Its political position seems to be rather strong, and it is ready to continue the present policy despite the criticism of isolationist and selective approach groups. Russia's defense minister, Pavel Grachev, during his meeting with the French defense minister, stated that Russian peacekeeping troops in Moldova, Tajikistan, and the Caucasus amounted to sixteen thousand. Further, there was a battalion of twelve hundred soldiers in Yugoslavia. The minister drew special attention to the fact that Russian peacekeeping forces already exceeded the UN peace contingent. He pointed out that these figures were one more argument for acknowledging Russia's unique mission as a guarantor of peace and stability in the post-Soviet space.[42]

Guarantor of Peace and Stability: Russia's Great Challenge

During the coming ten to fifteen years Russia will live in an unstable geopolitical space surrounded by states mired in deep political and economic crisis or involved in military conflicts. After a period of uncertainty in formulating Russian foreign and military doctrines, Russia now seems to be pursuing its geopolitical and regional objectives in a more consistent manner. In spite of the fact that the political groups analyzed above differ over the appropriateness of restoring Russia's might, they are united by the idea of creating a great Russian state in the place of the former Soviet Union. This means that the government will do everything it can to prevent the dissolution of the Russian Federation, including strengthening its borders and giving its military forces the responsibility not only for protecting their own country but also for preventing the spread of conflicts now raging on parts of its borders. The idea of an active Russian foreign policy in the former Soviet Union has also been stressed by Foreign Minister Andrei Kozyrev: "Russia has a unique mission in the territory of the former Soviet Union. . . . Russia can perform its mission using the centrist approach. It should avoid both the extreme policy of force, sending tanks for the restoration of the former empire, and the complete retreat from near abroad countries, giving up close historical ties, Russian history, those unique relations that have been established and cemented by the common history and culture of the Russian-speaking population."[43]

It is in Russia's interest to minimize its military involvement in conflicts when possible and to avoid being "dragged" into long-term military conflicts, especially when they escalate into civil wars. The idea of a unique Russian position in the post-Soviet space and a Russian willingness to accept the concept of collective international efforts in conflict zones do not contradict each other and can become important elements of a peacekeeping strategy in the region. Of course, the question of NATO and UN involvement in conflicts in the successor states of the USSR is still a point of controversy in political, military, and academic circles. This idea has not garnered strong support among the elites and the public. There are at least two reasons for this. First, the international community itself has not developed a consensus on the conduct of collective peacekeeping. Second, the whole question of NATO involvement in civil wars seems dangerous and nonproductive to many observers, and Russia's role in such an effort is far from clear.[44]

This is not to suggest that Russia is presently opposed to cooperation with the West. The pivotal players in any Russian decision to engage in such cooperation are in favor of a stronger Russian peacekeeping presence in the republics of the former Soviet Union that is consistent with international norms. As for the military, the active role of Russian military forces in managing conflicts has been given special attention in the new Russian military doctrine.[45]

To serve as a guarantor of peace and stability in the post-Soviet space, Russia will have to prove its ability to survive economically and politically and to appear as a great and democratic power, rather than a threat to the freedom and democratic development of its neighbors. This is a great challenge for Russia, but a very appealing one for its leaders, the Russian elite, and the Russian people. Such a policy is possible only in a stable Russia with a moderate leadership and a foreign policy course formulated by realistically thinking representatives of different political groups.

Notes

1. *Nezavisimaia gazeta*, 1 April 1992, pp. 1–3.
2. See, for example, A. Kortunov, *Rossiia i Zapad: Modeli integratsii* (Moscow: Rossiiskii nauchnyi fond, 1994).
3. *Russian Security After the Cold War: Seven Views from Moscow* T.P. Johnson and S.E. Miller, eds., (Washington, DC, and London: Brassey's, 1994), p. 2.
4. Ibid., p. 26.
5. *Nezavisimaia gazeta*, 9 July 1994, p. 1.
6. There were a number of publications devoted to this question. See, for instance, A. Kortunov, *Dezintegratsiia Sovetskogo soiuza i politika SShA* (Moscow: Rossiiskii nauchnyi fond, 1993); idem, *Rossiia i Zapad*; A. Bogaturov, M. Kozhokin, and K. Pleshakov, *Posle imperii* (Moscow: Rossiiskii nauchnyi fond, 1992); A. Bogaturov, *Blizhnee zarubezhie i vozmozhnosti rossiisko-amerikanskogo partnerstva* (Moscow: Rossiiskii nauchnyi fond, 1993); A. Frolov, *Concepts and Views of Regional Security in the USSR and in Russia* (Moscow: Rossiiskii nauchnyi fond, 1994).
7. *Moscow News*, 2 January 1992, p. 3.
8. *Literaturnaia Rossiia*, 28 August 1992, pp. 2–4.
9. ITAR-TASS, 9 April 1992.
10. ITAR-TASS, 27 May 1992.
11. ITAR-TASS, 1 June 1992.

12. ITAR-TASS, 22 June 1992.

13. *Nezavisimaia gazeta*, 7 June 1994, p. 3.

14. For a more detailed analysis of Russian conservatives and their views, see T. Shakleina, *Ty gotov postoiat' za Rossiiu?* (Moscow: Rossiiskii nauchnyi fond, 1993). See also V. Batiuk and T. Shakleina, *Rossiia i Amerika: Rossiiskaia vneshne-politicheskaia mysl' o rossiisko-amerikanskikh otnosheniiakh* (Moscow: Rossiiskii nauchnyi fond, 1992).

15. *Nezavisimaia gazeta*, 19 August 1992, p. 4.

16. This idea was expressed by Marshal Evgenii Shaposhnikov in a broadcast by Radio Rossii on 11 December 1992.

17. *Nezavisimaia gazeta*, 19 January 1994, p. 1.

18. ITAR-TASS, 1 March 1993.

19. In an address to the CIS leaders on 17 March 1993, Yeltsin stated that a collective security mechanism, "including collective peacekeeping forces, ought to be started as soon as possible. Here the experience of international operations in keeping the peace, especially direct support for our joint efforts by the UN, the CSCE, and other organizations, will also be useful. In my opinion, we should strive to set up an effective security system within the structures of the CIS, which would become an important factor in sustaining peace in the entire Eurasian region." *Nezavisimaia gazeta*, 18 March 1993, p. 1.

20. *Demokraticheskaia Abkhazia* (Sukhumi), 3 October 1992.

21. See, for example, *Nezavisimaia gazeta*, 9 November 1993 and 24 November 1993; *Moscow News*, no. 36, 1993, p. 10A, and no. 42, p. 13A; *Izvestiia*, 17 March 1993, 28 July 1993, and 24 August 1993; *Novoe vremia*, 1994, no. 4, p. 13.

22. ITAR-TASS, 3 February 1994.

23. ITAR-TASS, 4 February 1994.

24. ITAR-TASS, 10 February 1994.

25. ITAR-TASS, 17 February 1994.

26. Shakleina, *Ty gotov postoiat' za Rossiiu?*, pp. 27–36.

27. Similar ideas were expressed by the Russian conservatives in 1992–93. See, for example, ibid., pp. 19–25.

28. *Nash sovremennik*, September 1992, p. 104; *Literaturnaia Rossiia*, 22 January 1993, p. 11.

29. *Nash sovremennik*, February 1993, p. 150.

30. *International Peacekeeping*, vol. 1, no. 3 (1994), p. 8.

31. *Nezavisimaia gazeta*, 15 June 1994, p. 3.

32. *Nezavisimaia gazeta*, 30 June 1994, p. 5.

33. *USIA Opinion Research Memorandum*, 3 August 1994, pp. 1, 17.

34. *Nezavisimaia gazeta*, 11 June 1994, p. 3, and 24 June 1994, pp. 1, 2; Kortunov, *Rossiia i Zapad.*

35. *Nezavisimaia gazeta*, 8 June 1994, pp. 1, 3; 2 July 1994, p. 3; 5 July 1994, p. 5; 6 July 1994, pp. 1, 3; *Rossiiskie vesti*, 1 July 1994, p. 2.

36. ITAR-TASS, 3 February 1994.

37. This assumption has been put forward by A. Arbatov. See his articles in *Nezavisimaia gazeta*, 24 June 1994, and in Johnson and Miller, *Russian Security After the Cold War.*

38. *Nezavisimaia gazeta*, 23 July 1994, pp. 1, 3.

39. ITAR-TASS, 23 February 1994.

40. The idea about establishing a new military alliance was expressed, for instance, by General V. Larionov. The creation of a new structure of collective security in Eurasia analogous to the NATO Security Council, with Russia as its main actor, has been sug-

gested as an alternative to NATO and UN participation in conflict management in the former Soviet Union. This approach is part of a new concept popular among Russian intellectuals and the military. The main idea of this new theory is the restoration of the Russian state as the center of a new alliance. It will unite the states that will be left outside NATO and European structures.

41. *Nezavisimaia gazeta*, 24 June 1994.
42. ITAR-TASS, 4 February 1994.
43. ITAR-TASS, 19 January 1994.
44. Kortunov, *Rossiia i Zapad.*
45. *Izvestiia*, 18 November 1993, pp. 1, 4; *Nezavisimaia gazeta*, 9 June 1994, pp. 1, 5.

II

State-Building and Military Power in the Western Newly Independent States

6

National Security in the Baltic States

Rolling Back the Bridgehead

Elaine M. Holoboff

It is one of the ironies of history that the full independence of the three Baltic states came only on the backs of Soviet conservatives trying to preserve the centralized power structures of the crumbling union. By the end of President and General Secretary Mikhail Gorbachev's tenure, every region in the country had issued either declarations of sovereignty or independence. In large part because of this, they suffered brutal repressions in January 1991 as Gorbachev struggled to convince his conservative opponents that he was capable of acting resolutely in the face of anarchy.

After the failed August 1991 coup, President Boris Yeltsin of the Russian Federation became the first to acknowledge the Baltic states' full and legal right to independence, even though many understood that there was every likelihood that this break would presage the collapse of the entire union. International diplomatic recognition followed quickly, and with it the urgent task of building security structures for these small nations and finding a modus operandi with large neighbors such as Russia.

One of the greatest quandaries for Baltic security has been the fact that the region has traditionally occupied a role as a bridgehead between east and west. Owing to their geographical position, the three Baltic states have historically been viewed as little more than outposts for larger neighbors. From the east, tsarist Russia utilized the Baltics as a window to Europe, and from the west, Germany, Poland, Denmark, and Sweden all took turns in usurping these lands for their own benefit. Periods of independence have been fleeting, though remarkably, cultural identities have been preserved despite this.

It has been virtually impossible for these small countries, centrally located within the heart of Europe, to relinquish their role as a bridgehead. Yet much of what is found in the postindependence discussions on national security and defense in the Baltic states attempts to rectify just this situation. With the death of the ideological competition between East and West, the Baltic states now see new opportunities to become full and autonomous members of the European community, rather than the victims or instruments of great-power politics. But the years of Soviet occupation still loom large, this time with Russia (and Russian citizens) occupying the role previously held by the communists.

In order to understand how the Baltic states are attempting to reverse their historical role as a bridgehead, this chapter will look first at the ways in which they went about securing state structures after independence.[1] Specifically, this will involve a look at the successful attempt to reverse Soviet occupation; the difficult task of defining citizenship; and the task of forming national armed forces. After this, evolving concepts of national security and defense policy will be discussed in greater detail, including an examination of the type of threats to security that are of some concern in the Baltic states. Then the broader question of Russian interests in the region will be examined, with a view to understanding how Russia may or may not present a threat to the Baltic states. Finally, the Baltic states' attempts to enter Europe will be explored.

Securing the State

One of the defining features of Baltic postindependence national identity is the fact that Lithuania, Latvia, and Estonia all understand themselves to have been, above all else, occupied states during the Soviet period.[2] There is, hence, a fundamental objection to being labeled as countries belonging to either the Soviet Union or the former Soviet Union (FSU). Victims of great-power manipulation under the 1939 Nazi-Soviet pact, these countries were occupied in 1940 by Soviet troops; the birth of independence and democracy there is understood to have suffered, if not a still-birth, at least an early childhood death. Though the annexation of the Baltic states was never recognized by Western powers, neither was a great deal of attention paid to the ensuing political repression and large-scale exile of Baltic citizens to the Soviet hinterland by Stalin in the postwar period.

The first task of independence was to rid Lithuania, Latvia, and Estonia once and for all of the vestiges of occupation, most importantly by securing the full and complete withdrawal of Soviet (de facto Russian) troops on Baltic territory. The second task has been to define the parameters of citizenship, again reinforcing a complete break with the previous period by disallowing any individuals who might have actively participated in the Soviet occupation. And the third task has been to establish armed forces capable of defending the newly independent countries.

Reversing Soviet Military Occupation

At the beginning of their independence, the three Baltic states found themselves burdened with approximately 150,000 Soviet troops.[3] With the collapse of the

Soviet Union, Russia in its self-defined role as "successor to the Soviet Union" assumed the burden of this occupation and reluctant responsibility for rectifying it. Moscow had initially hoped that it could take up to eight years to withdraw some of the troops, and that it might obtain basing rights in places such as the Liepāja naval base, the Skrunda ABM radar station, the Ventspils space monitoring station in Latvia, and the Paldiski submarine base in Estonia, as well as guaranteed transit rights through Lithuania to the Russian enclave of Kaliningrad.

Lithuania was the first of the Baltic states, and indeed of any state in the FSU, to secure the complete withdrawal of Russian troops on 31 August 1993. Even at the last moment, however, Russia refused to sign the main document in the agreement, which involved a commitment to withdraw troops in order to fulfill "international obligations" (i.e., to rectify the occupation status of the forces). In the end the main document remained unsigned, though a timetable and two other agreements governing the withdrawal were agreed to.

An early agreement on withdrawal, signed 8 September 1992, was made possible for a number of reasons. First, a relatively low percentage of Russians resided in Lithuania (9.4 percent, compared with 30.1 percent in Estonia and 34 percent in Latvia). Second, a so-called zero option on citizenship was implemented (i.e., granting citizenship to those residing in the country at the time of independence). In addition, there was clear public support for making the withdrawal a centerpiece of Lithuanian foreign policy. In a referendum on 14 June 1992, 91 percent of voters agreed that troops should leave by the end of the year.[4] The withdrawal process was also assisted by the fact that Lithuanian Defense Minister Audrius Butkevičius had a good working relationship with the Russian Ministry of Defense, and mutually agreeable solutions were found to the problem of the withdrawing troops. For example, Lithuania agreed to build housing for the troops in the Kaliningrad region. In partial exchange, the Russian side agreed to supply Lithuania with some much-needed equipment for its developing armed forces.

Russia was also anxious to secure transit rights to the Kaliningrad region; however, as of mid-1994 a formal agreement had not been signed. One of the sticking points is that Russia refuses to submit to the type of notifications desired by Lithuania. The overall population in Kaliningrad is 900,000, and the total armed forces are estimated to be somewhere between 30,000 and 60,000. There is also a high concentration of equipment (six hundred tanks; nine hundred armored combat vehicles; seven hundred artillery pieces).[5] With such a highly militarized region on its doorstep, Lithuania is constantly reminded that, if it so desired, Russia could overwhelm this small country in a matter of hours. Fortunately for Lithuania, it has neither contentious citizenship laws, a large Russian population, nor an anti-Russian government in power since the parliamentary and presidential elections of the former communists (renamed the Lithuanian Democratic Labor Party) in the autumn of 1992 and early 1993.

After prolonged discussions, threats, and counterthreats, agreements on Russian troop withdrawals were finally signed with Latvia (30 April 1994) and Estonia (26 July 1994). In the case of the latter, the agreement came only weeks before the troops were completely withdrawn on 31 August 1994. There was considerable pressure from the United States for Latvia to sign an agreement with Russia, and immediately after its signing, the treaty came under criticism for making too many concessions to Moscow. For example, Latvia agreed to give Russia the right to stay at the Skrunda radar base for another four years, in addition to eighteen months for dismantlement. Also, 22,320 retired military officers (retired before 28 January 1992) were to be allowed to stay in Latvia; of these, 3,000 were already citizens. It is important to note that those retired military officers who are not already citizens are ineligible to become nationals unless they marry a Latvian citizen. In addition, some four thousand officers retired after January 1992 were required to leave by the end of 1994. The issue of the retired officers was a particularly difficult aspect of the negotiations.

In Estonia, the agreement was looked upon with trepidation because it immediately put Latvia's northern neighbor on notice that it too would be subject to the same pressure to compromise with Russia. However, in this case it was Russia that came under even greater arm-twisting from the United States Senate, which, in mid-July 1994, threatened to stop all aid to Russia if troops were not withdrawn by the end of August. On the Estonian side, there was widespread anxiety that, of 10,700 retired former Soviet officers, at least 1,600 were a potential threat to the stability of the country. (This included especially a group of officers retired *after* 1990 who were between the ages of thirty-five and fifty.) The fact that Estonia's regular army totaled only twenty-five hundred members meant that this portion of the Russian population, if armed, could easily present a challenge to local forces. Nonetheless, an agreement between Estonia and Russia was signed in July, and military pensioners were to be guaranteed the same rights as all Estonian citizens. Estonia did gain the right to disallow residency to anyone considered a national security risk (this will involve roughly one thousand Russian officers who will be required to leave); however, it was agreed that the commission considering such cases will have to include a CSCE representative.[6] Russia was given fourteen months to dismantle its base at Paldiski. By 31 August 1994, troop withdrawals from all the Baltic states were complete.

Russia used two strategies in negotiating a withdrawal with Latvia and Estonia. First, there was a continued insistence on linking Russian troop withdrawals with the treatment of ethnic Russians in the region, particularly while citizenship laws remained undefined. Second, Moscow used a "stop-start" strategy on troop withdrawals, threatening to halt the exit of troops whenever there was displeasure with political or military events. In actual fact Russia's rhetoric rarely seemed to match its actions, and on a number of occasions withdrawals proceeded despite pronouncements to the contrary.

Ironically, Russian Foreign Minister Andrei Kozyrev suggested that once troop withdrawals were complete Moscow would have a freer hand to pursue the interests of ethnic Russians in the Baltic states, because it would not have to be sensitive to the legal issues involved. In Kozyrev's words:

> After this [troop withdrawals] our activity will not diminish regarding all the other problems of the Russian population, but to the contrary, this will actually create a more favorable situation to fight for the rights of the Russian-speaking population in these Baltic states.[7]

Thus, it may be that strong diplomatic pressure will continue on the Baltic states as Russia pursues new political and economic goals in the region. In this sense, rectifying the Soviet occupation has solved some problems but has left in its wake the continued necessity of finding a modus operandi with Russia.

Defining Citizenship

Determining who may and who may not become a citizen has proven to be one of the most contentious problems faced by the Baltic states. Lithuania resolved citizenship questions almost immediately, but Latvia and Estonia struggled with this issue for several years. Though legislation is largely in place, many problematic aspects remain, not least of which is the continued alienation of much of the ethnic Russian population.

Lithuania passed a citizenship law as early as 3 November 1989 that guaranteed that all individuals residing in the country at the time of independence would be given the right of citizenship. This ensured that relations with Russia proceeded fairly smoothly, in stark contrast to the often acrimonious discussions on this issue between Russia and Latvia and Estonia. Russia's frequent insistence on linking citizenship issues with troop withdrawals further complicated relations with these three countries.

Latvia developed its first guidelines for citizenship on 15 October 1991; however, this guaranteed citizenship only to those persons who were already citizens during independence (i.e., prior to June 1940) and descendants of such persons. A first draft of a citizenship law, passed by the Saeima on 25 November 1993, put forward further restrictions on the right to citizenship and was clearly designed to exclude the large numbers of ethnic Russians residing in the country. The most controversial aspects included a ten-year residency period, Latvian language tests, and restrictive annual naturalization quotas. A second reading of the law passed through the Saeima with few changes on 9 June 1994, this despite the fact that Latvia had received clear indications from the Conference on Security and Cooperation in Europe (CSCE) and the Council of Europe (CE) that the proposed quota system was undesirable. The law was passed on 21 June 1994, but under pressure from President Guntis Ulmanis the Saeima removed the quota system on 22 July 1994. The new citizenship law, without the controversial quota system, came into effect on 11 August 1994.[8]

Estonia's original position on citizenship was similar in content to Latvia's, though in practice an even harder line was taken on the granting of citizens' rights to non-Estonians. The country's first act was to reinstate the 1938 Law on Citizenship in February 1992.[9] Only those who were citizens during the previous period of independence and their descendants would be allowed automatic citizenship. Personnel in the former Soviet army could obtain citizenship only if they fulfilled this condition and if they had retired before 20 August 1991 (i.e., independence), or if their spouse or child already had residency. All other persons would have to complete a two-year residency period (which could start only as of 30 March 1990), followed by a one-year waiting period. The latter appeared designed to deliberately disallow ethnic Russians from participating in the parliamentary elections of September 1992, and hence having a say in the future of the country. This trend continued in May 1993, when the parliament passed a law allowing all residents to vote in local elections but not to stand as candidates.

It was especially Estonia's Law on Aliens that has come under severe criticism from bodies such as the CSCE.[10] Initially noncitizens had only two years to apply for residency and work permits, and if this was not accomplished they would be required to leave the country. Lack of permanent residency meant that persons without official status could not, for example, purchase properties or receive social benefits. By July 1994, Estonia was forced by pressure from the CSCE, the Council of Europe, and Russia to guarantee work permits to anyone who was eligible for permanent residency and had been in the country before 1 July 1990, thus abolishing this discriminatory aspect of the law with regard to temporary residents.

Moscow has repeatedly expressed deep concern about the situation of ethnic Russians in Latvia and Estonia since independence. In each country there are approximately 450,000 individuals without citizenship, the vast majority of whom are ethnic Russians. Citizenship laws are viewed as discriminatory, and it is not uncommon for Russian politicians to refer to a system of "apartheid," "genocide," and/or "ethnic cleansing" in the Baltic states. Russia's concerns about both the content and application of the laws have apparently not been assuaged despite their reformulation.

There can also be no doubt about the grave dissatisfaction that exists among large portions of the ethnic Russian population in Latvia and Estonia. In many ways they view themselves as a disenfranchised people, abandoned by both the local governments *and* the Russian government. There is a suspicion that Moscow is using them to pursue its own political ambitions and extract concessions from the Baltic states, while offering ethnic Russians nothing of real substance. Many ethnic Russians have understood that in their new countries of residence, to quote the words of a Russian nationalist who has lived in Latvia for several decades, "You are not even a people of second choice, you are nobody."[11] Thus there is a perception that they have been abused by their state of residence and abandoned by their state of ethnic origin.

While the CSCE is generally satisfied with the treatment of ethnic Russians in Latvia and Estonia, and the human rights organization Helsinki Watch determined that "no systemic, serious abuses of human rights in the area of citizenship" are taking place in Estonia, it is obvious that individual abuses do occur frequently, leading to many cases of despair among the Russian population.[12] The major problem is in the implementation of existing legislation and the fulfillment of citizens' rights. Lack of personnel, bad management, and unwieldy bureaucracies have been criticized for slowing down application procedures. A lack of language classes in some regions makes the requirement of language tests impossible. Similarly with the elderly, few concessions are given despite the fact that acquiring the local language might prove too difficult. In regions such as eastern Estonia, the Russian population is as high as 90 percent, and the Estonian language is rarely heard, much less studied. Other serious problems along the way have included the procedures for dealing with Russians living in temporary housing, such as that allocated to many in the former Soviet military; the inability to purchase property; the lack of proper passports, which imposes travel restrictions on individuals; the lack of voting rights; and the lack of access to normal medical care and social benefits.

Though it is not often stated publicly, a certain percentage of Estonians and Latvians would simply have preferred ethnic Russians to return to Russia.[13] Such anti-Russian sentiments are often stimulated, in part, by "expatriates" who have returned home, but who often have little understanding of local conditions, not to mention relations with Russia and Russians. Thus, rather than being viewed as victims of the vicissitudes of the Soviet regime (with the obvious exclusion of those in the KGB and Military Intelligence), ethnic Russians are singled out as the unsavory remains of communism. It should thus come as no surprise that many Russians consider themselves to be discriminated against.

Defining citizenship is obviously one of the most difficult and sensitive issues involved in establishing statehood and a national identity. Though these questions have thus far been resolved in a peaceful manner, it remains to be seen whether a just understanding of citizenship can be implemented over the long term, both legally and practically.

Building New Armed Forces

The Baltic states have faced two major problems when building their armed forces: breaking once and for all the links with the past Soviet army, and establishing a credible defense force able to deal with potential threats to security.

Breaking the reliance on Soviet (and then Russian) expertise, personnel, and equipment has presented a difficult challenge to the Baltic states. The defense forces of these countries still rely on the expertise and manpower of former Soviet officers. For example, in Lithuania military training courses are taught largely by officers from the former Soviet army because of a lack of local expertise; in Latvia over 50 percent of the Interior Ministry is staffed with noncitizens. In some cases, there are fears about where the allegiances of these groups reside. For example, a senior official from the Latvian Interior Ministry has suggested that loyalty is questionable in at least 25 percent of his force.[14]

Equipment is another difficult issue, and the shortage of weapons and combat equipment has been described as one of the weakest aspects of the armed forces in the Baltic states.[15] Ideally, each of the Baltic states would like to acquire equipment that is compatible with their political goals of entering NATO; however, the costs involved in such an undertaking are highly problematic. Reliance on Soviet/Russian equipment dominates the defense forces, with the exception of the occasional donation from European countries such as Sweden or Germany. With shortages of equipment a continual problem it is difficult to carry out defense tasks properly. For example, the Estonian navy is equipped with only four to five small vessels, though at least three times this number is needed in order to adequately patrol territorial waters.[16] The Latvian navy is only slightly better equipped, with a dozen small vessels and a minesweeper. The process of breaking links with the Soviet past will be a long one, and a shortage of funds and expertise will necessarily limit national goals for some time yet.

In addition, the defense forces suffer from the limitations of finance and manpower. Each country has aimed to develop a total defense force of 10,000 to 20,000 persons. Lithuania has built an armed force of almost 21,000 persons (a 4,300 regular army/rapid reaction force, a 250-person navy, a 250-person air force, 5,000 border guards, and 11,000 volunteer territorial and national guards). Eight percent of the state budget goes to defense. Latvia has a total defense force of roughly 21,000 (a 1,600-person regular army, 3,500 border guards, a 300-person naval force, and a volunteer home guard, called the Zemessardze, of 16,000). Over 3.5 percent of the state budget goes to defense. Finally, the Estonian defense forces total roughly 10,500 persons (a 2,500-person regular army and a home guard, called the Kodukaitse, 2,000 border guards, and also a 6,000-person volunteer defense league, called the Kaitselitt, to carry out territorial defense).[17]

Creating credible armed forces has proven to be a formidable task, and far-reaching goals have frequently been thwarted by practical limitations. However, the problem is greater than one of simply acquiring the desired number of troops. Determining the potential threats to the nation and the way these troops might be used has been another urgent task for the newly independent states.

Defining National Security and Defense Policies

If building national armies has been a difficult task, an even greater challenge has been the construction of national security and defense policies to guide both politicians and military personnel in their task of making the nation secure. In most cases, considerable public debate remains on these issues, and final versions of national security and defense concepts have yet to be formally accepted.

Latvia is the only country to have adopted a defense concept (November 1992), but it too began considering an updated version in March 1994. Draft concepts focus on several issues, in addition to detailing the proposed structure of defense forces. Most importantly, they outline the general principles by which the building of the armed forces should proceed and the nature of threats these forces may face. It is these two aspects of the emerging national security and defense concepts that are focused on below.[18]

"Total Defense"

In each of the draft concepts, there are plans to rely on a concept of "total defense" that should take account of military, economic, social, and psychological factors in defense planning. These concepts rely on a strong defensive posture for the armed forces, augmented by territorial and civilian-based defense.

For each of the Baltic states it has obviously been necessary to take account of available resources in the formulation of realistic defensive aims, and this has been part of the impetus behind the "total defense" concepts. There have been few illusions about the ability of each country to repel an attack from a major military power. In the event of an armed attack, military forces should (ideally) be designed to be adequate for two to three weeks of defensive engagements. Once the fighting capacity of regular forces is worn down, the strategy would then turn to one of guerrilla warfare, as well as citizen defense and nonviolent resistance. The armed forces in wartime would rely heavily on volunteer territorial forces to carry out a guerrilla war should normal means fail. It is hoped that up to one hundred thousand to three hundred thousand troops could be mobilized, though in practice the uppermost figure is probably far too optimistic. In the case of Estonia, there have been some discussions that suggest that a full mobilization of the population would also be joined with an attempt to transfer the military operation to the territory of the aggressor. In practice, however, this would seem an impossible task for a small armed force. In peacetime, civilian populations could be trained in passive or nonviolent resistance with the intention of presenting any aggressor with further obstacles and disincentives for attack.

In addition to the regular armed forces, territorial defense units, and civilian resistance, defense against an aggressor would also involve "internationalization" of any conflict, or "CNN defense," as it has sometimes been referred to.[19] The idea is that aggression by an enemy would be met with such widespread public opposition (nationally and internationally) that the potential costs (diplomatic and possibly economic) would outweigh any possible gains.

Though "total defense" concepts are seen as one of the only options for real defense in the Baltic states, they are not without problems. Of gravest concern is the use of so-called volunteer defense groups to carry out territorial defense. These bodies have already come under some criticism in Estonia, Latvia, and Lithuania for their apparent lack of control, and it seems evident that proper training and chain of command have sometimes been lacking. For example, in Estonia the Kaitselitt (the defense league charged with carrying out territorial defense) was accused of various attacks on Russian units in 1992. In 1993, one unit in western Estonia flatly refused to obey orders to relocate their unit, and the scandal ultimately resulted in the resignation of the defense minister. In Lithuania, a defection of a group of soldiers from the home guard also ultimately resulted in the resignation of Defense Minister Butkevičius. Both the Estonian Kaitselitt and the Latvian Zemessardze (the volunteer home guard) have in the past had poor relations with local police forces, again adding to the view that they represent an undisciplined force.[20] Neither of these groups was under the administrative control of the Ministries of National Defense, though this situation has since been rectified and discipline is understood to be much improved (Latvian forces have received training assistance from Great Britain that has led to an increased performance level, and undesirable elements have been "purged" from the home guards of both Latvia and Estonia).

The Baltic emphasis on territorial defense is quite obviously modeled on countries such as Sweden and Switzerland.[21] It is useful to recall, however, that the latter are exceedingly homogeneous, wealthy, and stable societies. But is territorial defense really appropriate in cases where a state is ethnically divided, as is the case in Latvia and Estonia? Or do such defense plans contain within them the seeds of a Yugoslav-style scenario? One cannot, after all, train two-thirds of the population in civilian defense, and not the other one-third (e.g., ethnic Russians). On the other hand, if ethnic tensions continue to divide Baltic societies, and if the entire population is trained in territorial defense, one runs the risk of a civil war layered on top of any outside aggression. Territorial defense may work well for societies such as Sweden and Switzerland, but the Yugoslav case has also demonstrated the inherent dangers of adopting territorial defense when a society is unstable economically and divided socially.

The difficulty for the Baltic states is that there are not a great number of other options. While Western states are generally supportive of the Baltic states, most have quietly made it known to the Baltic states that they would not support any of these countries militarily in the event of an attack (the one exception is Sweden, where it has been suggested that it might find it difficult to remain neutral in such an event). An alternative is the Israeli model; however, it seems obvious that at this stage in their economic development neither Lithuania, Latvia, nor Estonia can afford such an option. In addition, any attempt to militarize the region would only antagonize Russia and could in itself precipitate a crisis. Moscow would doubtless react with alarm to an influx of new weaponry and see this as an attempt by the West to bring NATO to Russia's doorstep, if only by proxy.

Threats to National Security

Although threats are perceived by each of the Baltic states in somewhat different ways, strong common themes can be found. Ostensibly none of the three states regards any other country as an enemy. However, in practice, though rarely named in public documents, Russia and ethnic Russians in the Baltics are understood to constitute one of the greatest potential threats to national security. Whether stated explicitly or not, the primary purpose of defense forces is to guard against a Russian threat, both internally and externally.

How are the potential threats from Russia or Russians understood? *Internal* threats (i.e., those emanating from within each country) could include extremist activities of antigovernment groups (e.g., communists, "imperialists," and other antidemocratic forces); "utilization of the demographic situation" by anti-democratic forces (i.e., radical Russian groups using the high percentage of Russians within the country to foment trouble); and intelligence activities of "unfriendly neighboring countries" (i.e., Russia). Until their complete withdrawal, Russian troops were also viewed as a major threat to security, and in the case of Lithuania, the large number of Russian troops in Kaliningrad still constitutes an obvious concern.

Are ethnic Russians in the Baltic states a threat to the security of the state? It remains difficult to assess the likelihood of the Russian population taking matters into its own hands. Despite widespread grievances, most ethnic Russians in Latvia and Estonia remain apolitical, and the chances of a so-called fifth column emerging seem doubtful. It may be that further radicalization could come with an increasing awareness of democratic political rights, and a simultaneous understanding of their disenfranchisement from these processes, but so far this has not been the case.

In Latvia alone, there are over fifteen groups involved in one way or another with the situation of Russians in the country. Over half of these have been described as borderline or disloyal social and/or political groups. Some, such as the Association of Russians in Latvia and the Union for the Defense of Veterans' Rights, have advocated the organization of a coup in Latvia.[22] However, while many of these groups are strong on rhetoric, there is little evidence that they have the capacity to act beyond this.

In Estonia, too, there is an evident lack of leadership and organization among Russian groups. A quasi parliament was set up in Tallinn on 30 January 1993; however, it does not appear to have at any time constituted a threat to the central government.[23] Serious tensions did exist in the Russian-dominated populations of Narva and Sillamäe in eastern Estonia; however, these reached a zenith in the summer of 1993, when serious demonstrations occurred. In July 1993, the majority Russian population held a referendum on regional autonomy that was overwhelming supported by locals, but declared illegal by the Estonian government. After local elections in October 1993, in which a majority of hardline communists failed to win seats in local government, the situation stabilized considerably. What is unclear is whether these hardline elements have left the political scene for good. It is conceivable that Narva could become a flash point again at some future date if pro-Russian forces become better organized. Meanwhile, periodic exchanges of rhetoric continue. For example, in April 1994 members of the ethnic Russian community accused the Estonian government of developing a policy of "ethnic cleansing" aimed at incarcerating Russians in "concentration camps" with the intent to deport them.[24]

Concerning the threat from intelligence forces of "other countries," it is certainly the case that the Baltic states found themselves ill-prepared for counterintelligence activities. There is every likelihood that the majority of KGB and Military Intelligence forces in these countries at independence elected to stay rather than return to Russia. At least a portion of these forces would have infiltrated state structures and doubtless continue to work for the Russian government. Thus, it would be naive to assume that Russian intelligence activities do not take place, though how widespread these are is impossible to gauge. It is also difficult to determine how significant a threat this constitutes. For example, are there conditions under which Russian intelligence forces would shift from espionage to actual sabotage of the Baltic governments? This would seem an unlikely pattern of activities for the Yeltsin government, despite the fact that it has moved significantly to the right since the December 1993 parliamentary elections in Russia. However, one cannot exclude a threat emanating from this sphere if an ultranationalist president and government come to power in Russia. The capacity for bringing about the downfall of any one of the Baltic states certainly exists, and it would be relatively easy for Russian intelligence forces to inflame and manipulate the dissatisfaction of the ethnic Russian population in order to destabilize these small countries.

In terms of *external* threats, the unstable situation in the FSU and Russia, unchecked nationalism, and ethnic conflicts are also major concerns in the Baltic states. There are also fears about the lack of control of nuclear weapons in the FSU. It is difficult to see how these threats might emerge in the future, but this does not stop them from being real considerations in the development of national security and defense policies.

The growth of antidemocratic, pro-imperialist forces in "neighboring countries" has been a growing concern since 1993, particularly if political developments bring with them the possibility that the Baltic states might be brought back into a Russian sphere of influence, perhaps by the use of military force. In this respect the December 1993 parliamentary success of Vladimir Zhirinovsky and the Liberal Democratic Party in Russia was viewed with some alarm by all the Baltic states, as were the perceived changes in Russian foreign policy beginning in January 1994.

By early 1994, many in the Baltic states were openly worried about the "deepening imperialistic tendencies in Russian foreign policy," particularly those that included the Baltic states in Russia's de facto sphere of influence.[25] A speech on 18 January 1994 by Kozyrev to a conference on Russia's policy toward the CIS and Baltic states served only to confirm worst-case fears. Kozyrev spoke about the threats to Russia emanating from the so-called 'near abroad,' and of the danger of a "security vacuum." This speech was taken as evidence of a shift in Russian foreign policy by both the Baltic states and the Russian press.[26] The Baltic states were further alarmed on 6 April 1994, when, in what appears to have been a diplomatic blunder, Yeltsin gave a speech on Russia's intentions to establish a number of military bases in the FSU, including facilities in Latvia. Various Russian government ministries quickly issued denials about the intent to include Latvia, but nonetheless serious suspicions remained about Russia's real aims.[27]

In the longer term there are fears that the victory of an ultranationalist or far-right candidate in Russia could result in highly belligerent actions toward Moscow's neighbors, especially in those regions that contain large numbers of ethnic Russians. Though the presidential elections in Russia are not scheduled until 1996, there is already concern that someone like Zhirinovsky could gain power. Zhirinovsky himself has often expressed the opinion that Russia is not a nation but rather a collection of peoples. In this view, an external conflict, far from being perpetuated for military or political reasons, would instead be carried out for "ideological" purposes. The "ideology" or myth of extending the Slavic nation could (indeed does) serve useful purposes domestically by uniting the Russian population, and the fear is that the alleged ill-treatment of ethnic Russians could easily serve as a pretext for intervening in the domestic affairs of Russia's neighbors.[28]

In the case of Estonia, Andrus Park discussed four possible scenarios that could conceivably require the use of the armed forces. These include: (1) a "1940 scenario," which would involve an all-out conquest by Russia; (2) a "Trans-Dniester scenario" involving the northeast Russian-populated region of Estonia; (3) a "Russian disintegration scenario," in which uncontrolled military forces enter Estonia; and (4) a "Georgian scenario," in which violence breaks out because of uncontrolled paramilitary forces (e.g., a clash between pro-Estonian forces within the country).[29] Obviously, all these variants except the last involve a potential threat from Russia, and while it is impossible to evaluate their likelihood, they are useful for understanding the type of fears that exist in the Baltic states.

Baltic economic dependency on Russia is also viewed as an ever-present threat. There is still a heavy reliance on trade with Russia, though in the case of Estonia exports and imports to and from Russia have declined substantially (exports declined from 56.5 percent in 1991 to 19.9 percent in 1993, and imports for the same years declined from 45.9 percent to 18.6 percent). Conversely, with Lithuania and Latvia, 40 and 48 percent (respectively) of exports still go to Russia, with Moscow demanding a 30 percent Russian tariff barrier against all imported goods in the case of Lithuania. Lithuania also has the greatest dependency on goods from Russia, with at least 73 percent of its imports coming from this source. Latvian imports from the CIS are approximately 39 percent of total goods. The Baltic states have all sought most-favored-nation (MFN) status from

Russia, though only Latvia and Lithuania have been successful in achieving an agreement. Moscow used the "sweetener" of MFN status as leverage in gaining concessions from Estonia and Latvia in negotiations on the withdrawal of Russian troops. Lithuania was granted MFN status on 18 November 1993, but the agreement remains unratified by the Russian parliament. The newly elected Russian Duma insisted on linking MFN status with the achievement of an agreement on transit rights to Kaliningrad.[30] Latvia was given MFN status after the treaty on troop withdrawals, but again has seen few practical results from this as of the end of 1994.

Energy dependency on Russia is of even greater concern than general trade relations. Since Moscow decided to charge world prices for its oil and gas, energy debts to Russia have skyrocketed. Russia has on more than one occasion used energy leverage as a method for exerting pressure on the Baltic states in order to achieve political goals. On 27 June 1993, Yeltsin accused Estonia of implementing a system of "apartheid" and turned off gas supplies to Estonia in an effort to stimulate changes in citizenship laws. The process was immediately effective, and the next day Estonian President Lennart Meri suspended a law that would have required five hundred thousand ethnic Russians to adopt Estonian citizenship or permanent residency within two years, or presumably leave the country.[31]

There is also the question of outstanding border disputes between the Baltic states and their neighbors. Though not explicitly addressed in the draft national security and defense concepts of these nations, this question of redrawing borders has obvious implications for regional security. There are three outstanding claims. In 1940 certain districts of Belarus were ceded to Lithuania; Latvia claims 1,293.5 square kilometers of Russia's Pskov region; and Estonia claims 2,449 square kilometers of the border region near Narva and south of Lake Peipus/Chudskoe, in accordance with the 1920 Tartu treaty.

Estonia in particular has taken a hardline position on the issue, antagonizing Russia in the process. In January 1994, Russian Deputy Foreign Minister Vitalii Churkin responded to Estonia's claims by threatening that "there is no need to create additional irritants, which, as a matter of fact, will bring no practical results. We can take retaliatory measures, and our Estonian partners will not like it."[32] Russia is determined to physically guarantee that the borders existing in December 1991 are immutable. It has set about putting in place border markings and posts, much to the consternation of the Estonian government.[33] Precisely why Estonia would challenge Russia on the border issue is difficult to understand, especially given the fact that the area beyond Estonia's existing border is populated largely by Russians, and that harassing Russia on this issue can only result in a serious deterioration of relations.

While Russia is obviously understood to constitute one of the greatest potential threats to security, it is not the only one. Other threats that have been identified include organized crime, ecological problems, general economic and social instability, the slow development of proper state structures (e.g., the armed forces, a judicial system), threats to the local culture, and even health problems. Organized crime is a serious problem, especially considering the issue of porous borders and the lack of adequate numbers of border personnel. In this situation, the Baltic states find themselves easy transit routes for drug smuggling, illegal arms traffic, and various other types of illegal activities. In terms of the environment, threats include old Soviet-style nuclear reactors; nuclear waste; warehouses of ammunition, fuel, and waste left by the Russian forces; and dumping in territorial waters. While the economies of the Baltic states are progressively strengthening, there are still fears that the transition to a free market economy will exact an unacceptable toll on certain segments of the population, thereby stimulating social unrest. And finally, the immaturity of government structures is frequently viewed as a threat in and of itself. The armed forces are a case in point, for as long as there is no ultimate consensus on the nature of the threats facing the state (reflected in the acceptance of national security and defense policies), it is difficult to know what the armed forces should look like, both in terms of size and function.

Gulliver's Travels: Russian Policy Toward the Baltics

Russia is geographically and politically a giant next to the three Baltic states. In understanding this, Moscow has not hesitated to throw its weight around, both for reasons of domestic consumption and to achieve concessions from the Baltic states themselves. A number of ways in which Russia has sought to pressure the Baltic states have already been referred to.

Yet in order to understand Russian interests in this region it is necessary to first take a brief look at the general trends in the Russian foreign and defense policy over the last few years. In April 1993, Russia published its first foreign policy concept, followed by its new military doctrine in November 1993.[34] Several common themes can be detected in these documents. Not unusually, Russia asserted its right as a great power to defend its vital national interests. Most importantly, these interests included first, the protection of the rights, freedoms, and legitimate interests of Russian citizens in foreign states, or stated another way, the protection of "human rights" in the "near abroad" (i.e., the protection of ethnic Russians); and second, the containment of local wars and conflicts, especially those involving instability along Russia's borders. The military doctrine in particular contains an overwhelming emphasis on the potential external and internal threats that might arise from a variety of sources of instability in the FSU. In addition, a direct military threat to Russia would include a buildup of groups of forces on Russia's borders, and/or the introduction of foreign troops in states neighboring Russia (other than those deployed under a United Nations Security Council mandate, or by Russia's agreement with a regional collective security body such as the Commonwealth of Independent States).

Of greatest concern to many of Russia's neighbors are its increasingly assertive actions in the "near abroad," for example, in the sphere of "peacekeeping." Lennart Meri, the president of Estonia, remarked in early 1994 that "we have noticed a growing tendency among some states to interpret the concepts of peacekeeping in a capricious fashion, selectively borrowing only those ideas that happen to conform with the political agenda of the moment."[35] Russia now supports four ongoing military operations outside Russia (Tajikistan, South Ossetia, Moldova, and Abkhazia) and may send additional troops to Nagorno-Karabagh should a Russian-brokered cease-fire be achieved. With over eighteen thousand "peacekeeping" troops committed to the "near abroad," a suspicion is beginning to develop among Russia's neighbors that perhaps Moscow's intentions are not so benign or lacking in self-interest.[36] At the root of these suspicions is the fear that Russia intends to establish another division of Europe, with the newly independent states of the FSU substituting for the former Warsaw Pact states. The situation is not helped when senior military figures in Moscow state publicly that the concept of sovereignty does not apply to the FSU and that Russia's borders must be understood as those of the FSU. Even more worrisome is testimony from South Ossetians, Abkhazians, and Trans-Dniestrians who are quick to sing the praises of Russia as a "liberator."[37]

As 1994 progressed, Russia also became more intent on defining the type of assistance it is prepared to give to ethnic Russians in the "near abroad," including those in the Baltic states. In May 1994, the Russian Foreign Ministry produced a draft program aimed at safeguarding the interests of ethnic Russians in the FSU. This would include measures such as economic support, priority treatment of Russian companies run by ethnic Russians, and the establishment of a broadcasting network targeted at Russian populations.[38] A commission on minority rights was also set up under the Russian president to examine citizenship questions.[39]

Also in May 1994, the influential Council on Foreign and Defense Policy advocated a series of measures designed to support ethnic Russians in the FSU.[40] One of the council's central assumptions is that integration of the states of the FSU is inevitable, though the terms of this process remain to be defined. Rather than forced integration by military means, for example, the council recommends a strategy of "leadership instead of direct control," in which economic, political, and military support from Moscow would be withdrawn from those who refused to cooperate with Russia's interests. Interestingly, however, the council suggested that, while Russia should be the "guardian angel" for minorities in the FSU (i.e., ethnic Russians in the "near abroad"), Russia should also develop a special policy toward the Baltic states because of their unique historical, geographical, and cultural characteristics.

What then are Russia's interests in the Baltic states, given that it has now withdrawn all its troops from the region but still has concerns about the large ethnic Russian population? A summary of these interests would include: (1) the establishment of a cordon sanitaire on the western rim to ensure that NATO's reach does not extend into the FSU (thus the inclusion of any Baltic state in NATO would be strongly opposed); (2) defense of ethnic Russians, at least rhetorically; (3) protection of the rights of remaining military forces (e.g., transit rights through Lithuania to Kaliningrad; basing rights at the Skrunda radar base in Latvia; access to a submarine training facility in Estonia in order to dismantle the two nuclear reactors there); and (4) defense of Russia's economic interests (e.g., establishing an acceptable environment for Russian businesses; gaining control of certain "strategic" factories and industries). Beyond securing these interests, the Yeltsin government probably understands that at a practical level the Baltic states must be treated rather differently than other regions of the FSU, especially insofar as a reassertion of Russian influence goes. There are clear Western interests in the region, and European governments have quietly made it clear that, if there are to be spheres of influence in Europe, the Baltic states must be considered part of Western Europe. However, whether the next Russian government can be relied upon to accept the same operating rules remains to be seen.

Rolling Back the Bridgehead

Integration with European security and economic structures is seen as one of the fundamental ways the security of the Baltic states can be guaranteed and the historical role of this region as a bridgehead finally relinquished. It is also seen as one of the only ways to counter the perceived threat from Russia. To this end, each of the Baltic states has actively pursued political, economic, and military relations with Europe, both as an end in itself and as a means for reducing the threat from the east. Membership, associate membership, or participation in the European Union (EU), the Council of Europe (CE), the Western European Union (WEU), NATO, the North Atlantic Cooperation Council (NACC), the Partnership for Peace (PfP), and the CSCE are all seen as priorities. Even the socialist-oriented government in Lithuania has turned toward the West after it realized that it would find little favor in Moscow with a parliament dominated by nationalists.

As of mid-1994, all three countries were members or associate members of the Council of Europe (Lithuania and Estonia joined in May 1993, though associate membership for Latvia was held up because of difficulties in its naturalization requirements); the PfP (Lithuania was the second country to join the partnership on 27 January 1994, followed by Estonia on 3 February, and Latvia on 14 February); the WEU (all three acquired associate membership on 9 May 1994), and the CSCE. However, much to their disappointment, it is likely to be some time yet before the Baltic states gain entry into either the EU or NATO. In the former case, a free trade agreement was signed with Lithuania, Latvia, and Estonia on 18 July 1994 (effective 1 January 1995),[41] but full membership in the EU will not come for several years at least. Nonetheless, a free trade agreement will go some way at least toward loosening Baltic economic dependency on Russia.

The issue of NATO enlargement is perhaps the most sensitive for both the Western and Baltic states. Lithuania was the first country from East-Central Europe and the FSU to request NATO membership, on 4 January 1994, only six days before the PfP offer was made. The question of new members was an uncomfortable one for the Western alliance. To begin with, NATO was itself struggling to define a new post–Cold War identity, and the issue of enlargement came as an unwelcome complication. Second, the Western alliance was acutely sensitive to the issue of antagonizing and alienating Russia, especially in view of growing nationalist sentiments within the country. With this background, NATO, especially the United States, sought a compromise solution for enlargement, which took the form of the PfP.

Despite an all-around attempt to put a brave face on the issue, the PfP was a poor consolation prize for the Baltic states. Disappointment revolves around two issues. Membership in NATO, however unlikely, was seen as a just reward for the democratic progress that the Baltic states had made in the short period since 1991. Membership would obviously have been an important practical and symbolic validation of this progress, and a confirmation of the Baltic states' West European identity. Even more important was the security issue. Real fears about "Russia resurgent" stimulated the desire for concrete security guarantees from the Western alliance. Instead, the PfP proved a weak substitute, offering only "consultation" in the event of a "direct threat to (the) territorial integrity, political independence, or security" of a partner state.[42] The Baltic states still anticipate their eventual entry into NATO. In the words of Lennart Meri, "PfP is an important first step. Without a doubt, however, our long-term goal is eventual full membership in NATO. We regard this goal . . . as part of a natural and completely normal progression with the overall process of European integration."[43]

In addition to membership in European bodies, there is also the issue of membership in local alliances. For example, during the first few years of independence there has been discussion of a Baltic-Black Sea alliance, a Baltic-Nordic bloc, and closer cooperation on a variety of issues between the Baltic states themselves. In many cases, however, not a great deal of progress has been made. While there are relatively good relations between the Baltic states and the Black Sea states, the idea of a regional alliance remains underdeveloped for many reasons. For example, conservative Belarus constitutes a major obstacle to the process, and the problems facing a large nation such as Ukraine are rather different from those facing the smaller Baltic states.

More similarities are to be found with the Nordic states, and considerable links have already been forged in this direction—for example, in agreements on military cooperation (Latvia and Denmark signed a military cooperation agreement on 3 January 1994, and Estonia and Denmark signed a similar agreement on 30 March 1994). Latvia in particular has close relations with Denmark and

Sweden, and Estonia has close ties with Finland and Sweden. There has been some discussion of a Nordic-Baltic pipeline, which would go some way toward alleviating the Baltics' energy dependency on Russia. Lithuania, on the other hand, has turned many of its efforts toward Central Europe, though Denmark has also cooperated with this country to a large degree as well. A Council of Baltic Sea States (CBSS) involves annual meetings of the foreign ministers of ten states (including Russia).

Common foreign and defense policies have been an aim within the Baltic states for some time, though as Park noted, "In 1992–94, it was almost a ritual to regret that there is not enough cooperation between the three Baltic States."[44] In a perfect world, each state would hope to re-create the cooperation of the 12 September 1934 Baltic Entente, but thus far nothing as comprehensive has emerged. The entente provided for trilateral foreign ministers' conferences at least twice a year to coordinate foreign policy and diplomatic affairs, though cooperation eventually broke down in 1939. The Council of Baltic States, formed in 1990, has attempted to re-create this previous collaboration and involves meetings between the heads of state and government and foreign ministers. However, the zenith of this body would appear to have been the 1990–92 period, and there have been doubts and disappointments about the way forward since then. Similarly, the Baltic Assembly, which was established in 1991 for parliamentarians, has·been criticized as being ineffective. A Baltic Council of Ministers to coordinate meetings of the prime ministers was formed in June 1994, and its relative success or failure remains to be seen.

On defense issues, there have been some practical steps taken toward Baltic cooperation. There has been a great deal of discussion about the coordination of military information, training, and operations such as coastal control. The first joint maneuvers between the Baltic states were held on 12–15 July 1994, and plans are also being made for the formation of a 650-person Baltic peacekeeping battalion that would function under a UN mandate.[45]

Conclusion

The process of state formation is never easy, and even less so when the development of a country is frozen in time for several decades. To make the task even more complicated, the Baltic states must not only throw off the legacy of the Soviet Union but also their historical role as a bridgehead for both the East and the West. Only by doing so will a tangible security be achieved and their entry into Europe finally guaranteed. It is, of course, not only entry into European institutions that will guarantee a relinquishing of this role, but the establishment of secure relations with all regional actors.

Thus far, good progress has been made in this direction. In the short three years since independence, all former Soviet troops have left the Baltic states. Rather than Russian troops being in the majority, it is now national armed forces that ensure the security of the Baltic states. Though these will require many years before they develop to their full potential, a considerable degree of movement forward has been made in defining the various branches of the armed forces, securing basic resources, and bringing them under the control of government ministries. At the same time, national security and defense policies need to be defined in greater detail and accepted by national parliaments. There needs to be a more public discussion about the question of threats to national security and clearer distinctions between those that might arise from within the state and those arising from external sources.

Many issues also remain on the question of defining citizenship, though the legal situation regarding noncitizens is gradually being clarified according to European standards. The real task of securing the state, in terms of citizenship issues, will be whether the question of Russian minorities in Latvia and Estonia can be resolved without severe social tensions. The issue of ethnic Russians, and Russia itself, will remain a serious one for the three Baltic states for some time to come.

By reasserting their national identities, the Baltic states must ideally strike a balance between respect for *all* the citizens in their small nations *and* an awareness of the activities of other states that may infringe on this process. This is by no means an easy task. Yet to paraphrase a sentiment expressed in a draft defense policy concept of one of the Baltic states, the hope is that the traditional role of a bridgehead can be transformed by turning the Baltic states into "a bridge of trust between East and West."

Notes

This paper is dedicated to Academician Andrus Park of the Estonian Academy of Sciences, who passed away unexpectedly in September 1994. The truly objective and professional analysis of this great scholar will be very sadly missed by many colleagues throughout Europe and further afield.

1. This chapter is based in part on a series of interviews conducted in Latvia, Estonia, and Russia in June 1994. The author would like to express thanks to those government and nongovernmental experts interviewed, particularly individuals from the Latvian Prime Minister's Office, the Latvian Ministry of Interior, the Latvian Institute of International Affairs, the Latvian Association for the Advancement of the Rebirth of Russia, the "Equal Rights" group of Latvia, the Latvian Human Rights and International Humanitarian Cooperation Committee, the Estonian Ministry of Foreign Affairs, the Estonian Ministry of Defense, CSCE officials in Estonia and Latvia, and Russian officials dealing with the question of Russia's role in the "near abroad." I am also grateful to Audrius Butkevičius (former Lithuanian defense minister), Talavs Jundzis (former Latvian defense minister), and Česlovas Stankevičius (MP in the Lithuanian Seimas) for invaluable discussions on the region. Finally, I am especially grateful to Atis Lejins (director of the Latvian Institute of International Affairs) for his careful reading of a draft of this chapter and his valuable comments. Nonetheless any errors of fact or interpretation are the author's alone.

2. For a more detailed consideration of the question of national identity as well as a

historical review, see Romuald Misiunas, "National Identity and Foreign Policy in the Baltic States," in *The Legacy of History in Russia and the New States of Eurasia*, ed. S. Frederick Starr (Armonk, NY: M.E. Sharpe, 1994).

3. Only a year earlier there were upwards of 600,000 troops in the Baltics, many there temporarily on their return from Germany (the numbers included 300,000 in Latvia, 200,000 in Estonia, and 100,000 in Lithuania). For a summary of the progressive decline in forces from 1990 to 1994, see Ben Lombardi, *Russian Troop Withdrawal from the Baltic Region*, Research Note 94\09 (Ottawa: Operational Research and Analysis, Directorate of Strategic Analysis, Department of National Defence, 1994), p. 8.

4. On the referendum, see Saulius Girnius, "Relations Between the Baltic States and Russia," *RFE/RL Research Report*, 26 August 1994, p. 29.

5. "Crisis in Russia: Facts and Figures," *SIPRI Fact Sheet*, October 1993. The frequently cited figure of two hundred thousand armed forces is generally understood to have been overinflated. The Lithuanian government estimates the total armed forces in Kaliningrad to be in the range of sixty thousand, whereas other observers suggest the figure could be as low as thirty thousand.

6. Girnius, "Relations Between the Baltic States and Russia," p. 32.

7. Comments made at a meeting with local Russians during his visit to Tallinn, 25 May 1994; transcript provided by Estonian government officials. For example, in mid-1994 the Russian parliament was considering a "compatriots assistance program" to give economic aid to Russians in the "near abroad."

8. *RFE/RL Research Report*, 8–12 August 1994, p. 20.

9. For details on the 1938 Law on Citizenship and the Law on Aliens (discussed below), see "Integrating Estonia's Non-Citizen Minority," *Human Rights Watch* (Helsinki), October 1993.

10. See, for example, "HCNM Recommendations on the Estonian Law on Aliens," *CSCE Newsletter*, 19 May 1994, p. 2.

11. Reported to the author by a Russian political activist in Riga.

12. For a number of examples of complaints by individuals, see "Integrating Estonia's Non-Citizen Minority."

13. For a discussion of anti-Russian sentiments in the Baltics, see Misiunas, "National Identity and Foreign Policy in the Baltic States," pp. 10–11.

14. Interview by the author, June 1994, Riga.

15. I. Skrastins, "The Armed Forces of the Baltic States: Current Status and Problems of Development," paper from the Republic of Latvia, Defense Academy, Defense Scientific Center, 1994, translated and distributed by the Conflict Studies Research Center, Royal Military Academy, Sandhurst.

16. Mark Galeotti, "Baltic Military Structures," *Jane's Intelligence Review*, August 1993, p. 353. Lithuania also had only four vessels until it acquired two frigates from Russia in late 1992.

17. Information on force levels comes from *The Military Balance 1993–94* (London: Brassey's, 1993), pp. 78–79, 82–83. For a summary of some of the planned force levels, see Galeotti, "Baltic Military Structures"; and Roy Allison, *Military Forces in the Soviet Successor States*, Adelphi Paper 280 (London: International Institute for Strategic Studies, 1993), pp. 51–53.

18. Unless stated otherwise, the following discussion is based largely on unpublished draft documents of proposed national security/defense policies for the three Baltic states. These include "The Fundamentals of National Defense," Estonian Defense Ministry, 1993; "The Republic of Latvia's Defense System Concept," Latvian National Security Council document (decision no. 11), 28 March 1994; "The National Security and Defense Concept of the Republic of Lithuania," draft of an ad hoc group of 50 Seimas MPs, March

1994; "National Security Concept of the Republic of Lithuania," draft of the ad hoc working group headed by G. Kirkilas, chairman of the National Security Committee of the Seimas of the Republic of Lithuania, 23 June 1993; and "Lithuanian Defense Doctrine," 1 December 1993. In the case of Lithuania, in November 1994 a parliamentary committee was charged with developing a unified national security and defense doctrine from the several existing drafts. I am grateful to Evaldas Nekrasas and Arminas Lydeka for helping me obtain copies of the Lithuanian documents.

19. Galeotti, "Baltic Military Structures," uses this term to refer to the use of the media to bring international opinion to bear on a conflict situation.

20. Ibid., p. 353.

21. For a description of the total defense concepts of these and other countries, see Adam Roberts, *Nations in Arms: The Theory and Practice of Territorial Defence* (London: Macmillan Press, reprint 1988).

22. This information comes from an unpublished summary of non-Latvian groups and their activities in the country collected by Nils R. Muiznieks, visiting fellow, Baltic Academic Center. I am grateful to Guntis Stamers for drawing my attention to this article.

23. Andrus Park, "Ethnicity and Independence: The Case of Estonia in Comparative Analysis," *Europe-Asia Studies*, vol. 46, no. 1 (1994), pp. 80–81. Park confirms this view of a fragmented Russian population.

24. "Russians in Estonia Appeal to Yeltsin," *Foreign Broadcasting Information Service Daily Report—Central Eurasia* (hereafter FBIS *Daily Report—Central Eurasia*), 15 July 1994, p. 69.

25. Andrus Park, "Russia and Estonian Security Dilemmas" (unpublished paper, March 1994), discussed in detail Baltic fears about the emerging Russian threat.

26. See, for example, the Baltic response in *RFE/RL Daily Report*, 21 January 1994; and the Russian response in *Krasnaia zvezda*, 20 January 1994; as well as "Speech Signals 'Revision' of Foreign Policy," *FBIS Daily Report—Central Eurasia*, 19 January 1994, p. 9.

27. For a summary of the various exchanges on this issue, see *RFE/RL Daily Report*, 7 April 1994.

28. Audrius Butkevičius views this as a distinct possibility should a pro-nationalist government come to power in Russia, whether under Zhirinovsky or someone else.

29. Park, "Russia and Estonian Security Dilemmas," pp. 30–35; each scenario is discussed in far greater detail in Andrus Park, "Fighting for the Mini-State: Four Scenarios" (unpublished paper, March 1994).

30. Girnius, "Relations Between the Baltic States and Russia," p. 30.

31. *International Herald Tribune*, 26–27 June 1993 and 28 June 1993.

32. Cited in *RFE/RL Daily Report*, 31 January 1994.

33. *RFE/RL Research Report*, 16–19 August 1994, p. 17.

34. See "Basic Provisions of the Concept of Foreign Policy of the Russian Federation," *Nezavisimaia gazeta*, 29 April 1993; and "The Basic Provisions of the Military Doctrine of the Russian Federation," *Rossiiskie vesti*, 18 November 1993, pp. 1–2.

35. Lennart Meri, "Estonia, NATO and Peacekeeping," *NATO Review*, April 1994, p. 9.

36. Park, "Russia and Estonian Security Dilemmas," discusses these concerns in detail, pp. 11–13.

37. Comments from senior Russian military representatives and senior military and political representatives from South Ossetia, Abkhazia, and Trans-Dniestria made during a conference on "Partnership for Peacekeeping," 20–24 June 1994, Moscow, organized by the Center for Political and International Studies in conjunction with a number of Russian government ministries.

38. A summary of these plans is provided in *RFE/RL Daily Report*, 8 February and 19 May 1994.

39. *RFE/RL Daily Report*, 30 March 1994.

40. See "Strategy for Russia: Theses by Foreign and Defense Policy Council," *Nezavisimaia gazeta*, 27 May 1994.

41. *RFE/RL Research Report*, 18–22 July 1994, p. 13.

42. "Partnership for Peace: Framework Document," article 8. Issued by the Heads of State and Government participating in the meeting of the North Atlantic Council held at NATO Headquarters, Brussels, 10–11 January 1994.

43. Meri, "Estonia, NATO and Peacekeeping," pp. 7–8.

44. Park, "Russia and Estonian Security Dilemmas," p. 20.

45. *RFE/RL Research Report*, 18–22 July 1994, p. 13.

7

Ukrainian Perspectives on National Security and Ukrainian Military Doctrine

Nicholas S.H. Krawciw

When, in 1991, Ukraine entered the world forum of independent states, it also embarked on the uncharted waters of international diplomacy. While elites of established nations were suddenly confronted by the end of the Cold War and the emergence of a more chaotic world, Ukraine had to cope with all of that while trying to define itself, its interests, and its capabilities. What is more than that, Ukrainian statesmen, who possessed no expertise in international diplomacy or in building a nation as well as a state with all the necessary institutions, quickly had to come up with threat assessments and notions of national security that would help secure their new state's independence. All this had to be done in embryonic governmental structures whose personnel had no experience in what they were doing and no idea how to work together.

The difficulties encountered by Ukrainians in their efforts to solidify their national security concepts are closely linked to their political, economic, ecological, and social dilemmas. Furthermore, these challenges are compounded by fear of Russia, Western pressures for nuclear disarmament, and inherent insecurities resulting from centuries of subservience, persecution, and internal disharmony.

This chapter attempts to describe how a handful of Ukrainians developed their national security policy and military strategy during the formative years (1990–94) of their new state. Highlighted below are some of the doubts, hesitations, considerations, problems, accomplishments, and remaining challenges of Ukrainian national security as seen by Ukrainian leaders and scholars who were and are now shaping that policy. Much of what is presented is based on this writer's observations of events and Ukrainian reactions to them, and on his work with some of the Ukrainians involved in security policy formulation. Thus, events and actions are the framework of this chapter. They help readers understand the Ukrainian perspectives on security that this chapter attempts to highlight. Another large part of the material in this chapter is based on the very perceptive analysis of Western scholars who are cited in the notes. The period covered includes primarily the years from 1990 through the present.

In this work, Ukraine is considered a multiethnic nation. References to Ukrainian elite, leaders, statesmen, and so forth, include persons of all persuasions and all ethnic minorities who participated or are participating in the process of building the new nation, its institutions, and its policies.

The Impact of Recent History on Considerations of National Security

The Ukrainian approach to foreign policy and national security is an amalgam of various perceptions that stem primarily from experiences in World Wars I and II and the Cold War. It is a product of the unique circumstances experienced by various parts of Ukraine during each of these periods and since their independence.

Prior to World War I, in Galicia, the western part of Ukraine, which at that time was part of Austria-Hungary, there existed near-total cultural and educational freedom, at least for most of the male population. Ukrainians served in local administrations and could serve as officers in the army. Consequently, during World War I—by 1917—when the Austro-Hungarian Empire was dissolving, Ukrainian Galicians formed units of Ukrains'ki sichovi stril'tsi, or Ukrainian Sich Riflemen (Sich was the name of the ancient Cossack stronghold on the Dnipro River). Many educated Ukrainians joined these formations in 1917 and participated in local engagements against Poland, in actions on behalf of the briefly independent Ukrainian republic in 1918–19, and as Polish allies in the war against the Bolsheviks in 1920. From these experiences and as a result of Polish repression during the interwar years sprang the Organization of Ukrainian Nationalists (OUN), which became the nucleus of western Ukrainian ethnonationalism (later ultranationalism) and a source of military thought as well as the keeper of the traditions of the Ukrainian Sich Riflemen.[1]

The OUN survived in one form or another into the present era. During World War II it was instrumental in forming the Ukrainian Insurgent Army (UPA), which fought both the German and Soviet forces. After the war, the UPA continued its struggle against the Soviet Army and Soviet security forces until about 1953. Today, the OUN is a very small party in western Ukraine, but its outlook on national security matters has been adopted by the extreme nationalist parties like the Ukrainian National Assembly (UNA) and the Ukrainian Conservative Republican Party. These parties advocate strong, ethnic armed forces, retention of nuclear weapons, and no compromises with Russia on the Black Sea fleet. In the March 1994 legislative elections to the new Rada, of the 338 available seats, the UNA won three seats, the Conservative Republican Party two, and the OUN none.

The moderate nationalist parties and coalitions like Rukh (Movement), the

Ukrainian Republican Party, the Congress of Ukrainian Nationalists, and the Democratic Party also advocate a strong national armed force and a tough line on the Crimea and the Black Sea fleet.

In central, eastern, and southern Ukraine, people's experience during Ukraine's struggle for independence between 1917 and 1921 had been suppressed during the Soviet era. Instead, the population of these regions has been indoctrinated with the glory and sacrifices of the Red Army during the "Civil War." Similarly, the history of the 1941–45 period, depicted as the "Great Patriotic War," focused on the gallant accomplishments of the Soviet armed forces. From a historic and military perspective, these sacrifices and accomplishments were respectively tragic and truly remarkable. More important, since they live in the minds of many older people, they tend to shape a unified view of a threatening West among both Ukrainians and Russians in these regions.

Following from the experiences of World War II, it was only natural for Ukrainians in the central, eastern, and southern parts of their nation to take pride in the victory achieved and to help fortify their state—the Soviet Union—against any further "perfidy" of the West. In this aftermath, even the memories of the great famine of 1933 (in which millions of Ukrainians died as a result of Stalin's confiscation of the harvest) faded. Their nuclear status and achievements in space made the people feel that they truly were a superpower. It was not until late in the Cold War, in the mid-1980s, that people's attitudes started changing. The costly involvement in Afghanistan, the Chernobyl disaster, and the failure of perestroika shook their confidence in the viability of the existing state and made them join with the more nationalistic western Ukrainians in opting for independence and a new quest for economic and political security. Nonetheless, because they felt secure and taken care of during most of the Soviet era, the central, eastern, and southern people of Ukraine still harbor ambivalent attitudes about the West, about nuclear weapons, and even about total independence from Russia. Now that the political and economic crisis in Ukraine has deepened, many are in favor of some sort of reintegration with the Russian Federation or with the Commonwealth of Independent States (CIS). Throughout the country there is a pervasive feeling that the most important security is economic security.

Thus, there is a mixture of historical experience within Ukraine. Those who are ethnically conscious and those other citizens of Ukraine, including some Russians, who view Ukraine as a multiethnic state and value what it may be able to provide for its people are aware of the importance of a coherent security policy backed by military strength. Most of them attribute Ukraine's inability to maintain statehood during the Cossack era or to regain it during the world wars of this century to a lack of sizable and unified armed forces. Another portion of the population, particularly those who have not overcome their Russian or Soviet allegiance, feel that Ukraine has no business standing on its own and that it would be of much greater benefit for everyone in the CIS if security policy and the defense forces were again subordinated to Moscow. As in all distributions of opinion, there are sizable groups with views somewhere in between or with no opinion of their own. For example, despite Ukraine's current troubles, a January 1994 SOCIS-GALLUP opinion poll indicates that out of 1,215 persons questioned, 51.4 percent answered yes to the question of whether Ukraine should join NATO to ensure its security, 20.8 percent answered in the negative, and 26.9 percent had no opinion. The other interesting aspect of this poll is that 45.9 percent of Russian Ukrainians answered in the affirmative.[2]

There are a fair number among the current ruling elites and among Ukrainian scholars who contributed to the design of the nation's security policy and who had the foresight to create an independent armed force quickly as the Soviet Union was dissolving. They are the reformers who, so far, have succeeded in the very difficult task of maintaining stability while striving for social and institutional change.

Main Security Considerations: The Threats of Erosion, Subversion, and Invasion

Most Ukrainian statesmen, as well as the country's cultural and intellectual leaders, recognize the great need for institutional reform and modernization to stem economic and social decline. But they fear disintegration from within. The threat of erosion could occur as a result of a number of factors. Among them are the lethargy, inaction, and often strong political activism of some parts of the large bureaucracy[3] remaining in place from the Soviet era; ethnic rivalries and orientations between the Russian and pro-Russian "left bank" (eastern Ukraine) and the nationalistic "right bank" (central and western Ukraine); and divisions over political and economic policy.[4]

The senior Ukrainian leadership, which included both communists and democrats, backed by a broad national consensus for independence in 1991, was able to harness part of the nomenklatura to support the new state. In this salvaged bureaucracy are a few old institutions that are critical for nation-building. Among them are the armed forces, the internal security forces, and the local police. Two new institutions, the Ministry of Foreign Affairs and the Ministry of Culture, also played a significant role in helping secure stability and define the new state and its interests.

Adding to Ukraine's fear of internal disintegration is Ukrainian ambivalence concerning Russia. Most moderate central and western Ukrainian nationalists (both the educated elite and the common people) as well as the ultranationalists see Russia as an eternal imperial enemy—as it is portrayed by Russian nationalist politician Vladimir Zhirinovsky. His many hostile pronouncements and the perception that he exerts considerable control over the foreign affairs and military committees of the Russian Duma add to their apprehension. Meanwhile, nearly all Ukrainian easterners and southerners, most of whom speak primarily Russian and among whom many Russians live, have a different view of Russia.

Most of them do not fear Russia. They want accommodation and restoration of economic ties with the CIS, particularly the Russian Federation. They complain that Ukraine's independence did not improve their lot as they expected. Many of them wishing the days of the Soviet cornucopia would return want closer ties with the Russian Federation. All this is causing a polarization that in turn is nurturing the growth of illegal paramilitary formations. Thus, a very important security problem for Ukraine is how to deal with this rift, how to defuse growing hostilities, and how to quell any internal disorders quickly. Any serious internal conflagration could lead to subversion, which in turn could be followed by a Russian intervention (or invasion threat) to seize/secure nuclear warheads or to protect the large Russian ethnic minority in eastern Ukraine or the Crimea. Therefore, prevention of any situation that could lead to Russian intervention is a widely recognized national security imperative that leads some Ukrainian statesmen to proclaim reliance on nuclear deterrence. Others argue for large conventional armed forces. Still others clamor for accommodation with Russia backed by great-power security guarantees.[5]

On the whole, external military threats from neighboring nations other than Russia are, for most thinking Ukrainians, a distant third security priority. Relations with nations along Ukraine's western and southwestern borders have been normalized, because Ukraine has treated fairly the Hungarian and Romanian minorities living on the Ukrainian side of the border.[6] However, strains with Romania over policies toward Moldova remain. In this case, Ukraine is concerned that the armed conflict that raged in Moldova's Trans-Dniester region in 1991–92 will recur, endangering Ukrainian and Russian citizens and drawing Russian involvement into that area. Most importantly, relations with Poland, Ukraine's historic western archenemy, are generally friendly and mutually supportive. In an excellent (June 1993) study, Ilya Prizel states:

> For the first time since the onslaught of the Tatars in the thirteenth century a symbiotic relationship between Poland and Ukraine has emerged.[7]

Many of Ukraine's leading statesmen and scholars recognize the abovementioned regional concerns and threat perceptions of the people. They are searching for an optimum security policy that will help them preserve the state while advancing reform and trying to build new chains of authority and new political institutions.

Events and Issues in 1990 and 1991

What makes Ukrainian national rebirth and development of a sense of identity particularly complex to accomplish is the fact that successive generations of conquest, be it Polish, Russian or Soviet, have managed either, at worst, to destroy Ukraine's political elite or, at best to thoroughly "de-nationalize" it. As a result, although an old nation, Ukraine is currently engaged in the process of nation-building, a process which entails not only assertive remaking of internal institutions but also a new sense of history and new symbols. The development of foreign policy, especially toward powers that previously dominated a country, is a key ingredient of nation-building.[8]

National security policy includes foreign policy. Both are essential elements of nation-building. However, a nation's security policy in today's world has to be broader. It must embrace considerations and activities oriented toward internal stability, a strengthened economy, and other aspects of security. Attempts to formulate national security concepts for the new Ukraine became visible in 1990 among increasingly bold adherents of Rukh, the umbrella organization of various parties and individuals in western Ukraine modeled after the Polish Solidarity. At that time most pronouncements concerning national security were general in nature and linked to Rukh's drive to secure Ukrainian independence.

The March 1990 parliamentary elections produced a partially democratic legislature (the Verkhovna Rada—Supreme Council, or Rada for short) in the Ukrainian SSR. Included in it were such senior Rukh leaders as Viacheslav Chornovil, Stepan Khmara, Mykhailo Horyn, Bohdan Horyn, and younger ones like Ihor Derkach. Acting on their insistence and eager to defuse the nationalist ferment caused by student strikes of that summer, the new Rada declared Ukraine's state sovereignty on 16 July 1990—more than a year before the August 1991 coup in Moscow. That declaration also laid the foundation for Ukraine's initial security policy. Two of its provisions are of particular importance in that regard: (1) the Ukrainian SSR declared the right to establish its own armed forces; and (2) the Ukrainian SSR solemnly declared its intention to become, in the future, a permanently neutral state that does not participate in military alliances and that holds to the three nonnuclear principles—not to accept, manufacture, or acquire nuclear weapons.[9]

The amazing thing about this declaration, in addition to its future applicability to security policy, is that with it the Ukrainian Rada clearly signaled its intention to distance Ukraine from the Soviet Union. At that time, in 1990, a path toward neutrality and nonnuclear status must have appeared to the communist and noncommunist leadership in the Rada as a viable option toward full Ukrainian independence.[10]

In September 1990, Leonid Kravchuk was elected chairman of the Rada and resigned from his position as second secretary of the Ukrainian Communist Party. His popularity rose, and he began championing sovereignty.[11] For the rest of that year and during the first half of 1991 not much happened in terms of further pronouncements or actions concerning Ukraine's independence or security. However, Ukrainians in government, scholars, and the general public were watching the events in Eastern Europe, the Russian SSR, and the Baltics. Strong winds of change were blowing across all of Central and Eastern Europe. Gorbachev's glasnost, by this time, allowed much more access to news and opinion carried by Western mass media, previously prohibited texts on history and political science, and reports with interpretations of internal debates. It was a time of reorientation and new thinking. Those who had visions of independence also started developing thoughts on national security.[12]

The opportunity to act came at the time when the Moscow coup collapsed. On 24 August 1991, the Rada declared Ukraine's independence (subject to popular ratification on 1 December 1991). That same day, the leading western Ukrainian representatives mentioned earlier and many "centrist nationalists," like Dmytro Pavlychko (a poet and writer who held the chair of the Rada's Foreign Affairs Committee) and Ivan Drach, another poet, and even many Communists who were in the process of abandoning their soon-to-be-outlawed party, were joined by Kravchuk in an extraordinary session of the Rada to pass a resolution calling for the following: (1) the subordination of all Soviet military formations deployed on the republic's territory to the Ukrainian Verkhovna Rada; (2) the creation of a Ukrainian Defense Ministry; and (3) the creation of Ukrainian armed forces, a national guard, and a subdetachment to protect the Ukrainian Verkhovna Rada, the Cabinet of Ministers, and the National Bank.

Kravchuk and most of the legislators accepted the argument of the various new democrats that had the coup not gone sour, Ukraine's independence and governmental institutions would have have been without defense as in 1918.[13]

A few days later, on 29 August 1991, the Presidium of the Rada (this is a powerful grouping in the Ukrainian parliament that consists of the Rada's chairman, his two deputies, heads of standing committees, and party or faction leaders) approved edicts that placed under Ukrainian jurisdiction the border troops and the internal security troops on Ukrainian territory. And on 3 September 1991, the full legislature approved the appointment of Major General Konstantyn Morozov minister of defense with the rank of colonel general. He became a significant and somewhat independent player in the formulation of Ukrainian security policy.

Events and Conventional Defense Issues in 1991 and 1992

Morozov sensed that he had to move quickly if trouble with Moscow was to be avoided. Others in leadership positions felt the same. By the end of 1991, with the close cooperation of the Rada, and with the full backing of Kravchuk (who was elected Ukraine's first president on 1 December 1991, the day Ukrainians overwhelmingly approved their independence), Morozov achieved the "redesignation" of what had been a Soviet force of probably more than seven hundred thousand into a force that now would be called Ukrainian.[14] That fall and winter the legislature passed some basic laws pertaining to the Ukrainian armed forces and their internal security and border troops. At the same time, despite harsh criticism from Moscow, Minister Morozov ordered the commanders and soldiers of all units to start taking loyalty oaths to Ukraine. These two actions could be considered the beginning of the actual "transformation" of the old Soviet force into a Ukrainian one.

The basic laws that were enacted gave the armed forces some general missions, such as to "defend the territorial integrity of Ukraine," but provided no specific scenarios and tasks that are usually found in a national military strategy. As far as security policy is concerned, Kravchuk and other members of his government continued to declare Ukraine "nonnuclear and nonaligned." Furthermore, the Ukrainian leadership, while trying to define what Ukraine stood for, was also just starting to visualize the threats to the new state, but the armed forces were not provided with any scenarios for which they could organize and train. In other words, there was no national security policy guidance from which a military strategy could be developed.

There was, however, awareness that institutions capable of providing the government with some in-depth analysis were needed. There was also an awareness that senior Ukrainian leadership of all branches of the government needed to be exposed to Western institutions, laws, and models of governmental structures. Initially, only a few Western governments picked up on this need and invited senior Ukrainians for visits to their institutions in the fall of 1991.

Bohdan Havrylyshyn, a Ukrainian-Canadian, had been assisting Ukraine in its nation-building processes for more than a year by that time. As president of the International Renaissance Foundation in Kiev, a Soros Foundations arm in Ukraine, he arranged invitations from a number of governments in Europe for visits by Ukrainian ministers, parliamentary committees, and various senior staffs to view West and Central European structures and to discuss Western approaches to fundamental national policies and practices.

As one example of these internships, at the end of October 1991, a Ukrainian delegation, consisting of the Committee on Defense and Security, with Vasyl' Durdynets as its chairman, and with Ievhen Marchuk, the minister of internal security participating, visited West Germany, Czechoslovakia, and Switzerland to learn what laws these nations have and what practices are used in control of intelligence, internal security, and police forces. The Ukrainian group spent a number of days in each country, visiting security organizations, discussing legal issues with senior judges, and taking many notes. Two months later, toward the end of January 1992, the Ukrainian Rada was debating proposed legislation that would establish the Ukrainian National Security Service. That law contained many provisions gleaned and discussed during the October trip, such as civilian/parliamentary oversight over police functions and the role of the judiciary in police activities. Minister Marchuk responded to hours of questioning by the full legislature and, while showing clear concern for capabilities to deal with internal and external threats, he was able to reassure them that the draft law contained adequate provisions to safeguard the individual rights of citizens. More important, the law drafted by Durdynets and his committee contained more of a balance between individual rights and state security needs than Soviet-era laws had. In many ways it was similar to the West European examples studied by that committee in October 1991.[15]

It is worth mentioning that, during the discussions in October 1991 in Switzerland, the Ukrainian members of the delegation showed a wide range of strategic understanding and clearly had already prioritized for themselves and for anyone who cared to listen the threats facing Ukraine. Marchuk, Durdynets, and the other delegates all agreed that the possibilities of regional instability in eastern and southern Ukraine (meaning primarily the Crimea) were of greater concern than external threats. While showing this personal strategic awareness, they also requested during that trip that this author, an American of Ukrainian roots, assist them in their security research by developing a concept for an independent "think tank" in Ukraine such as the International Institute for Strategic Studies (London) (IISS), RAND, or others. In other words, they voiced a need to broaden and deepen their security perspectives. The result of this request was the establishment in Kiev of the International Institute on Global and Regional Security (IIGRS) in May 1992.[16]

And now back to the armed forces. As was mentioned earlier, solidifying the few functional institutions on Ukrainian territory was the government's first security priority. There was near unanimous agreement in government and among the educated elite that the armed forces were the main institution that needed the new state's attention. Therefore, with considerable backing from many quarters, including the powerful (at that time) Union of Ukrainian Officers (SOU), Minister Morozov pressed on with what had to be done. He now considers the period of January through May 1992 as most critical for the firm establishment of the Ukrainian armed forces. After that time, Russia, having realized that it had lost the army on Ukrainian territory, started applying pressure on Ukraine through the footholds it still retained: the strategic formations, the military-industrial complex, and the Black Sea fleet.[17]

During the January–May 1992 period, loyalty oaths and attestation boards were Morozov's tools to ensure that the armed forces would be reliable in a crisis. More than ten thousand officers who refused to take the loyalty oath were separated from the army. Six thousand others who took the oath but who were political officers or Communist Party members in Soviet times were screened by the attestation boards before assignment or rejection.[18] Programs to introduce Ukrainian language, history, and military heritage were designed and sent out for implementation. Also, by mid-1992, the reorganization of the military educational system was undertaken. It envisioned a gradual contraction of thirty-four formerly Soviet army schools into eight or nine Ukrainian military institutions.

A more pressing issue was the need to move on with the reorganization and drawdown while also rebuilding the shattered morale and combat readiness of a force whose resources were dwindling and that had done little training for over a year—since the previous summer. To rebuild morale and infuse a Ukrainian national spirit into his forces, Morozov created a directorate called the Socio-Psychological Service. Over one thousand ethnically ardent Ukrainian officers were assigned to it and were then further subassigned to every level of staff and command. Also, they were to ensure that Ukrainian armed forces commanders, most of whom at the senior command levels were Russians, were executing the prescribed programs of what has been called "re-Ukrainization." The programs included intensive Ukrainian language and history studies for everyone. Unfortunately, the charter of this directorate was too broad. It clearly infringed on the responsibilities of the chain of command. A serious backlash, evidenced by the intentional inaction of many commanders and their outspoken criticism, caused Minister Morozov to rein in this new directorate and slow down "re-Ukrainization." The officers of the Socio-Psychological Service were told to stop acting like commissars and were directed to become staff assistants to the commanders. Meanwhile, the better commanders were also slowly making inroads to eliminate the traditional hazing among the lower ranks.[19]

Concerning the drawdown (which was necessary because of economic pressures) and reorganization of the armed forces, early in 1992 Morozov created a small strategic planning cell headed by Major General Vadim Grechaninov. Initially this cell recommended that the armed forces be reduced over time to a ceiling of 450,000. Later that year this figure was adjusted downward to 420,000, or 8 percent of the Ukrainian population.[20] Grechaninov's strategic planning cell envisioned a ground force structure of some seven to eight combined arms divisions, six to seven tank and motorized infantry brigades, six to seven artillery brigades, and two to three army aviation brigades, all of which would be located in two operational commands replacing the Carpathian and Odessa military districts. That placed most of Ukraine's combat forces in the western and southern regions. There were no major ground force combat units in eastern Ukraine. The former Soviet army air force was made a separate service and was named the "air-space defense" command, which was subdivided into four air defense groups. For Ukraine's navy, Morozov and his planners envisioned a force of sixteen naval squadrons, with naval aviation and coastal defense units manned by some forty thousand servicemen.[21] At that time, in mid-1992, Morozov was hoping that Ukraine would obtain a fair share of the Black Sea fleet through already frustrating but ongoing negotiations, despite the fact that he was not allowed to take over that fleet earlier in the year.

These dispositions were partially due to the locations of former Soviet bases, but, since there was almost no discussion of why a part of the force should not also be placed closer to the borders with Russia, the stationing plan was also an obvious effort not to provoke "Big Brother." As this author recalls, the only parliamentarian who raised questions about this mal-deployment was Ihor Derkach, a young nationalist from western Ukraine who was also a member of the Committee on Security and Defense in the Rada. The dispositions also lacked a centrally located strategic reserve.[22]

As for combat readiness in the conventional deterrent sense, not much could be done in 1992. The economic situation continued to deteriorate. There were barely enough funds to pay all the people in the armed forces. Very little was left over for training and maintenance of equipment, two very important elements of combat readiness.

In one area of conventional security policy formulation, Ukrainians could not find consensus during their first year of statehood. That area concerned how to approach the issue of the Black Sea fleet. Western Ukrainian leaders, led by Stepan Khmara, who had already written his own version of a military strategy for Ukraine, wanted the government to stick to the Rada's resolutions and to act on the Black Sea fleet as it did on the ground and air forces. Morozov also favored quick action but wanted it to be worked out with Russia. Kravchuk, Fokin (the prime minister at that time), Zlenko (the foreign minister), Pavlychko, and other "centrists," as well as most former communists in the Rada, all favored a more gradual approach.

Apparently, Morozov started taking some action to take control of the fleet. He says:

> In March of 1992 the Ukrainian Ministry of Defense had actual control over the Black Sea Fleet. Almost 85 percent of the naval officers were prepared to transfer to the service of Ukrainian naval forces. They were waiting to receive from the Ukrainian government a decision on their fate.
>
> The only condition of their loyalty to Ukraine was a change of commanders. This did not take place. Ukraine was waiting for concessions on the part of Russia, while Russian policies in the Ukrainian Crimea were gaining momentum.[23]

The Crimea and the Black Sea fleet pose special problems for both Ukraine and Russia. Much heritage and emotion can come into play when Russians and Ukrainians start dealing with issues concerning that picturesque but poor peninsula or the fleet that has little strategic value. In the spring of 1992, Ukrainian Rada member Stepan Khmara and Russian Federation Vice President Aleksandr Rutskoi visited Sevastopol at different times, inflaming passions among the people of the Crimea and escalating tensions. While most Russians view the Crimea as a historical warm-water naval foothold for which many wars were fought with the Turks (between 1700 and 1855) and two campaigns with the Germans (1941 and 1944), the majority of Ukrainians, fearful of possible gradual dismemberment, want to maintain Ukraine's existing territorial integrity.

In Ukraine, strong popular opinion demanded that a Ukrainian navy be formed as soon as possible. However, political negotiations with Russia on the division of the fleet were not moving quickly. Finally, in June 1992 in Yalta, Kravchuk managed to get Yeltsin's agreement to divide the fleet, and there was some hope in the air in Kiev that things were finally moving. Morozov appointed Admiral Kozhyn commander of the Ukrainian navy, a Ukrainian fleet staff was formed, and about half of the sailors being drafted into the Black Sea fleet were Ukrainians. But as the year wore on, Russian and Ukrainian committees meeting periodically to develop a scheme for the fleet's division made little progress.

Regarding the internal security forces, General Ievhen Marchuk, who upon the Rada's January 1992 passage of the law concerning Ukraine's internal security structure became director of the Ukrainian Security Service (and had to give up his portfolio as minister of the interior), performed screening measures similar to Morozov's in the former Ukrainian KGB. By the end of May 1992, Marchuk dismissed thirteen or more generals and many others from the service.[24]

In summary, by mid-1992 Ukrainian leaders had, generally speaking, carried out their most basic needs toward the establishment of institutions that would secure Ukrainian internal stability and provide for conventional defense on land. Not resolved were the issues of the huge nuclear arsenal on their territory and the Black Sea fleet.

Ukrainian Views on Nuclear Disarmament in 1992

By all indications, Ukraine's transfer of tactical nuclear weapons to Russia in the spring of 1992 was carried out in the spirit of the 1990 parliamentary declaration and to fulfill its Minsk agreement with Russia of 30 December 1991. Most of the Ukrainian leadership wanted to continue to garner world recognition for Ukraine's independence and induce economic assistance from the West for its future disarmament obligations. There were no new analyses made to support some broader or more refined security policy objectives. In that vein, in April 1992, Kravchuk committed Ukraine to START I and signed the Lisbon Protocol to that treaty as a nonnuclear state. That implied Ukraine's eventual accession to the Nuclear Nonproliferation Treaty (NPT).

The results of these gestures were disappointing for Ukraine's leaders. Instead of Western applause for its promises and for ridding Ukraine of tactical nuclear weapons, they started to receive immediate intense pressure from the United States and others to ratify START I quickly and join the NPT regime. Most Ukrainian leaders, including Kravchuk and Morozov, many in the parliament, and a sizable proportion of the population perceived that pressure as the West's refusal to treat Ukraine as an equal member in the family of nations. They saw themselves being driven back into a position of subservience to Russia. The backlash against nuclear divestiture set in and started growing in terms of political and popular strength.[25]

Another factor that reinforced Ukraine's hesitation to go the extra mile toward nonnuclear status in the fall of 1992 was the very deep-rooted fear of Russia by the majority of the population, which identified with Ukrainian aspirations for true political independence. Russian claims to Sevastopol and the Black Sea fleet, pronouncements by various Russian politicians and generals on the rights of intervention and peacekeeping in the area of the former Soviet Union, and the possible spillover from various crises and instabilities occurring in Russia all contributed to the belief by many Ukrainians that strategic nuclear weapons could somehow play a deterrent role against Russia. On the other hand, no scholar or statesman in Ukraine in 1992 seemed to have developed a deeper understanding of what nuclear possession really foreshadows. Few in Ukraine seemed to have analyzed contingency scenarios with second- and third-order consequences. Such an analysis would have shown, as it did later for Volodymyr Selivanov, the national security advisor to President Kravchuk, that Ukraine, which does not have adequate strategic reconnaissance and command and control capabilities, would open itself to preemption and catastrophic destruction during any serious crisis. In addition, an adequate command and control infrastructure would take years to build, would squander billions of dollars, and would surely condemn Ukraine to more decades of poverty.

Faced with these feelings and concerns, and recognizing the need for a national security policy and military strategy ("national military doctrine," as Ukrainians call all that), Morozov, without much help from the president's office or from the Ministry of Foreign Affairs, submitted a draft doctrine for approval by the parliament in October 1992.[26] It was a weak document because its security policy portion did not provide a way out from what some legislators perceived as the contradiction between Ukraine's status as "neutral, nonaligned, and nonnuclear" and its need for some counterweight to the Russian threat. Thus, the document was wide open to criticism from various quarters of the legislature. And so this first attempt to define Ukraine's security policy was defeated by opponents in the legislature.

Meanwhile, in the United States there was no one to bolster Ukraine's self-confidence. The election campaign, the electoral loss by the Republicans, their subsequent lame-duck period, and then the transition period under a new Democratic administration produced no new initiatives from the West until the spring of 1993. Ukraine continued to smart under real and imagined pressures through the winter.

Progress and Problems of 1993:
National Security Theory and Practice

During the early months of 1993, some leaders in the governmental structures of Ukraine progressed in the development of a number of significant institutions. Selivanov continued to refine the organization and charter of Ukraine's National Security Council, which had been established in July 1992. By March 1993, the council accepted a study with proposals for its membership and functions developed by scholars of the International Institute on Global and Regional Security (IIGRS) mentioned earlier. Among them were Dmitri Vydrin, Leonid Tupchienko, Oleh Bodruk, Eduard Lisytsyn, and the institute's first Western scholar, Ian Brzezinski. Bodruk and Lisytsyn were also coauthors (with Oleksandr Honcharenko and Nina Maslova-Lysychkina) of a widely published series of articles entitled "A Concept of Ukraine's National Security: Problems and Perspectives of Its Formulation." These articles outlined the theoretical approach to policy based on Western models. The authors describe how Western nations define their national interests, develop national objectives, and then formulate security policy from which a national military strategy is then evolved. They point out the responsibilities of executive agencies and the legislature in this process.

At the time of his departure from the National Security Council in May, Selivanov's own views on Ukraine's national security had crystalized to the point where they were probably the basis of Ukraine's current national security policy. In a spring 1993 interview, he clearly outlined: (1) the construction of a multiethnic Ukrainian state united by a certain cultural and historical heritage as well as by the values of all its people; (2) the integration of the interests of all Ukraine's citizens in the formulation of national security policy; (3) the inclusion of political, economic, social, scientific, humanitarian, and other spheres into an understanding of security; (4) the adherence to the law regulating activities of Ukraine's Security Service in order to safeguard the rights of individual citizens; (5) the close relationship between internal security and aggression from external threats, or how internal instability or conflict could lead to a wider war; (6) a complete listing of plausible external and internal threats to Ukraine; (7) the dangers of overmilitarization and the use of the armed forces for internal security functions; (8) the use of creative political methods and conflict prevention techniques to reduce internal threats and maintain internal stability; (9) the participation in international organizations in order to develop mutual trust and understanding among states; (10) the balancing of national interests, rather than the creation of a balance of forces, as the main objective of national security policy; and, most important; (11) the formulation of policy toward the issue of nuclear weapons in Ukraine from a perspective far broader than a purely military one. Those who argue for Ukraine to remain a nuclear power do not understand the long-range economic, social, and political consequences—the costs, the ensuing international isolation, and the danger during a crisis.[27]

The last point made by Selivanov sounds as if he had read the works on nuclear issues by a number of well-known U.S. authors.[28] Selivanov lists the following as external threats: actions designed to violate Ukrainian borders; efforts to diminish Ukrainian political independence; attempts to draw the Ukrainian state into conflicts outside its borders or to use Ukrainian territory; and interference in Ukraine's internal affairs, such as inciting of ethnic strife. About internal threats, he says, "In general, internal threats are most pronounced when a new nation and its society are trying to get on their feet. The reasons for that can be found in political instability, in crisis situations due to economic and social turbulence, and in ethnic, religious, or ultra-nationalistic extremism." He further explains that these conditions create an environment in which various extremist factions wishing to achieve their political goals could turn to the use of illegal paramilitary formations and other radical methods such as terrorism, organized crime, or narcotics trade. All of these activities would undermine political stability and could lead to armed conflict or even civil war.[29]

In addition to the National Security Council, state institutes such as the Strategic Institute of Ukraine, which functions under the president of Ukraine and is headed by Dr. Perizhkov, the Ukrainian Institute of International Relations of the Taras Shevchenko University, the Institute of World Economy and International Relations of the Ukrainian Academy of Sciences, and a number of others were breaking out on their own and publishing increasingly sophisticated works on issues of national security. All of them were benefiting from the freedom of speech now in existence in Ukraine.

Concerning force and military strategy development, Morozov and his reformers pressed on during 1993, despite opposition, to carry out their vision of the Ukrainian armed forces. There was slow but steady progress in almost all the main areas of the "transformation" that had been enumerated so far. By the summer of 1993, the number of men in uniform fell to below six hundred thousand, the operational commands were functioning, re-Ukrainization was also coming along better than expected now that the methods used were relaxed, and, last but not least, the draft military strategy paper was much better than the first version. Even with respect to the fleet, a solution seemed on the horizon after Kravchuk and Yeltsin agreed to divide it evenly during their May meeting near Moscow. At that conference, Yeltsin also acknowledged Ukrainian territorial sovereignty over Sevastopol and the Crimea.

In the spring and summer of 1993, beginning efforts were made in the contingency planning functions of the main staff of the Ukrainian armed forces. General Anatolii Lopata was appointed and confirmed as the new chief of the main staff in April 1993. As a seasoned commander and staff officer, he energized all the staff activities, particularly contingency and mobilization planning. Mobilization concepts were developed, and work was in progress to establish a mobilization system. Lopata also worked closely with the Committee on Defense and National Security to develop a sorely needed budget process for the armed forces.[30] The most impressive political progress in Ukraine's search for relevance in the national security arena came suddenly in the fall of 1993. The Ukrainian parliament, which in September 1993 decided on its own reelection in March 1994, approved Ukraine's national security policy statement (known in Ukraine by the term *voienna doktryna*—military doctrine) on 19 October 1993. Kravchuk secured the vote on this document with the backing of the newly appointed minister of defense, General of the Army Vitalii Radets'kyi, and by saying to the Rada, "if you don't approve this doctrine, every officer will make his own." He could have added, "every politician will make his own." Ukraine's security objectives listed in the document include: defense of the country's sovereignty and political independence; preservation of its territorial integrity; and participation in international organizations to safeguard political, economic, and military stability in Europe and in the whole world.

The doctrine, in a sense, responds to the greater interest shown by the United States toward Ukraine in the spring of 1993 (reflected in the visits by such U.S.

officials as Strobe Talbott and Les Aspin). The document reaffirms Ukraine's goal to become a nonnuclear state but links its disarmament process to security guarantees by other nuclear states and to compensation. Like the Russian military doctrine adopted a few weeks later, the Ukrainian paper prohibits use of the armed forces for political purposes. But its overall thrust is much more defensive in nature and seems to be more genuinely oriented toward conflict prevention. It places significant reliance on international treaties and calls for an all-European security arrangement.

This report on Ukrainian national security perspectives would be incomplete if it did not also mention the persistent and dedicated work of Deputy Foreign Minister Borys Tarasiuk and a small cadre of able assistants. A career foreign service officer, Tarasiuk often traveled with the president, drafted important communiqués, and consistently argued for major world power backing of Ukraine's independence in return for its nuclear disarmament. Throughout 1993, he could also be seen as an active participant in international conferences such as the biannual conference between Russia's Institute on Europe and Ukraine's IIGRS, at the workshops at the Stiftung Wissenschaft und Politik (SWP) (in Ebenhausen, Germany) on Ukraine sponsored by RAND, SWP, and IIGRS, and at many other gatherings where Ukraine's views were sought.[31]

Issues and internal Ukrainian views concerning the Black Sea fleet remained on the problematic side of the ledger during 1993. Ukraine's plunge into hyperinflation added to pressures to find a solution quickly. At the Massandra meeting of September 1993, Kravchuk indicated that Ukraine might be willing to give up its nuclear missiles and its portion of the fleet for Russian debt forgiveness and for continued supplies of energy. Just the willingness even to consider such a quid pro quo caused an uproar throughout Ukraine. Even Morozov publicly objected to this proposal. The Black Sea fleet is old and its operational potential is marginal, but receiving a portion of it is symbolically important for Ukraine. Russian recognition that the fleet is now in a foreign (Ukrainian) port is also important for most Ukrainians. The possibility that Ukraine may not get part of the fleet disturbed many Ukrainian naval officers and sailors. Morozov had to spend some time in the Crimea putting out fires of discontent among Ukrainian sailors.

Also on the negative side of this assessment for 1993 is the fact that conventional combat readiness of the Ukrainian armed forces deteriorated even further. The importance of this reality is that it can easily shake whatever confidence Ukrainians may have in their national security concepts and posture. The Ukrainian navy had a few new ships by the end of the year, but the ground and air forces, which have plenty of military hardware, were doing very little to improve their capabilities. Other than classes in military schools, there was little ongoing field training; ammunition to conduct live fire exercises was scarce, and there was no fuel to exercise military vehicles. All that plus continued instances of hazing in the armed forces lowered the morale and discipline of the troops.[32] In one area, combat readiness improved. That involved the battalion sent to Bosnia for United Nations peacekeeping in 1992. Special measures have been taken to overcome criticism received from the United Nations Command in Bosnia that the leadership of the Ukrainian unit was weak and that its soldiers cared more about black market activities than about their mission. By all indications, the Ukrainian unit in Bosnia has been performing much better.

And so, 1993 ended on a mixed note. It was unfortunate that, at the time when Ukraine needed to move into the exploitation phase of its early accomplishments in building its armed forces, Minister Morozov had to resign and then failed to be reappointed. Maybe that was the price he had to pay for speaking out against the Massandra proposals and for not succumbing to unbelievable pressures from those who wanted quicker accommodation toward Russia. On the hopeful side of security issues for Ukraine there were the signs, by the year's end, that a breakthrough in nuclear disarmament negotiations with Russia, brokered by the United States, was approaching and that a number of new and energetic players such as Valerii Shmarov, a deputy prime minister for armament and conversion, and Vitalii Radets'kyi, the new minister of defense, were pursuing moderate and sensible national security goals.

Change and Continuity in 1994

Ukrainian leaders in and out of government entered the new year with considerable apprehension. The economy continued its free fall, and the upcoming legislative and presidential elections foreshadowed possible changes in political direction. Nonetheless, President Kravchuk continued to carry out Ukraine's nuclear disarmament pledges by signing the Trilateral Agreement with Russia and the United States on 14 January 1994.[33] The "lame duck" Rada ratified it in a stormy session in February but left Ukrainian accession to the Nuclear Nonproliferation Treaty in doubt. Western Ukrainian legislators, led by Viacheslav Chornovil and Serhii Holovaty, criticized this accord for not containing adequate security guarantees and for insufficient economic benefit for Ukraine. Eventually, the accord was backed by the chairman of the parliament, Ivan Pliushch (at that time a presidential candidate who had generally backed Kravchuk over the years on security policy issues), by moderates, and by the leaders of the left bloc—the socialists and the legally revived communists.

Next came Leonid Kravchuk's visit to Washington in early March 1994, when he gained U.S. promises of additional economic assistance. He brought with his delegation, among other senior officials, Ievhen Marchuk, who speaks fluent English and continues to maintain friendly ties with his Western counterparts. He was also accompanied by Minister of Defense Radets'kyi. That was Radets'kyi's first visit to the United States. During his discussions in Washington, Radets'kyi reaffirmed his commitment to the program of military-to-military contacts with the United States initiated in 1993 by Minister Morozov, and he displayed a genuine interest in the Partnership for Peace program with NATO. Radets'kyi also showed deep concern over the situation in the Crimea and the lack of progress in the talks with Russia over the Black Sea fleet. The defense minister's greatest problem, however, was how to restore morale, a high level of professional training, and combat readiness in the Ukrainian armed forces.[34]

The March 1994 legislative elections were the next significant event, that has changed, to some degree, the cast of players on the Ukrainian scene. The new legislature's leader is Oleksandr Moroz, leader of the Socialist Party of Ukraine. For that position, he defeated Vasyl' Durdynets, who was backed by the right and center parliamentary factions. In the previous Rada, he frequently criticized Kravchuk and Morozov, but now he is sounding like Durdynets on many issues. In addition to early actions intended to revive the economy, Moroz promises reforms that will strengthen the government and enable it to govern.[35]

On 16 June 1994, the new Rada, as a result of secret balloting, approved Vitalii Masol as prime minister of Ukraine. In the 1987–90 period, Masol had headed the Council of Ministers of the Ukrainian SSR but had to step down following the student strikes. His candidacy for prime minister was advanced by Moroz and "acknowledged" by Kravchuk. Masol has sounded much like Moroz in his initial pronouncements. He too wants to focus on building a strong government and institutions capable of resolving Ukraine's problems.[36]

Beyond their focus on governmental organization and their preoccupation with what to do about the economy, Moroz and the new legislature have displayed their attitude toward Ukrainian sovereignty and security. The Rada's action had to do with the Crimea. On 20 May 1994 and again on 30 May 1994, the Crimean parliament voted to revitalize the constitution enacted in 1992, which would have made the Crimea almost fully independent of Ukraine, but which was suspended that year by the Ukrainian Rada. The Ukrainian legislature, after a long debate, approved a compromise bill that called on the executive branch to take appropriate constitutional action to bring the Crimea into Ukraine's fold. A mission was formed that was to work with the Crimean leadership to resolve the crisis.[37] At the time of this writing, the results of this mission and of other actions by Ukraine's new leaders to defuse the crisis are not clear. However, the serious approach to this issue by the Ukrainian Rada's mostly new membership and their concern for what is a dangerous national security problem for Ukraine are quite clear.

On 14 June 1994, Minister of Defense Radets'kyi traveled to the United States for his own official visit on invitation from U.S. Secretary of Defense William Perry. Their discussions were fruitful in terms of planning further bilateral cooperation, Partnership for Peace (PfP) participation, for which Ukraine signed up in February, and the next steps in the implementation of the Trilateral Agreement. Radets'kyi reported that Ukraine was ahead of schedule in its shipment of missiles and warheads to Russia. However, when during activities with the U.S. navy discussions turned to issues of the Black Sea fleet, he showed concern over Russian intransigence in the negotiations over the fleet's division and basing. Throughout his visit to the United States, he made it clear that he is committed to the PfP process and that he intends to do all he can to make it a meaningful series of military exchanges. [38]

On 26 June 1994, Ukrainians went to the polls to vote for the next president. Leonid Kravchuk and Leonid Kuchma received the largest number of votes among seven candidates. They competed in a runoff election on 10 July 1994. Despite poll predictions to the contrary, Kuchma won. While Kravchuk was backed by the electorate in central and western Ukraine, Kuchma received an overwhelming majority of votes in all the large urban centers of eastern and central Ukraine, as well as in the Crimea. He immediately took steps to assure central and western Ukraine that he will address their concerns for economic reform and will not abandon Ukraine's quest for closer ties with the West. Concerning the Crimea, he declared that since it voted overwhelmingly for him, he considers it a vote of confidence not only in him but also in Ukraine. As expected, he also indicated that his government will pursue closer economic ties with Russia and the CIS.

In mid-August 1994, Kuchma sent Deputy Prime Minister for Security Affairs Ievhen Marchuk to Moscow, where talks about the division of the Black Sea fleet were restarted. Negotiations on base rights and basing will follow in the future. To help him shape foreign and national security policies, late in August, Kuchma appointed Gennadii Udovenko as foreign minister and Valerii Shmarov as the first civilian minister of defense. Udovenko had been Ukraine's first ambassador to the United Nations and its acting ambassador to the United States from the time of independence in 1991 until spring of 1992. The appointment of Shmarov is a historic step for Ukraine. It expands significantly the nation's civilian control of the armed forces and presents an opportunity to create a civilian cadre within the Ministry of Defense. Shmarov quickly indicated that, in his new position, he will concentrate on policy and the preservation of critical elements of the military-industrial complex, leaving day-to-day management of military affairs to the chief of staff of the Main Staff, General Anatolii Lopata.[39] Also, as a key member of the Ukrainian team that worked out the Trilateral Agreement with the United States and the Russian Federation, he can be expected to continue close relations with both countries.

All present indications are that Ukraine's national security directions under the new team will continue to follow the cumulative wisdom and experience gained by the majority of Ukraine's political and scholarly elite along principles outlined by Selivanov and contained in Ukraine's military doctrine.

Conclusion

Three years have passed since Ukraine became an independent state. During that time, in terms of international recognition, it has carved out for itself a place on our globe. At the same time, it has maintained internal stability and has gained experience as a "player" on the world arena while avoiding bloodshed and external conflict. It has also become one of the first nations in history to voluntarily bargain away nuclear might for some security assurances and for economic benefit. On the other hand, Ukraine has not found consensus for sorely needed political and economic reform and modernization. And that, in the long run, may become the most significant threat to its survival.

Nonetheless, considering the complexities of what had to be done, one cannot help but admire what Ukraine has accomplished. While the new nation was groping to define what it is and while governmental institutions were being established, often under crisis conditions, Ukrainian leaders also had to develop foreign and internal security policy, begin some strategic planning, and restructure the Soviet armed forces on their soil. To be sure, much of what was formulated and set up was done in haste and often without adequate study or debate. Nonetheless, a basic national security system and a Ukrainian armed force were organized and are now in existence. Still, some of what was done will have to be reshaped and fine-tuned to accommodate the remaining political and economic realities of the post-Soviet era and the changing geopolitical landscape of Eurasia.

As to the future, the thoughts and actions of Ukrainian leaders concerning national security will benefit from the experience gained since 1991. Their main effort will be oriented toward gaining economic security while reducing their military establishment to prudent defense levels, and while maintaining the internal political stability needed for modernization of political institutions and for other important reforms. "The major security challenge for Ukraine seems to be that it has to do all these things at once, in extremely fluid circumstances that make each task logically contingent on the solution of the others."[40]

Notes

1. The author's father, Bohdan Krawciw, a Ukrainian poet and writer, frequently talked about the Galician autonomy under Austria-Hungary as compared to the rather authoritarian rule over Galicia by Poland between 1921 and 1939. As an ardent Ukrainian nationalist Bohdan Krawciw became a member of the OUN in the 1920s and 1930s and was imprisoned a number of times by Polish authorities. Later, as the OUN adopted a more radical ultranationalistic approach in its policy and politics, he broke away from it, suffering personal hardships in consequence. During an in-depth discussion of that period with the author in 1971, Bohdan Krawciw mentioned that some of the OUN's political theory bordered on fascism. Like many western Ukrainians and Poles who lived through that period, he harbored no enmity against the people of the opposing nation.

2. Nikolai Kulinich, "Ukraine in the New Geopolitical Environment: Issues of Regional and Subregional Security," in *The Making of Foreign Policy in Russia and the New States of Eurasia,* ed. Adeed Dawisha and Karen Dawisha (Armonk, NY: M.E. Sharpe, 1995) pp. 113–39.

3. When Gorbachev shut down the Communist Party in the Soviet Union, he eliminated the governing control infrastructure of Soviet society. Previously, when the Communist Party was strong, the party officials as well as the party and nonparty members of

the state apparatus, or nomenklatura as all of them were called, simply carried out the will of the party's Politburo. The nomenklatura, as such, had no vision, will, or direction of its own. But it did have administrative control and great privileges. After the demise of the Soviet Union, a large segment of that huge bureaucracy is opposing change while still clinging to its positions, benefits, and functions. In Ukraine, part of the nomenklatura, which includes the bureaucracies of the large military-industrial complexes and the coal mines in the Donbas region (eastern Ukraine), refuses to carry out orders of the government or obey the laws promulgated by the parliament. It also opposes reform and has significant political influence because most of its members belong to the communist or socialist blocs or parties. As a result, very little gets accomplished.

4. Sherman Garnett, "The Sources and Conduct of Ukrainian Nuclear Policy: November 1992 to January 1994," in *The Nuclear Challenge in Russia and the New States of Eurasia,* ed. George Quester (Armonk, NY: M.E. Sharpe, forthcoming). In this excellent treatise on Ukrainian nuclear policy, Sherman Garnett also analyzes Ukraine's security policy orientations. He states, "The great danger is not that Russians and Ukrainians cannot live together, but rather that conflicting economic and political interests will politicize ethnicity and bring an ethnic dimension to the current internal crisis."

5. Ibid. Garnett calls this Ukrainian orientation toward Russia "accommodationist." He calls the orientation that favors a strong national armed force, retention of nuclear weapons, disengagement from the CIS, and closer links with the West "nationalist." His full discussion of these orientations and their fluidity is well worth reading.

6. Karen Dawisha and Bruce Parrott, *Russia and the New States of Eurasia: Politics of Upheaval* (New York: Cambridge University Press, 1994), p. 71.

7. Ilya Prizel, "The Influence of Ethnicity on Foreign Policy: The Case of Ukraine," in *National Identity and Ethnicity in Russia and the New States of Eurasia,* ed. Roman Szporluk (Armonk, NY: M.E. Sharpe, 1994), p. 109; also pp. 105–14. Also see his in-depth discussion of the Ukrainian-Polish relationship, pp. 4–21.

8. Ibid., pp. 104–5.

9. For a more complete presentation of all military aspects of Ukraine's July 1990 declaration of state sovereignty, see John Jaworsky, *The Military-Strategic Significance of Recent Developments in Ukraine,* Project Report 645 (Ottawa: Department of National Defense, Operational Research and Analysis, 1993), p. 79.

10. Kulinich, "Ukraine in the New Geopolitical Environment," pp. 113–39. Kulinich states that the history and advantages of neutrality were being studied by Ukrainians in 1990, well before full independence.

11. Taras Kuzio, *Ukrainian National Security Policy* (a very comprehensive, soon-to-be published manuscript). See especially chapter 2, "Domestic Sources of Security Policy."

12. The author had lengthy discussions on this subject in the fall of 1991 with a number of key players on the Ukrainian scene. Among them were Vasyl' Durdynets, at that time chairman of the Rada's Committee on Defense and Security; Ievhen Marchuk, Ukraine's minister of security and head of the National Security Service (successor to the KGB in Ukraine); Bohdan Havrylyshyn, director of the International Management Institute in Geneva, Switzerland, and chairman of the International Renaissance Foundation in Kiev.

13. Jaworsky, *Military-Strategic Significance of Recent Developments in Ukraine,* p. 80.

14. Ibid., p. 82. Jaworsky shows that Ukraine inherited from the Soviet Union twenty tank and motorized infantry divisions, one air assault division, one coast guard division, three artillery divisions, a large number of special units, and four air armies, representing about a quarter of the air asset holdings of the Soviet Union.

15. The author participated in the Switzerland portion of this trip and later, in January 1992, monitored the mentioned discussions of the Rada.

16. The author developed the requested concept and delivered it through Bohdan

Havrylyshyn to the Ukrainians at the end of November 1992. This concept was accepted by Marchuk and Durdynets during discussions with the author in January 1993. The concept for the new institute included Ukrainian and Western scholars and a board of directors who were prominent Ukrainians and Westerners but not high governmental officials. This action resulted in the establishment of the International Institute on Global and Regional Security (IIGRS). Its director is Dmitri Vydrin and its executive director is Leonid Tupchienko.

17. Konstantyn Morozov, "Current Ukrainian Military Policy and Issues in Its Formulation" a paper presented at the colloquium on "The Military Tradition in Ukrainian History: Its Role in the Construction of Ukraine's Armed Forces," sponsored by the Ukrainian Research Institute, Harvard University, and the Institute for National Security Studies, National Defense University, Cambridge, MA, 12 May 1994.

18. Ibid.

19. See the chapter by Taras Kuzio in this volume.

20. Roy Allison, *Military Forces in the Soviet Successor States*, Adelphi Paper 280 (London: International Institute for Strategic Studies, 1993), p. 41.

21. Ibid., p. 43. Also, the author had many discussions about all this with General Vadim Grechaninov and with members of his staff.

22. Ihor Derkach mentioned this problem to the author during one of their periodic meetings in Kiev in 1992. Also see Allison, *Military Forces in the Soviet Successor States*, p. 39.

23. Morozov, "Current Ukrainian Military Policy."

24. Discussion in Kiev, at the end of May 1992, between Ievhen Marchuk and three American members of the board of directors of the IIGRS (see note 16): John W. Nicholson, George Williams, and Nicholas Krawciw.

25. During the spring and summer of 1992, the author had a number of discussions concerning Ukrainian security policy and nuclear issues with Mykola Mykhalchenko, President Kravchuk's political advisor. Also Dmitri Vydrin, director of IIGRS, commissioned a poll in the fall of 1992 that showed that popular opinion in Ukraine was shifting toward a more hawkish line over nuclear weapons.

26. Coordination between ministries in Kiev in 1992 was nearly nonexistent. The author heard frequent complaints of nonsupport by officials from one ministry talking about another.

27. Volodymyr Selivanov, "National Security: The Guarantee of Independent Ukraine's Existence," interview by Viktor Korobkov, *Army of Ukraine*, no. 7 (May 1993), pp. 19–28.

28. See, for example, Stephen E. Miller, "The Case Against a Ukrainian Nuclear Deterrent," *Foreign Affairs*, vol. 72, no. 3 (summer 1993); or Bruce G. Blair, *The Logic of Accidental Nuclear War*, (Washington DC: Brookings Institution, 1993).

29. Selivanov, "National Security," p. 22.

30. John Baker of the Atlantic Council in Washington, DC, organized an internship in Washington for nine or ten Ukrainians from the Rada's Standing Committee on Defense and National Security and the Ministries of Defense and Finance. Ian Brzezinski and the author assisted in this effort in Kiev. The author provided General Lopata sample budget presentation models.

31. The author attended a number of discussions with Borys Tarasiuk in 1992 and 1993. The IIGRS conference series with the Russian Institute on Europe is attended by many prominent scholars, government officials, and politicians on both sides; four have been held so far, providing an informal forum for dialogue between Russia and Ukraine. Borys Tarasiuk and the author attended most of these conferences.

32. See the chapter by Taras Kuzio in this volume.

33. Russia, Ukraine, and the United States signed an agreement on 13 January 1994 in Moscow for the dismantlement and shipment to Russia of Ukraine's entire nuclear arsenal of 176 former Soviet nuclear missiles and 1,804 warheads. Under the agreement, Russia is obligated to provide Ukraine with nuclear fuel rods containing 100 tons of uranium for Ukrainian nuclear power plants. The United States will buy 500 metric tons of highly enriched uranium from Russia for $11.9 billion over the next twenty years for reprocessing into low-enriched uranium fuel rods and sale around the world. For greater detail, see *Washington Post*, 15 January 1994, p. A15.

34. The author met with General Radets'kyi a number of times during that visit and took him on a tour of West Point.

35. *Svoboda* (Jersey City, NJ), 21 May 1994.

36. *Svoboda*, 18 June 1994.

37. *Ukrainian Weekly* (Jersey City, NJ), 5 June 1994.

38. The author accompanied Minister Radets'kyi on his U.S. tour, 14–19 June 1994.

39. *Ukrainian Weekly*, 11 September 1994.

40. Comment of Bruce Parrott on an earlier draft of this chapter. I am grateful to Professors Bruce Parrott and Karen Dawisha for their encouragement and assistance in this project. This soldier needed it.

8

Ukrainian Civil-Military Relations and the Military Impact of the Ukrainian Economic Crisis

Taras Kuzio

The election of Leonid Kuchma as president of Ukraine on 10 July 1994 ended the post-Soviet transition period associated with Leonid Kravchuk, who had been elected on the same day that Ukraine's December 1991 referendum indicated 90 percent support for independence from the former USSR. President Kravchuk had played a key role in arranging the meeting of the heads of state of the three East Slavic former republics—Russia, Belarus, and Ukraine—that led to the disintegration of the former USSR and its replacement by the Commonwealth of Independent States (CIS). It was also Ukraine's drive to nationalize all former Soviet security forces on its territory that initiated the disruption of the former Soviet armed forces.

The role of civic groups and the politicization of civil-military relations are likely to grow if the new president, elected with only a slim 6 percent majority, attempts to fundamentally change Ukraine's geopolitical orientation. After the Massandra Russian-Ukrainian summit in September 1993, Kuchma was accused of having "sold out" to Russia, leading to rumors of a coup d'état by military officers. Kuchma's alleged "pro-Russian" orientation has already brought assassination threats by the Union of Ukrainian Officers (SOU) and military intelligence.[1]

It is perhaps not coincidental that Kuchma asserted his control over the armed forces by appointing a civilian defense minister on 26 August 1994. The new defense minister, Deputy Premier Valerii Shmarov, is a close Kuchma ally from the military-industrial complex and the National Space Agency. The first civilian defense minister in the former USSR, Shmarov stated that "a civilian minister must resolve political issues, international issues, economic issues, integrating the armed forces and industry."

Civil-military relations have played and will continue to play an influential role in the formulation of Ukrainian security policy. Public opinion, for example, played a significant part in forging the hardline position on nuclear weapons by the Ukrainian leadership, in contrast to positions on nuclear weapons in both Kazakhstan and Belarus.[2] Nevertheless, as in Soviet times, the public is largely divorced from national security issues, which are still broadly perceived as the prerogative of the elite. Although the armed forces are held in widespread esteem due to a combination of both Soviet propaganda concerning the "Great Patriotic War" and Ukrainian nationalism, the armed forces and the threats that they are meant to defend against are not regarded as a priority by the average person on the street. The public continues to perceive questions of economics and law and order as those of primary importance, in contrast to nationalistic symbols, something reflected in the 1994 election results.

There is a plethora of civic groups that have a stake in the domestic debate on security policy in Ukraine and the sources of external and domestic threats. Many of the civic groups that are active in the armed forces are a double-edged sword. On the one hand, they are welcome as an invaluable source of support for molding the inherited *Homo Sovieticus* into the armed forces of the newly independent Ukrainian state with its own myths and symbols. But on the other hand, they are a source of politicization of the officer corps, agitating against "pro-Russian" or "treasonous" decisions by the country's political leadership.

Ukrainian political parties and civic groups are often interconnected through the media and membership in the armed forces, acting as a "watchdog" over the Ukrainian leadership's perception and defense of the country's national interests. Any lurch too far in a pro-Russian direction or toleration of regional separatism that would be perceived as a threat to Ukraine's independence and territorial integrity could lead to intervention in domestic politics by military and civic groups.

The failure to implement economic reform, mismanagement of the economy, and Russian economic pressure have created a severe socioeconomic crisis in Ukraine. This has had a negative effect on military reform, discipline, morale, and combat readiness, while giving greater public support to paramilitary and secessionist groups that thrive in times of crisis. Can the armed forces fulfill the role they are entrusted with? Or will this role increasingly be given over by default to paramilitary nationalist and specialist forces?

This chapter will survey civil-military relations in Ukraine before and after the disintegration of the former Soviet Union (FSU). It will cover the multitude of civic and paramilitary groups and their relation to the military authorities, as well as survey the role of public opinion and public threat perceptions in the formulation of Ukrainian security policy. Civil-military relations will also be discussed with regard to the growing domestic threat of separatism,[3] especially in the Crimea.

The second half of the chapter will deal with the impact of the economic crisis in a number of military realms: Ukraine's inability to absorb its Soviet military inheritance; financial and social problems; professional training and the provision of spare parts; low prestige of the armed forces; and officer loyalty and morale. Finally, the chapter will point to the impact of the economic crisis on Ukraine's military plans, combat readiness, and ability to implement planned reforms.

Civil-Military Relations Prior to the Disintegration of the FSU

The campaign to launch separate Ukrainian armed forces was begun in Ukraine in autumn 1989 by radical right nationalist groups, especially, but not exclusively, in western Ukraine. When nationalist groups first espoused such radical demands they were criticized as "provocative" by leading democratic figures, such as the writer and poet Ivan Drach.[4]

Between 1989 and 1991, the demands espoused by these small nationalist groups were first taken up by mainstream opposition groups, such as the Ukrainian Popular Movement, Rukh, and the Ukrainian Helsinki Union (renamed the Ukrainian Republican Party [URP] in April 1990) and later even by the national communist wing of the nomenklatura. Within ten months, these demands were included in the 16 July 1990 Declaration of Republican Sovereignty. Fourteen months later, Ukraine declared independence and began to launch its own armed forces in the face of opposition from Moscow.

Historical experience supported the nationalist demand for separate armed and security forces, a demand that was echoed by a wide spectrum of public opinion, democratic opposition, and the national communist nomenklatura. Andrii Haisins'kyi, a commander in the National Guard, pointed out that "from history we know that the UNR [Ukrainian National Republic], Sub-Carpathian Rus' and the western UNR were broken up precisely because they did not solve the crucial question—they did not form their own army." Another author pointed to the "need to prevent a Ukrainian repeat of 1920."[5]

In addition to the need to avoid repeating historical mistakes, two other arguments were mustered in favor of separate Ukrainian armed forces. First, a sense of urgency pervaded the state-building process due to the widely held fear that this was the last chance, after repeated failures and centuries of Russification and ethnocide, to achieve an independent state. Second, the need for a separate armed forces and the urgency of state-building were a direct outgrowth of the perceptions of threat within the loose and uneasy alliance of anticommunist groups and national communists that had propelled Ukraine to independence in late 1991. This perception of threat toward the state and nation was directed at Russia, a threat brought sharply into focus by its demands for border changes almost immediately after Ukraine declared independence on 24 August 1991.

The launching of the Ukrainian armed forces after the Declaration of Independence, therefore, did not occur within a vacuum. Democratically controlled councils elected in March 1990 and the Ukrainian parliament under Leonid

Kravchuk's chairmanship from July 1990 to August 1991 had already outlined the legal and intellectual basis for Ukraine's right to possess separate security forces.

On 30 July 1990, the Ukrainian parliament adopted a resolution that called for Ukrainian conscripts to serve only in Ukraine, while on 10 October 1990 another resolution demanded that all Ukrainian conscripts currently serving outside the republic be allowed to return to serve in Ukraine. This demand referred particularly to Ukrainian conscripts serving in "hot spots" of ethnic conflict and was supported by the activities of the Association of Independent Ukrainian Youth (SNUM) aimed at preventing conscripts from being sent to serve outside the republic,[6] activities that were repeatedly condemned by the Soviet military press.[7]

But one commentator at the time noted that "Unfortunately, the mechanism for fulfilling these decrees was not made. The decision remained on paper."[8] In addition, then parliamentary chairman Kravchuk, always the cautious politician, was still uncommitted to separate armed forces and was unwilling to undermine the authority of the Soviet armed forces.[9] Nevertheless, the demands raised in these parliamentary resolutions have since become widely accepted in the public mind and have an impact on Ukrainian security policy. If Ukraine joins the Commonwealth of Independent States (CIS) Treaty on Collective Security, like the more conservative and less independence-minded Belarus, Kiev is likely to refuse to allow its armed forces to be deployed outside the republic (Ukrainians serving in the Black Sea fleet were withdrawn from intervention in the Georgian civil war in the summer of 1993).[10]

By early 1991, "in parliament, and not only in Ukraine, as well as in the mass media there [was] an ongoing discussion of the idea of forming republican armed forces."[11] The repressive actions of the Soviet authorities against national movements in Tbilisi, Baku, Vilnius, and Riga also swelled the ranks of those clamoring for separate security forces that would defend the local population against Moscow and protect the republic's sovereignty and territorial integrity. Vladimir Gryniov, a Russian from Kharkiv who was then second deputy chairman of parliament, argued that these acts of repression "showed that the general sovereignty of any republic can be asserted and the rights of its citizens defended only if we have our own army."[12]

Civic and informal groups also took the lead in developing another theme that has since become widely accepted, namely, that one of the necessary attributes of an independent state is an army. In the words of Levko Luk'ianenko, then leader of the URP, "If a state has its own independent external and domestic policies, armed forces, financial-monetary system independent from foreign forces, and law enforcement organs, then it is independent; without these it is colony, a dependent territory, a protectorate."[13]

In addition to parliament and the democratically controlled councils,[14] civic groups were also highly active in propagating the concept of separate security forces. These civic groups, such as the Committee of Soldiers' Mothers (KSM),

Rukh's Military Collegium, and even Afghanistan veterans' groups, helped publicize the brutality of life for conscripts in the Soviet armed forces, while the democratically-controlled councils even gave refuge to deserters. This brutality was often seen as having ethnic overtones, as Ukrainian conscripts were subjected to abuse by Russian officers or were killed in interethnic conflicts that were not Kiev's business.[15]

These cases of brutality, repression, poor service conditions, and suspicious deaths were widely publicized in the *samvydav* (samizdat) press, in the independent newspapers established by democratically controlled councils,[16] and at conferences.[17] Democratically controlled councils in western Ukraine even formed their own municipal police, many of whom were Afghan veterans.[18] They not only encouraged desertion but applied greater pressure for conscripts to be allowed to undertake their military service in Ukraine while increasing public hostility to all-union institutions, such as the Soviet armed forces, and Moscow's rule.

The Civic Committee for the Revival of a Ukrainian National Army (HKVUNA) was established in Lviv in February 1990 with its own newspaper, *Kris*. The HKVUNA united under its wing the entire range of civic groups that backed its aims (the KSM, Rukh, Memorial, the URP, the Greens, the Ukrainian language society Prosvita, youth groups, the Association of Ukrainian Women, and other anticommunist political parties). Through meetings, its newspaper, and the media, the HKVUNA supported deserters from the Soviet armed forces, publicized incidents of brutality, attacked Marxist "indoctrination" in the Soviet army, and demanded the removal of Ukrainians from "hot spots" outside Ukraine. Reflecting the radicalism of its leaders, the HKVUNA joined the Interparty Assembly, forerunner of the Ukrainian National Assembly (UNA), a radical alternative to more mainstream democratic groups.[19]

The inaugural congress of the KSM, held in September 1990 in Zaporizhzhia focused on three issues: the fate of conscripts in hot spots outside Ukraine, their use in construction battalions (*stroibaty*), and prosecution of officers who caused the death of conscripts.[20] It also demanded that KKSM members be included as advisors within military commissariats in order to ensure the implementation of the parliamentary resolutions on military affairs, the revival of Ukrainian military traditions, and the proper classification of conscripts who left their military units as "runaways," not "deserters."[21] The KSM also helped to hide "runaways" from eastern Ukraine within the democratically controlled oblasts of western Ukraine.[22]

During the second half of 1990 and first half of 1991, Rukh and all the other newly established political parties included sections devoted to military affairs and demands for separate armed forces within their programs.[23] The culmination of this campaign was the widely publicized two-week hunger strike in Kiev in October 1990 by students; one of their six demands included the right to undertake military service within Ukraine. Kiev Marine School cadets supported the students and prevented the militia from undertaking any repressive acts against them. The Ukrainian parliamentary resolution of 17 October 1990 accepted the student demands, which ended the hunger strike.[24]

But the opposition was not united, and two strands developed over military policy during this period. The radical nationalists openly supported desertion and refusal to serve in the Soviet armed forces, while the moderate democrats argued only for the right of conscripts to serve in Ukraine. The HKVUNA advised conscripts to refuse the draft on the basis of their citizenship in the occupied Ukrainian National Republic (the 1949 Geneva Convention outlaws forcible conscription into the ranks of the occupying army).[25]

Radical nationalists also argued that the disintegration of the Soviet armed forces into republican armies would prevent civil war. Other demands raised by the HKVUNA (the majority of which have since been implemented) included a Ministry of Defense, a law on alternative service, the right of servicemen to religious instruction, nationalization of military academies, reorganization of the Ministry of Interior Troops into a National Guard, banning of the Communist Party from the armed forces, and social-legal guarantees for servicemen.

The demands for a total boycott of Soviet conscription did not achieve such popularity as in the Baltic republics. Whereas 87 percent of Lithuanians supported the draft boycott, only 31 percent of Ukrainians did so: "For many Lithuanians, serving in the Soviet army was seen as serving in an army of occupation, while the Russians and Ukrainians were more likely to perceive the Soviet armed forces as being their own."[26]

This problem of Ukraine's "two faces" with regard to the Soviet legacy and relations with Russia has bedeviled Ukraine since 1993, as reflected in the results of the parliamentary and presidential elections in 1994. The Baltic approach would have worked in western Ukraine, but not central and eastern Ukraine, which had been under tsarist-Soviet rule for centuries and was a founding republic of the FSU. The Baltic zero option of rejecting all the Soviet inheritance, including the military, on its territory at the time of independence would have created the potential for "Trans-Dniester Republics" to be created by the former Soviet military in areas of southern and eastern Ukraine, where large numbers of Russians lived. In addition, nationalizing all the conventional armed forces in Ukraine neutralized any potential threat they may have posed to the newly independent state, both domestically and externally, because such an action broke the back of the Soviet military.

Civil-Military Relations in Independent Ukraine

The growing chorus of Ukrainian demands for separate armed forces and hostility toward all-union structures undoubtedly played a role in the disintegration of the former Soviet armed forces, as most visibly seen in their failure to act to support the coup d'état in August 1991. The Ukrainian drive to establish separate armed forces between mid-1991 and mid-1992 was a highly popular move, backed by all of Ukraine's political parties and civic groups and the newly elected president and parliament (the Communist Party of Ukraine [CPU] was banned between August 1991 and October 1993).[27]

The nationalization of all Soviet conventional forces on Ukrainian territory was undertaken relatively quickly and without conflict (except in the case of the Black Sea fleet). Besides the factors previously outlined, the motive behind this action was to prevent another pro-Soviet/Russian coup d'état—a military rebellion along the lines of that undertaken in Moldova by the Soviet (from April 1992, Russian) Fourteenth Army—and thereby neutralize or remove any domestic threats to Ukrainian independence.

Other factors contributing to the successful nationalization of the former Soviet armed forces were the lack of any ethnic conflicts in the republic at the time of independence (unlike Moldova or Transcaucasia), a large number of Ukrainian officers (unlike most other former Soviet republics apart from Russia), the willingness of Russian or Belarusian officers to take the loyalty oath of a fellow Slavic republic, and the removal of the CPU from control of the military.

Since the successful takeover of the former Soviet armed forces on Ukrainian territory, civil-military relations in Ukraine have become politicized, especially at times of crisis (e.g., negotiations over the Black Sea fleet, elections, and in response to Russian territorial claims). Seventy percent of military officers often think about political problems—only enterprise directors have a higher figure.[28] The armed forces also have the highest public support of any state institution; only the Church comes a close second, with 69 percent.[29]

But civilian and military priorities are divided at a time of acute economic crisis in Ukraine. During the 1994 parliamentary and presidential elections, the two most acute voter concerns were the economy and crime. The Soviet inheritance is reflected in the widespread aloofness of the majority of the population from foreign and military affairs, regarded traditionally as areas exclusively the preserve of the elite. Although the threat of Crimean secessionism may be of acute concern to the president, the parliament, and the armed forces, it is much lower on the list of priorities for the person on the street than the economic crisis and declining living standards.

Sixty-five percent of Ukrainians believe that the only force capable of guaranteeing law and order is the armed forces (reflecting the low public status of the militia). But 89 percent of officers believe that their main function is also to protect the territorial integrity of the Ukrainian state[30] (in comparison to only 9 percent of the population who believe that this should be a first priority of the state).[31] Newly elected President Kuchma has placed greater emphasis on the economy and law and order, but, coming from the military-industrial complex, he is unlikely to neglect the military. Ukraine's armed forces, launched at the same time as independence was gained, therefore have a natural raison d'être— the preservation of the state's independence.

In order to defend the independence of the state, it has been necessary to imbue the Ukrainian armed forces with the "ideology of statehood" as the "only priority and object of defense against internal and external enemies." This policy, which to some degree would be pursued in any newly independent state, was constantly criticized by radical left political parties (communists and socialists) who were opposed to anti-Russian, Ukrainian nationalism and were motivated by the hope that the armed forces of the former USSR would join together again within the CIS.

That an independent state cannot exist without its own armed forces is a fact widely accepted within Ukrainian society. The Ukrainian military, in comparison to Russian armed forces, is therefore more politically bipartisan, although civic groups such as the Union of Ukrainian Officers (SOU) have closer ties and sympathies to national democratic and nationalist groups and parties (as opposed to the radical left or liberal democrats, both groups that backed Kuchma for president).[32]

At the same time, nearly 54 percent of civilian respondents believed that a violent conflict similar to that which took place in Moscow in September–October 1993 could occur in Ukraine.[33] This figure could increase with the election of Kuchma, whose support for economic reform is likely to bring him into conflict with the left-wing bloc in parliament, which is in favor of a weak presidency. Civic groups and political parties with a stake in the national security debate will also continue to act as a watchdog over the ability or willingness of Ukraine's leadership to deal with perceived internal and external threats. Ironically, former President Kravchuk will also adopt a similar role (as well as that of the nation's grand elder statesman).

The aloofness of the Ukrainian military from direct involvement in the domestic political process, which distinguished Ukraine from Russia until late 1993, could change with the election of Kuchma. All the civic groups and political parties with a stake in civil-military relations voted for the incumbent, President Kravchuk. Kuchma won with a small majority, based primarily in eastern and southern Ukraine, which would not allow him to drastically alter Ukraine's geopolitical balance between Europe and Eurasia. Any attempt to move Ukraine too close to Russia and the CIS would generate domestic instability and sharpen regional divisions. It also would increase the potential for a military coup d'état and paramilitary action, which until now have been relatively unlikely.

The presidential vote clearly reflected how Ukraine is equally divided between its northern and western regions, including Kiev (which voted for Kravchuk), and its southern and eastern areas, including the Crimea (which voted for Kuchma). If Kuchma strays from his predecessor's path of carefully balancing eastern and western Ukrainian interests, which are radically different concerning the question of foreign orientation, then the growth of regional separatism could become dangerous. Residents of the Donbas and the Crimea do not regard Russia as a threat and harbor positive views of their northern and eastern neighbor. Whereas 32 percent of Ukrainian citizens generally believed that conflict with Russia was likely, this figure varied sharply from region to region. Only 18 percent in the Donbas region of eastern Ukraine and the Crimea believed that conflict with Russia was likely, which is in sharp contrast to 79 percent in western Ukraine.[34]

Kuchma's initial support for federalization, dual state languages (Russian and Ukrainian), dual citizenship, lease of Sevastopol and other naval bases to Russia, as well as a treaty relationship with the Crimea, are all positions that are hotly opposed by civic groups such as the SOU and large elements of the officer corps within the armed forces and National Guard. If these policies are pursued, the military, whose major raison d'être is defense of Ukraine's independence and territorial integrity, and paramilitary groups could be drawn into the domestic political process, with dangerous ramifications (in the same manner as parts of the Soviet armed forces were drawn into supporting the August 1991 coup d'état in an attempt to forestall the collapse of the former USSR).

Ukrainian armed forces do not suffer from an "Afghan syndrome," as do their Russian counterparts, except in their unwillingness to undertake military missions outside Ukraine. Ukraine's profession of neutrality is oriented primarily against Russian pressure to join the CIS Treaty on Collective Security established in the summer of 1992; it is not oriented against joining Western structures such as NATO's Partnership for Peace (PfP). The latter is the most popular option among officers, because even NATO membership is considered preferable to the CIS Treaty on Collective Security.[35] Although the idea of a CIS economic union has grown in popularity as the economic crisis has escalated, military and political integration with Russia in the CIS remains unpopular.[36]

Ukrainian leaders have espoused the necessity of departicization, the effort to remove the influence of political parties from the armed forces. In 1992 this policy was directed primarily against the communists and pro-Soviet elements in the military. But, at the same time, the military cannot become completely depoliticized: "the army cannot stay on the sidelines of processes that are taking place in the country, remaining a passive observer of conflict situations."[37] "In the event of domestic or external conflict, the military should stand on the side of the constitutional authorities and state interests—not the interests of political forces," Colonel Vitalii Chechylo, a leading military author, points out. In his view, this would be best achieved by civilian control of the Ministry of Defense (which newly elected Kuchma has undertaken). "To attempt to achieve the complete depoliticization of the army is not possible; but it is imperative that it be fully departicized," the same author argues.

If the armed forces were to become completely depoliticized, they could begin to act as an independent force with their own political agenda or support a particular political party, a danger that Ukrainian authors are aware of. But the military will have to tread a fine line if the political leadership of Ukraine is perceived as "treasonous" with regard to its two sacred objectives (defense of the country's independence and maintenance of territorial integrity), a possibility that exists with the election of Kuchma. The leadership of the armed forces supports in principle a democratic polity. But in the event of widespread internal threats of secessionism or growing external threats (for example, the election of Aleksandr Rutskoi as Russia's next president), or a combination of the two, the armed forces could intervene with the support of nationalist parties to establish an authoritarian state "in the national interest."

The dividing line between departicization and depoliticization is a fine one, however. Although the SOU is a registered civic group, it has been accused of adopting the role of a political party and even a "war party," leading to calls for it to be made illegal. Members of the SOU argue that it is not a political party because it does not seek power (although seven members were elected in the 1994 parliamentary elections).[38] "But that does not mean," according to Oleksandr Skipalskyj, then head of the SOU, "that the army and the SOU, which some would like to be the case, should be indifferent toward the fact as to in whose hands power lies."[39] The SOU therefore will be closely monitoring Kuchma's policies concerning questions of national security.

During the election campaigns it proved difficult to separate the armed forces from the political campaigns, and debates raged across Ukraine in the spring and summer of 1994. In nearly half of the voting districts in the Carpathian military district, both civilians and military servicemen voted together. The military authorities also had to attempt to prevent election speeches by candidates that were not cleared with them beforehand.[40]

At a meeting of the Ministry of Defense collegium on 29 April 1994, General Major Volodymyr Petenko, a former presidential military advisor, asked the generals who were present to collect signatures within the armed forces in support of Kravchuk, to ensure his place in the presidential elections on 26 June 1994 (candidates required one hundred thousand signatures to be registered). Yet there were also six other presidential candidates.[41] Defense Minister Vitalii Radets'kyi also called upon the armed forces to vote for Kravchuk (one factor that contributed to his dismissal in August 1994).

Officer Loyalty and Inculcation of Patriotic Values

In January 1992, President Leonid Kravchuk ordered all conventional military officers in Ukraine to take the oath of loyalty to the newly independent state. The majority of officers agreed to do so for a variety of reasons, not all patriotic. The remainder were initially allowed to stay in the armed forces, although they were not given appointments or work of a highly classified nature.[42] In order to appease the large number of non-Ukrainian officers and in line with the Ukrainian policy of not building a narrow ethnic state, the loyalty oath refers only to the "peoples of Ukraine," not the Ukrainian nation.[43]

The SOU was one of the first to demand that those officers who had refused to take the oath be dismissed from the Ukrainian military. This view was backed by then Defense Minister Morozov six months later.[44] In February 1994, new Defense Minister Radets'kyi, also ordered all officers of the reserve who had not sworn allegiance to Ukraine to be struck off the military register. At the same time, Ukraine demanded that the strategic rocket forces take the oath; nine hundred out of twenty-three hundred officers refused to do so, together with one out of three top commanders. Those officers who refused to take the oath were repatriated to Russia.[45]

The remainder within the strategic rocket forces who took the Ukrainian oath of loyalty now take their orders directly from Kiev—not Moscow—and come under Ukraine's administrative control of its nuclear bases. The implications of this action are that Moscow has lost control over nuclear weapons in Ukraine (although operational capability remains in Russia's hands). Ukraine now has greater leverage to extract concessions for denuclearization as well as the ability to prevent Russia from firing nuclear weapons from Ukrainian soil without Kiev's authorization.

Although most of the officers took the Ukrainian loyalty oath, their motives for doing so have always been questionable, a factor contributing to Ukrainian insecurity. Hryhorii Omel'chenko told the fourth SOU congress that only 30 percent of officers were ready to defend Ukrainian independence. In a poll of officers in one military academy, only 8 percent responded positively to the question, "Are you ready to defend Ukraine with weapons in your hands?"[46] In another survey, 60 percent had taken the oath because of housing, the stable social situation, and access to foodstuffs.[47] Defense Minister Morozov complained that some officers had taken the oath believing that eventually the armed forces of Ukraine would be united again with Russia in the CIS (a belief that the SOU and other nationalist groups suspect Kuchma of supporting).

Although Ukraine was successful in nationalizing peacefully the former Soviet armed forces on its territory, it was faced with two problems, the first of which was to build loyalty to the newly independent state among the officer corps. The officers had been trained in Soviet and communist values, but Ukrainian authorities needed to forge a willingness on their part to defend Ukraine against external threats, one of which—Russia—was a country that Soviet nationality policy had constantly portrayed as Ukraine's ally, partner, and elder brother. The second problem was that the Ukrainian armed forces (like the education system) would henceforth need to be made channels for the Ukrainization of denationalized young conscripts.

The difficulties facing the Ukrainian authorities and their newly created Socio-Psychological Service could be seen in the effort to forge a new set of loyalties and myths around which to unite Ukrainians from different regions of the country with a variety of historical experiences. In answer to the question as to what traditions should be used to build the Ukrainian military, the majority of officers disagreed with using that of the nationalist Ukrainian Insurgent Army

(UPA) (although they did not voice explicit disapproval of its cultivation). In order of importance, Ukrainian officers upheld the use of the traditions of the Russian tsarist army, the Soviet armed forces, and the Cossacks.[48]

The UPA (and the Organization of Ukrainian Nationalists [OUN], its political arm) is a complicated and divisive legacy for the newly independent state and its armed forces to digest. The main area of UPA-OUN activity was western Ukraine, together with Kiev, and it was an object of constant condemnation and vilification by the Soviet authorities, who linked the UPA to émigré nationalists who "collaborated" with the Nazis and were then funded by Western espionage services against the USSR. Soviet officers were the target of much of this anti-nationalist propaganda, as were Ukrainian citizens themselves, especially in eastern Ukraine, where it often found fertile soil among the Russified population.

Ukraine lost six million people in World War II, and the country suffered heavily from the Nazi occupation. To convince the population that the UPA-OUN fought both the Nazi and Soviet occupiers of Ukraine will take persuasion and patience, not always virtues that nationalists possess. The Ministry of Defense newspaper, *Narodna armiia*, for example, plays a careful balancing act between publicizing the exploits of Soviet Ukrainian veterans and introducing the UPA-OUN legend, both of which are now used to educate Ukraine's conscripts and officers.

Seven decades of Soviet totalitarianism and communist indoctrination needed to be overcome to create a new Ukrainian soldier. The Socio-Psychological Service had to overcome decades, if not centuries, of denigration of the Ukrainian national idea and the right to independence, the falsification of its history, and the Russification of its language and culture. National heroes, which are now needed to build new myths and symbols for the newly independent state and armed forces, were castigated as "bandits and traitors to the people" in both tsarist and Soviet times.[49]

The task laid out for the Socio-Psychological Service and the SOU, which heavily dominated it, was to change these orientations toward Ukrainian national and military traditions. Besides inculcating Ukrainian patriotism and language into the nationalized former Soviet armed forces, the Socio-Psychological Service would also deal with morale, repression within the ranks, improving discipline, humanitarian support, and cultural-educational work.[50] In the Odessa military district, then commander (and later defense minister between October 1993 and August 1994) Radets'kyi admitted that "The role of the military-psychological department keeps growing. The Union of Ukrainian Officers and official organizations of the district work jointly to improve the combat readiness of the troops. I greatly respect the union and always try to help it."[51]

In these tasks, the Socio-Psychological Service utilizes not only the SOU but also leading nationalist thinkers such as Volodymyr Iavors'kyi,[52] the Cossacks, and civic groups, such as the Ukrainian-language society Prosvita. Because of their affiliation with the Ministry of Defense Socio-Psychological

Service, radical nationalistic thinkers, such as Iavors'kyi, actually have a wider readership and influence than otherwise would be the case. The service is therefore indispensable in promoting morale, fighting spirit, and discipline and in creating a historical-national framework for the armed forces and their principal role of defending Ukraine's independent statehood and territorial integrity.[53]

The Union of Ukrainian Officers

During late 1991 and early 1992, when the Ukrainian armed and security forces were launched, the bulk of the demands raised by civic groups such as the KSM, the HKVUNA, Rukh, and the SOU were implemented. Then parliamentary chairman Kravchuk had to co-opt the existing Kiev military district as his Ministry of Defense, although the loyalty of many of its staff was no doubt suspect. The Ukrainian leadership also had to rely during this uncertain period upon an alternative power structure at the local level for organizational and political support. This reliance on the SOU gave it an influence far greater than its membership would suggest.

In many ways, the SOU took over the functions of the former Main Political Administration (MPA) in the Soviet armed forces, and it has been criticized for resembling another "military party."[54] In early 1993, 155 communist and socialist deputies officially complained about the growing politicization of the SOU and its depiction of Russia as "the main enemy of Ukraine" (in actual fact, the SOU had always been a highly political body, with one foot in politics and another in the military).[55] In September 1993, the Board of the Ministry of Defense criticized statements by the SOU condemning the Massandra accords with Russia to divide the Black Sea fleet, which "prove that the union has been actually transformed into a political organization." Threats of dismissal from the armed forces were leveled against SOU members who signed the statements.[56]

The SOU gathered intelligence, particularly in hostile units such as the Black Sea fleet, conducted political campaigns, recommended personnel on the basis of their reliability and loyalty, propagandized Ukrainian military traditions, and helped draft laws. The SOU was therefore entrusted with organizing an alternative civil-military paradigm, working closely with the then defense minister, Morozov. The SOU was also heavily represented in the various military publications, such as the newspapers *Narodna armiia* (formerly *Leninskoe znamia* of the Kiev military district), *Ukrains'kyi flot* (Sevastopol), *Slovo i chest'* (Odessa), *Ukrains'ka armiia* (Liviv, formerly *Slava rodiny*), and the journals *Viis'ko Ukrainy* and *Surmach*.

The SOU was established at two congresses in July and November 1991, with the active support of the Military Collegium of Rukh and the Ukrainian Republican Party (URP). The demands of the SOU resembled those of other civic groups, such as HKVUNA. These demands included that the military be departicized, officers should take an oath of loyalty to Ukraine, that the draft should consist only of

Ukrainian citizens, that political officers should be forcibly retired, and that Ukrainian officers serving outside the republic should be financially helped to return to Ukraine. In addition, the SOU demanded the restructuring of the military-industrial complex, reform of the Ukrainian KGB as well as a legal framework for Ukrainian armed forces, and the creation of a National Security Council and Ukrainian Ministry of Defense. All of these demands were implemented by mid-1992.[57]

The SOU's demands became progressively more radical in the first year of independence. By the autumn of 1992, the SOU had swelled to seventy thousand members, making it the largest civic group in Ukraine (Rukh, the second largest, has fifty thousand).[58] In contrast to Russia's Union of Officers, which was always allied to the National Salvation Front on the radical right of Russian politics, the SOU maintained close ties to its original cofounders, center-right democratic groups (Rukh and the Congress of National Democratic Forces).[59] In addition, the SOU has no competitor among Ukrainian officers, except the Union of Officers in the Crimea (whose size is unknown), whereas in more denationalized Belarus, officers are divided between the (nationalist) Belarusian Association of Servicemen and the (pro-Russian) Union of Officers of Belarus.[60]

No such pro-Russian officers' union was formed in Ukraine, because its military policies destroyed the former Soviet armed forces in the winter of 1991–92, forcing officers to take the Ukrainian oath of loyalty. Any structure formed in opposition to this course of action, which the SOU backed, would have been quickly labeled "treasonous." In Belarus, a watered-down oath of loyalty was not administered until a year later than in Ukraine.

The SOU has always remained distrustful of the higher officer corps, where 70 percent of generals and 50 percent of the Ministry of Defense were Russian.[61] The SOU subjected the Ministry of Defense to a great deal of criticism over the slow pace of Ukrainization in society and the armed forces, the growth of organized crime, and the continued presence of officers who had refused to take the Ukrainian loyalty oath. Their demand for a Ukrainian naval command separate from the Black Sea fleet was heeded in April 1992, and administrative control by Ukrainian citizens over strategic nuclear weapons was implemented in the autumn of 1992. The SOU, as well as the SOU of the Ukrainian navy,[62] also remained strongly critical of Russian-Ukrainian agreements over the Black Sea fleet. "Antistate, anti-Ukrainian organizations, parties, and groups" in Ukraine in general should be banned, the SOU argued.[63]

The SOU was particularly influential within the Socio-Psychological Service and the Higher Attestation Commission[64] of the Ministry of Defense. The Socio-Psychological Service replaced many of the functions of the MPA.[65] Led until late 1993 by Major General Volodymyr Muliava,[66] a member of the SOU, the Democratic Party, and the Rukh Military Collegium, the service indeed co-opted some of the political officers from the MPA of the former Soviet armed forces.

The growing radicalism of the SOU was reflected in the demands and resolutions adopted at its fourth congress in April 1993, which was attended by then Defense Minister Morozov.[67] These included the cancellation of Ukraine's nuclear-free status, the creation of a strategic rocket command, the change of "Victory Day" to "Day in Memory of Victims of World War II," parliamentary recognition of nationalist groups from the 1940s, and the introduction of religious chaplains into the armed forces. The SOU also condemned Russian aggression in the Caucasus, criticized the head of the Government Committee for the Social Protection of Servicemen, and called for the amalgamation of the air force and air defense commands.

The SOU condemned the intelligence services for their lack of resolute action against external and internal enemies and demanded that they be subordinated directly to the president and defense minister. The SOU has also agitated against the CIS economic union and joined the Anti-Imperialist–Anti-Communist Front, established in the winter of 1992–93 to campaign against the revival of the CPU.[68]

The SOU has played a considerable role in unofficially aiding the central authorities where their position was weak. SOU members nationalized Black Sea fleet vessels and shore infrastructure in Mykolaiv Oblast to forestall their inclusion within the future division of the fleet between Ukraine and Russia. Whether these actions were undertaken with the consent of Kiev, or whether the government simply "turned a blind eye," is difficult to tell, but the outcome is undoubtedly welcomed by the Ukrainian authorities. Similarly, the first elected chairman of the Ukrainian Civic Committee of the Crimea, the only all-Crimean Ukrainian body established with Kiev's official financial support in October 1993, is Serhii Lytvyn, also head of the Crimean branch of the SOU.[69]

Hryhorii Omel'chenko, deputy chairman of the SOU and head of the Department to Combat Organized Crime and Corruption within the Security Service, helped establish the secret organization Anti-Mafia, which regularly publishes compromising materials on high-ranking officials in the media.[70] Despite the left-wing majority in the newly elected Ukrainian parliament and its past hostility toward the SOU, Omel'chenko's authority as a moral force campaigning against the mafia gave him the largest number of votes to head the parliamentary Committee Against Organized Crime and Corruption.[71]

At its sixth congress, in June 1994, the SOU intervened in the presidential elections by backing Kravchuk for the presidency and Volodymyr Cherniak, a member of Rukh, for the post of mayor of Kiev. A major area of discussion at the congress was the Crimean crisis. SOU delegates from the Crimea complained that the Ukrainian authorities were preventing the Ukrainian People's Self-Defense Forces (UNSO) and Ukrainian Cossacks from traveling to the peninsula while allowing free passage to Don Cossacks and the Union of Soviet Officers (an ally of the Union of Russian Officers of the Crimea). They demanded that the Ukrainian authorities "put a stop to a rampage of antistate forces in our country and uphold the territorial integrity and inviolability of Ukraine's borders." Demanding the withdrawal of Russian troops from Ukraine and discussion of

Russia's "anti-Ukrainian policy" in the United Nations Security Council, the SOU warned with an eye to the future that "We reserve the right to do our utmost to defend Ukraine's statehood from its enemies."

The SOU also discussed which candidates to support in the local elections on 26 June 1994, the further introduction of the Ukrainian language into the armed forces, and the social welfare of officers. In the words of Ivan Bilas, a National Guard officer, a member of the SOU and the Congress of Ukrainian Nationalists (KUN), and a newly elected deputy, "This congress could be our last if the organization does not unite its ranks around the idea of statehood and Ukrainian independence. The union should become a barrier to oppose socialism in the armed forces."[72]

In order not to be upstaged by the relationship between moderate democratic groups and the SOU, the Ukrainian National Assembly (UNA) established a Union of Ukrainian Officers in the Diaspora (SOUD) in June 1992 in Baku, led by Colonel Oleksandr Slusarev.[73] Between 300,000 and 400,000 Ukrainians served in the former Soviet armed forces outside Ukraine at the time of the FSU's disintegration. The SOUD demanded the creation of a State Committee and Fund to help facilitate the return of those officers who wished to do so (over half have returned to date). Many of the officers who are helped by the SOUD to return to Ukraine join the UNA and help train its paramilitary arm, the UNSO.[74]

Paramilitary Groups

A variety of paramilitary groups exist in Ukraine and play a role in its civil-military relations. The most visible example of this was the election of three members of the UNA-UNSO in the March–April 1994 parliamentary elections in Lviv and Ternopil' (one of whom, Oleh Vitovych, was elected leader of the UNA in August 1994). All three UNA-UNSO deputies have attended parliamentary sessions in their military fatigues. No Russian paramilitary groups exist in Ukraine, except in the Crimea, where they are supported logistically by the Don Cossacks, and by the Trans-Dniester Republic located in eastern Moldova.

Ukraine has six political parties on the radical right of its political spectrum: the Congress of Ukrainian Nationalists (KUN), the Ukrainian Conservative Republican Party (UKRP), the Union for Ukrainian State Independence (DSU), the Organization of Ukrainian Nationalists in Ukraine, the Social National Party of Ukraine, and the UNA. Only the KUN, the UKRP, and the UNA were able to obtain parliamentary representation, and only from western Ukraine (although the UNA also did well in Kiev). Together they have twelve seats in the new parliament. Although the main threat as perceived by these radical right groups is Russia, their xenophobic nationalism is directed against the majority of Ukraine's neighbors, who have historically harbored territorial claims. The radical right groups demand that Ukraine's borders include all of its "ethnographic territories," which would incorporate lands from Russia, Belarus, Poland, Slovakia, Romania, and Moldova.

The DSU has launched a paramilitary organization called Varta (Guard), though it is still in an embryonic stage, but only the UNA has developed a relatively large paramilitary arm, the UNSO.[75] The UNSO was formed after the failed coup d'état and declaration of Ukrainian independence in August 1991, with the initial noble aim of launching a partisan war in the event of Russian occupation. Since then, it has taken part in military engagements in the Trans-Dniester Republic, defending the Ukrainian population against Moldovan forces, and in Georgia against the Russian-backed Abkhaz separatists.

The UNSO has been deliberately careful not to brandish weapons publicly in Ukraine, although its members undoubtedly possess weapons from their military activities outside Ukraine, from sympathetic members of the security forces (including possibly SOU members), and through theft and purchase on the black market or from the military.[76] Besides the SOUD, the UNA-UNSO has also created both the Association of Manufacturers Engaged in the Sphere of National Security, to obtain political and financial support within Ukraine's large military-industrial sector, and the National Assembly of Labor, to create a popular electoral base and to apply pressure on the authorities through strikes and demonstrations.

Although the UNSO has been active against Russian, Romanian, and Ruthenian separatists in the Crimea, Chernivtsi, and Transcarpathia oblasts, respectively, it did not attempt to overthrow the authorities under former President Kravchuk, unlike its counterparts in the Transcaucasus. The Ukrainian historical fear of losing state independence is reflected in the concentration of UNSO activities against foreign or externally inspired threats (e.g., in the Crimea). But the UNSO and other paramilitary groups, who all voted for Kravchuk in the presidential elections, may have fewer reservations about undertaking action against Kuchma.

The UNSO would become increasingly active on the domestic front in the event of a breakdown of law and order, civil war, or secessionist armed rebellion. Thus far, the UNSO and similar radical right groups have not opposed the Ukrainian leadership by working for a military coup d'état. But if President Kuchma were to attempt to alter Ukraine's geopolitical orientation toward Russia or grant too many concessions to separatists, which the UNSO would regard as "treasonous," the threat of internal disorder and a military coup could grow.

Two other paramilitary forces in Ukraine include the All-Ukrainian UPA (Ukrainian Insurgent Army) Brotherhood and the All-Ukrainian Cossack Union (VUKS). The former unites veterans of the UPA and the Organization of Ukrainian Nationalists from the 1940s and 1950s, many of whom were imprisoned in the Soviet gulag. It held its first congress on 27 April 1991 in Lviv after being formed on 6 October 1990 in Ivano-Frankivs'k. The UPA Brotherhood cooperates most closely with the KUN and other anticommunist organizations while helping the SOU to propagate the memory of the nationalist struggle of the 1940s within the security force in military academies and the Socio-Psychological Service of the Ministry of Defense.[77]

The VUKS has always maintained close links with the same center-right democratic groups as the SOU, with which it is more likely to cooperate because the UNSO is regarded by a significant proportion of SOU members as "extremist."[78] The close links between the civil organization VUKS and the military were evident in the election of Major General Volodymyr Muliava, then head of the Socio-Psychological Service of the Ministry of Defense, who became Cossack hetman (chief) in late 1992. Many military officers are also members of the VUKS, and therefore there is undoubtedly overlap with the SOU.[79] The VUKS has fifteen thousand to twenty thousand members, slightly more than the UNSO, with its most radical branch in Volyn' Oblast.[80]

The VUKS held meetings with President Kravchuk and with the Ministry of Defense, the border troops, and the National Guard over cooperation in joint patrols against crime, incorporation of Cossack units, and transfer of facilities from the former DOSAAF (Union of Voluntary Societies for Cooperation with the Army, Air Force, and Navy, currently named the Society in Support of the Defense of Ukraine) to enable Cossacks to help prepare young people for conscription.[81] In August 1993, the VUKS was given the right to help patrol Ukraine's borders. Relations between Russian and Ukrainian Cossacks are poor in the Crimea and Donbas. High-level meetings have been held with the Kuban Cossack Host, a region populated by Ukrainian Cossacks after the destruction of their autonomous state in the eighteenth century, but overwhelmingly Russified since the 1930s.[82] Like the SOU, VUKS leader Major General Muliava told his members to vote for Kravchuk during the presidential elections. Tense relations will therefore exist between paramilitary groups and newly elected President Kuchma. The VUKS signed a statement with other national democratic parties in protest of Kuchma's inaugural speech, which "does not serve the goals of national accord." They warned that "If Mr. Kuchma supports the plans of Russia on turning the CIS into a single state, this would lead to the bloody conflict of war, since Ukraine is not going to voluntarily become part of a new empire."[83]

Civil-Military Relations and Ethnic Conflict

The former Soviet armed forces were nationalized without the ethnic conflict that has proved common to most other former Soviet republics (for example, Moldova and the Transcaucasus). Yet there does exist ethnic tension within the Ukrainian military and between Ukrainian civic groups and non-Ukrainians in the military.[84]

The SOU has demanded a veto in military appointments in order to replace Russians with Ukrainian officers. In the spring of 1993, the then head of the SOU, Omel'chenko, complained that 53 percent of officers in the Ukrainian military were from Russia. He also criticized the fact that the Russian language—not Ukrainian—still dominated the majority of military units.[85] In the same month as this complaint by Omel'chenko, at the fourth congress of the SOU the then Defense Minister Morozov issued an order whereby by the end of 1995 all military matters and communications will be conducted only in the Ukrainian language (which is unlikely to be accomplished).[86]

The growing economic crisis has exacerbated regionalism and separatism in Ukraine. The electorate in eastern and southern Ukraine is more likely to vote for candidates who put these regions' interests above national ones.[87] In an opinion poll in Kharkiv among seventeen- and eighteen-year-olds in 1994, the majority stated that they would change their negative attitude toward serving in the military if they were to serve in their oblast.[88] In a similar poll in the former Odessa military district, more than half of the soldiers questioned stated their desire to serve near home.[89]

The deep crisis in relations between the Crimean (autonomous) republic and Ukraine in the first half of 1994 also involved civil-military relations. The Crimean peninsula is highly militarized, with over fifty-one thousand Ukrainian security troops, double the number during the Soviet era. These include forces from the Ministry of Internal Affairs (MVS) (which includes the red-bereted Berkut riot police and black-bereted Spetsnaz state protection service), the army, the navy, the air defense forces, the air force, the Security Service (SBU), the border troops, and the National Guard.[90] In addition, the Black Sea fleet, theoretically under joint management but de facto under Russian control, has forty-eight thousand personnel in the Crimea and southern Ukraine.

In April 1994, President Iurii Meshkov, elected four months earlier on a separatist platform, attempted to wrest control of the MVS and the SBU from Kiev by appointing his own men to head these structures. Whereas the SBU remained loyal to Kiev, the MVS, with its large cache of weapons and two specialist elite units, is now divided in its loyalties between Kiev and Meshkov.[91] In addition, the restoration of the May 1992 Crimean constitution as a step toward secession was coupled with a resolution demanding that Crimean draftees be allowed to undertake their military service on the peninsula.[92]

Meshkov has demanded that Ukrainian military personnel be withdrawn from the Crimea and that its security be guaranteed by the Russian Black Sea fleet and the creation of a "Crimean republican guard." The Russian military leadership backs these demands by demanding the removal of the Ukrainian navy from the Crimea and the sole right to utilize the Sevastopol naval base. Meanwhile, Ukrainian and Tatar political and civic groups from the Crimea have picketed the Ukrainian parliament, demanding presidential rule, the abolition of Crimean autonomy, and the removal of all Russian armed forces from the peninsula.

At issue is the division of responsibilities between the Crimean and Ukrainian authorities. Whereas Ukraine argues that security questions cannot be delegated to a regional authority such as the Crimea, Meshkov points to the treaty signed between Tatarstan and the Russian Federation. Ukraine, however, is not a federal state (unlike Russia), while Tatarstan does not control its own foreign policy or state security, areas delegated to the federal Russian authorities.[93]

The officers of the Black Sea fleet have long played a political role by refusing to implement agreements between the Russian and Ukrainian presidents on a 50 : 50 division of the fleet, an act that should have been declared mutiny against the civil powers and their commanders in chief. The city council of Sevastopol held a public opinion poll on presidential election day on 26 June 1994 in which the question, "Are you in favor of the status of the city of Sevastopol as the main base of the Russian Federation Black Sea fleet, in accordance with the Russian-Ukrainian protocol dated 3 September 1993?" received a 90 percent endorsement. On 23 August 1994, the Sevastopol city council voted to recognize the former Russian parliament's jurisdiction and decision to grant it the status of a subject of the Russian Federation, a move condemned by the Ukrainian Justice Ministry. These moves are tantamount to direct interference by the civil authorities in military and foreign affairs.[94]

Finally, any conflict in the Crimea would inevitably drag in paramilitaries from Ukraine and Russia and the Muslim peoples of the North Caucasus. Russian Cossacks are already cooperating with the militia defending Crimean public buildings. The UNSO meanwhile has recruited volunteers for an "active holiday" in the Crimea during the summer of 1994 and has created a Crimean "military command" that would go into action in the event of conflict on the peninsula.[95]

Economic Crisis and the Military

Ukraine's severe socioeconomic crisis has placed a great strain on the operational effectiveness of the armed forces as well as its morale and discipline. In mid-February 1994, General Ivan Shtopenko admitted that the armed forces were hardly surviving financially. The Ministry of Defense had barely received 10 percent of funds allocated to it in 1994. Officers and their families were often living at subsistence levels, he claimed.[96]

The defense budgets in 1993 and 1994 were quite high as a proportion of the total budget (and thereby unsustainable in the medium and long term), but there was little left for procurement, research, and development. The bulk of the defense budget is apparently taken up by the social needs of officers and servicemen. Little is left over for training, new equipment, and maintenance. During 1992–94, the Ukrainian parliament adopted budgets that remained on paper. Nationalist and national democratic parties and civic groups clamored for a larger percentage of the budget to be allocated to security needs due to the perceived widespread external and domestic threats to the newly independent state.

Ukrainians' plans for military reform by the end of the decade are ambitious. Ukraine inherited three-quarters of a million servicemen in December 1991, which is to be reduced to a third of this figure by the year 2000. The armed forces, national guard, and border troops that will remain at the end of the decade are planned to serve on professional contract. These plans include seven to eight combined arms divisions, six to seven motorized rifle and tank brigades, six to seven artillery brigades, two to three army aviation brigades, four air force groups, sixteen naval squadrons, and naval aviation and coastal defenses with dozens of ships and upwards of forty thousand naval seamen. But these ambitious plans are dependent upon overcoming the socioeconomic crisis, obtaining Western aid, and clarifying the prevailing threat perceptions within the Ukrainian leadership and public.[97]

The economic crisis has also affected the combat capability of the armed forces. Ukraine inherited a large volume of military equipment at the time of independence due to its location as the first strategic echelon of the former Soviet armed forces, which were poised for a western offensive against NATO. The bulk of these forces were based in the Carpathian military district of western Ukraine, an area where they are today least required. There are few bases in eastern Ukraine, where the threat perceptions are currently greatest for the security forces and nationalist groups. To build a military infrastructure in eastern Ukraine would be economically prohibitive. Although "the equipment left to Ukraine is sufficiently powerful, if maldeployed at present, to form a deterrent against Russia,"[98] much of it is being held on to in order merely to deny it to Ukraine's eastern neighbor. It often has little practical military use, maintenance is unavailable, and training facilities are absent. Air force pilots no longer fly their required training hours due to the lack of fuel. On average, pilots fly only twenty-five exercises per annum, when their number should be at a minimum sixty. One-third of aircraft were out of order: "Repair is impossible since there is not enough fuel even to check the engines. This has led to the suspension of combat training."[99] Ukraine inherited forty-two strategic bombers that have little use for a country that has announced its intention to denuclearize. The commander in chief of the Russian air force, Colonel General Deinekin, has claimed that if they are not transferred to Russia in 1994, "they will very simply turn into scrap metal in the near future." Ukraine has proposed that in exchange for the bombers it have access to maintenance for its fighter aircraft and spare parts for military equipment.[100]

A large proportion of the military budget, which is small and eaten away by inflation, is taken up by social welfare and Ukraine's international obligations (the CFE and START I treaties). Little is left for spare parts and maintenance. In the 1994 budget, only 8 percent was allocated for the purchase of spare parts and maintenance, when the Ministry of Defense had requested that it be 80 percent. If this is allowed to continue, it will have a disastrous effect on the air force and military aviation. Many of the spare parts for airplanes and tanks come from Russia; Ukraine does not possess a closed production cycle within its military-industrial complex.

Ukraine inherited a large quantity of military equipment from the FSU, but, in terms of quality, it is poor (especially if the armed forces are to become professional by the end of the decade, as current military plans outline). The large volume of military equipment also has a drawback in that it ties up a large proportion of (the already small intake of) conscripts in guard duties, rather than military exercises (although shortages of fuel have nearly prevented regular exercises). The destruction and sale of weapons is taking place at a rate slower than the decline in the conscript intake.

The situation within the Ukrainian navy is little better. Ambitious plans announced in 1992 by then Admiral Borys Kozhyn have been quietly shelved. The state does not have the resources to build such an ambitious navy; it has therefore asked each oblast to pay for one ship each. Not surprisingly, the western Ukrainian oblasts have proved most supportive of the idea.

Maintenance of Ukrainian naval vessels is a severe problem; of forty-five ships, in June 1993 fifteen were in need of repair and twenty-nine were docked and immobile. The Black Sea fleet has complained that the Ukrainian navy owes large debts for energy and construction services. The Ukrainian navy counters that the Black Sea fleet owes taxes, pension fund payments, and payments for utilization of onshore repair facilities to the tune of 120 billion coupons.[101]

Ukrainian naval personnel also complain of the fact that 75 percent have no housing and, because of the low value of the coupon in relation to the ruble in the region (the exhange rate is 20 : 1), they are paid in real terms only half of what Black Sea fleet personnel receive.[102] Ukrainian monetary policy, which was extremely slack in 1992–93 and led to hyperinflation of nearly 100 percent per month in December 1993, damaged Ukraine's ability to maintain the pay of its naval forces. At a time when Ukraine was attempting to win over the loyalties of officers from the Black Sea Fleet (and retain those who had already defected to the Ukrainian navy), its economic and monetary policies proved disastrous.

These factors, in turn, have led many military officers with specialist skills to resign their commissions. In early 1993, each air force regiment had fourteen combat crews; now each has only four.[103] During the first ten months of 1993, over nine thousand officers, a third of whom were young, resigned their commissions.

The economic crisis has affected the elite of the armed forces, as well as regular units. The First Airborne Division, based at Bolgrad in the Odessa oblast, was formerly the elite Ninety-eighth Soviet Airborne Division, which was successfully divided with Russia in the spring of 1993. Although the division inherited a large volume of military equipment, there is a serious lack of parachutes (one for every two to three soldiers), and many specialists have left for Russia (especially in air transport, flight control, and maintenance). Fuel and lubricants are in short supply. Perhaps the most acute problem, as in the Ukrainian navy, is pay. Russian airborne troops obtain up to two hundred times higher allowances for each parachute jump they undertake than do their Ukrainian counterparts.[104]

Just as in the Russian armed forces, the movement of young officers away from the Ukrainian armed forces is leading to its "graying," with the remaining lower- and higher-ranking officers left to dominate the ranks. The Ukrainian armed forces are dominated by officers with fifteen to nineteen years experience at the top end, and those with less than three years of service at the bottom end. The former are afraid of unemployment outside the armed forces due to their age levels, while the latter are new officers who are only just learning new skills (but are likely to leave in the medium term for better-paid posts outside the military). A large proportion of young people enter military academies because obtaining qualifications is easier than in other higher educational establishments. After they finish the military academy, they often leave for the civilian sector.

Officers who are leaving the armed forces tend to be doctors, lawyers, economists, topographers, and communications and radio electronics engineers. In response, the Ministry of Defense has issued special instructions not to allow officers to resign their commissions early.[105] Many officers are also resigning to join the Russian and other CIS armed forces, 40 percent of whose officers are from Ukraine. In 1993, over one thousand air force and strategic rocket force officers from Ukraine joined the Russian armed forces for higher wages.[106] Officers also become mercenaries, selling their military skills to warring sides in the various hot spots of the FSU. In May 1994, a Ukrainian pilot was sentenced to death in Nagorno-Karabagh for flying in the Azerbaijani air force.

Discipline within the armed forces is in decline due to the socioeconomic and political crisis, which, in turn, erodes the prestige of military life. In this respect, the armed forces are not isolated from general negative developments within society as a whole.[107] Ninety-three percent of officers in the armed forces are dissatisfied with their financial status (pay in the civilian sector is 1.5 to 2 times higher on average). The same share of officers believe that their material situation is "critical;" they are surviving only with help from parents. The bulk of their salaries covers only foodstuffs.[108] One in two young officers would like to resign his commission; many officers are attracted by the greater rewards offered by the private sector.[109]

The decline in discipline coupled with low financial pay has encouraged officers to fend for themselves by either working part-time in commercial structures, stealing military equipment, building dachas, or working as security guards. As the weekly newspaper *Kyivs'ki vidomosti* (2 June 1994) lamented, it was a pity the building of Ukraine's armed forces was being undertaken at a slower pace than that of officers' dachas. The rise in corruption and theft within the military was linked in the bulk of cases to organized crime in society. As crime and corruption grew in the armed forces, discipline declined. Regulations for penal battalions, two of which exist in Kiev and the Crimea, setting out the procedure and conditions for punishing conscripts, were introduced in June 1994 to meet these growing problems.[110]

The SOU was a major pressure group for the creation of the Main Control-Revision Inspectorate, established in March 1993 on orders from Defense Minister Morozov.[111] The commercial center under the Ministry of Defense was closed on orders of President Kravchuk, who accused it of "serious violations of economic and financial discipline" in real estate, equipment, and funds received from the sale of military assets. Much of the surplus equipment Ukraine inherited is designated ahead of time as "coming to the end of its working life," stored, and then illegally sold. During the course of 1992–93, five generals were dismissed (often with evidence provided by the SOU) for corruption, including Lieutenant General Oleksandr Ignatenko, chief of the directorate on personnel of the Ministry of Defense.[112] Many of these dismissed officers remained hostile toward the SOU and Defense Minister Morozov.

Violations of the law and "mass legal nihilism" within the armed forces were caused by the economic crisis. The creation of the inspectorate was not welcomed by all officers, especially as it cooperated with the Security Service. "The life of those who regarded military service as a convenient way to line their own pockets became too strenuous," one newspaper remarked.[113] It cited the case of Lieutenant General Volodymyr Tolubko, a former deputy from Kharkiv and commander of the Kharkiv garrison, against whom criminal proceedings were instituted for large-scale theft of military property.[114]

The SOU was also instrumental in establishing a department to deal with the social concerns of servicemen within the Cabinet of Ministers. Led by the first chairman of the SOU, Vilen Martyrosian, an Armenian from western Ukraine and a former deputy to the USSR Supreme Soviet, the new department would deal with housing, unemployment, and officers returning from the CIS.[115] According to Omel'chenko, by the spring of 1993, over 150,000 officers and midshipmen remained outside Ukraine in the FSU. Between 1992 and 1993, forty thousand of them requested to be transferred to Ukraine; of these, twenty-one thousand were released from duty. Seventeen thousand of these officers eventually found their way back to Ukraine.[116] The number of officers wanting to return may show an increase in 1994, placing added strain on the military budget, if reports prove to be correct that the Russian minister of defense issued instructions to release Ukrainian officers from their duties.

Although the SOU has remained critically disposed toward Martyrosian and his government committee, SOU members have still agreed to work with the committee at the local level and head nineteen of its oblast branches. The majority of officers believed that the government was insensitive to the social problems affecting them and that the legislative protection of their rights remained ineffective. This lack of faith among officers in the highest organs of the land directly affects the fighting morale of the officers, especially at a time of crisis (as was most vividly seen in August 1991, when the Soviet military refused to obey the commanders of the junta).

Ukrainian military commentators have pointed out that the poor quality of officers is often responsible for the fact that, whereas some bases are well organized and orderly, others are run-down. These discrepancies cannot be blamed on the lack of funds, because all officers are in a similarly difficult position. If the base is allowed to run down, this will affect discipline, morale, military preparedness, and order within the ranks. Often the question is not simply costs: "There is a need merely for attention, the will of the commander, their conscious approach to the carrying out of their duties, [greater] attention paid to younger staff, and a strict control over the carrying out of decisions that have been taken."[117]

Some officers believed that trade unions were the only means left open to them to defend their rights, although unions were banned by the Ministry of Defense, in an act backed by the SOU. An alternative, the Ukrainian Congress of Servicemen and Businessmen, was formed in November 1993 on the initiative of the government's Committee for the Social Protection of Servicemen, and therefore was immediately seen as a competitor by the SOU.[118] Despite the Ministry of Defense ban, Oleksandr Slusarev, also chairman of the SOUD, heads the Independent Trade Union of Servicemen of Ukraine. Both organizations are rivals to the SOU and are linked to the Ukrainian National Assembly (UNA),[119] which is attempting to spread the influence of radical right nationalism within the armed forces by exploiting their social problems.

One of the most acute social problems remains housing: sixty thousand officers are without apartments.[120] "Today the housing problem for servicemen has become political and it demands an immediate solution," Omel'chenko told the fourth SOU congress. The severity of officers' social problems has led directly to their politicization. Ninety percent of officers had no faith in the ability of the authorities to dole out housing in a just manner. Omel'chenko warned that 78 percent of officers would be willing to take "extreme steps" if their social problems were not dealt with, up to and including the torching of illegally built dachas and physical attacks on generals (no source was given by Omel'chenko for the origin of this figure).[121] The fact that many top officers are Russian could therefore produce a lethal combination of ethnic and social grievances to be exploited by groups such as the UNA.[122]

Besides housing, officer discontent also concerns diet, living standards, free time, and fear of the future and unemployment as the armed forces are reduced in size. Sixty-three percent of officers believed they had now made the wrong career move, yet over 70 percent expressed alarm at the thought of the unstable economic situation outside the armed forces. The resultant reluctance to remain within the armed forces except as a last resort rather than be unemployed outside, has eroded discipline, morale, and productivity.

Unless democratization and social welfare go hand in hand within the armed forces, "it is difficult to see how to form a strong army able to stand up to any aggressor."[123] Ukraine inherited many of the social problems that affected its Soviet predecessor, which were publicized by civic groups in 1990–91.

The economic and social crisis in Ukraine also affects the military through conscription problems. Over three-quarters of young Ukrainians remain skeptical of and uninterested in undertaking military service. They have maintained a critical view of the idea that military service helps instill patriotic qualities. At the same time, more than half recognize that the armed forces are necessary to ensure peace, while one-third regard the army as a guarantor of the state and national interests.[124] Even in Lviv Oblast, a region with the strongest nationalist sentiment in Ukraine, 61 percent of draftees would not go to military service voluntarily. The reasons for this state of affairs include the low prestige of the military (17.6 percent) and fear about its effect on health and life (22.3 percent); 11 percent are put off by the harsh discipline; and 41.6 percent are afraid of brutality by older officers and conscripts.[125] Although not cited, undoubtedly the ability to earn higher pay in the private sector is also an enticement to young draftees and officers.

The draft intake varies between a low of 12 to 18 percent of men of conscript age in some oblasts and a high of 40 to 42 percent in other regions. First selections from among these conscripts are made for specialist units (National Guard, border troops, strategic rocket troops, airborne, and Spetsnaz). With the lower conscript base this means in effect that the worst-quality conscripts remaining after specialist units have taken the best are assigned to the motor rifle, tank, and artillery units of the armed forces.[126]

The yearly conscript base is between seventy thousand and eighty thousand, three times less than military requirements. This figure is likely to worsen, due to draft dodging and Ukraine's demographic plight.[127] Ukraine's mortality rate, worsened by poverty, medicine shortages, and the Chernobyl nuclear disaster, continues to rise sharply. Deaths began overtaking births in Ukraine in 1991 for the first time since World War II—and the trend has worsened since. Not only is mortality rising, but so are incidences of cancer, blood diseases, and suicides. These trends will undoubtedly negatively affect the conscription intake of Ukraine's armed forces.

Up to 70 percent of conscripts can use existing legislation to avoid military service on legal grounds, including health and conscientious objection[128] (eight hundred conscripts undertook alternative service in 1993).[129] Only one-third of the total number of conscript age men will undertake military service, because draft dodging and going absent without leave have "become unprecedently widespread."[130] Parents increasingly help their sons to avoid the draft;[131] 78 percent of parents supported their sons' opposition to serving in the armed forces in Dnipropetrovs'k Oblast alone.[132] Not only parents, but half of military officers did not want their children following them into service in the armed forces.[133]

Few draft dodgers were punished for not observing the law On General Military Duties and Military Service due to shortcomings in the law. The number of draft dodgers grew during 1992–93 due to the growing apathy of young people toward politics as well as the ability to earn high salaries from commercial and trading activities in the civilian sector. The quality of conscripts also declined. The number of those with criminal records grew, reflecting the severe rise in crime in society, and the health of draftees worsened, due to a variety of factors linked to the socioeconomic crisis (nuclear aftereffects of Chernobyl, the decline in protein in people's diets, the lesser availability and higher price of medicines and vitamins, as well as the growth of previously uncommon diseases, such as diptheria).

To help encourage draftees to enlist, an "Agit-Train" was utilized at different enrollment centers where Soviet and UPA veterans helped military commissars, another example of civic groups cooperating with the military.[134] Military commissars have complained that the MVS and militia are not interested—although more likely they are unable to help due to overextended resources—in cooperating with them in looking for draft dodgers.[135] The lack of fuel even prevented the military on some occasions from collecting draftees, and many had to walk to enlistment centers.[136] Desertion from units has remained another problem. In the first nine months of 1992, several thousand servicemen from all regions of Ukraine, including the nationalistic western oblasts, deserted due to a dislike of the military, the desire to be transferred to their home regions, or mistreatment by officers.[137]

This mistreatment, or *didovschina* (hazing),[138] of conscripts is a major factor discouraging draftees from undertaking their military service, a phenomenon inherited from the Soviet army and one of its more troublesome legacies.[139] The publicity given *didovschina* in the Soviet army in 1990–91 in the Ukrainian press and by civic groups may have damaged popular attitudes toward the military in general. *Didovschina* decreased the prestige of the military[140] and led to suicides (the most widespread cause of death in the armed forces)[141] and desertions. In Odessa oblast alone, in 1993 over one thousand deserters were on the run, probably related to the rise in *didovschina*.[142] While on the run, many draftees and conscripts go on to commit crimes, such as theft and even murder. Between 1992 and 1993, the number of abuses in the armed forces rose by one-third, according to the KSM.[143]

Conclusions

The launching of the Ukrainian armed forces between mid-1991 and mid-1992 was a popular move backed by the majority of public opinion, civic groups, parliament, and the newly elected president. The two previous years of agitation by civic groups and political parties through demonstrations, pickets, and conferences and in the media, parliament, and local councils had prepared the intellectual and moral climate needed to ensure that the question of separate armed forces remained a high priority for the newly independent state.

The reasons for this were numerous, and they continue to play a role in the formulation of security policy, shaping the domestic debate on military policy and threat perceptions. A major influence on the popularly felt need to possess armed forces was historical—in order to ensure that Ukraine did not lose its independence again, as in 1920–21. This, in turn, coupled with the high degree of threat perception within which the public debate on security policy was conducted, particularly as regards the territorial integrity of the state. Finally, the rapid pace of the construction of armed forces and their prioritization in 1992–93 was linked to the widespread feeling that this was the last chance available to consolidate independent statehood.

Several lessons and conclusions follow from these political and military circumstances. First, military service outside Ukraine, especially in hot spots, will continue to remain unpopular. This is unlikely to change even if Ukraine signs the CIS Treaty on Collective Security under newly elected President Kuchma (although this is unlikely, due to strong domestic hostility). But Ukraine, which lacked a foreign policy vis-à-vis its own CIS "near abroad" under President Kravchuk, is likely to become more involved in inter-CIS affairs, such as peacekeeping (an area in which Ukraine has experience in Bosnia-Herzegovina and where it is regarded as more neutral than Russia).

Second, one of the much-touted successes of Ukrainian military policy is the removal of foreign bases from its territory as the basis for its professed course of neutrality. Only Russian forces within the Black Sea fleet remain in the Crimea and southern Ukraine. Third, one of the many attributes of independent statehood for a country with a large number of perceived threats to its borders (Ukrainians talk of only one neighboring country—Belarus—never historically harboring claims to its territory) is separate armed forces.

The consensus on threat perceptions to the Ukrainian state that existed in 1992 began to break down in 1993–94, hampering the consolidation of a commonly held view of national interests and security policy. If the 1994 presidential elections are taken as a rough guide to the foreign orientation of Ukraine's citizens, then they are divided fairly evenly. A nationalistic, anti-Russian, and pro-Western vision, on the one hand (represented by Kravchuk), was pitted against a pro-Russian, pro-CIS, and cautious, distrustful view of the West, on the other (represented by Kuchma).

Civil-military relations within Ukraine remained stable and relatively without conflict during President Kravchuk's tenure in office. This could change under Kuchma if integration with Russia becomes a policy priority, separatism grows unhindered, and policies such as federalization and dual citizenship are introduced—policies that are strongly opposed by the nationalist lobby and large elements within the security forces.

In the case of the Crimea, the newly elected pro-Russian president and parliament with a secessionist agenda are backed by the majority of Russian public opinion and political leadership. Conflict with Kiev hinges on the unfinished questions of the Black Sea fleet, with its highly politicized officer corps, the presence of Ukrainian armed and security forces in the Crimea, and the Crimea's attempts to take control of branches of these forces (MVS, Judiciary, and SBU). These various conflicts are likely to continue to fester for a long time to come, although relations between Kuchma and Meshkov are unlikely to be as personally antagonistic as those under Kravchuk. Kuchma would not be able to tolerate a Crimean drive for independence, and he regards the Crimea's vote for himself as a vote for it to remain within Ukraine.

The campaign of the Crimean authorities and pro-Russian civic groups against their conscripts serving in the Ukrainian armed forces resembles the campaign four years earlier by Ukrainian groups against the Soviet armed forces. The Crimean branch of the KSM seceded from its Ukrainian organization and has come under the umbrella of the RDK, Meshkov's party. The Crimean CSM has launched a propaganda barrage claiming that Crimean conscripts are being killed and injured in the Ukrainian armed forces.[144] It is still too early to ascertain how this will develop, but what is already clear is that the Ukrainian-Soviet conflict relationship over security policy has now been transferred to the Crimean-Ukrainian relationship, with the Soviets now replaced by the Ukrainians as the "oppressors."

The armed forces have the highest degree of public confidence of any state institution, much higher than the president or parliament. The first priority of the armed forces, according to its officers, is defense of the country's territorial integrity and independence. Therefore, they are closely tied to the very raison d'être of the state. But Ukraine inherited a large gulf between its citizens and elite over the policy priorities that the state should pursue. While it recognizes the importance of the armed forces, the public perceives other issues closer to home as more important and as requiring the urgent attention of the country's leadership (the economic crisis, organized crime, and so forth).

Ukraine is faced with a number of challenges in dealing with the armed forces it inherited from the FSU. Although the majority of Soviet officers resident in Ukraine at the time of the disintegration of the FSU took the oath of loyalty, only a minimum of 30 percent, or 50 percent at a maximum, did so for patriotic reasons. The majority of the officers Ukraine inherited spoke Russian and had been indoctrinated with Marxist ideology and Soviet nationality policy. The very idea of now regarding Russia as a threat after decades of advice stating that Moscow was, in fact, Ukraine's best friend and paternalistic elder brother undoubtedly created confusion, divided loyalties, and conflict.

The role of the SOU and other civic groups with an interest in military affairs therefore was, and is likely to remain, crucial. The SOU dominates the Socio-Psychological Service, the Higher Attestation Commissions, the government's Committee for the Social Protection of Servicemen, and the Main Control-Revision Inspectorate. The SOU has no challenger to its status as the sole officers' organization, unlike in Russia and Belarus, although the left-wing majority of the newly elected parliament is hostile toward the SOU's Ukrainian nationalism and anti-Russianism.

The economic crisis has affected the armed forces in a number of direct ways. The lack of attention paid by President Kravchuk to the economic crisis and reform is partly attributable to the prioritization of his administration in 1992–94 to security questions (diplomatic representation, placing Ukraine on the international map, building separate armed and security forces). This prioritization aimed to ensure that Ukraine's independence had become irreversible and no longer vulnerable (as it had been historically) to external threats and lack of Western interest in its fate. Yet Kravchuk's popularity within the armed forces was lower than expected during the presidential elections. The armed forces were disappointed by Kravchuk's failure to fulfill promises made earlier on socioeconomic questions, and therefore they proceeded to vote against their commander in chief. "The problems troubling Ukrainian society cannot but affect morale among the armed forces," Muliava, chief of the Ukrainian Cossacks, commented.[145]

Incorporating the Soviet military inheritance is proving to be difficult: maintenance of equipment is unsatisfactory, training is below standards, pay is low, and younger officers are resigning their commissions. This in turn has led to a rise in corruption, politicization of the officers (as reflected in the SOU), and decline in military prestige, morale, and discipline. These factors will damage the capabilities and operational effectiveness of the armed forces, especially at a time of crisis.

Although the armed forces remain the most popular official institution, with a recognized role to play in safeguarding domestic peace and the country's independence, they are highly unpopular among young people of draft age. Ukraine inherited many of the negative aspects of the Soviet armed forces, such as *didovschina*, and many draftees would prefer to be stationed close to home. The demand of the new Crimean leadership that conscripts from its region undertake their military service on the peninsula is therefore likely to be greeted as a popular action (as it was when Ukrainians demanded in 1990–91 from the Soviet Ministry of Defense that their conscripts be allowed to serve in the republic).

The importance of civil-military relations is therefore likely to grow with the election of Kuchma as Ukraine's second president. The policies of the newly elected president will be scrutinized by civic groups, political parties, paramilitary groups, and military officers for any hints of a pro-Russian bias or leniency on domestic threats to Ukraine's territorial integrity.

Notes

1. See "Coup Talk in Ukraine," *Foreign Report (Economist)*, 9 December 1993; *Segodnia*, ITAR-TASS news agency (Moscow), and UPI (United Press International), 12 July 1994. An assassination scheme was allegedly hatched by Major General Oleksandr Skipal'skyi of military counterintelligence, who is also a former head of the SOU. The SOU called on its members to vote for Kravchuk in the presidential elections. For details of earlier accusations of treachery by the Ukrainian armed forces against former president Leonid Kravchuk after the Massandra Russian-Ukrainian summit in September 1993, see "Coup Talk in Ukraine."

2. See Taras Kuzio, "From Pariah to Partner: Ukraine and Nuclear Weapons," *Jane's Intelligence Review*, May 1994.

3. See T. Kuzio, "Ukrainian Election Results Point to Increasing Regionalism," *Jane's Intelligence Review Pointer*, no. 6 (April 1994).

4. *Literaturna Ukraina* (Kiev), 23 November 1989. See the replies by Vasyl' Smohytel, secretary of the National Party, in *Perspektyva* (Kiev), nos. 2, 3 (February 1990).

5. *Za vil'nu Ukrainu* (Lviv), 20 September 1991; *Visti Slobozhanshchyna* (Kharkiv), 1990, no. 3.

6. *Ukrains'ke slovo* (Paris), 18 February 1990, 8 April 1990.

7. *Krasnaia zvezda* (Moscow), 14 March 1990.

8. *Molod Ukrainy* (Kiev), 20 December 1990.

9. See Kathleen Mihalisko, "Ukraine Ponders Creation of a National Army," *Report on the USSR*, 22 February 1991.

10. *Holos Ukrainy*, 17 November 1993.

11. *Robitnycha hazeta* (Kiev), 23 February 1991.

12. Radio Kiev, 4 February 1991.

13. *Za nezalezhnist'* (Ivano-Frankivs'k), 23 March 1991.

14. See the Lviv oblast resolution On the Autumn Draft of Military Conscripts in Lviv Oblast and the Undertaking of Their Military Service, in *Za vil'nu Ukrainu*, 9 September 1990, and the resolution by Ivano-Frankivs'k oblast in *Zakhidnii Kur'ier* (Ivano-Frankivs'k), 7 September 1990. These resolutions were implemented, unlike those of the Ukrainian parliament.

15. See the report of the return of the body of Liubomyr Fitko a conscript who was killed as a "Banderite" (slang for nationalist), from Voronezh to Lviv, in *Za vil'nu Ukrainu*, 8 December 1990. On similar incidents see *Zakhidnii kur'ier*, 25 October 1990; *Za vil'nu Ukrainu*, 12 March 1991; *Holos* (Kiev), 13 November 1991; and *Vechirnii Kyiv* (Kiev), 2 December 1991.

16. One serviceman described how he ran away from his unit after "becoming acquainted with the contents of literature of a democratic character that we regularly received from Ukraine. Under its influence on 23 February I, and those of like mind, hung up a blue and yellow flag in our unit." *Molod Ukrainy*, 20 December 1990.

17. See *Za vil'nu Ukrainu*, 3, 10, 17 September 1991; *Narodna hazeta* (Kiev), no. 11 (October 1991); and *Narodna armiia*, 26 December 1991.

18. See *Moloda Halychyna* (Lviv), 10 April 1990; and *Ratusha* (Lviv), 4 December 1990.

19. *Spadshchyna* (Lviv), 1990, no. 8; *Ukrainian Review*, vol. 38, no. 1 (spring 1990), pp. 67–68, and no. 4 (winter 1990), pp. 46–48.

20. *Za vil'nu Ukrainu*, 12 January 1991. See also R. Shreeves, "Mothers Against the Draft: Women Activists in the USSR," *Report on the USSR*, 21 September 1990.

21. *Literaturna Ukraina*, 11 October 1990.

22. See *Za vil'nu Ukrainu*, 5 February 1991, 20 April 1991, and 27 September 1991.

23. See the appeal to servicemen and the resolution On Service in the Army, in *Druhi Vseukrains'ki zbory narodnoho rukhu Ukrainy: Dokumenty* (Kiev, 1990; Newark, NJ: Prolog, 1991), pp. 62–63, 66.

24. *Ukrain'ski novyny* (Warsaw), 1990, no. 12; and *Washington Times*, 18 October 1990.

25. *Shliakh peremohy* (Munich), 3 June 1990.

26. A.H. Miller, W.M. Reisinger, and V.L. Hesli, "Public Support for New Political Institutions in Russia, the Ukraine and Lithuania," *Journal of Soviet Nationalities*, vol. 1, no. 4 (winter 1990–91), p. 97.

27. See Taras Kuzio, "Nuclear Weapons and Military Policy in Independent Ukraine," *Harriman Institute Forum*, vol. 6, no. 9 (May 1992).

28. *Politychnyi Portret Ukrainy* (Kiev: Academic Research Center Democratic Initiative) 1993, no. 3.

29. *Robitnycha hazeta*, 22 March 1994.

30. *Uriadovyi kur'ier*, no. 135 (7 September 1993); and *Narodna armiia*, 10 March 1994.

31. *Politychnyi portret Ukrainy* (Kiev: Academic Research Center Democratic Initiative), December 1993, no. 5.

32. *Rozbudova derzhava* (Kiev), no. 2 (February 1992).

33. *Politychnyi portret Ukrainy*, 1993, no. 3.

34. *Politychnyi portret Ukrainy* 1993, no. 5.

35. *Narodna armiia*, 10 March 1994.

36. *Politychnyi portret Ukrainy*, 1993, no. 5.

37. *Narodna armiia*, 8 July 1993.

38. See Taras Kuzio, "The Implications of the Ukrainian Elections," *Jane's Intelligence Review*, June 1994; and idem., "From Romanticism to Pragmatism: Ukraine Since the Elections," *Jane's Intelligence Review*, December 1994.

39. *Rozbudova derzhava*, no. 2 (February 1994).

40. *Narodna armiia*, 26 February 1994.

41. *Kyiv'ski vidomosti* (Kiev), 12 May 1994.

42. Radio Ukraine, 11 June 1992. See also Serge Schmemann, "Russia Angry Over Ukraine Demand for Loyalty Oath," *International Herald Tribune*, 6 January 1992.

43. *Vidomosti Verkhovnoi rady Ukrainy* (Kiev), no. 5 (4 February 1992).

44. *Postfactum* (Moscow), 26 January 1992; *Independent*, 8 June 1992.

45. UNIAN News Agency (Kiev), 1 February 1994; *Izvestiia*, 22 February 1994.

46. *Vechirnii Kyiv*, 20 May 1993.

47. *Narodna armiia*, 30 April 1993.

48. *Visnyk Natsional'noi hvardii Ukrainy* (Kiev), no. 5 (June 1993). Another poll gave support for the traditions of the Soviet armed forces (55 percent), Cossacks (48 percent), and last, the UPA (22 percent). See *Narodna armiia*, 17 March 1994.

49. See the article by Colonel Hryhorii Temko, head of the directorate on humanitarian work within the main department of the Socio-Psychological Service, in *Narodna armiia*, 11 March 1994.

50. See *Narodna armiia*, 19, 28 August 1992, 16 September 1992.

51. *Narodna armiia*, 8 September 1992.

52. Iavors'kyi is employed as a "specialist on the ideological-theoretical basis for Ukrainian state independence" in the head section of the Educational and Socio-Psychological Department of the Ministry of Defense. See *Narodna armiia*, 13, 18 November 1993, and 10, 17, 23 December 1993, for his material prepared for local branches of the service.

53. The objectives of the Socio-Psychological Service are outlined in *Narodna armiia*, 29 July 1992 and 22 January 1993.

54. *Narodna armiia*, 4 April 1992. See also the criticism of former SOU member Vitalii Chechylo in *Narodna armiia*, 2 October 1992, and replies in the 10 and 16 October 1992 issues.

55. *Vechirnii Kyiv*, 12 February 1993; and *Robitnycha hazeta*, 12 May 1993.

56. *Narodna armiia*, 18 September 1993. The statements denouncing the Massandra accords were similar to the criticisms made by then Defense Minister Morozov, who later resigned. See Taras Kuzio, "Ukrainian Defense Minister Resigns," *Jane's Intelligence Review Pointer*, no. 2 (December 1993).

57. See Taras Kuzio, "Ukraine's Young Turks: The Union of Ukrainian Officers,"

Jane's Intelligence Review, January 1993. See the Statute of the SOU in *Narodna armiia*, 12 August 1993.

58. *Vechirnii Kyiv*, 4 September 1992. By mid-1994 the SOU's membership had reportedly risen to one hundred thousand (*Ukrains'ke slovo* [Paris], 29 May 1994). But other reports suggest that after the SOU became progressively politicized in 1992–93 membership declined to approximately twenty thousand. As with all political and civic groups in Ukraine, membership is often exaggerated and difficult to check. At the sixth SOU congress there were complaints that it had lost its "mass" base. *Narodna armiia*, 14 June 1994.

59. Support for private farming and economic reform, for example, has remained very high among the armed forces, Ministry of Internal Affairs, and Security Service (91 percent). See *Politychnyi portret Ukrainy*, 1993, no. 5.

60. See Ustina Markus, "Belarus Debates Security Pacts as a Cure for Military Woes," *RFE/RL Research Report*, vol. 2, no. 25, 8 June 1993.

61. *Uriadovyi kur'ier*, 25 September 1992.

62. *Molod Ukrainy*, 29 December 1992.

63. *Narodna armiia*, 6 June 1992; and *Literaturna Ukraina*, 18 June 1992.

64. The SOU may have been successful in reducing the number of non-Ukrainians in the officer corps, making it more loyal, but this did not neccesarily mean that the quality of officers also increased.

65. Then head of the Socio-Psychological Service, Major General Muliava, counters this criticism that it is a new MPA in *Narodna armiia*, 25 November; and *Narodna hazeta*, nos. 50–51 (December 1992).

66. Muliava was relieved of his post after the change of defense minister in October 1993. In October of the previous year he was elected hetman (chief) of the Ukrainian Cossacks, another civic paramilitary group. *Kyivs'ka pravda* (Kiev), 15 October 1992.

67. On the congress, see *Narodna armiia*, 13 April 1993; and *Holos Ukrainy*, 22 April 1993.

68. *Narodna armiia*, 14 August 1993.

69. *Narodna armiia*, 17 May 1994.

70. *Nezavisimost'* (Kiev), 16 April 1993.

71. See *Nezavisimost'*, 1 June 1994.

72. *Narodna armiia*, 14 June 1994. See also UNIAR News Agency, 11 June 1994; and UNIAN News Agency, 29 June 1994. The newly elected head of the SOU is Colonel Viacheslav Bilous, a Poltava deputy from the Democratic Coalition Ukraine election bloc.

73. *Financial Times*, 10 March 1992. The Azerbaijan branch of the SOU had five thousand members who requested permission to work under contract for the Azeri armed forces.

74. *Zamkova hora* (Kiev), 1992, no. 11; *Ukrains'ki Obrii* (Kiev), 1993 no. 1; and *Vechirnii Kyiv*, 19 January 1993.

75. Information about the UNSO is mainly taken from Taras Kuzio, "Ukrainian Paramilitaries," and idem, "Paramilitary Groups in Ukraine," *Jane's Intelligence Review*, December 1992 and March 1994. On the politics of the radical right, see Bohdan Nahaylo, "The Politics of Intolerance: Ukraine," *RFE/RL Research Report*, 22 April 1994.

76. During 1992–93, serious crimes rose by 376 percent in the Ukrainian armed forces, including theft of weapons and military property. *Krasnaia zvezda*, 3 March 1994.

77. On the UPA Brotherhood, see *Zakhidnii kur'ier*, 18 October 1990; *Poklyk sumlinnia* (Lviv), 1991, no. 15; *Shliakh peremohy*, 19 and 26 May 1991; *Literaturna Ukraina*, 6 February 1992; *Shliakh peremohy*, 24 July 1993; and *Statut Vseukrains'koho bratstva UPA* (Kiev: Ukrainian Information Service, n.d.).

78. The VUKS and the SOU were both members of the Democratic Coalition Ukraine, the election bloc of center-right national-democratic groups based primarily in western and central Ukraine.

79. On Ukrainian Cossack groups see *Literaturna Ukraina*, 22 October 1992; *Vechirnii Kyiv*, 27 January 1993; *Narodna armiia*, 29 January 1993, 10 February 1993, 28 April 1993, and 19 November 1993.

80. *Vechirnii Kyiv*, 2 November 1993.

81. Former Defense Minister Radets'kyi pointed to the problem of a lack of pre-conscription induction to prepare for the armed forces, which reduced the quality of conscripts. On pre-conscription military education, see *Narodna armiia*, 28 May 1994.

82. *Vechirnii Kyiv*, 4 March 1993.

83. *Molod Ukrainy*, 26 July 1994.

84. *Narodna armiia*, 24 February 1993.

85. *Narodna armiia*, 30 April 1993.

86. *Holos Ukrainy*, 8 April 1993. See also "The State Language—The Language of the Military," and "Forcible Ukrainization or a Conscientious and Nonrepressive Return to a Natural State," *Narodna armiia*, 28 August and 14 September 1993. In response to complaints about forcible Ukrainization, *Narodna armiia*, 25 January 1994, published an article entitled "Ukrainian Army—State Language: To Learn Does Not Mean That It Is Forced."

87. *Politychnyi portret Ukrainy*, 1993, no. 3.

88. *Rada* (Kiev), 2 June 1994.

89. *Narodna armiia*, 20 February 1993.

90. *Krasnaia zvezda*, 1 March 1994.

91. See the presidential decrees annulling the appointments by Meshkov of his own men in charge of the MVS and Security Service. *Holos Ukrainy*, 25 May 1994.

92. See the following articles: Taras Kuzio, "Will Crimea Be Europe's Next Flashpoint?" *European Security Analyst*, no. 30 (April 1994); idem, "Crimea—Europe's Next Bosnia?" *Conflict International*, vol. 9, no. 3 (March 1994); and idem, "Crimean Crisis Deepens," *Jane's Intelligence Report Pointer*, no. 8 (June 1994).

93. See Elizabeth Teague, "Russia and Tatarstan Sign Power-Sharing Treaty," *RFE/RL Research Report*, 8 April 1994.

94. *Krasnaia zvezda*, 2 June 1994.

95. UPI and Reuters, 1 June 1994; UNIAN News Agency, 2 June 1994. See Slavko Artmenko, "Orhanizatsiini ta taktychni zasady UNCO," *Holos natsii* (Lviv), no. 22 (August 1994). Cossacks in the Crimea are divided between pro-Ukrainian and pro-Russian groups. *Kyivs'ki vidomosti*, 2 June 1994.

96. *Narodna armiia*, 16 February 1994. Top officers' pay in the armed forces was 1.5 million coupons (approximately $45).

97. Roy Allison, *Military Forces in the Soviet Successor States*, Adelphi Paper 280 (London: Brassey's for the IISS, 1993), pp. 42–43.

98. Ibid., p. 42.

99. UNIAN News Agency, 21 February 1994.

100. Ekho Moskvy Radio (Moscow), 18 May 1994; and UNIAN News Agency, 19 May 1994.

101. *Narodna armiia*, 4 May 1994.

102. Ustina Markus, "The Ukrainian Navy and the Black Sea Fleet," *RFE/RL Research Report*, 6 May 1994, pp. 38–39.

103. UNIAN News Agency, 21 February 1994.

104. The difference is again due to the weakness of the Ukrainian coupon in relation to the ruble. Whereas Ukrainians earned two thousand to eight thousand coupons for each

parachute jump, Russians earned ten thousand to twelve thousand rubles (the exchange rate is roughly 20c : 1r). See the series of articles on the First Ukrainian Airborne Division in *Narodna armiia*, 28–30 April, 4 and 6 May 1994.

105. UNIAN News Agency, 29 November 1993.

106. *Moskovskii komsomolets* (Moscow), 25 February 1994.

107. *Narodna armiia*, 17 March 1994.

108. *Narodna armiia*, 8 July 1993. In February Ukraine's minister of defense had to travel to Odessa and Ivano-Frankivs'k after officers went on strike over delays in the payment of their wages. UNIAN News Agency, 21 February 1994.

109. ITAR-TASS, 22 November 1993.

110. UNIAN News Agency, 22 June 1994.

111. *Narodna armiia*, 19 May 1993. See also Omel'chenko's comments to the fourth congress of the SOU in *Narodna armiia*, 30 April 1993.

112. *Krasnaia zvezda*, 30 March 1993.

113. *Narodna hazeta*, 7 September 1993.

114. On the criminal case against Tolubko, see *Nezavisimost'*, 6 August 1993.

115. *Narodna armiia*, 28 March 1992.

116. *Narodna armiia*, 30 April 1993.

117. *Narodna armiia*, 31 May 1994.

118. The Ministry of Defense statement is published in *Uriadovyi kur'ier*, nos. 97–98 (1 July 1993) and that of the SOU in *Narodna armiia*, 13 March 1993. On the Congress of Servicemen and Businessmen, see *Holos Ukrainy*, 2 November 1993; and *Narodna armiia*, 18 December 1993. Leading members of the SOU accused Martyrosian of attempting to split the officer corps. *Molod Ukrainy*, 29 April 1993.

119. *Narodna armiia*, 1 December 1993. See also *Ukrains'ki Obrii* (Kiev), no. 12 (June 1993). Eighty-four percent of officers were opposed to joining civilian trade unions, while 94 percent would not take part in strikes (*Robitnycha hazeta*, 22 March 1994). Unions are unlikely therefore to be a popular option in the armed forces.

120. See *Narodna armiia*, 9 June 1994.

121. *Narodna armiia*, 30 April 1993.

122. On a visit to the United States in June 1994, Defense Minister Radets'kyi asked the Ukrainian diaspora to help deal with the social problems of the armed forces, especially housing.

123. *Visnyk Natsional'noi hvardii Ukrainy*, no. 5 (June 1993).

124. Radio Ukraine, 31 October 1993.

125. *Shliakh peremohy*, 4 December 1993. In 1993 in Lviv and Ternopil' oblasts of western Ukraine, the call-up was poor. Other oblasts with a poor record included Kharkiv, Zaporizhzhia, and Kirovohrad. *Narodna armiia*, 15 February 1994.

126. *Narodna armiia*, 27 May 1994.

127. *Strategii rozvytku Ukrainy: Vyklyky chasu ta vybir, Naukovi dopovidi 22* (Kiev: National Institute for Strategic Studies, 1994), p. 119. Population growth rates in Ukraine between 1991 and 1994 were negative. Only 30 percent of Ukrainian children are born healthy. UNIAN News Agency, 2 June 1994.

128. Radio Ukraine, 16 December 1992.

129. These figures are by Major General Valerii Venher, head of the main organization and mobilization directorate of the general headquarters of the Ministry of Defense. UNIAR News Agency (Kiev), 26 May 1994.

130. ITAR-TASS, 22 July 1993; and *Demokratychna Ukraina* (Kiev), 10 August 1993.

131. *Narodna armiia*, 26 November 1993.

132. *Narodna armiia*, 8 June 1993. Eighty-eight percent of draftees did not want to

serve in the armed forces, while 61 percent threatened to desert in Dnipropetrovs'k Oblast.

133. *Robitnycha hazeta*, 31 March 1994.

134. *Narodna armiia*, 16 June 1993. UPA veteran Roman Kharkhalis was invited to speak to pre-conscript draftees taking part in a sports competition. *Narodna armiia*, 14 May 1994.

135. *Narodna armiia*, 8 February 1994.

136. *Narodna armiia*, 15 February 1994.

137. *Krasnaia zvezda*, 6 November 1992.

138. On *didovschina*, see *Holos Ukrainy*, 26 March 1993; *Narodna armiia*, 14 April 1993, 17 August 1993, 7 September 1993, and 17 December 1993.

139. See *Vechirnii Kyiv*, 18 December 1993. Forty percent of Kharkiv youths asked in one survey pointed to *didovschina* as their reason for not wanting to undertake military service, while another 14 percent were afraid of it harming their health. *Rada*, 2 June 1994.

140. On the link between bullying *(didovschina)* and the low prestige of the military, see *Narodna armiia*, 23 September 1993.

141. Forty servicemen committed suicide in the first quarter of 1994. *Kyivs'kyi visnyk* (Kiev), 21 June 1994.

142. UNIAN News Agency, 10 August 1993; and UNIAR News Agency, 13 August 1993.

143. *Narodna armiia*, 13 May 1994.

144. Ibid.

145. Reuters, 10 July 1994.

9

Belarusian Perspectives on National Security and Belarusian Military Policy

Anatolii Rozanov

One of the main functions of every state is to secure its own safety. This is done by demonstrating resistance to all kinds of external threats, and especially by demonstrating the capacity to fight if war should come. The basic requirements and provisions concerning the rules and methods by which this security function is fulfilled are usually outlined in the national security strategy. An integral part of this strategy is a military doctrine that provides a strategic concept for a state to maintain and use its armed forces so that they can withstand attack in case of war.

Military doctrines have undergone drastic transformation since the end of the Cold War. The most prominent aspect of this change has been the shift in the essence of doctrinal guidelines from the problems of conducting war to those of preventing it. This redirection is connected with the tendency to create a Euro-Atlantic system of collective security that might ensure a greater sense of security for each country at less cost than that incurred under the confrontational security arrangements of the past.[1]

The vision of Euro-Atlantic security presupposes that each country relies on the sense of security of other states. Obviously, in order to be a reliable partner in this mutual security arrangement, each state must develop and pursue a concept of national security that is fundamentally cooperative and compatible with evolving collective security frameworks.

Therefore, one of the principal tasks facing the newly independent Republic of Belarus is the formulation and implementation of a prudent national security strategy and a well-defined, far-sighted defense policy within the context of the European security setting.

Unfortunately, so far neither the Ministry of Foreign Affairs nor the Ministry of Defense of the Republic of Belarus has issued any detailed, comprehensive statement or report on this subject. There is almost no available information about the steps to be taken by the republic in the security sphere. To understand this void, one must take into account the absence of a tradition in Belarus of open and free discussion of such issues. Formerly the republic had no real opportunity to articulate its position on these matters because all the major decisions related to the formulation and implementation of the foreign policy and security strategy of the former Soviet Union were made in Moscow.

The purpose of this chapter is to interpret the fundamentals of an emerging Belarusian line in the realm of security and to provide appropriate information about practical steps taken by the republic in this sphere.

Basic Principles of Belarusian Security Policy

The general principles of the security policy of Belarus were outlined in the Declaration of State Sovereignty on 27 July 1990 and were confirmed in the constitution of the Republic of Belarus adopted by the Belarusian Supreme Soviet on 15 March 1994. These principles include the intention to be free of nuclear weapons and neutral in the foreseeable future. Article 18 of the constitution states:

> The Republic of Belarus shall proceed in its foreign policy from the principles of states' equality, the nonuse or threat of force, the sanctity of borders, the peaceful settlement of disputes, noninterference in internal affairs, and other generally recognized principles and rules of international law. The Republic of Belarus aims to make its territory a nuclear-free zone, and the state neutral.[2]

One can see that the principles of the Belarusian foreign and security policy are outlined in the constitution in a very concise form. It would therefore be appropriate to formulate and explain the conceptual guidelines that have shaped the Belarusian foreign policy.

By the middle of 1994, several versions of a general foreign policy concept were developed by the Ministry of Foreign Affairs, but not one of them was accepted by the Presidium of the Supreme Soviet. What is really surprising is that these options are regarded by Belarusian officials as "classified" information. The habit of treating important information and documents as secret has rather deep roots in Belarusian political life. This is but one example of Belarus's totalitarian legacy.

For understandable reasons, Western politicians and observers have paid considerable attention to the process of denuclearization within the former Soviet republics. The policy of Belarus in this respect does not cause any considerable fears in the West.

As distinct from Ukraine and Kazakhstan, Belarus has been consistent in its adherence to the first Strategic Arms Reduction Treaty (START I) and to the Nuclear Nonproliferation Treaty (NPT). Belarus will definitely become a nuclear-weapon-free state by 1997. Technically, it is not so difficult for the republic to rid itself of nuclear weapons deployed on its territory, because the intercontinental ballistic missiles (ICBMs) based at Lida and Mozyr are SS–25 mobile missiles. Furthermore, from the standpoint of strategic stability, the single-warhead SS–25 is much more defensive in nature than the multiple-warhead SS–24s and SS–19s deployed in Ukraine, or the multiple-warhead SS–18s based in Kazakhstan.

By the autumn of 1992, all strategic nuclear weapons in Belarus had been put under Russian control. The removal of ICBMs from Belarus to Russia started in the middle of 1993. Nine SS–25s (out of a total of seventy-two) were withdrawn in 1993, thirty-six more are to be transferred to Russia in 1994, and the rest were to be transferred in 1995.[3] These missiles will be redeployed to Valdais to replace the older SS–17 missiles. This action will not violate any provisions of the START I Treaty or the START II agreement.

When the Belarusian parliament ratified the NPT and START I and the Lisbon Protocol in February 1993, however, the agreements with Russia governing the status of Belarusian nuclear weapons and the coordination of Russian and Belarusian military activities were criticized by some Belarusian deputies from the opposition who demanded more Belarusian control over the process of withdrawal of nuclear weapons to Russia.

Earlier, several Belarusian military leaders and security analysts had proposed that a limited number of ICBMs remain in Belarus to safeguard its security.[4] Some analysts noted that in Cold-War West Germany, American tactical and intermediate-range nuclear weapons had been deployed to serve the purpose of extended deterrence, and that Russian ICBMs could play a similar role for Belarus by virtue of its geographic location.

This point of view was not shared by a majority of deputies. In Belarus, the influential political players were not interested in maintaining ICBMs on Belarusian soil. But as Roy Allison insightfully put it, by accepting that the nuclear weapons in Belarus belonged to Russia, Minsk placed itself "under a de facto Russian nuclear umbrella, covered by a form of 'extended deterrence,' with or without specific nuclear guarantees from Russia."[5]

Belarus's ratification of the START I Treaty and unconditional adherence to the NPT were widely applauded in all quarters. Belarus thereby signaled its reliability as a partner in post–Cold War international politics. The Belarusian government has also been supportive of the Russian government's stance on nuclear weapons in other republics of the former Soviet Union.

Following the Belarusian ratification of START I and the NPT, the United States offered $65 million in aid and technical assistance toward the secure dismantlement and safeguarding of nuclear weapons on Belarusian territory. This amount is in addition to the $11 million provided by previously concluded agreements. As a result, the United States signed aid agreements with Belarus in

August 1993 in such areas as export controls, environmental restoration, and defense conversion, totaling $59 million, and has continued to explore with Belarus the best use of the remaining funds. The Belarusian projects to be funded by the United States include (in millions of dollars):[6]

Emergency Response	5.00
Export Controls	16.26
Communications	2.30
Environmental Restoration	25.00
Defense Conversion	20.00
Strategic Nuclear Delivery/ Vehicle Dismantlement	6.00
Military-to-Military Contacts	1.50
TOTAL	76.06

In January 1994, President Bill Clinton visited Belarus during his European tour. The six-hour visit was regarded by some Western observers as Belarus's "reward" for relinquishing the nuclear weapons it inherited from the Soviet Union.[7] By visiting Minsk, President Clinton evidently also meant to signal Ukraine that it would not be forgotten if it followed Belarus's lead.

An important point that deserves to be raised in relation to Belarusian security policy is the question of neutrality and its potential impact on Belarus. It seems that considerable problems are likely to arise if Belarus tries to achieve its desired neutral status as soon as possible without taking account of the cessation of East-West politico-military confrontation and the fundamental changes in Europe that have emerged with the end of the Cold War. A discussion as to the wisdom of becoming neutral immediately is now taking place, as Belarus tries to react to different initiatives aimed at the creation of new collective security structures.

In 1992–93 Prime Minister Vyacheslau Kebich stressed that, given Western Europe's alliance policy, it was doubtful that Belarus could become a neutral state in practice. Citing the examples of Finland, Austria, and Sweden as neutral countries that were currently reconsidering their positions, he came to the conclusion that Belarus's neutrality option would prove counterproductive and could serve to isolate Belarus.

The most ardent advocates of Belarusian neutrality have been the opposition Belarusian Popular Front (BPF) and its leader, Zenon Pazn′iak. The policy of neutrality is favorably viewed by the BPF because it wishes to distance Belarus from Russia and redirect Belarusian foreign policy more toward the West.

When the Treaty on Collective Security was signed in Tashkent on 15 May 1992 by representatives of six newly independent states (former republics of the Soviet Union, including Russia), Belarus at first decided not to join, on the grounds that its future neutral status would not allow it to take part in any military alliances. But after heated debate in the Supreme Soviet, Belarus decided on 8 April 1993 to accede to the treaty, with several reservations.

The vote was 188 deputies in favor, 34 opposed, and 30 abstentions. The deputies approved the treaty only under the condition that Belarusian troops never serve beyond the republic's borders. Zenon Pazn'iak, however, accused the pro-Russian parliamentary majority of betraying the Belarusian national interest by supporting participation in the pact. Indeed, the chairman of the Supreme Soviet, Stanislau Shushkevich, voted against the Treaty on Collective Security; he argued that entering it is at odds with Belarus's proclaimed aim of neutrality.

The supporters of the pact state that the Tashkent treaty itself does not mean the formation of a military bloc. They argue that the treaty was designed to create a regional collective security system that corresponds to the principles of the United Nations charter. They also stress that the strong military ties with Russia that accompany participation in collective security mechanisms are un-avoidable during the current period of transition, and should therefore be institu-tionalized through the Tashkent treaty.

Nevertheless, many supporters of the pact openly doubt whether Belarus can become neutral while occupying such a geostrategically important position in Eastern Europe. Most of Belarus's neighbors are knocking on the door of the North Atlantic Treaty Organization (NATO), trying to obtain NATO military guarantees in one form or another. In the future NATO may become the central military pillar of an all-European security system. In light of this possibility, the nonparticipation of Belarus in future security structures that might be built under NATO auspices would hardly be prudent. The prospect of a NATO-centered European security system is not unrealistic. We should therefore look to the future with an open mind.

It is noteworthy that Western analysts are rather skeptical about the prospects of neutrality for such countries as Belarus and Ukraine. For example, the authors of a report on the new European security order, prepared in May 1993 for the Political Committee of the North Atlantic Assembly, state that if a country chooses to be neutral in the emerging international situation in Europe, it as-sumes that there are going to be political, military, ideological, or other divisions in Europe. But if those divisions are disappearing with the end of the Cold War, it is a rather strange option for states to proclaim neutrality—vis-à-vis what and whom?[8]

Of course, a country can choose not to align itself with any multilateral, collective, or bilateral security arrangements. But practically speaking, this ap-plies to either small peripheral countries or countries with an established tradi-tion of neutral status, such as Switzerland.

Moreover, even Switzerland's traditional foreign and security policy has been called into question by the changes in Europe. For Manfred Rosch, "According to Bern's new basic stance, neutrality is no longer valid if the international community takes collective action against law-breakers."[9] Some Swiss experts argue that Switzerland should in the future exploit every opportunity for external political involvement.

According to Swiss Defense Minister Kaspar Villiger, Switzerland cannot avoid a wide-ranging discussion about neutrality over the coming years. Addressing an April 1994 international conference in Zurich titled "Institutes and Security Dialogue," Villiger said, "We are adapting our neutrality policy to the new circumstances of our strategic environment. Neutrality cannot preclude us from contributing to European stability. . . . Neutrality is an instrument, not an objective of Swiss security policy."[10]

These remarks seem relevant to the ongoing discussion in Belarus on the merits and possible negative side effects of the neutrality option. Stanislau Shushkevich was in favor of an unconditional shift of the republic toward neutrality and against participation in any form of the Tashkent treaty. At first he proposed that this matter be decided through a referendum. Then his position became more vague. This ambiguity was one of the main reasons for his dismissal by parliament. The new chairman of the Supreme Soviet, Mycheslau Hryb, who previously headed the parliamentary Commission for Questions of National Security, Defense, and Crime Prevention, unequivocally supported the treaty.[11]

The policy of neutrality obviously should not be an end in itself, but rather a means of safeguarding the security of Belarus. It could be a pragmatic option, open to reconsideration. To include the neutrality objective in the Belarusian constitution seems unneccessary. It is perhaps worth recalling that in 1847 the Swiss founding fathers chose not to incorporate neutrality into their constitution. Rather, they saw neutrality as an instrument that might, in an emergency, have to be surrendered.

According to the *Economist*, "Neutrality may be going out of fashion. The famous European neutrals—Sweden, Switzerland, Finland, and Austria—are all to some extent moving away from it."[12] Indeed, as the Swedish minister for foreign affairs, Baroness Margaretha af Ugglas, has stated, "As the pace of history accelerates and our involvement with the rest of Europe deepens, the policy we pursue could no longer be labeled neutrality."[13]

With the disappearence of the Soviet Union and the dissolution of the Warsaw Pact, there are no longer two alliances to be neutral between. The dramatic changes in the political and strategic map of Europe make the Belarusian goal of becoming neutral somewhat out of date. In fact, the stubborn adherence of some Belarusian leaders to the neutrality option clearly reflects their provincial mind-set and their inability to understand the tendencies of international development. The viewpoint is being disseminated that Belarus could become "a second Switzerland" if it pursues the policy of neutrality. Any disinterested observer can see that this view is groundless, though, of course, appealing.

In the entirely new European security setting it would be wise for Belarus to face the changes while keeping open all foreign and military policy options, without overemphasizing any one of them, especially neutrality.

Belarusian Military Doctrine and Military Reform

On 16 December 1992, the Supreme Soviet of Belarus formally adopted a document embodying Belarusian military doctrine. The complete text of the document has not been published, but the main features and characteristics have since been revealed by the defense minister, Colonel General Pavel Kazlouski.[14]

Military doctrine is officially regarded in Belarus as a system of fundamental principles on the prevention of war, the preservation of peace, defense development, preparation of the armed forces for countering possible aggression, and methods of engagement of the armed forces in the defense of the sovereignty and territorial integrity of the republic.

The military doctrine of Belarus has a strictly defensive orientation. It is aimed not at waging war but preventing war and bolstering international security and stability. The Republic of Belarus, according to the doctrine, will pursue its own independent course in the military and security realm. At the same time, the doctrine, while emphasizing the requirements for a policy of "armed neutrality," provides an opportunity for military cooperation with other countries for defensive purposes. This possibility, however, is mentioned in the document only in the context of organizing coordinated counteractive measures in case of aggression.

The military doctrine of the Republic of Belarus, as presented by Kazlouski, has two basic dimensions: military-political and military-technical. Thus, it incorporates some traditional Soviet approaches to military doctrine, thereby demonstrating a shortage of original strategic thinking on the part of the Belarusian defense establishment.

The military-political facet of the doctrine emanates from the so-called concepts of the prevention of war and cessation of aggression. The concepts of deterrence and active defense determine the military-technical part of the doctrine. These concepts are developed within the doctrine only in the most general terms. They hardly look convincing. It is difficult to imagine, for instance, how the Belarusian armed forces would incorporate or implement the concept of deterrence under present or future circumstances. It is wise not to overestimate the significance and real meaning of this document. In fact, it is only an interim statement.

In practical terms, the official doctrine calls for substantial reductions in the armed forces of Belarus. This reduced force is to be made up of airborne, air defense, and smaller mobile assault units, replacing the earlier massive tank formations.

As the western front of the former Soviet Union, Belarus was always considered to be on the front line of any confrontation with NATO. As a result, the republic had one of the largest concentrations of new heavy weapons, particularly main battle tanks (1,850, to be precise), and one of the largest concentrations of service personnel per capita of any republic of the former Soviet Union.[15] In fact, because of its strategic position, Belarus was one of the most

militarized parts of Europe. Six of the thirty-two tank divisions of the Commonwealth of Independent States (CIS) were located in Belarus.[16]

The armed forces of Belarus were set up on the basis of the Soviet Belarusian
military district and the military contingents and units deployed in the republic.
The troops constituting the Belarusian military district numbered 130,000. In
addition, there were forty thousand troops in the strategic forces stationed in
Belarus.[17]

By the end of 1992, the number of military personnel declined to 115,000 (a
20.6 percent reduction) and,[18] by the autumn of 1994, it was slightly more than
100,000. In adopting the new military doctrine, the Belarusian Supreme Soviet
decided that military personnel should not exceed 100,000—1 percent of the
population. This indicator is regarded by Belarusian officials as a generally
accepted standard for European countries.

One of the problems within the Belarusian armed forces has been the ethnic
makeup of the officer corps. At the time of the breakup of the Soviet Union,
ethnic Belarusians accounted for only 16 percent of the army's officers. Russians
constituted over 50 percent, and even Ukrainians outnumbered Belarusians, representing over 20 percent of the officer corps. This distribution has had repercus-
sions for the armed forces, as the loyalties of these officers have been questioned
by the BPF and the Belarusian Association of Servicemen. Both of these groups
share the view that Belarus should have a national army. Efforts have been made
to alleviate this situation by banning all political organizations from the armed
forces. The depoliticization of the army was directed mainly at the Belarusian
Association of Servicemen, which has been responsible for generating ethnic
tensions within the armed forces.

At the same time, measures have been taken to gradually de-Russify the
forces as a whole. In June 1992, the Ministry of Defense declared that Belarusian
was to be the official language spoken in the military. In June 1994, it was
reported that 47 percent of the officers and a majority of the conscripts were
native Belarusians. In as little as one year, it was said, Belarusian-born servicemen would account for 65 percent of the Belarusian army.[19]

The army's public image has suffered. Domestically, there is a common view
that Belarus does not need any significant military force and, furthermore, that
the republic cannot afford such a force, owing to economic constraints. In 1994,
only about 4 percent of the republican budget was earmarked for the Ministry of
Defense. This money was enough only for the army to survive.[20] As a result of
negligence toward the army's problems and needs, lack of suitable housing for
officers, and inadequate social conditions, morale is not high among the servicemen. A poll conducted among officers of the Minsk Higher Military Engineering
College in 1994 showed that 52 percent of those surveyed did not see any
prospects for their continued service, and 25 percent had already decided to leave
the Belarusian armed forces. As many as 96 percent of the servicemen expressed
their dissatisfaction with the legal status and material security of Belarusian

officers.[21] Not surprisingly, the Belarusian army is now short of about fifteen hundred junior officers.[22]

For decades the military-industrial complex has placed a heavy burden on the Belarusian economy. During the Cold War about one-half of machine-building output was devoted to military needs.[23] More than two hundred thousand specialists were employed in the defense sector of the economy.[24] Defense employment constituted as much as 20 percent of the industrial workforce.

The time has come to demilitarize the Belarusian economy. Since the breakup of the USSR, orders for military-technical equipment from Russia and other countries of the CIS to Belarus have decreased from 42.6 percent of the total output in 1991 to 9.5 percent in 1993.[25]

So far, however, Belarus's economic conversion efforts have not been impressive. Not surprisingly, the directors of militarily oriented enterprises were among the most active supporters of Belarus's participation in the CIS Treaty on Collective Security. They vigorously backed the government in its efforts to forge an economic union with Russia.

During his visit to Minsk in March 1994, U.S. Defense Secretary William Perry offered Belarus more aid and contracts with U.S. firms for defense conversion. Perry also provided $30 million to Belarusian authorities to proceed with conversion programs in industry, housing, officer retraining, and the destruction of conventional weapons.[26]

When Belarus was a part of the USSR, it had approximately one hundred enterprises that participated in the production of individual components for military equipment, but it had no integrated system for the production of weapons. Therefore, despite the fact that about 50 percent of Belarusian industry had been engaged in military production, as of today only 3 to 5 percent of the listed requirements of the Belarusian army can be satisfied by the republic's industry.[27]

Current Foreign and Security Policies of Belarus

In the current foreign policy of Belarus, there is a trend toward more active participation in the Conference on Security and Cooperation in Europe (CSCE), which is regarded by leading Belarusian experts as the most suitable way of strengthening the republic's security environment. The CSCE remains the only real all-European forum for political dialogue. One of the advantages of the CSCE is that it covers almost all aspects of security—political, military, economic, ecological, humanitarian, and so forth. In the 1991 Charter of Paris for a New Europe, the CSCE outlined the vision of a comprehensive security setting for Europe built on a foundation of democracy and cooperative security. Since then, significant progress has been achieved.

But this vision is far from being realized. The crisis in the former Yugoslavia has also shown the limitations of the CSCE framework. The CSCE, which has developed various mechanisms for crisis management, is not a true collective security organization, because it lacks the necessary instruments of enforcing adherence to its principles.

The time has come to build and extend the institutional and operational dimensions of the CSCE process. Belarus strongly supports these efforts. The CSCE is faced with the necessity of streamlining its decision-making process and improving its capacity for early warning and prevention of conflicts. If it is successful in these efforts, the CSCE can do much more to promote regional stability, especially through the untapped potential of its Forum on Security Cooperation.

It is clear that in the process of elaborating the security and defense priorities of Belarus, policy makers should not ignore corresponding concepts developed by NATO countries. A useful channel of mutual information on security and defense matters can be obtained through Belarus's membership in the North Atlantic Cooperation Council (NACC). It is in the interest of Belarus to take advantage of its membership in the NACC. Belarus would like to see a greater operational role for the NACC, although this institution seems to be only an interim solution to the security concerns of Central and East European countries. The future of this structure is by and large uncertain. NATO has declared that it is prepared to make itself available for international peacekeeping operations. It has taken steps in this direction up to the use of military force. Nevertheless, NATO has been and remains primarily an alliance for the purpose of collective defense rather than collective security. At the moment it is not ready—or willing—to extend its security guarantees to cover greater Europe. These guarantees still apply only to NATO members. NATO's role outside its area is not entirely clear. One of the pertinent topics for discussion in strategic and political circles is the question of NATO's eastward enlargement. The expansion of NATO to the east seems to be premature and difficult to achieve at this juncture. It would be easier to extend the obligation to consult under Article 4 of the Washington treaty with NACC partners, first of all with the countries of the Visegrad Group, than to extend the guarantees of Article 5.

NATO can hardly disregard the position of the Russian leadership with respect to the enlargement of the alliance, although NATO officials have indicated that Russia has no veto over NATO policies. There is sense in the opinion expressed by Russia's security analysts that NATO's expansion should be synchronized with its transformation.[28] Such a transformation should even occur first. But so far nobody knows exactly how NATO will be transformed and to what extent it could strengthen its political component at the expense of a military one.

Certainly, NATO will remain the central point of engagement for the United States in European security. The U.S. government is now working with its European allies to adapt NATO to the new challenges of an undivided Europe and to turn former adversaries into new partners for peace.

The United States has initiated NATO's Partnership for Peace (PfP) program, which will extend practical security cooperation to the NACC partners and other European nations. The United States and its allies do not exclude the possibility of opening the door to an evolutionary expansion of NATO's membership. But in the words of former U.S. Defense Secretary, Les Aspin, the PfP "puts the question of NATO membership where it belongs, at the end of the process rather than at the beginning."[29]

In Belarus, although the Partnership for Peace was from the beginning viewed favorably, the idea of NATO's expansion to the east was regarded as controversial. It appears that a positive response of Belarus to the PfP is a reasonable option. When Defense Secretary William Perry visited Minsk in March 1994, however, earlier predictions that Belarus would seek to gain membership in the Partnership for Peace program unfortunately failed to materialize. Belarusian officials said that they wanted to see whether Russia would proceed with its plans to join.[30] It is a pity that the government of Belarus was so inflexible, stubbornly following the Russian line, and allowing itself to be motivated by considerations that have nothing to do with Belarusian national interests.

In September 1994, the new minister of foreign affairs of Belarus, Vladimir Senko, announced that Belarus would soon join the PfP, but in the immediate future would not take part in military exercises owing to financial considerations.[31] The new defense minister, Colonel General Anatolii Kostenko, has indicated the necessity, from the point of view of the Ministry of Defense, of participating in the PfP.[32]

Today Belarus faces a serious dilemma in its relations with Russia. The Belarusian government is inclined to expand its ties with Russia to the utmost. The idea of confederation has already been aired in Russia and Belarus. Some Western observers treat Belarus as "the Soviet-style outpost that has subordinated most of its economic and military policies to Russia."[33]

Since 1993, the Belarusian government has been flirting with the doubtful idea of merging the monetary system of Belarus with that of Russia. The proposal articulated by Vyacheslau Kebich would make the Russian ruble the only legal tender in both countries. In the opinion of Zenon Pazn'iak, the proposed ruble zone constitutes Russian "economic blackmail." Adrian Karatnycky, in an article in *National Review,* argues that "Russia has virtually annexed Belarus by integrating the republic's economy and military into its own."[34]

The issue, however, is more complex than it appears to be at first sight. The views mentioned above may represent an oversimplified, one-sided version of events. It would be incorrect not to take the current economic situation in Belarus into account, as it contributes to the popular appeal of potential economic and monetary union with Russia. The Belarusian interim currency, the *zaichik,* has rapidly lost value since it was introduced in 1992. In March 1994, the Belarusian ruble was worth about 0.15 Russian rubles. Inflation reached 40 percent per month in August 1993, and in August 1994 approached the 50 percent level. The government has been unable to introduce radical market reforms, and no full-scale privatization program has been adopted. Under these circumstances, many people in Belarus view an economic union with Russia as a means to improve their basic living conditions. And it is clear that Russia is far ahead of Belarus in the process of economic transition.

On 12 April 1994, in a move that increased concern in the West about Russian neoimperialism, Russian Prime Minister Viktor Chernomyrdin and his Belarusian counterpart, Vyacheslau Kebich, signed a treaty aimed at unifying the monetary systems of the two countries and lifting customs barriers between them. In a set of agreements that were to be implemented in stages, Belarus was to give up the right to control its money supply, handing over monetary and credit controls to the Russian Central Bank. Russia was to receive a free lease on military bases for its strategic forces still deployed in Belarus.

In return for this limitation on its sovereignty, Belarus was promised cheaper oil and gas from Russia. As *Izvestiia* noted at the signing of the treaty, Belarus "exchanged a part of its sovereignty for Russian rubles."[35] At the same time, the *New York Times* noted that "Western diplomats in Belarus fear that economic union will bring pressures for a more political union, beginning with the potential reintegration of some of the old Russian empire."[36] Western experts, preferring a permanent Belarusian currency, are steadfastly against the monetary union, which they say would prevent Belarus from ever becoming a truly independent state.

So Belarus, the republic most closely linked with Russia, is likely to establish even closer ties with its eastern neighbor. Surely, it will have to pay a considerable political cost for monetary union. And as Russian foreign and military policies in the "near abroad" have become more assertive, generating speculation about a Russian Monroe Doctrine, these linkages will undoubtedly stimulate Western anxiety. The *Calgary Herald* has already formulated the crucial question: "Does this signal the beginning of the putting together of the pieces of the Soviet Union?"[37]

The prospect of a restoration of the Soviet Union in its previous ill-fated form now looks like a fantastic vision. But one can foresee Russian efforts to reverse the process of economic, political, and military disintegration within at least portions of the former Soviet Union in the years to come.

On 10 July 1994, Aliaksandr Lukashenka, the anticorruption campaigner, won the presidential elections in Belarus, garnering over 80 percent of the vote against Vyacheslau Kebich. His decisive victory was to a considerable degree due to popular weariness with old-style Soviet-era leaders who failed to conduct any coherent market reforms in three years of independence.

During the election campaign Lukashenka supported economic and monetary union with Russia. He even suggested that the alliance be extended to the political sphere. But after victory he became more cautious in his estimates of the benefits for Belarus of merging its monetary system with that of Russia.

As a result of President Lukashenka's visit to Moscow and his talks with President Boris Yeltsin, it became clear that the idea of a monetary union with

Russia would probably not materialize. The proposed union has already been criticized within Russia as economically unprofitable. The new Belarusian leadership evidently, began to realize that such a liaison could in effect turn Belarus into a Russian province.

Instead of making a monetary union the first priority, Lukashenka and his team started to concentrate on reaching a comprehensive political modus vivendi with Russia. The treaty on friendship and cooperation between the two countries, according to this approach, would establish the framework for the development of their relations of all aspects.

Lukashenka's economic program during his electoral campaign (to impose strict state control on the economy, confiscate "ill-gotten gains" in the private sector, and the like) led Western observers to describe the new president's likely economic policies as "hair-raising."[38] In practice, however, he adopted a rather pragmatic line on economic reforms and stressed the inevitability of the transition to a market economy. Still, he has given little clue as to how he might implement his economic program.

In the realm of foreign policy and security strategy, no fundamental revisions are envisaged. The so-called eastern vector of Belarusian foreign policy is said to be the dominant feature of the international engagement of the republic. The efforts to bolster collective security within the CIS have not been relinquished.

At the same time, some corrections in the security policy of Belarus are likely to follow. One of the signals is the inclination to join NATO's PfP. The idea of participating in both Eastern and Western security arrangements is gaining ground. Defense Minister Anatolii Kostenko has indicated that the military reform in Belarus is still in its initial phase and has promised to speed it up.[39]

It is worth noting that Foreign Minister Senko stated that the document on Belarus's foreign policy preferences, which was under discussion by the Presidium of the Supreme Soviet, should not be confidential and designed only for experts. In his words, this document must be clear to the ordinary person on the street.[40]

In conclusion, it would be wise for Belarus to pursue a more balanced course in relations with Russia and the West. Finland's model of cooperation with the former USSR might be a useful example of a prudent policy that could be relevant to Belarus. The political leadership of the republic so far has been unwilling to develop such a policy. Belarus needs fresh intellectual and conceptual input into its foreign and security policy-making process in order to gain a respected place within the community of democratic European nations.

Notes

1. Stanislaw Koziej, "A Non-Confrontational Model of Military Doctrine in the Future European Security System," *Military Doctrine and Military Reconstruction in Post-Confrontational Europe* (Prague: Czech Military Review, 1994), p. 22.

2. *Konstitutsiia Respubliki Belarus'* (Minsk: Polymia, 1994), p. 6.

3. *Izvestiia*, 17 March 1994.

4. Roy Allison, *Military Forces in the Soviet Successor States*, Adelphi Paper 280 (London: IISS, 1993), p. 46.

5. Ibid.

6. U.S. Department of State Dispatch, 3 January 1994.

7. *Christian Science Monitor*, 14 January 1994.

8. North Atlantic Assembly, Working Group on the New European Security Order, Interim Report (Brussels: International Secretariat, 1993), p. 14.

9. Manfred Rosch, "Switzerland's Security Policy in Transition," *NATO Review*, vol. 41, no. 6 (December 1993), p. 21.

10. Federal Councillor Kaspar Villiger, Keynote Address, International Conference on "Institutes and the Security Dialogue," Zurich, Switzerland, 26 April 1994.

11. *Sovetskaia Belorussiia*, 9 April 1993.

12. *Economist*, 11 June 1994, p. 31.

13. Margaretha af Ugglas, "Sweden's Security Policy in Post–Cold War Europe," *NATO Review*, vol. 42, no. 2 (April 1994), p. 11.

14. *Vo slavu rodyny*, 23 March 1993.

15. By the end of the Cold War, Belarus had on its soil one soldier per 43 civilians. In contrast, Russia had one soldier per 634 civilians, and Ukraine had one per 98. *Izvestiia*, 20 November 1993.

16. Ustina Markus, "Belarus Debates Security Pact as a Cure for Military Woes," *RFE/RL Research Report*, 18 June 1993, p. 70.

17. *Izvestiia*, 20 November 1993.

18. Ibid.

19. Minsk Radio, 20 June 1994, as reported in *Foreign Broadcast Information Service Daily Report—Central Eurasia*, 22 June 1994, p. 58.

20. *Sel'skaia zhizn'*, 26 May 1994.

21. *Vo slavu rodyny*, 17 May 1994.

22. *Sel'skaia zhizn'*, 26 May 1994.

23. Marion Cutting, "Belarus: Return to the Fold?" *Ostekonomisk Rapport*, vol. 5, no. 9 (24 September 1993), p. 2.

24. *Sovetskaia Belorussiia*, 30 March 1993.

25. Markus, "Belarus Debates Security Pact," p. 68.

26. *Boston Globe*, 24 March 1994.

27. *Zviazda*, 6 May 1994.

28. *Christian Science Monitor*, 14 January 1994.

29. Les Aspin, "New Europe, New NATO," *NATO Review*, vol. 42, no. 1 (February 1994), p. 12.

30. *Boston Globe*, 24 March 1994.

31. *Vo slavu rodyny*, 14 September 1994.

32. *Narodnaia gazeta*, 22 September 1994.

33. *Christian Science Monitor*, 14 January 1994.

34. Adrian Karatnycky, "Another Chance for NATO?" *National Review*, 7 February 1994.

35. *Izvestiia*, 14 April 1994.

36. London *New York Times*, 13 April 1994.

37. *Calgary Herald*, 29 January 1994.

38. *Times*, 12 July 1994.

39. *Sovetskaia Belorussiia*, 22 September 1994.

40. *Sovetskaia Belorussiia*, 7 September 1994.

III

**State-Building and Military Power in the
Southern Newly Independent States**

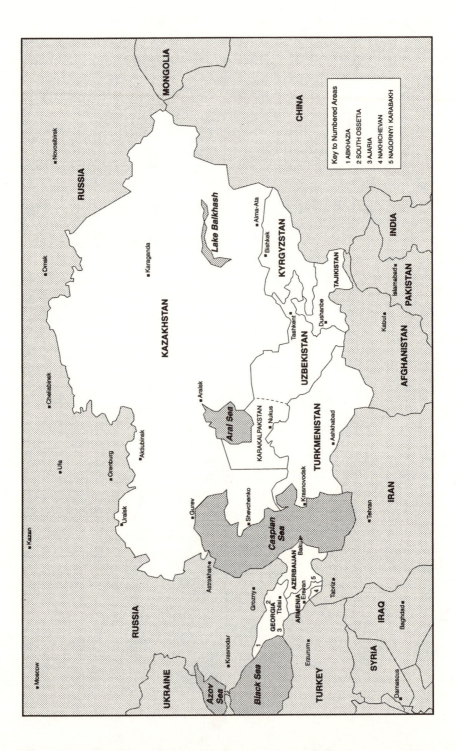

10

National Security and Military Issues in the Transcaucasus

The Cases of Georgia, Azerbaijan, and Armenia

Jonathan Aves

The leaderships of the three internationally recognized states[1] that emerged in Transcaucasia in the wake of the dissolution of the Soviet Union at the end of 1991—Georgia, Azerbaijan, and Armenia—have faced enormous difficulties in enhancing their national security since independence. All these countries found themselves in poor condition to begin establishing themselves as full-fledged members of the international community, and without exception their national security has deteriorated sharply over the past three years. All have had to face the reality of their insignificance in the international order and have had to accept painful and frequently substantial restrictions on their sovereignty.

There has been a strong tendency in discussions concerning the Transcaucasian republics, both in the region and outside, to stress the structural character of their weaknesses and to locate these weaknesses in their inherently difficult geopolitical situation. This argument tends to depict the Transcaucasian republics as pawns in a game being played by powerful neighbors. Much is made of the historical rivalry among Russia, Turkey, and Iran for hegemony over the region, and the inability of local leaderships to affect decisively the national security of their states is taken for granted. The deterioration in their national security since 1991 is seen as confirmation of the correctness of this point of view.

This chapter takes a rather different line. Of course, it would be foolish to suggest that the Transcaucasian republics have not faced a difficult international environment or that the legacy of Soviet rule and, even more crucially, its precipitate collapse, left them in a strong position to consolidate their independence;

but the chapter seeks to redress the balance by highlighting the record of political leaderships in either damaging or enhancing the national security of their states.

It is not surprising that commentators have stressed the inherent weakness of the Transcaucasian states. For outsiders, their emergence as independent states came as something of a surprise that has tended to be regarded more as the by-product of processes in larger and longer-established regional powers than as the expression of local political realities. For Transcaucasian commentators who emerged out of almost complete isolation from the outside world into a largely indifferent international environment, it is more comfortable to blame their disappointments on the scale of the problems they faced than on their own ignorance or mistakes.

This syndrome is particularly apparent in the tendency to ascribe all the problems of the Transcaucasian states to the machinations of Russian imperialists. It would be idle to deny that there are many Russian politicians, officials, and particularly military personnel who are motivated by revanchist and imperialist sentiments in formulating and implementing policy toward Transcaucasia; nor can it be denied that such imperialist tendencies are often informed by a contempt toward the Caucasian peoples that borders on racism. But this is not the whole story.

First, it would be wrong to overestimate the importance of Transcaucasia in the calculations of Russian national security decision makers. It is true that, since the collapse of the Soviet Union, the Russian military has progressively sought to identify a new role for itself in the CIS republics, particularly in combating national-ethnic and religious disputes.[2] However, decisions about whether to intervene and about the type and scale of intervention have tended to stem from circumstantial factors (e.g., the personality of a local commander such as Lieutenant General Aleksandr Lebed' in Trans-Dniestria, or the pattern of existing deployments, which has helped make Abkhazia and the Crimea centers of tension because Russian forces were stationed there as a result of prior Soviet deployments) or domestic considerations (e.g., the escalation of tensions in Abkhazia and the Crimea as the power struggle between Yeltsin and the parliament came to a head in the autumn of 1993).

Second, it would be wrong to overestimate Russian power. While Russia is clearly far more powerful than the Transcaucasian republics, it has been experiencing a severe political and economic crisis for at least five years that has had a significant impact on its capacity (including its military capacity) to project its power externally. Thus, increasingly hawkish Russian rhetoric has been accompanied, in practice, by the withdrawal of forces from Azerbaijan, Lithuania, and Latvia and (as of the summer of 1994) agreements on their future withdrawal from Estonia and Moldova.

Third, skillful behavior by the leaderships of the non-Russian republics concerned in preventing internal political divisions that can be exploited by Moscow and especially in ensuring the smooth management of civil-military relations can make a significant contribution toward enhancing national security. An additional factor that can contribute to the enhancment of the national security of the post-Soviet states is successful state-building, that is, the creation of legitimate and effective political-administrative structures that can mobilize resources toward the achievement of national security goals. This chapter will seek to demonstrate the applicability of these remarks regarding the behavior of local political leaderships and successful state-building to the cases of Georgia, Azerbaijan, and Armenia.

National Security in the Transcaucasian Context

For all three Transcaucasian republics, the primary national security tasks are consolidating independence, breaking their dependence on Russia, acquiring diplomatic recognition from the international community, and establishing direct bilateral contacts of all kinds with other states. This aspiration for independence is in strong contrast to the situation in 1917, when the leading political movements in the Transcaucasian republics restricted themselves to raising demands for autonomy when faced with the collapse of the tsarist empire. In the late 1980s, independence was the unqualified demand of all the leading Transcaucasian political movements, even, surprisingly, in Armenia, although strong pro-Russian sentiments remained, especially in the diaspora.

Identifying the factors that affect national security has become the subject of considerable debate in the academic literature in recent years. Traditional definitions of national security have stemmed from the concerns of established states and have emphasized the defense of national territory by building up military potential and concluding alliances with other states to minimize external threats.[3] Such narrow definitions are less helpful when we are dealing with new states, such as the Transcaucasian republics, which face pressing threats to their sovereignty and even survival stemming from their weak legitimacy. Of course, traditional definitions of national security still have a great deal of relevance to the problems faced by the Transcaucasian republics. All three have attempted to pursue the usual strategies of building up military potential and seeking alliances with other states to enhance their national security, but as this chapter will demonstrate, their success has also very much depended on their record in state-building.

There are also some crucial differences of emphasis in the immediate national security tasks faced by the three Transcaucasian republics. For Georgia and Azerbaijan, the main task is the need to combat potential and actual secessionist threats, but by contrast, for Armenia, the main task is the need to protect the rights of Armenians living outside its borders, principally the Armenian community of Nagorno-Karabagh, and, if possible, unite them in one political unit.[4] This perception is linked with vivid memories of the genocide of the Armenian communities in eastern Anatolia in 1915 and a view of the present Armenian national territory that stresses its unviability, especially due to the paucity of its natural resources and its landlocked character.

In essence, national security is the product of an interaction between relatively fixed factors, such as population size, economic strength, and geopolitical situation, and more intangible factors, especially the skill of political leaders in mobilizing available resources and, through effective diplomacy, securing the support of other states to achieve national security goals. In established states the task of political leaders is facilitated by the existence of legitimate (usually representative) institutions and effective (usually bureaucratic) administrative structures to carry out these functions. Naturally these institutions and structures are either weak or absent in new states such as the Transcaucasian republics, which places much more of an onus on the skill, choices, and even luck of their political leaders in enhancing their national security than in established states.

As this chapter makes clear, the resources and alliances with other states that are potentially available to the three Transcaucasian republics vary considerably and, as noted above, so does the respective nature of their national security tasks. But, crucially for the argument of this chapter, there is not an obvious fit between the endowment of resources and available alliances and the success of the three Transcaucasian republics in realizing their national security tasks. The long-term national security of the Transcaucasian republics is very difficult to predict, but to put it crudely, the record so far shows that Georgia has played a weak hand poorly, Azerbaijan has played a relatively strong hand poorly, and Armenia has played a weak hand relatively skillfully. The operative factor in determining these outcomes has not been predetermined structural factors but the quality of political leadership.

State-Building

Since the late 1980s, the political leaderships of all three Transcaucasian republics have found themselves having to breathe life into the administrative structures bequeathed to them from the Soviet regime. On the surface, these structures seemed almost like the institutions of full-fledged states in embryo. The federal form of the Soviet constitution had granted union republics like Georgia, Azerbaijan, and Armenia many of the trappings of sovereign states—national assemblies (supreme soviets) and administrative bureaucracies, including many of the ministries that exist in independent states, such as foreign and interior ministries, as well as regional and local administrative bodies (local soviets).

However, endowing these bodies with real legitimacy and enforcing normal bureaucratic procedures proved to be a very complex task. In all the Transcaucasian republics, to a greater or lesser extent, political leaderships have proved to be incapable of maintaining a basic level of law and order, let alone mobilizing resources for the military tasks that all have faced over the past three years. This is largely because the institutions prescribed by the Soviet constitution did not reflect the real distribution of power, which grew out of Communist Party networks held together by economic and ethnic ties.

The weakness of the institutions that the Transcaucasian republics inherited from the Soviet system led in all three instances to a formal concentration of power in executive presidencies, as the military emergencies that all three republics faced seemed to demand. However, the task of breathing new life into hitherto moribund institutions, such as republican supreme soviets, and especially the creation of powerful new institutions, such as executive presidencies, touched on the perquisites of powerful interest groups and elites and required leaderships willing to engage in a complex process of bargaining. Their relative success in doing so can be measured by the level of violent political factionalism and corruption as well as by the extent to which elementary law and order are upheld and resources effectively mobilized for military purposes.

It is also true, of course, that all the former Soviet republics lacked some of the basic attributes of sovereign states, including, most significantly for this chapter, armed forces. The creation of armed forces in the Transcaucasian republics proved to be a singularly tension-ridden business. For a variety of reasons—some political (distrust of commanders who had secured promotion under the communist system), some to do with timing (all had to begin the creation of armed forces before the disintegration of the Soviet Union had given them an unambiguous legal right to do so), and some to do with ethnic/cultural reasons (particularly a lack of ethnic Caucasian trained personnel)—none of the Transcaucasian republics could follow the Ukrainian example and simply assume control of Soviet forces deployed on their territory. Certainly, the great bulk of the military equipment employed by the armies of the Transcaucasian republics originated from the Soviet army, but most of it had to be acquired through semilegal commercial means.

The need to create armies from scratch and equip them very quickly meant that in all the Transcaucasian republics, to a greater or lesser extent, political leaderships had to look to figures within their respective national movements with either the organizational ability or the financial clout to play a key role in setting up armed forces. The restricted control over the military (in terms of political loyalty and control over financial resources) that inevitably resulted from these origins[5] has created that characteristic feature of the military scene in post-Soviet Transcaucasia, the militia warlord. It is no exaggeration to say that these warlords have represented and continue to represent the most serious threat to the national security of the Transcaucasian republics.

Georgia

The successive Georgian leaderships in Tbilisi faced particularly difficult problems in consolidating their authority over the territory of the republic. First, the country had three autonomous entities on its territory. Of these, two—Abkhazia and Ajaria—had the status of autonomous republics under the Soviet constitution and, with it, some of the attributes of sovereignty.[6] The third, South Ossetia, although granted fewer formal rights (it was an autonomous region), had a population in which ethnic Ossetians formed a clear majority, and the local communist leadership established links with the "conservative" Soiuz bloc in the USSR Supreme Soviet in the late 1980s.

The authorities in Tbilisi rapidly lost effective control over these autonomous entities and, in South Ossetia and Abkhazia, fought unsuccessful campaigns to reestablish their authority, with the result that both entities had established de facto independence by the end of 1993. As far as Ajaria is concerned, the local leader, Aslan Abashidze, has tended to confine himself to promoting the economic autonomy of his fiefdom. The majority of the population of Ajaria is Muslim, unlike the rest of Georgia, but they are predominantly ethnically Georgian, and this has allowed Abashidze occasionally to play the role of mediator between Georgian factions and even to be suggested as a potential national leader.[7]

Tbilisi's policy toward these autonomous entities has been relatively consistent under changing political leaderships in attempting to assert strong central control. In terms of national security, this policy has arguably as much to commend it as any other, but implementation was attempted in the face of strong opposition from influential groups in Moscow and the North Caucasus and, most important, the Tbilisi authorities were unable to enforce their claims because of the absence of effective military sanctions at their disposal. As a result, they have found themselves entering into negotiations on the future political relationship between Tbilisi and the autonomies in an extremely weak position, from which they could be forced to make greater concessions than if they had avoided or postponed a military showdown.

In terms of fixed resources, Georgia has both strong and weak points. Its total population of around 5.5 million is larger than that of Armenia, Estonia, Latvia, and Moldova, and it is a fertile country, even though in agricultural terms it is dependent on imports of crucial staples such as grain, meat, and sugar from other former Soviet republics. Georgia has an extended Black Sea coastline, but most of its trade passes through rail and road links that lie across Abkhazia; the alternative route lies through Azerbaijan, which gives Baku potentially unwelcome extra leverage.

Of the three Transcaucasian republics, Georgia is the most ethnically heterogeneous. In 1989, roughly 70 percent of the population was ethnically Georgian. However, it is interesting to note that, in national terms, the Ossetians and Abkhazians were the fourth and fifth largest minorities, respectively. The largest minority group was the Armenians, followed by the Russians, and then the Azerbaijanis.[8] The existence of significant Armenian and Azerbaijani minorities, both with concentrations in border areas, creates a potentially serious source of tension, not least from conflicting demands to enforce central control over minority areas and latent secessionist tendencies. This is one area, at least, where Georgian policy has been relatively successful. This is mainly the result of Tbilisi's success in steering a middle course between the two republics of Armenia and Azerbaijan in their conflict over Nagorno-Karabagh and, particularly in the case of the Armenian minority in the Akhalkalaki district, not enforcing its claims for central control.[9]

Despite these economic and demographic weaknesses, it is clear that the Tbilisi authorities should have had more than sufficient resources at their disposal to crush the rebellions of the sixty-six thousand Ossetians in South Ossetia and one hundred thousand Abkhazians. Tbilisi's strength vis-à-vis Abkhazia was additionally boosted by the fact that within the Abkhazian autonomous republic, ethnic Abkhazians constituted only about 18 percent of the population, with Georgians making up about 45 percent.[10] While it was always likely that the Abkhazians and Ossetians would come into serious conflict with Tbilisi and forces in Russia would exploit those conflicts, the divisions between Georgians strengthened the secessionists' hand and provided revanchist Russians with opportunities to intervene. Indeed, it is the intensity of the violent conflict between different Georgian factions and, partially as a consequence, the failure to establish effective administrative structures that have been the most serious sources of Georgian weakness.

In the spring of 1991, in an attempt to create a new effective governmental apparatus that could circumvent what he felt were unreliable existing structures, Zviad Gamsakhurdia set up a strong executive presidency. However, the move was premature. Despite the fact that he was elected by an overwhelming majority in May 1991, his authority as president was, if anything, actually less than it had been when he was merely chairman of the Supreme Soviet, since he had alienated powerful interest groups and provoked charges of authoritarianism from his rivals in the nationalist movement who feared that they were being marginalized. Administrative upheaval (Gamsakhurdia attempted to carry out a radical reform of local government at the same time) and the tenuous legitimacy of the new structures meant that Georgia had begun to descend into chaos before Gamsakhurdia was ousted from the presidency at the beginning of 1992.

The return of the former Soviet foreign minister, Eduard Shevardnadze, to Georgia in March 1992 was greeted as a sign that the republic's leadership might evince a greater degree of competence and coherence in the future. However, Shevardnadze's overenthusiastic endorsement of what had essentially been a military coup as a "democratic revolution" left him in the power of the National Guard and Mkhedrioni militias.[11] While the appointment of Tengiz Kitovani and Jaba Ioseliani to responsible government positions (minister of defense and member of the defense council, respectively) could have been seen as a way of taming them in the chaotic situation in which Georgia found itself, it had the opposite effect.

The question of establishing a Georgian armed forces had first arisen in earnest at the end of 1990, after the victory of Gamsakhurdia's nationalist Roundtable bloc in elections to the Supreme Soviet. Coming to power on a wave of anticommunist emotion and himself a former dissident, it is not surprising that he should have looked outside the ranks of Soviet professionals for the leader of the National Guard, set up in January 1991, with a planned strength of twelve thousand men; however, his choice of his associate Kitovani, vainglorious and incompetent, turned out to be a disaster.[12]

Gamsakhurdia's downfall can be dated from the refusal of Kitovani to obey an order to disband the National Guard and place it under the control of the Ministry of Internal Affairs during the August 1991 coup in Moscow and his subsequent emergence as a focus for the opposition. After the fall of Gamsakhurdia, Kitovani successfully resisted an attempt by Shevardnadze to replace him as minister of defense with a professional soldier, Lieutenant General Anatolii Kamkamidze, at the end of 1992.[13] Amid persistent rumors that he was planning a new military coup, Kitovani was finally replaced by Gia Karkarashvili in May 1993. However, Karkarashvili was inexperienced and linked with factions in the National Guard. He was eventually dismissed in early 1994 and subsequently accused of having sold military secrets to the Abkhazians.[14] In April 1994 Shevardnadze finally appointed Vardiko Nadibaidze, an ethnically Georgian general in the Russian army (he could barely speak Georgian), to be head of a new Georgian army. Shevardnadze proposed that the size of the new army be a very modest "well-equipped and supplied" five thousand men.[15]

These maneuverings made a significant contribution to the poor Georgian performance in the Abkhazian war, but they had other deleterious effects as well. One of Shevardnadze's first priorities in early 1992 was securing a settlement of the conflict in South Ossetia. A military solution was ruled out, even if it was feasible, because that would have effectively given more power to the National Guard militia and would have exacerbated relations with Russia. Furthermore, the Ossetian conflict was strongly associated with the Gamsakhurdia regime, and one of the first acts of the interim Military Council was to release the Ossetians' leader, Torez Kulembekov, from prison. This made it easier for Shevardnadze to sign a peace agreement on 24 June that allowed for the deployment of a Russian-dominated peacekeeping force in the region. While a decision on the future political status of the region was postponed, Georgia's sovereignty over South Ossetia was seriously compromised.

Perhaps more seriously, brutal punitive expeditions spearheaded by the Mkhedrioni to suppress residual support for Gamsakhurdia in the western province of Mingrelia in the spring of 1992 provoked a festering rebellion in the strategically vital Georgian-Abkhazian borderlands.[16] The pro-Gamsakhurdia insurgency in Mingrelia reached its climax in the autumn of 1993, undoubtedly undermining the efforts of the Georgian government forces to resist the final assault of the Abkhazians and their allies on the capital, Sukhumi. Indeed, there is good evidence to suggest that Gamsakhurdia had even tried to do a deal with the Abkhazians.[17] Since the Georgian army disintegrated as it was expelled from Abkhazia, Shevardnadze was forced to patch up his differences with Ioseliani in order to secure the support of the Mkhedrioni against the Gamsakhurdia forces and to agree to the landing of Russian marines in western Georgia to secure important communication lines.

Apart from its predictable impact on law and order, the power of the militias brought a fatal incoherence into government policy making and implementation. This was most evident at the outbreak of the Abkhazian war, when Shevardnadze and Kitovani were pursuing contradictory strategies. Thus Shevardnadze's supporters subsequently criticized Kitovani for a unilateral attack on the Abkhazian parliament in Sukhumi, while Kitovani's supporters blamed Shevardnadze for preventing him from following up his attack on Sukhumi with an attack on the Abkhazian stronghold in Gudauta. Whatever the merits of their respective positions, the result was the worst of both possible worlds, with the Abkhazians outraged at the attack on Sukhumi but still in a position to fight back.

The collapse of administrative structures meant that the Georgians were almost totally unable to mobilize their resources for the military effort in Abkhazia. Whatever the extent of Russian military assistance to Abkhazia and South Ossetia, the Georgian military effort was very poor. For most of the Abkhazian war, the Georgian army consisted of ill-disciplined militia bands which frequently appeared to be more interested in obtaining booty than in achieving military objectives. Shevardnadze admitted to a Western correspondent in April 1993, "It is too early to talk about an army. We've just got armed units. . . . Mostly, they are patriots and volunteers. The level of training is none or very low. It is difficult to talk about discipline, it is so very weak."[18]

Intense factional infighting and the failure to create workable administrative and political institutions led not only to the effective loss of important chunks of territory by the end of 1993; it also led to a collapse of elementary law and order. While support for Georgian independence in 1991 was practically unanimous among ethnic Georgians, their political leaders' failure to construct legitimate and effective power structures, their almost total neglect of the economy, and their inability to ensure basic law and order meant that, by the beginning of 1994, it became almost impossible to mobilize the population against new external and internal threats to national security. In that respect, Georgia represents an example, if an extreme example, of the importance of social and economic factors to national security.

Azerbaijan

Azerbaijan is the largest of the three Transcaucasian republics in terms of both territory and population. According to the 1989 census, its total population was just over seven million; the country was quite homogeneous ethnically, with just over 80 percent of its population being ethnically Azerbaijani.[19] It has a long coastline and extensive reserves of oil and other minerals. It is also well endowed agriculturally, producing both staples and industrial crops such as cotton. It was one of the few non-Russian republics that paid more into the union budget than it received back in subsidies.

Together with its ethnic homogeneity and relatively favorable international position, Azerbaijan's human and natural resources should have given it a reasonable basis on which to enhance its national security. However, since independence, conflict between different factions has produced an even more rapid turnover in the national leadership than in Georgia. Since independence was declared in the autumn of 1991, Azerbaijan has been led by four presidents—Aiaz Mutalibov (November 1991–February 1992), Iagub Mamedov (March 1992–May 1992), Abulfaz Elchibei (June 1992–August 1993), and Gaidar Aliev (since October 1993). Changes of regime have included a coup and countercoup in May 1992 and a military coup in June 1993.

Changes in the political leadership have had a serious direct impact on the fighting capacity of the Azerbaijani military. First, although it is difficult to gauge the veracity of the claims and counterclaims, on a number of occasions at least it seems that local Azerbaijani military commanders have engineered setbacks in order to discredit the existing Baku leadership. Thus the Azerbaijanis lost the key town of Shusha (against practically no resistance) and the Armenians established their vital Lachin "corridor," in the first half of 1992, when the communist-dominated leadership in Baku was at loggerheads with the army, dominated by the Azerbaijani Popular Front (APF). Not surprisingly, some of the worst Azerbaijani defeats occurred in 1993, when the political struggle between the APF and its opponents was at its most intense.

Factional infighting has also hampered the effort to establish a national army. Under Mutalibov, little attention was paid to building up the armed forces. Evidently, he feared that attempts to create an Azerbaijani national army would simply provide the launchpad for an APF coup. Instead, he preferred to rely on his alliance with "conservative" elements in Moscow. This brought some short-term benefits, as the Soviet military assisted Azerbaijani internal forces in operations against Armenian villages in the spring and summer of 1991. The failure of the August 1991 coup in Moscow left Mutalibov very exposed, and in October 1991 he announced that an Azerbaijani national army would be established after all. On 10 October 1991, the Azerbaijani Supreme Soviet voted to place the Soviet Fourth Army under Azerbaijani jurisdiction and recall Azerbaijanis serving elsewhere in the Soviet Union.[20]

Inevitably, this was a half-hearted affair as long as Mutalibov remained in power, and when the APF took over in May 1992, little had been achieved. At the end of January 1992, five months after its creation, the Azerbaijani armed forces had only 150 men. A British correspondent observed that Azerbaijani soldiers deployed around the strategic town of Agdam in February were supplied with "useless equipment" and that food rations were totally inadequate.[21]

The election of Abulfaz Elchibei at the beginning of June 1992 was followed by a stiffening of Azerbaijani resolve. In the same month the Azerbaijani Ministry of Defense attributed some military successes to the fact that "this was the first time our military leadership managed to bring together some seven large army groups that hitherto acted mostly independently, like guerrillas, without any co-ordination whatsoever." In August 1992, Elchibei told a local journalist that "I should say that now we are witnessing a new turn in this conflict. . . . We are sure that Karabagh will soon be freed from the Armenian bandits."[22]

Elchibei's confidence turned out to be misplaced. Partly because there had been few Azerbaijani officers in the Soviet army and the pool of potential expertise was limited, and partly because the pressure to achieve military success quickly was so strong, considerable emphasis was placed on powerful figures within the APF in setting up army units. One of the most important of these was "Colonel" Suret Guseinov, who was a prominent figure in the republic's second city of Gandja and who had equipped a brigade from his own resources. The role played by Guseinov in Azerbaijani politics is strongly reminiscent of that played by Kitovani in Georgia and certainly highlights the dilemmas faced by new states that have to establish armed forces in the face of a national emergency.

As noted above, the Azerbaijani army scored some impressive successes in the summer of 1992 but was unable to achieve a breakthrough, and the loss of the Kelbajar district in the winter of 1992–93 was followed by reports that this had been the result of willful incompetence by Guseinov. Whether Guseinov began to plan his bid for political power before the loss of Kelbajar or only later after the Baku authorities tried to remove him in February 1993 is unimportant. Such a coup attempt was entirely predictable from an army that consisted of units loyal to their commanders (and perhaps most crucially, who were financially dependent on them) rather than the Baku authorities.

Guseinov made his move in June 1993 after a botched military operation by the Baku authorities to remove him from his Gandja stronghold. A series of defeats at the front had undermined the credibility of the APF government, and Guseinov and his soldiers moved on Baku, meeting practically no resistance. In the middle of July 1993, Elchibei fled the capital for his home village of Keleki in Nakhichevan. His flight was followed by a new power struggle in Baku between Guseinov and the former republican Communist Party boss Gaidar Aliev, who had returned to Baku in the meantime, which created yet more problems for the Azerbaijani army. For a short time in the summer of 1993, there were two ministers of defense, one loyal to Guseinov and one loyal to Aliev. However, Aliev steadily managed to consolidate his authority and marginalize Guseinov. One aspect of this power struggle was a purge of army commanders linked to Guseinov and the APF, such as army chief of staff General Safar Abiev and chief of border forces General Zakhid Rzaev.[23]

While the power struggle in Baku was working itself out, the Armenians were able to secure a string of important military victories in the summer and autumn of 1993, in particular the occupation of Agdam, which had had over forty thousand inhabitants before the war, in August. By the time Aliev established firm control over the army, the Armenians had achieved an almost impregnable defensive position. In the winter of 1993–94, the Azerbaijani army launched a massive offensive on all the Karabagh fronts. Although the Armenians suffered heavy casualties, the Azerbaijanis were unable to make a breakthrough.

If the command structures of the Azerbaijani army were now more impressive, the winter offensive revealed other weaknesses in the Azerbaijani war effort. First, Azerbaijani morale was low, as successive defeats had undermined soldiers' confidence in their commanders. A British correspondent noted that a high proportion of the soldiers were now "young conscripts press-ganged into training camps last summer and autumn."[24] Second, in a bid to overcome the ineffectiveness of the call-up of its own population, the Azerbaijani leadership had recruited numbers of foreign mercenaries, including Afghan guerrillas, to fight in the war. Not surprisingly, their performance did not live up to expectations.

Political turmoil in Azerbaijan has ensured that the existing administrative structures remain weak and ineffective. While it is undeniable that Armenia has received political, economic, and military support from Russia, it is surprising that the Azerbaijanis, with their much larger population and stronger economic base, have not been able to achieve greater military success. While the breakdown of law and order in Azerbaijan has not reached anything like the proportions it has in Georgia, administrative structures have been unable to mobilize the country's substantial resources for the war effort. Frequent changes in political leadership have been accompanied by frequent changes of personnel in the administrative apparatus, in ministries, and at the regional and district levels. Between September 1991 and mid-March 1992 alone, there were no fewer than five defense ministers, and the post of the chief of the General Staff changed hands six times between September 1991 and October 1992.[25]

On numerous occasions, the call-up of the male population has been decreed by the authorities in Baku with little noticeable result in terms of military effectiveness. In September 1992, Elchibei signed a decree mobilizing all men born between 1966 and 1974 for the war.[26] But as the author himself has observed, even by the beginning of 1994, Baku hardly gave the impression of being the capital of a country at war, and conscription seemed to bother the city's young men little. According to a Georgian source, by the summer of 1994, Azerbaijan had mobilized considerably more manpower for its army than Armenia, forty-nine thousand against thirty-two thousand, but the offensive of the winter of 1993–94 showed that superior numbers were not sufficient to produce results. Furthermore, Roy Allison has calculated that Armenia mobilized thirty thousand to thirty-five thousand men for the war and if Azerbaijan wanted to achieve a similar ratio between servicemen and civilians, it would have to raise forces of sixty-five thousand to seventy thousand.[27]

However, the impact of the political infighting and failed state-building in Azerbaijan was not such a threat to its national security as it was to Georgia's. This was partly because of wider international and economic factors, which will be discussed below, and partly because the civil strife in Georgia had deeper roots; but it is also important to bear in mind that Azerbaijan was not so susceptible to disintegration as Georgia. To start with, Azerbaijan was significantly more ethnically homogeneous than Georgia. Of the two autonomous entities on its territory, one, the autonomous republic of Nakhichevan, was ethnically predominantly Azerbaijani. Moreover, the second, the autonomous region of Nagorno-Karabagh, while it proved to be the cause of a debilitating and seemingly intractable military conflict, was not in a strategically vital position. Abkhazia lay across key supply routes to Russia and was the location for important Russian military facilities; Nagorno-Karabagh was situated away from Azerbaijan's border with Russia and other powerful regional neighbors.

Perhaps the most important reason for Azerbaijan's survival was the fact that the power struggle in 1993 between Elchibei, Guseinov, and Aliev failed to escalate into civil strife on anything like the scale of that in Georgia. This was partly because of the unwillingness or inability of Elchibei to mount serious armed resistance and partly because of the way Aliev was able to rapidly establish his authority. The only real threat to Azerbaijan's national integrity was posed by the declaration of a Talysh-Mugan republic in the far south of the country by a close associate of Guseinov, Alikram Gumbatov, in July 1993. This adventure rapidly turned into farce. The Talysh[28] character of the "republic" was minimal, while the clear threat to Azerbaijani territorial integrity posed by its mere existence only discredited Gumbatov and, by association, Guseinov.

Nonetheless, there are unavoidable parallels between the conflicts in Abkhazia and Nagorno-Karabagh. Much like the Georgian authorities, Baku has also pursued a consistent policy of attempting to assert strong control over Nagorno-Karabagh in the belief that the best way to combat secessionist movements is not to appease them. But in doing so it has found itself up against an Armenia bolstered by a firm alliance with Russia and without the political and administrative structures that would allow it to bring its much larger resources to bear on the conflict. By mid-1994, Azerbaijan had lost control over up to a quarter of its territory and had failed to mobilize its appreciable resources behind the war effort. Thus by any measure its national security had deteriorated sharply since independence; however, the relatively rapid stabilization of its internal situation under Aliev has meant that its long-term potential for recovery cannot be ignored by its neighbors, especially Armenia.

Armenia

Armenia faced independence in the late 1980s with a number of obvious basic weaknesses. Uppermost in the minds of most Armenians was the country's geopolitical isolation. In one respect, the fact that Armenia does not have a border with Russia was an advantage, since it minimized a potential source of conflict, but in overall terms its physical isolation from its only real source of supply both of foodstuffs for its population and fuel and raw materials for its industries was a very basic disadvantage. This has given Azerbaijan an exceptionally powerful lever over Armenia that it has taken advantage of in the form of an economic blockade that it has imposed effectively on Armenia since 1989. The deterioration of the internal situation in Georgia since the end of 1991 and in Armenia's relations with Turkey have made Armenia's physical isolation almost complete.

Armenia is the smallest of the three Transcaucasian republics in terms of both territory and population. According to the 1989 census, its total population stood at just over 3.3 million.[29] Furthermore, it has few natural resources, and much of its land surface is unsuitable for cultivation. On the other hand, it was the most ethnically homogeneous of the Transcaucasian republics (with over 90 percent of its population being ethnically Armenian according to the 1989 census)[30] and has no autonomous entities on its territory. While the dilemmas posed by Armenia's physical situation are immense, the republic's political leadership has pursued a skillful foreign policy to mitigate its impact, as will be discussed below. Less noticed has been the way the leadership's domestic policies have also worked to enhance the country's national security position.

Armenia's success in mitigating threats to its national security has undoubtedly been a by-product of the country's remarkable political stability since independence, certainly compared to the situation in the other two Transcaucasian republics. The Armenian Pan-National Movement (APNM) came to power in the summer of 1990 under its leader, Levon Ter-Petrossian, who was confirmed as the country's president in elections in November 1991 and who has retained the reins of government up to the time of this writing.

This stability would have been difficult to predict. The APNM faced challenges to its position both from the old communist nomenklatura and from opposition political movements, principally the Dashnaktsiutiun, which has been fiercely critical of the APNM's political line. The success of the APNM owes something to its heterogeneous social roots: the movement embraced both unofficial nationalist activists and representatives of the Soviet elite, particularly from the cultural world and the Komsomol, somewhat on the lines of the Baltic popular fronts. The APNM has perhaps been fortunate in that the Armenian Communist Party did not have within its ranks a figure of the stature of Shevardnadze or Aliev, but it has also been quite skillful in the way it has effectively bought off the old elite through its program of economic reform. As a result, prominent officials from the old regime frequently figure among the directors of newly privatized industrial concerns.[31]

The Dashnaks have certainly attacked the APNM government for its economic reforms, calling for more state intervention and a more effective social safety net for the vulnerable, but the main thrust of their criticisms has been directed toward the government's policy on Nagorno-Karabagh. Here they have demanded a more assertively nationalistic line—in particular, recognition of the declaration of independence by the Nagorno-Karabagh Republic (NKR). The main reason for the APNM's ability to resist a nationalist movement like the Dashnaktsiutiun is clearly the success Armenia has enjoyed in the Karabagh war. Dashnak energies have tended to be channeled into the defense of the NKR, where they constituted the political leadership for a while in 1992, and as long as the war continues many of their best activists will have their hands full. It is a moot question, however, as to what would happen if Armenia were to start losing the war or even if a peace were to be concluded; in that case, some sort of a Dashnak bid for power in Erevan, mounted from Stepanakert, the capital of the NKR, might well become conceivable.

While it is possible to imagine fighters in the NKR, particularly those affiliated with the Dashnaktsiutiun, posing a threat to the APNM in Erevan, Armenia has avoided the worst excesses of warlordism. A crucial moment was provided by the "militia crisis" of the summer of 1990, when Moscow put pressure on the newly elected APNM government to suppress "illegal armed formations" on its territory. These already included large groups such as the self-designated Armenian National Army (ANA), which had six thousand armed volunteers, four thousand of whom were deployed in Erevan. Ter-Petrossian was able to ensure that the ANA handed in enough weaponry to satisfy Moscow while satisfying his domestic nationalist constituency by absorbing large numbers of ANA fighters into official security structures. The creation of a genuine national army was set in motion that autumn by the new parliament. An eventual force of thirty thousand to thirty-five thousand men was envisaged and, as noted above, it seems to have been achieved.[32]

As in the other two Transcaucasian republics, the raising of financial resources for the war effort in Armenia has owed much to ad hoc and semilegal "tax gathering" from enterprise directors and businesspeople carried out by Internal and Defense Ministry officials.[33] The rounding up of recruits has also provoked charges of over-zealousness and illegality, but perhaps the fact that anyone feels constrained to complain is a mark of the difference between Armenia and Georgia and Azerbaijan, where conscription has been so ineffective it has provoked little public concern.[34]

The NKR represents perhaps the most effective example of state-building for national security in Transcaucasia, however. While it is undeniable that the NKR is entirely dependent on the flow of military and nonmilitary supplies from the Republic of Armenia, the way the NKR government has mobilized the extremely limited resources at its disposal is, by all accounts, impressive. Democratic institutions and procedures have been put into abeyance, and authority has been vested in a Defense Council, which has put Karabagh society and economy on a war footing. Conscription is effective, and the NKR army of fifteen thousand men is disciplined and, not surprisingly, enjoys high morale.[35] The extent of

Erevan's political control over the NKR is highly controversial. The Armenian government insists that the NKR is effectively independent, and there have certainly been occasions when they have appeared to diverge in their reactions to peace initiatives, but, particularly since the summer of 1992, close associates of Ter-Petrossian have occupied key positions in the NKR governmental structures, and in August 1993 the NKR minister of defense, Serge Sarkisian, was transferred to that post in Erevan.

Clearly it would be wrong to ignore the regular infusions of Russian financial and material aid to Armenia in weighing the various factors that have affected Armenia's national security since independence. But it would also be wrong to ignore the country's political stability, relatively smooth management of civil-military relations, and ability to mobilize its limited resources effectively.

Foreign Policy

The three Transcaucasian republics have very limited room for maneuvering on the international stage. As has been argued in the first half of this chapter, the failure to establish legitimate and effective state structures that could contain factional conflict and mobilize resources to achieve national security tasks placed further constraints. In broad terms, it is also true to say that while the three Transcaucasian republics had varying opportunities to seek and obtain support from regional powers and the wider international community, they all were in the position of small, weak states located in a region in which much more powerful neighbors sought to exert a dominating influence and where any sort of international regime was very weak.

Despite the disintegration of the Soviet Union, the key regional power in Transcaucasia remains Russia. The relationship between the three Transcaucasian republics and Russia is based on a very complex set of perceptions and interests. On the one hand, the Transcaucasian republics remain anxious to bolster their sovereignty and independence from Russia. On the other hand, many Russian politicians and officials remain unwilling to accept the reality of their independence; moreover, although Moscow's direct political control over Transcaucasia has been removed formally, this has not been reflected in a similar disintegration of Moscow's economic and military leverage. To complicate matters further, the political leaderships of the Transcaucasian republics have often tried to pursue the clearly contradictory policies of bolstering their political independence from Moscow and at the same time seeking Russian help to restore their economies and support them in local military conflicts.

As far as the two other key regional powers, Turkey and Iran, are concerned, their relationships with the Transcaucasian republics have become more significant and complex since the dissolution of the Soviet Union. Turkey, with its close alliance with the United States and, in the 1980s at least, a booming market economy, on one level has sought to act as the new dominant regional power. At the same time, however, it is continually under public pressure to support Muslims—especially Turkic Muslims in the former Soviet Union—which undermines its pretensions to act as a neutral arbiter in Transcaucasia. Iran has played a perhaps surprising role in the region. While the revolutionary Islamic ideology of the present Iranian regime prompted many people to believe that it would aggressively support Transcaucasian Muslims, Tehran has generally behaved in a pragmatic fashion, keen to promote itself as a neutral arbiter and ready to spread its influence mainly by normal diplomacy and trade, with the ostensible aim of creating a regional balance.

The three Transcaucasian republics have handled this extremely complex set of external relationships with varying degrees of skill. While in the final analysis none of them could do very much to resist a determined attempt by Moscow to reimpose its hegemony, this chapter once again stresses that the way they have played the diplomatic cards at their disposal has made a significant contribution toward either enhancing or impairing their national security.

Georgia

Georgia's basic international situation is very weak. The country has a long border with Russia that follows the natural barrier of the Caucasus Mountains; it is also a region of great ethnic complexity and has historically been the source of constant threat from the mountain tribes who live there. This instability has, historically, been utilized by Russia to gain leverage over Georgia. Although the Georgians are Orthodox Christians, like the Russians, the Georgian Orthodox Church has older and separate roots and has consistently sought to evade subordination to the Moscow Patriarchate. To the south, Georgia faces what has historically been the source of invasions from the Muslim powers of Turkey and Iran. Relations with Armenia and Azerbaijan have also historically been cool. Finally, Georgia does not have a substantial diaspora; even within the Soviet Union the great majority of Georgians lived in the Georgian republic.

Failures in foreign policy were one of the principal justifications for the overthrow of Gamsakhurdia, who was accused of both unnecessarily antagonizing Russia and alienating the West. Certainly his policy toward Russia only succeeded in provoking the old Gorbachevite center without building solid links with the emerging Yeltsinite center. Thus conflict in South Ossetia had already led to intervention by Soviet troops in the winter of 1990–91. The declaration of independence in April 1991 and a summary rejection of any discussion of the new Union Treaty provoked economic sanctions. A Yeltsin-Gamsakhurdia meeting in the spring of 1991 showed some signs of a potential alliance against the old center, but Gamsakhurdia's tendency to express strong suspicion of all Russian politicians meant that rumors that he had been in league with the Moscow plotters in August 1991 found ready ears. His subsequent refusal to consider joining the CIS and his readiness to lend aid to the Chechen nationalist movement in the autumn of 1991 during its standoff with Moscow meant that the new Russian leadership was, to say the least, sanguine about his eventual overthrow.

As has been noted, Gamsakhurdia made some attempt to play the North Caucasus card against Moscow. While the lack of Caucasian unity has historically been used by Moscow to strengthen its position in the Caucasus, such an orientation was unlikely to be universally popular in Georgia. Still, Gamsakhurdia did establish a close relationship with the president of Chechnia, General Dudaev, which later gave him a base to attempt a political comeback, but this achievement was more than outweighed by the Russian resentment that it caused. He also pursued a relatively soft line toward the Abkhazians, who were a key force in the Confederation of Peoples of the Caucasus, but his earlier aggressively nationalist rhetoric meant that they were extremely suspicious of his real intentions.

When Shevardnadze returned to Georgia, he put a high priority on improving relations with Russia. The Russian foreign minister, Andrei Kozyrev, visited Tbilisi in April 1992, and negotiations were begun to draw up a wide-ranging bilateral treaty. The South Ossetian cease-fire agreed on in June, mediated by the Russians, was an early product of the thaw in relations between Georgia and Russia. However, when the Abkhazian war broke out in August 1992, further progress proved impossible.

To complicate matters, Russian-Georgian relations rapidly became a pawn in the Russian domestic power struggle. While Shevardnadze continued to cultivate Yeltsin and the "democrats" who still figured large in the presidential apparatus and government, the Russian Supreme Soviet took a consistently hostile line toward Georgia and blocked the ratification of the bilateral treaty for the duration of the war. More crucially, the Russian military had identified Georgia as a convenient arena in which to assert its importance in the new Russia. The Russian defense minister, Pavel Grachev, claimed in February 1993 that Russia had vital strategic interests on the Georgian Black Sea coast. The actual conduct of relations with Tbilisi was placed more and more in the hands of the Russian military, and evidence of actual Russian military support for the Abkhazian separatists began to pile up. Meanwhile, Russian nationalist politicians continually evoked Russia's historic mission in the south.

In this context, it is not surprising that when the Russian power struggle came to a head in the autumn of 1993 it coincided with the culmination of the Abkhazian war. In July 1993, Grachev mediated a cease-fire, against strong Georgian reservations that left roughly half of Abkhazia in Georgian hands. Over the succeeding two months, the bulk of the Georgian heavy equipment was withdrawn from the autonomous republic. Then, in the middle of September 1993, as the standoff between Yeltsin and the Supreme Soviet was reaching its critical point, the Abkhazians launched a large-scale offensive, and by the beginning of October, to all intents and purposes, Georgian forces and almost all the Georgian population in Abkhazia had been swept back beyond the Inguri River, which marks the boundary between Abkhazia and Georgia.

The collapse of Georgian resistance in Abkhazia left Shevardnadze and his government helpless in the face of a reinvigorated offensive by supporters of Gamsakhurdia in western Georgia. In October 1993, Georgia joined the CIS and Russian troops landed in the republic to support government forces, which rapidly overwhelmed the rebel advance. The way seemed clear for Russo-Georgian relations to be put on a regular footing. However, in the two years since 1992 Georgia had been reduced to chaos, and the mood in Russia had moved dramatically in the direction of a more assertive nationalism. Nevertheless, when Georgia signed a bilateral treaty with Russia in February 1994, accompanied by a military agreement that effectively reduced Georgia to the status of little more than a strategic satellite, the country had been reduced to such a condition that there was no serious opposition.

The hopes that had been placed on Shevardnadze's achieving a breakthrough in relations with the West also turned out to be in vain. Visits to Georgia by U.S. Secretary of State James Baker and German Foreign Minister Hans-Dietrich Genscher, who came armed with promises of aid and the acceptance of Georgia into the United Nations, in July 1992—before elections had been held to legitimize the January coup—seemed to suggest that the return of Shevardnadze had obtained a new prominence for Georgia in Western foreign policy calculations. However, while Western countries have been relatively generous with their rhetoric toward Georgia, they have rarely been willing or able to do anything concrete. The outbreak of the Abkhazian war hardly enhanced Shevardnadze's reputation, and Western governments were becoming increasingly sensitive to Russian claims in the former Soviet republics. Although the United Nations did eventually approve the dispatch of observers to Abkhazia in July 1993, they were few in number, and the Abkhazian breach of the cease-fire provoked little international response. In October 1993, the Security Council passed a resolution endorsing the Russian role in Georgia.

Azerbaijan

In a number of respects, Azerbaijan enjoys some intrinsic advantages compared with its two Transcaucasian neighbors in attempting to enhance its national security through foreign policy. First, its relative internal strength, combined with its religious, cultural, and ethnic ties to Turkey and Iran, has allowed it, to some extent, to become an autonomous player in regional politics. Second, its significant reserves of oil have attracted international interest to the republic for over a century. Since 1991, Azerbaijan's potential for playing the regional political game has been obscured by the strong ideological orientations of its first two leaders—in the case of Mutalibov, a strong pro-Russian orientation, and in the case of Elchibei, a strong pro-Turkish orientation. This should not be taken to mean that Baku could resist a determined attempt by Russia to impose its direct control over Azerbaijan, but Aliev appears to have learned from his predecessors and has rejected a strong ideological element in his foreign policy.

Mutalibov was tied to Moscow not just by inclination and by his career path as an industrial manager but by the very direct way he owed his position to Moscow's intervention. At the end of 1989, the APF was effectively usurping the power of the republican administration; it was responsible for maintaining the transport blockade of Armenia and rallying support for maintaining Azerbaijan's claim on Nagorno-Karabagh. Amid widespread pogroms against the Armenian population of Baku at the beginning of 1990, the APF prepared to declare the end of Soviet power in Azerbaijan. On 7 January 1990, Soviet troops were sent into Baku and suppressed the APF at the cost of hundreds of civilian casualties. In the aftermath, APF activists were arrested, and the first secretary of the Azerbaijani Communist Party, Abdul-Rakhman Vezirov, was replaced by Mutalibov. Elections to the republican Supreme Soviet were postponed to the autumn and were conducted under martial law. Only a handful of APF supporters were elected.

Mutalibov's close relationship with Moscow brought some benefits to Azerbaijan at first; the center adopted a more sympathetic stance on the Nagorno-Karabagh conflict, including, as was mentioned earlier, the participation of Soviet forces in operations against Armenian-populated villages to the north of Nagorno-Karabagh. However, Mutalibov's future remained very much tied up with that of the "conservative" opposition to Gorbachev, and, even if he had not given such unambiguous support to the attempted coup in August 1991, it is unlikely that he would have survived its demise for long.

When Elchibei was elected president in May 1992, he brought with him a diametrically opposed set of ideological orientations. First, while his suspicions of Russia were not expressed as openly as Gamsakhurdia's, he made no bones about his desire to reduce Azerbaijan's political ties with Russia, and he firmly rejected Mutalibov's moves toward Azerbaijani membership in the CIS. Second, he saw Azerbaijan's future as being tied intimately with that of Turkey as Azerbaijan's closest ethnic neighbor. A pro-Turkish orientation had much to recommend it in early 1992, as Russian influence seemed very much on the decline and Turkey was seeking to establish its credentials as the new regional hegemon through initiatives such as the Black Sea Cooperation Organization. Turkish businesspeople flocked to Baku to take advantage of the generous credits being granted by Ankara. Azerbaijani students traveled in the opposite direction to take up fellowships in Turkish universities.

However, Turkey's ambitions were not matched by its capabilities. Crucially, Turkey was unable to do anything to stem the advance of the Armenians in Nagorno-Karabagh, as the occupation of Kelbajar in the winter of 1992 showed most clearly. While Turkey sent some military advisors to Baku, and some weaponry officially or unofficially probably got through, Turkey was either unwilling (because its hands were full with the Kurds) or unable (because of pressure from a West anxious to support Yeltsin) to do anything substantive to aid Azerbaijan. The death of Turgut Özal in the spring of 1993 signaled a softening of even the rhetoric.

Meanwhile, Armenia's success, combined with the ineffectiveness of the international mediation effort conducted by the CSCE, underlined Russia's continuing importance. The early signs were that Elchibei's desire to break free from Moscow's political control would not cost too high a price. Russia still needed Azerbaijani oil equipment, and negotiations on a bilateral treaty were successfully concluded. Most important, from the Azerbaijani point of view, by the beginning of 1993 all Russian troops had left the republic. But the mood was changing in Moscow, and the prospect of Azerbaijan's signing a deal with Western oil companies that would remove Russia's economic leverage over Azerbaijan forever was met with concern.

The fact of Russian military involvement in Guseinov's June 1993 coup is well established, but its character is more difficult to work out. The crucial question is who, if anyone, ordered the Russian commander in Gandja to hand over large quantities of weaponry to Guseinov—did the order come from the Transcaucasian military district, from the Ministry of Defense in Moscow, or from politicians? It is interesting to note, however, that from the occupation of Baku in January 1990 through Mutalibov's attempt to return to power in April 1992 to the Guseinov affair, there have been more direct Russian interventions in Azerbaijan's internal political affairs than in those of almost any other republic, with the exception of Tajikistan.

The return of Aliev to power prompted most commentators to believe that there would be a dramatic reorientation of Azerbaijan's foreign policy toward a close alliance with Russia. Turkey was clearly upset by the turn of events; it demonstratively continued to recognize Elchibei as president and negotiated behind the scenes to seek a reconciliation between the two leaders. Predictably, in October 1993, Aliev took Azerbaijan into the CIS, and the Russian oil company Lukoil was brought into the consortium being granted rights to exploit Azerbaijani oil. From that point, Aliev began to resist Russian demands, which center on the right to impose a cease-fire in the Nagorno-Karabagh conflict (to be policed by Russian troops) and to station Russian border guards on the Azerbaijani-Iranian border.

While he is clearly more pragmatic in his dealings with Russia than Elchibei was, Aliev has sought to balance this by strengthening relations with other interested states. One of his first moves on coming to power was to improve relations with Iran, which had suffered because of a number of early statements by Elchibei expressing concern for the rights of the substantial Azerbaijani minority in Iran. He also concluded a deal to hire numbers of Afghani mujahideen to fight in the Nagorno-Karabagh conflict. Then, as Russian pressure mounted in the spring of 1994, he visited Turkey to restore good relations and secure diplomatic support, making it clear to Russia that there would be a political price to pay, at least, for any dramatic attempt to force Azerbaijan into the Russian fold.

Armenia

Armenia's international position is particularly difficult and its foreign policy choices are limited. Foreign policy is effectively dominated by Armenia's relations with Turkey and the whole thorny question of the 1915 genocide, its recognition by Turkey, and possible compensation and even territorial claims. With Turkey on the western border and Azerbaijan on the southeastern and eastern border, Armenians have felt that they are effectively encircled by hostile neighbors. Armenia does have a short border with Iran, and Tehran has been willing, even under the Islamic Republic, to deal with Armenia, but this opening cannot compensate for the effective closure of an outlet to the Black Sea through Turkey.

In these conditions, Armenia has, not surprisingly, looked to Russia as its protector. By and large, Russia has responded, although, as Moscow's pro-Azerbaijan policy in 1990–91 shows, Armenia cannot count on Russia. Furthermore, while the absence of a Russian-Armenian border might have some advantages, the fact that Armenia's communications lie across Georgia, with which relations have traditionally been cool and which in the 1990s has been in such a state of turmoil it has been unable to guarantee the security of cargoes from Russia or even its own Black Sea ports, does undermine the value of a Russian alliance. The power of the Armenian diaspora to swing Western support behind Armenia has perhaps been exaggerated but, with the history of 1918–20 (when the Armenian Republic had to face numerous invasions from Turkey and Azerbaijan) more vivid in its collective memory, it has been able to bring to Armenian foreign policy debates an appreciation of Armenia's continuing external vulnerability.

If Armenia faced independence with fewer foreign policy choices than Azerbaijan, despite some early attempts to establish a new relationship with Turkey, it has also, in contrast to Azerbaijan, gradually found its already limited number of choices diminishing. In the late 1980s, both Armenia and Turkey made some efforts to establish a new and more constructive relationship. On coming to power in 1990, the APNM leadership resisted demands, mostly emanating from the diaspora, that recognition of the genocide be placed at the top of the foreign policy agenda. The idea of a new highway from Armenia to the Turkish port of Trabzon was also widely discussed. Later, Armenia joined the Black Sea Cooperation Organization, and Ter-Petrossian even went to the funeral of Turgut Özal.

However, these good intentions could not completely overcome history. Despite everything, Ankara consistently refused to establish diplomatic relations with Armenia unless Armenia gave up all claims on Turkey. What progress that had been made could not survive the strains being caused by the Nagorno-Karabagh conflict. Particular strain was caused by clashes on the border between Armenia and Nakhichevan in the summer of 1992. Turkey is a guarantor of the autonomous status of Nakhichevan according to a Soviet-Turkish treaty of 1921, and it backed up strong verbal condemnation of Armenia with military activity on their border. Matters came to a head in the winter of 1992–93, when Ankara withdrew an offer to supply Armenia with electricity and prevented shipments of grain from being transported across its territory.

The deterioration of Armenia's relations with Turkey has been accompanied by an ever-growing dependence on its alliance with Russia. At first, relations between Moscow and the new APNM leadership in Armenia were rather complicated. Relations between the pro-independence APNM and the Gorbachev center were poor, as Moscow's support for Azerbaijan in 1990–91 shows, but from an early stage Armenia enjoyed strong support from the Russian democratic movement and, when Yeltsin came to power at the end of 1991, Armenia moved to cement a close relationship with Russia. It became an enthusiastic member of the CIS and signed all subsequent political, economic, and military agreements.

Conclusion

Inevitably, analysis of the foreign policies of the three Transcaucasian republics tends to bring out their structural limitations. Georgia is revealed to be almost irretrievably weak in the face of a determined bid by Russia to reassert its hegemony. Armenia is strong more by the coincidence of its "natural" pro-Russian orientation and the close links it has forged with key elements in the Russian leadership. Finally, Azerbaijan's basic advantages lie in its opportunities to play regional politics. Structural factors will arguably become even more salient if there is a dramatic shift in Russian policy toward Baku, as so many Armenians fear, or if Russian power in the region begins to recede again.

However, this chapter has shown that predictions based on calculations of the structural strengths and weaknesses of the three Transcaucasian republics can turn out to be off the mark. Thus, while the almost irredeemable internal weakness of Georgia and its subjection to Russia make it difficult to see how it could benefit from or even survive a weakening of Russian influence, the relative internal coherence of Armenia means that, despite its dependence on Russia, its leadership will have some room to maneuver. Similarly, while Azerbaijan has managed to stabilize its internal situation and retain some international room for maneuvering, a new bout of civil conflict could greatly reduce its chances of a future revival.

Notes

1. The dilemmas faced by the leaderships of the unrecognized states that have emerged in the region (Abkhazia, South Ossetia, and the Nagorno-Karabagh Republic) in seeking to enhance their national security are not addressed directly in this chapter.

2. The evolution of Russian military doctrine between 1992 and 1993 clearly

illustrates this point. See Charles Dick, "The Military Doctrine of the Russian Federation," *Jane's Intelligence Review,* special report (January 1994), pp. 1, 7.

3. Hans J. Morgenthau, *Politics Among Nations: The Struggle for Power and Peace* (New York: A.A. Knopf, 1948), is the classic statement of this view.

4. This might lead one to expect more coordinated action by Georgia and Azerbaijan to resist any international moves to water down the present generally accepted principle of the inviolability of the post-Soviet borders. Significantly, the Nagorno-Karabagh Armenians have not been slow to make the link and are actively pursuing contacts with Abkhazia, the Crimea, and the Trans-Dniester Republic. Interview with the Nagorno-Karabagh Republic foreign minister, quoted in *Monthly Digest of News from Armenia* (June/July 1994), p. 34.

5. While it is popular, particularly in Russia, to see these militia warlords as only the latest manifestation of a venerable Caucasian tradition, it makes much more sense to see them as growing out of a very specific set of circumstances.

6. Under Mikhail Gorbachev's proposed Union Treaty in 1991, autonomous republics were granted the right to join the new union as separate entities, in an attempt to undermine the position of the union republics.

7. Elizabeth Fuller, "Aslan Abashidze: Georgia's Next Leader?" *RFE/RL Research Report,* 5 November 1993, pp. 23–26.

8. According to the 1989 census, Armenians made up 8 percent of the population of the republic, Russians, 6 percent, Ossetians, 3 percent, and Abkhazians, 2 percent. *Zaria vostoka,* 23 March 1990.

9. When the author visited the Akhalkalaki district in 1991, local Armenian leaders readily admitted that fighters from the Nagorno-Karabagh conflict came to "rest" in the area.

10. *Zaria vostoka,* 23 March 1990.

11. The Mkhedrioni were estimated to have around five thousand fighters in 1990. Elizabeth Fuller, "Paramilitary Forces Dominate Fighting in Transcaucasus," *RFE/RL Research Report,* 18 June 1993, p. 80.

12. Ibid.

13. *Eastern Europe Newsletter,* 16 February 1992, p. 2.

14. *COVCAS Bulletin,* 23 February 1994, p. 13.

15. *Georgian Chronicle,* February–March 1994, p. 1, and April 1994, p. 1.

16. See, for example, the account in *Russkaia mysl',* 18 September 1992.

17. *Georgian Chronicle,* September 1993, p. 8, and October 1993, p. 2.

18. *Independent,* 13 April 1993.

19. *Vestnik statistiki,* 1991, no. 5. These figures, based on the 1989 census, are open to question, since the Nagorno-Karabagh conflict had already generated outflows of Armenians and Russians at the time the data were collected. Furthermore, data for other minorities, such as the Lezgians, Kurds, and Talysh, seem to have been consistently underestimated in Azerbaijani statistics.

20. Richard Woff, "The Armed Forces of Azerbaijan," *Jane's Intelligence Review,* October 1993, p. 459.

21. Ibid. Also see *The Guardian,* 14 February 1992.

22. *COVCAS Bulletin,* 18 June 1992, p. 9, and *Baku Times,* 12 August 1992.

23. *Russia Briefing,* 25 January 1994, p. 8.

24. *The Guardian,* 1 February 1994.

25. Woff, "Armed Forces of Azerbaijan," p. 460.

26. *Nezavisimaia gazeta,* 23 September 1992.

27. *BBC Summary of World Broadcasts,* 25 June 1994, and Roy Allison, *Military Forces in the Soviet Successor States* (London: IISS/Brassey's, 1993), p. 68.

28. The Talysh are a Persian-speaking minority in the south of Azerbaijan.

29. There is also a substantial Armenian diaspora, particularly in Russia and Georgia, as well as in the United States, Latin America, Western Europe, and the Middle East.

30. *Vestnik statistiki*, 1991, no. 1. Crucially, this census was carried out too late to count the Azerbaijanis already expelled from Armenia in 1988.

31. As, for example, the most influential of the former Communist Party bosses, Suren Demirdzhan.

32. Richard Woff, "The Armed Forces of Armenia," *Jane's Intelligence Review*, September 1994, pp. 387–88; and Allison, *Military Forces in the Soviet Successor States*, p. 68.

33. *Nezavisimaia gazeta*, 20 November 1992.

34. *The Guardian*, 21 April 1994.

35. Felix Corley, "Nagorno-Karabagh—An Eyewitness Account," *Jane's Intelligence Review*, April 1994, p. 164.

11

National Security and Military Issues in Central Asia

Bess A. Brown

When the Central Asian republics of the USSR (Kazakhstan, Kyrgyzstan, Tajikistan, Turkmenistan, and Uzbekistan) declared their independence in the last months of 1991, national security—the necessity for a sovereign nation-state to provide for the defense of its territorial and political integrity against external threats—was not at first perceived to be a pressing need by the new countries. Deciding for or against rapid introduction of a market economy, seeking to prevent or minimize the political effects of a decline in living standards resulting from the loss of financial subsidies that had been provided by the Soviet state, and gaining international recognition and support were all issues that had greater priority than creation of a national military structure in each of the Central Asian states.

Central Asian Security Concerns

Although with the loosening of Moscow's control in the late 1980s all the Central Asian republics had initiated tentative contacts with the outside world and their political elites had begun asserting the primacy of national interests over all-union ones, by December 1991, when the USSR was formally dissolved, the economies of the Central Asian states were still closely bound up with the rest of the union. The rupture of those ties has resulted in sharp economic decline in all the new states. The dominant internal security issue for Central Asia, therefore, has been the avoidance of social and political unrest fueled by popular anger over high inflation rates and sinking living standards, or by regional, ethnic, or clan antipathies that emerged after the removal of Soviet repression. Although Kazakhstan and Kyrgyzstan were concerned about their common borders with China, no immediate external threat to any of the newly independent states of Central Asia was perceived by the political elites in the region until the outbreak of the civil war in Tajikistan in June 1992, when Muslim fundamental-ism exported by the Islamic government in Afghanistan was seen as a danger to Central Asian regimes that consisted largely of communist-era officials who had substituted nationalism for their previous ideological orientation.

In the immediate aftermath of the disintegration of the USSR at the beginning of December 1991 and the creation of the Commonwealth of Independent States (CIS), which all the Central Asian states immediately joined, the leaderships of the new countries of Central Asia recognized that provision for national defense is an aspect of national sovereignty, and in the first months of 1992 all except Kyrgyzstan set up ministries of defense and began assuming control, at least on paper, over Soviet-era military units stationed on their soil. With their weak postcolonial economies, none of the new states were able to assume the financial burden of fully independent military forces, nor was there any indication that they desired to do so. The Central Asian leaderships appeared to have some hopes that a common CIS defense force could lessen the burden of individual military forces on the commonwealth's mem-ber states. When an effective CIS military structure failed to develop in early 1992, the Central Asian states turned to Russia as the primary heir of the Soviet armed forces and, in addition to taking at least theoretical jurisdiction over the Soviet army units and border troops stationed within their territory, also entered into bilateral agreements with the Russian Federation to provide training, equipment, and an officer corps for their nascent national defense establishments. These agreements have been expressed in terms of relations between sovereign and equal states; there is no question of subordination to the Russian military structure, though some Cen-tral Asian troops continue to serve in the Russian military.[1] The new military struc-tures of the Central Asian states are modeled on the Soviet defense establishment and are reported to be thoroughly imbued with the spirit and traditions of the Soviet army.[2]

Because of the weak sense of national identity that characterizes all the Cen-tral Asian states—only Uzbekistan can make a more or less supportable claim to having had an experience of national statehood, the rest being artificial creations of the Soviet era—one of the first tasks of the political and intellectual elite of postindependence Central Asia has been the promotion of national patriotism in place of the local or clan loyalties that traditionally have dominated the region. In addition to the need to develop a sense of national statehood in the new countries, these efforts have had a practical side as well—the new armed forces of the Central Asian countries have been plagued since their formation by high rates of desertion, as young men have felt no inner compulsion to serve the colors of their newly independent homelands.

Central Asian Dependence on Russia

Well into their third year of independence, the Central Asian military establish-ments remained so heavily dependent on Russian support that one Russian military observer has estimated it will require at least fifteen years for these countries to develop genuinely national armies, staffed with their own citizens.[3] Because so few Central Asians became officers in the Soviet army, there is no pool of experienced indigenous military cadres from which commanders may be drawn, so the officer corps of the Central Asian armies are largely staffed by Russian officers who are lured into the service of the new countries on a contract basis. The percentage of Russian officers varies, from approximately 90 percent in Uzbekistan and Kazakhstan to some 70 percent in Kyrgyzstan.[4] With reductions in the Russian military, service in Central Asia has proved an attractive prospect for many Russian officers who might otherwise have to seek jobs outside the defense sector.

The ethnic situation is reversed for conscripts in the Central Asian armies, where the percentage of soldiers of the country's titular nationality in Tajikistan, Kyrgyzstan, and Uzbekistan exceeds the percentage of that ethnic group in the country's population as a whole.[5] According to the Russian military publication *Armiia*, Tajiks make up 90 percent of the conscripts in the armed forces subordinate to Tajikistan's government, while Tajiks make up 79 percent of the country's population. The lowest percentage of conscripts of a country's titular nationality is in Kazakhstan: the percentage of Kazakhs among enlisted men at the time of this writing was 45 percent, a figure that approximated the Kazakh share of the country's population (around 48 percent). Similar percentages were reported for Kyrgyz in Kyrgyzstan (60 percent of conscripts and 57 percent of the population), for Uzbeks in Uzbekistan (85 percent of conscripts and 82 percent of the population), and Turkmens in Turkmenistan (70 percent of conscripts and 75 percent of the population). These figures are unsurprising, given that the Soviet practice of universal conscription has been adopted by the successor states.

In the first months after the Central Asian states became independent, there was considerable speculation in the West and in Russia over whether the new countries would choose to follow the Turkish model of secular democracy or would opt for the revolutionary Islamic fundamentalism of Iran. This debate overlooked the crucial fact that the Central Asian states are adherents of Sunni Islam, with its deep respect for temporal authority, making the Iranian model unattractive even for Tajikistan, despite its cultural and linguistic ties to Iran. The ties of the new Turkic-speaking states to Turkey developed rapidly in the last months of 1991, and Turkish officials offered help to the Central Asians in setting up military establishments and training professional military forces. These offers have come to little, however—only Turkmenistan has sent a number of officers to Turkey for military training. The dominant influence on the nascent military establishments of the new states has been Russia, and despite some frictions between the Russian Federation and individual Central Asian countries, this situation is unlikely to change significantly in the foreseeable future.

Central Asia and the CIS

In reaction to the number of Central Asian conscripts who perished during their service in the Soviet army, most if not all of the Central Asian states adopted laws prohibiting the assignment of their citizens to CIS forces outside their borders; exceptions have been made to permit citizens of Central Asian states to serve voluntarily in the Russian army and to permit the participation of border guard units from Kazakhstan, Uzbekistan, and Kyrgyzstan in CIS peacekeeping operations in Tajikistan. The CIS unified command, established after the setting up of the commonwealth, involved primarily Kazakhstan, which demanded a role in the unitary CIS control of strategic nuclear missiles, since some of these missiles were stationed on its soil.

At a CIS summit in Tashkent in May 1992, all the Central Asian states except Turkmenistan signed a Treaty on Collective Security with other CIS members. The only concrete result of the CIS collective security pact to date has been an agreement in January 1993 under which Uzbekistan, Kazakhstan, and Kyrgyzstan promised to join Russia in setting up a volunteer peacekeeping force for Tajikistan, and another signed in August 1993 that involved the same group of states and Tajikistan in an arrangement to defend the Tajik-Afghan border against incursions from Afghanistan. Although a Central Asian role has been proposed at CIS summits for peacekeeping forces to be stationed elsewhere in the CIS, particularly in the Caucasus, as of mid-1994 their function as peace-keepers was limited to Tajikistan.

The civil war in Tajikistan in the last six months of 1992 and the fighting on the Tajik-Afghan border that has continued sporadically since the beginning of 1993 have been the only regional conflicts that have affected the Central Asian states—and not all of them agree on its significance. Russian and many Western observers have been inclined to accept the assessment of Uzbekistan President Islam Karimov, who maintains that Afghan help for Tajikistan's Islamic opposition represents a threat to regional stability if not a danger to the entire common-wealth; the result has been a greater degree of Russian military presence in the region than Karimov may have bargained for, though he has had only praise, at least in public pronouncements, for the Russian military role in Tajikistan. Turkmenistan's President Saparmurad Niiazov, however, has said that Afghani-stan poses no threat to his country, and he has flatly refused to contribute to commonwealth peacekeeping forces in Tajikistan.

Draft guidelines for a system of collective defense for those CIS states which signed the 1992 CIS defense agreement were to have been considered at the October 1994 summit of CIS heads of state but were abruptly withdrawn a week before the meeting. When the draft was drawn up and initialed by the CIS defense ministers in June 1994, Uzbekistan had expressed reservations. Although there was little sign that Uzbekistan or any of the other Central Asian states was considering withdrawing from the Treaty on Collective Security as long as fighting continued on the Tajik-Afghan border, a settlement of the Tajik strife might well bring further questioning of CIS collective security arrangements.

Regional Security in Central Asia

Attempts to create mechanisms for coordination of economic, political, or security policies between the Central Asian states have had limited success. On four occasions between June 1990 and January 1993, the Central Asian heads of state gathered for highly publicized summits that were supposed to result in the creation of mechanisms for the regional coordination of economic relations and development; coordination of defense policies was given little attention at these meetings. The most promising coordination effort, organized in January 1994 by the presidents of Kazakhstan and Uzbekistan, the two most important states of Central Asia, and later joined by Kyrgyzstan, was designed as an economic union; by autumn 1994 the three states were discussing coordinating defense policy as well, though there were no reports of plans for a common military establishment.

The differences between the five states of Central Asia, which were considerable before the collapse of the USSR, have increased since these republics gained their independence, and to some extent they have become rivals for foreign aid and investment. Despite the efforts at coordination of policies within the region, each country has tended to go its own way in foreign policy, economic reform, political orientation, and security concerns. Kazakhstan and Kyrgyzstan have committed themselves to rapid economic reform, while Uzbekistan and Turkmenistan reject any transformation that their political elites perceive to endanger the political and social stability on which their own rule is dependent. Uzbekistan's President Karimov claims to fear the export of Muslim fundamentalism from Afghanistan through Tajikistan, while his Turkmen counterpart Saparmurad Niiazov, who shares Karimov's communist past and authoritarian bent, rejects the concept of an Islamic fundamentalist threat. These differences of orientation have proved increasingly divisive with the passage of time since the Central Asian states gained independence.

In May 1993, Kazakhstan's President Nursultan Nazarbaev told a group of media officials in Kazakhstan that there will be no confederation or unitary state structure in the Central Asian region because "everyone wants to live in his own room, not a communal apartment."[6] While Central Asian heads of state and many members of the nationally conscious intellectual communities in these countries celebrate the common historical, cultural, and—with the exception of Tajikistan—linguistic ties among the Central Asian states, Nazarbaev's assertion remains an accurate assessment, and the creation of regional security structures that would reduce the dependence of the Central Asian states on Russian support remains unlikely.

Kazakhstan

Prior to the dissolution of the USSR, the presence of a large Russian population concentrated in the northern regions of Kazakhstan that adjoin the Russian Federation seemed to ensure that the republic would be bound permanently to Russia. As a result, the largest of the Central Asian states and the second most populous after Uzbekistan was the last of the republics of the former Soviet Union to claim its independence, and the least prepared psychologically to do so. Its legislature adopted a declaration of independence only on 15 December 1991, almost a week after the creation of the commonwealth and the demise of the USSR. In its three years of independence, Kazakhstan's demographic structure has forced the country into a closer relationship with Russia than that experienced by any other Central Asian state except, for very different reasons, Tajikistan.

As a result of historic settlement patterns, the northern regions of Kazakhstan (and also the capital, Almaty) have a population in which the majority is Russian, while the southern parts of the country are primarily Kazakh. Therein, in the view of much of the Kazakh intellectual and political elite, lies the most acute danger to the territorial integrity of the country. Should the Russian population in the north become dissatisfied with their status as citizens of an independent Kazakhstan, they could demand, as Aleksandr Solzhenitsyn and others have proposed, that the northern regions of Kazakhstan become part of the Russian Federation.

Discouraging interethnic frictions that could alienate the Russian population is one of the policy cornerstones of Kazakhstan's leadership. But the efforts of the government to restrict nationalist assertiveness on the part of either of the country's two major ethnic groups have had limited success, as Russian inhabitants of Kazakhstan have become increasingly disaffected with the Kazakh takeover of most responsible positions in government and the management of the economy. Within the government, Kazakhs hold most important posts, including minister of defense and minister of foreign affairs and the chairmanship of the National Security Committee (formerly KGB), though until October 1994 the prime minister was a Slav.

In the spring of 1994, the disaffection of Kazakhstan's Russians with growing "Kazakhization" was worsened by the demands of Russian government officials that Russian citizens of Kazakhstan be allowed to assume citizenship of the Russian Federation in addition to their Kazakhstani citizenship. After considerable discussion, the constitution of Kazakhstan adopted in January 1993 had prohibited dual citizenship. Apparently encouraged by the successes of extreme nationalists in parliamentary elections in the Russian Federation—Vladimir Zhirinovsky is, after all, a Russian from Kazakhstan—Russians in Kazakhstan increased their demands for dual citizenship. These demands became more vocal after a tour of Central Asian capitals by Russian Foreign Minister Andrei

Kozyrev, who sought to deflect right-wing criticism of his pro-Western policies by displaying concern for the Russian populations in the "near abroad." As a result of the rising level of Russian nationalism within the Russian Federation, the neighbor with which Kazakhstan has the closest ties could easily become the greatest threat to Kazakhstan's national security.

Many in Kazakhstan's political establishment as well as in the population at large have a deep distrust of China inherited from the Soviet era, when articles by Chinese academics claiming that vast tracts of Central Asia had once been under Chinese dominion were widely republished in those Central Asian republics having common borders with China. The belief that the People's Republic of China had territorial ambitions in Central Asia was unaffected by the warming of relations between China and the USSR in the 1980s which brought a flood of Chinese consumer goods to Central Asia. Since independence Kazakhstan has developed relations with its neighbor to the east that are correct but less than cordial—Kazakhstan registers formal diplomatic protests with Beijing after every Chinese nuclear test, though Westerners question the extent to which these tests actually affect Kazakhstan. During an official visit to Central Asia in the spring of 1994, Chinese Prime Minister Li Peng signed a statement formally recognizing Kazakhstan's border with China; the statement was hailed by both sides as removing the main cause of distrust between the two states. Kazakhstan continued, however, to protest China's nuclear tests and, though the Kazakhstani authorities promised Li they would restrain the activities of Uigurs in Kazakhstan who were actively promoting the independence of their homeland in China, Xinjiang, there has been little indication that the Uigurs' strivings have been curtailed.

Kazakhstan's Nuclear Inheritance

The dominant issue in Kazakhstan's security policy since independence has been the presence on its soil of strategic nuclear missiles inherited from the Soviet military. Kazakhstan's leadership went on record as accepting unified CIS control of nuclear weaponry,[7] but despite the appeals of numerous foreign officials, Kazakhstan was as reluctant to give up its missiles as was Ukraine. Early in 1992, one Kazakhstani official explained that his country has two large nuclear-armed neighbors—Russia and China—and the missiles provided Kazakhstan a guarantee of its own security. Subsequent agreements with Russia and an agreement with China on mutual reduction of the military presence on the Chinese-Kazakhstan border seem to have reduced the fears that Kazakhstan might be under threat from its nuclear-armed neighbors,[8] although during a visit to Washington in May 1992 Nazarbaev told a *Washington Post* reporter that Kazakhstan wanted security guarantees from Russia, the United States, and China before it would agree to give up its nuclear weapons.[9]

After visits early in 1992 by the foreign ministers of a number of Western states, whose first order of business in Almaty was persuading Kazakhstan either to hand over the missiles to Russia or to destroy them, Kazakhstan's leadership declared that the country would sign the Nuclear Nonproliferation Treaty as a nonnuclear state. Kazakhstani representatives signed both the START I Treaty and the Lisbon Protocol, and the agreements were ratified by Kazakhstan's Supreme Soviet.[10]

During 1992 and 1993, officials from Kazakhstan visiting abroad made a ritual of promising that the country would sign the Nuclear Nonproliferation Treaty as a nonnuclear state, but it did not do so until the spring of 1994. In November 1992, U.S. experts visited Kazakhstan to discuss the technical aspects of destroying the missiles within the country rather than shipping them back to Russia.[11] The following February, Nazarbaev told journalists in Almaty that Kazakhstan would have to have both U.S. funding and technical help to destroy the missiles;[12] this appeal was made by Kazakhstani government officials to visiting Americans throughout 1993. The continual temporizing on the issue of giving up the missiles indicated that Kazakhstan's policy makers found it very difficult to reconcile themselves to the loss of the nuclear inheritance that had gained their country considerable status in the world community.

Kazakhstan's status as a nuclear power has been particularly ironic in view of the environmental damage the country sustained from the Soviet Union's nuclear weapons testing program. One of the first and most influential noncommunist political organizations to appear in Kazakhstan was the antinuclear Nevada-Semipalatinsk Movement, which experienced its greatest triumph when the nuclear weapons test site was shut down after the August 1991 coup. The weapons tests left behind a legacy of shattered health and nuclear waste dumps that have been patiently studied and catalogued by a government-sponsored geological expedition whose report appeared in early 1993. Kazakhstan's leadership had to weigh the antinuclear convictions of many of the country's citizens against the influence Kazakhstan has gained from its possession of nuclear weapons. It seems certain that most citizens of Kazakhstan prefer nonnuclear status for their country. The exception has been some of the more hot-headed Kazakh nationalist groups, who demanded Nazarbaev's resignation each time he promised foreign leaders that Kazakhstan would give up the missiles.

Kazakhstan's missiles also complicated the country's relations with Russia, which resorted to both direct and indirect pressure to persuade Kazakhstani authorities to honor promises to hand the missiles over to the Russian Federation. On several occasions during 1992 and 1993 rumors circulated inside and outside the CIS that Kazakhstan was selling, or considering selling, nuclear weapons or weapons components to states such as Iran or Iraq; in each case the rumors proved unfounded, and officials in Kazakhstan suggested that the stories were being circulated in order to demonstrate that Kazakhstan could not guarantee the security of its nuclear arsenal. In November 1993, Russian Deputy Minister of Defense Boris Gromov complained in an *Izvestiia* interview that Kazakhstan was ignoring its obligation to give Russia complete jurisdiction over the missiles, warning that some of the warheads had exceeded their service life and might become dangerous.[13] The dispute ignored the fact that Russian, rather than Kazakh, troops actually had control of the weapons.

Kazakhstan's legislature finally ratified the Nuclear Nonproliferation Treaty on 13 December 1993 during a visit by U.S. Vice President Al Gore, with Nazarbaev noting that he had promised that his country would accede to the treaty before the end of 1993.[14] Gore and Nazarbaev signed an agreement under which the United States obligated itself to provide $70 million to dismantle SS–18 silos and $14 million to ensure the safety of the weapons. A few weeks later, Nazarbaev announced at an economic summit in Switzerland that Kazakhstan had received security guarantees from its nuclear-armed neighbors, and that the United States and Russia had agreed to compensate Kazakhstan for the enriched uranium in the warheads of the missiles being scrapped.[15] With this agreement, Kazakhstan's adventures as a nuclear power seemed to be at an end.

Kazakhstan's Military Relations with Russia

At the beginning of March 1993, Kazakhstan and Russia concluded a series of wide-ranging agreements on cooperation between the two countries that included a statement of intent to draw up an agreement on military cooperation. This was characterized in official announcements as the first step in the creation of a joint defense zone and coordination of the use and conversion of military-industrial installations.[16] Nazarbaev commented that Kazakhstan's government already regarded the territory of the two countries as a joint defense zone, and in view of the close relationship between the two states, the creation of mixed military units should be considered.

The spirit of cooperation between the military establishments in the two countries cooled considerably at the end of 1993, after Russian financial demands on Kazakhstan and Uzbekistan as the price of their participation in a closer economic union proved to be too high for the two Central Asian states to accept. Large numbers of officers of Slavic origin started leaving Kazakhstan, a process that is reported to be continuing despite several agreements on military cooperation that were signed during Nazarbaev's visit to Moscow in March 1994.[17] Kazakhstan further distanced itself from close military cooperation with Russia when during his visit to Washington in February 1994, Nazarbaev pledged to explore opportunities for military cooperation with the United States; the possibility of joint United States-Kazakhstani military exercises was raised at that time. At the end of May, Kazakhstan joined the NATO Partnership for Peace program, the second Central Asian state to do so, thereby taking a further step away from the military integration with Russia espoused by Kazakhstan's leadership soon after independence.

Kazakhstan's military doctrine, anchored in a series of laws on military policy and organization adopted by the country's Supreme Soviet at the end of 1992, rejects first use of weapons of mass destruction and declares that Kazakhstan's defense posture will be committed purely to protection of the country's independence and territorial integrity.[18] Like the other Central Asian states, except for Tajikistan, which became embroiled in its civil war before such a step could be taken, Kazakhstan assumed control over all military forces and installations as well as property of the CIS armed forces stationed on its soil in mid-1992, an arrangement later approved by the CIS Treaty on Collective Security.[19] In August 1992, Nazarbaev issued a decree creating border troops on the basis of existing border guard units of the Eastern Border District, which then ceased to exist.[20] In addition to setting up its own army, Kazakhstan has declared its intention to establish its own navy, and it has claimed part of the Caspian Sea fleet.[21] The law on military structure adopted in December 1992 permits Kazakhstan's armed forces to participate in peacekeeping missions, but the president may authorize their use in such missions only with the agreement of the Supreme Soviet.[22] Nazarbaev agreed early in 1993 to the participation of troops from Kazakhstan in a CIS peacekeeping force in Tajikistan, but the necessary approval of the legislature was given only in April.[23]

Even before Kazakhstan became an independent state, Nazarbaev floated a scheme for an Asian equivalent to the Conference on Security and Cooperation in Europe (CSCE). In early 1992, Kazakhstan joined the CSCE along with the other successor states to the USSR, but Nazarbaev has continued to seek support for his Asian security plan.[24] Two preparatory meetings of potential member countries were held in 1993, but interest in actually setting up an Asian security structure has been limited.

Kyrgyzstan

The small and mountainous state of Kyrgyzstan shares some of the ethnic characteristics of Kazakhstan. A third of the population is non-Kyrgyz, and Kyrgyzstan's president, Askar Akaev, has sought to create a multinational government for his multinational state. Akaev is the only Central Asian head of state who does not have a Communist Party career behind him—he is a physicist who lived for many years in Leningrad, and who has committed himself to creating a Western-oriented democracy in Kyrgyzstan. Some members of the Kyrgyz nationalist opposition have accused Akaev of using authoritarian methods to reach his goals, but on the whole Kyrgyzstan under his guidance has made great strides toward political liberalization and economic reform. Both democratization and Akaev's ambitious privatization scheme have been endangered by the social and political stresses resulting from a severe decline in living standards as a result of the breakdown of Soviet-era economic ties.

During a visit to Japan in mid-1993, Akaev boasted that Kyrgyzstan was the only CIS country without its own army.[25] It had no Ministry of Defense; defense functions were carried out by a State Committee on Defense. The reduction of national security to a relatively minor role reflects Akaev's own determination that Kyrgyzstan will avoid all military blocs—he envisages Kyrgyzstan as the "Switzerland of Central Asia"[26]—and also economic reality: the country has little hope of supporting a large military establishment. Apparently, however, a significant segment of the population agrees with the proposition that an army is a necessary part of state sovereignty: in February 1993, the newspaper *Svobodnye gory* published a poll showing that 78 percent of respondents considered that Kyrgyzstan should have its own army.[27] In the course of 1993, Kyrgyzstan's government agreed with popular sentiment, and by September the formation of a national army was under way.

During 1992, foreign visitors were assured by officials in Kyrgyzstan that the country would drastically reduce the number of troops on active service on its territory.[28] Despite statements earlier in the year that former Soviet troops would not be taken under Kyrgyzstan's jurisdiction, in June 1992 Akaev issued a decree assuming jurisdiction over Soviet military units stationed in the country.[29] At the same time, Kyrgyz Vice President Feliks Kulov enunciated Kyrgyzstan's military doctrine as "armed neutrality," adding that the number of existing troops (he did not provide concrete figures) could be reduced by half without endangering Kyrgyzstan's security, and that the country's defense needs could be met without expensive equipment.[30]

When Kazakhstan took over what had formerly been the USSR's Eastern Border District, Kyrgyzstan found itself without leadership, support, or even medical supplies for its border guards, and the Kyrgyz government appealed to Russia for help. Under an agreement between the two countries that was signed in October 1992, Russian border troops assumed responsibility for guarding Kyrgyzstan's borders until other arrangements could be made.[31] This understanding was followed in April 1993 by an agreement on military cooperation between the two countries. Under the terms of this agreement, Kyrgyzstan permits Russia to operate a naval communications center on Kyrgyz territory; the Interfax news agency commented that Kyrgyzstan readily agreed to host Russian military installations because they create badly needed jobs at defense plants in the Central Asian state.[32] Shortly after the agreement was signed, Akaev told correspondents in Japan that he hoped Russia would soon remove those troops that were subordinate to the Russian army from Kyrgyz soil.[33]

Akaev's wish for the removal of Russian troops may be less an expression of unhappiness at their presence than a reflection of his realization that the presence of troops further burdens an economy that is already in desperate straits, and for whose presence there is little need because of a lack of a credible military threat. The only apparent danger to Kyrgyzstan that might have called for military action was the fighting in neighboring Tajikistan in 1992, and the possibility that it might spill across the border. Apparently some forces of the Tajik opposition took refuge in Kyrgyzstan in January 1993, when pro-government forces triumphed in the civil war.[34] Kyrgyzstan has been reluctant to become involved in Tajikistan; however, the country's legislature refused to send peacekeeping troops in the fall of 1992, and border guards from Kyrgyzstan who had been sent to the Tajik-Afghan border at that time were withdrawn in March 1993. In August, Kyrgyzstan was a party to the agreement with Russia, Kazakhstan, Uzbekistan, and Tajikistan to organize a common defense of the Tajik-Afghan border, and border guards from Kyrgyzstan have subsequently served there without, apparently, objections from the Kyrgyz parliament.

The official reaction of the Kyrgyz government to military exercises that troops from Uzbekistan conducted in Kyrgyzstan's Osh oblast in March 1993 without proper permission from Bishkek is indicative of the country's security priorities; while Kyrgyzstan's independent press raised a scandal over the unauthorized incursion of Uzbek troops, the Kyrgyz government tried to hush up the incident, fearing complications with neighboring Tajikistan.

Uzbekistan

The most populous state in Central Asia, Uzbekistan sees itself as the region's natural leader, a view not shared by its neighbors. Uzbek assertiveness has been a major factor militating against regional cooperation. Uzbekistan's relations with Moscow were affected in the last years of the Soviet Union by a growing perception in the Central Asian republic that the demand for ever greater cotton production had ruined the Uzbek environment and the health of many of its people and had deformed Uzbekistan's economic development.

The former Communist Party leadership still dominates political life in the country. Former Communist Party chief Islam Karimov has been president since 1990; he maintains an authoritarian rule that he defends by pointing to the dangers of social and political instability. There is some validity to his arguments: in 1989, bloody riots erupted in Uzbekistan's Fergana Valley, followed by sporadic attacks on Russian inhabitants of various parts of the republic, particularly in the Fergana Valley. When price restrictions were lifted throughout the CIS in January 1992, Uzbekistan was the only Central Asian state to experience street violence.

Karimov fears not only violence caused by economic and social hardship, however. He reacted to political unrest in Tajikistan by first trying to seal the common border, and later by branding the Tajik opposition coalition of nationalists, democrats, and Islamists as Muslim fundamentalists who pose a threat to all of Central Asia and beyond. The creation of a coalition government in Tajikistan, in which noncommunist opposition forces received a share of power, represented a major threat to Uzbekistan's conservative ruling elite, in Karimov's view, and he set about trying to undermine the Tajik government. As pro- and anticommunist forces battled each other in southern Tajikistan during the last six months of 1992, Karimov appealed to the CIS and even the United

Nations for help in limiting the damage and preventing the involvement of Muslim fundamentalist forces in Afghanistan which sympathized with Islamic groups in Tajikistan. The specter that Karimov conjured up of a repetition of the war in Afghanistan on commonwealth soil brought home to other CIS states the magnitude of the danger and led the presidents of Russia, Kazakhstan, and Kyrgyzstan to agree to send volunteer peacekeeping troops to Tajikistan.

Uzbekistan set up a National Guard on the basis of its own Ministry of Internal Affairs troops in January 1992.[35] Development of a defense establishment and military doctrine proceeded slowly, as other concerns, especially economic and social issues, took precedence. During the summer of 1992, the Uzbek legislature adopted a law on defense that specified that the makeup of the country's armed forces was to consist of land and air units, air defense forces, a special task force, and the National Guard.[36] The same law also specified that Uzbekistan would be a neutral state whose military establishment would exist for purely defensive purposes. Uzbekistan's military doctrine was still being formulated in January 1993, but the country's military establishment was already taking an active role outside the country's borders, helping Tajikistan's conservative government mop up opposition resistance.[37]

Karimov told a correspondent for the French daily *Liberation* in September 1992 that in the face of threats from Tajikistan, and from revolutionary Afghanistan via Tajikistan, Russia had become the chief guarantor of Uzbekistan's security and stability.[38] Responding to Karimov's eagerness for increased cooperation between the two countries, Russian Defense Minister Pavel Grachev visited Tashkent in February 1993 to explore possibilities for an agreement on military cooperation to include use of strategic installations. According to Grachev, agreements were envisaged by both sides on joint mobilization plans and plans for joint Russian-Uzbek maneuvers.[39]

Without the impetus provided by events in Tajikistan, it seems doubtful that Uzbekistan would have been interested in such close military cooperation with the Russian Federation. The Uzbek leadership continues to be suspicious of Russia because of criticism in the liberal Russian press of Karimov's authoritarianism and intolerance of opposition, and also of the Uzbek role in the Tajik civil war. Many Russian liberals are convinced that Tajikistan's conservative government could not remain in power without Uzbek support. According to Russian sources, on many occasions in 1993 Uzbekistan's air force carried out attacks on Tajik opposition forces fighting the government. Karimov has played a pivotal role in convincing the Russian government and the leaders of neighboring Central Asian states that the security of the entire commonwealth is dependent on sealing the Tajik-Afghan border against raids by the Tajik opposition and their Afghan supporters. In the view of many observers, Karimov fears less for the security of the CIS than he does for the stability of his own authoritarian rule, which might be effectively challenged by Uzbek Muslim forces supported by Islamic groups in Tajikistan or Afghanistan.

Turkmenistan

Soon after Turkmenistan was recognized as an independent state by the outside world, foreign observers assessed it as the Central Asian country most likely to extricate itself from the economic decline that affected the entire CIS. This prediction was based on Turkmenistan's possession of proven resources of natural gas and petroleum. During the first two years of its independence, the country's leadership concluded a number of agreements for building pipelines to ship its gas to likely customers in Europe, India, and even Southeast Asia. Many foreign firms have bid on petroleum exploration rights, and exploratory drilling is under way in several parts of the country.

Turkmenistan's high degree of success in integrating itself into the world economic community is a major element in President Saparmurad Niiazov's independent-minded approach to the CIS. He is unwilling to sign any collective agreement, including one on collective security, preferring that all relations with other CIS states be conducted on a bilateral basis.[40]

In June 1992, Turkmenistan signed a bilateral accord with Russia under which the Ministry of Defense of the Russian Federation would provide assistance in setting up a national army in Turkmenistan, providing equipment, training, and funding.[41] This army was to be under joint Russian-Turkmen command and could not become involved in military actions without the agreement of both countries. According to Niiazov's close associate and deputy prime minister, Valerii Otchertsov, the Russian Foreign Ministry rejected a proposal by officials in Turkmenistan for a joint army.

By April 1993, there were sixty thousand troops stationed in Turkmenistan, of which fifteen thousand were under direct Russian command and the remainder under joint command. Few Turkmens were in the officer corps, and three hundred men had been sent to Turkey for training. Niiazov, describing Turkmenistan's military establishment to a delegation from the World Economic Forum, announced that he planned to ask NATO for help in training Turkmen officers.[42] The Turkmen president explained his country's lack of concern about defense matters by saying that he could not imagine a threat to Turkmenistan's security for at least the next ten years. The civil war in Tajikistan, according to the Turkmen leadership, poses no threat to Turkmenistan, which, despite its proximity to Iran and increasingly close relations with that country, is immune to Muslim fundamentalism.

Typical of its leader's independent-mindedness, Turkmenistan was the first Central Asian state to join the NATO Partnership for Peace program.[43] Turkmen Vice Premier Boris Shikhmuradov, who signed the partnership documents at NATO headquarters, was quoted as saying that Turkmenistan was not looking for help from NATO but rather sees membership in the Partnership program as a confirmation of its independence and acceptance by the international community. Turkmenistan is already discussing the training of officers and other types of military cooperation with NATO members, according to Shikhmuradov.

Tajikistan

The one non-Turkic-speaking state in Central Asia, Tajikistan was the poorest of the republics of the USSR. It is the only one of the new Central Asian countries to experience large-scale violence since independence. The civil war that erupted there in mid-1992 and Afghan support for elements of the Islamic opposition that took refuge in Afghanistan at the beginning of 1993 have provided a graphic illustration of Russia's role as a stabilizing force within the CIS, at least in the perception of some member states, particularly Uzbekistan.

In early 1992, Tajikistan's communist-ruled government announced that like its neighbors in the region it would turn to the Russian Federation for help in creating military forces. These plans were forgotten in the political tumult that began in March and continued until May, when a coalition government was installed in power. Former communists held a majority of the seats in the new government, but one-third were given to members of opposition nationalist, democratic, and Islamic parties and movements. The support for these opposition groups was rooted in certain regions of the country; their opponents have been characterized as pro-communist, but it is probably more accurate to describe them as anti-opposition. Because of regional antipathies, these forces rejected a coalition government that included the former opposition, and by early June 1992 fighting had broken out between the supporters and opponents of the new government.[44]

During the six months of fighting in the latter half of 1992, the Russian 201st Motorized Rifle Division, stationed in Tajikistan under an agreement with Russia, played a prominent, if largely noncombatant, role. The division was commanded by a Tajik general, M. Ashurov, who ordered his troops to stay out of the fratricidal fighting. The Tajik nationalist-democratic-Islamic opposition accused the Russian troops of clandestinely supplying weapons to the pro-communists. Ashurov and his subordinates insisted that if any of their weapons came into the hands of either side, it was because they had been stolen. Reports from Tajikstan indicated that such thefts were fairly common, as were reports of Russian troops selling their weapons. In late 1992, Russian sources reported that the 201st had reluctantly begun recruiting inhabitants of Tajikistan to fill out its ranks.

While the 201st was trying to maintain neutrality, the Russian border guards, who had been stationed on the Tajik-Afghan frontier and remained in place at the request of Tajikistan's government after the country became independent, fought almost daily battles with Tajiks who had slipped into Afghanistan to supply themselves with weapons from the Afghan resistance.

Uzbekistan was particularly concerned about the regional security aspects of the Tajik civil war, but Kyrgyzstan also reported incursions into its territory by armed groups from the neighboring state. Kyrgyzstan's Vice President Feliks Kulov attempted to mediate in the civil war and earned himself a reprimand from the country's Supreme Soviet for offering Kyrgyz troops as peacekeeping forces as early as the fall of 1992. The legislature voted resolutely that no Kyrgyz troops would be allowed to become involved in Tajikistan.

Unable to prevail over its opponents or devise a peace plan that would be acceptable to those who sought a restoration of pro-communist forces, the coalition government resigned in November 1992, opening the way for a return to power of the conservatives who had been supported by Uzbek President Islam Karimov. Liberal Russian sources have claimed that Tajikistan's present regime is dependent on Uzbekistan to remain in power. A Russian who had been employed in Uzbekistan's Ministry of Defense, Aleksandr Shishliannikov, was appointed Tajikistan's minister of defense. Tajikistan's present leadership makes no secret of its dependence on Russian and Uzbek military as well as humanitarian assistance. Popular opinion of the government's need for outside support is unrecorded; the once vocal opposition is in prison, has been silenced, or has fled the country. Despite frequent assurances by government officials that resistance has been nearly wiped out within Tajikistan, pockets of resistance continue to exist in the Pamir Mountains in the southeastern part of the country. Throughout the summer of 1993, Tajik government troops skirmished with resistance groups in an attempt to open the road from Dushanbe to Gorno-Badakhshan, an autonomous region high in the Pamirs that has tended to support the opposition. The leadership of the region promised the Dushanbe government to disarm the opposition if Tajik government troops stayed out of the Pamirs; incursions by government forces into the region worsened relations and strengthened Badakhshani antipathy to the conservative government.

After gaining power in November 1992, Tajikistan's conservative leadership planned to base a national army on the troops of the so-called Popular Front of Tajikistan, one of the main pro-communist forces during the civil war. This plan seems to have had limited success, as the Popular Front, a loosely organized guerrilla group, was largely the creation of one man, an ex-convict named Sangak Safarov, who was killed in a shootout with a former ally in June 1993, after which his troops lost what little discipline he had been able to impose on them. By late 1993, Tajikistan's army was largely a Russian and Uzbek creation with Tajik recruits.

Despite the continued presence inside Tajikistan of anticommunist, pro-Islamic forces, after mopping-up operations in the early part of 1993 the government perceived Afghanistan as the source of the greatest danger. Former Afghan resistance fighters were accused by Russian border troops and Uzbek officials of running training camps and providing weapons to Tajik oppositionists who had taken refuge across the border. Some three hundred thousand Tajiks had fled to Afghanistan in January and February of 1993, fearing the wrath of the restored conservatives in the new government; by September, the Tajik leadership had had very limited success in persuading the refugees to return home. The government's reasoning on the refugee issue was easy enough to follow: the

Tajik refugees in Afghanistan were likely to be recruited by the Tajik Islamic opposition for a holy war against the Dushanbe regime.

Conclusion

In the third year of their existence as independent states, the countries of Central Asia faced no credible security threats from outside forces. Even the fighting on the Tajik-Afghan frontier is primarily a struggle between Tajiks; Afghanistan's role is almost incidental, largely confined to providing support for antigovernment forces. The very real threats to the Central Asian states are internal—primarily, weak economies and the danger of political and social instability. Although both Kazakhstan and Kyrgyzstan profess to be fearful of China's intentions, recent border agreements seem to have defused some of the concern in those two states. The only threat to the independence of the Central Asian states in the foreseeable future is likely to come from a Russia where nationalist and imperialist sentiments are experiencing a rebirth—ironically, the country on which the Central Asians are most dependent for the development of their military establishments.

Notes

1. For example, *Der Spiegel*, no. 22 (1994), contains an interview with a Kyrgyz soldier completing his service with Russian forces in Germany.
2. P. Mukhin, "Slavianskii faktor v armiiakh 'musul'manskykh' gosudarstv SNG," *Armiia*, 1994, no. 10.
3. Ibid.
4. Ibid.
5. Ibid.
6. ITAR-TASS, 5 May 1993.
7. Interview with Nazarbaev in *Le Monde*, 27 September 1992.
8. Xinhua, 24 November 1992.
9. *Washington Post*, 6 May 1992.
10. ITAR-TASS, 21 January 1993.
11. KazTAG-TASS, 5 November 1992.
12. Interfax, 19 February 1993.
13. *Izvestiia*, 27 November 1993.
14. *Washington Post*, 14 December 1993.
15. ITAR-TASS, 30 January 1994.
16. *Kazakhstanskaia pravda*, 9 March 1993.
17. Mukhin, "Slavianskii faktor."
18. *Krasnaia zvezda*, 28 January 1993; *Nezavisimaia gazeta*, 24 December 1992.
19. *Izvestiia*, 12 May 1992.
20. *Izvestiia*, 26 August 1992.
21. Interfax, 5 April 1993.
22. Interfax, 21 and 22 December 1992.
23. Interfax, 13 April 1993.
24. *Nezavisimaia gazeta*, 9 October 1992.

25. Kyodo News Agency, 23 April 1993.
26. Interview with Akaev, *Slovo Kyrgyzstana*, 14 February 1992.
27. *Svobodnye gory*, 23 February 1993.
28. Interfax, 25 March and 5 November 1992; *Kazakhstanskaia pravda,* 3 June 1992.
29. KyrgyzTAG-TASS, 1 June 1992.
30. *Kazakhstanskaia pravda*, 3 June 1992.
31. Radio Rossii, 8 November 1992; and *Slovo Kyrgyzstana,* 16 February 1993.
32. Interfax, 9 April 1993.
33. Kyodo News Agency, 23 April 1993.
34. *Nezavisimaia gazeta*, 13 January 1993.
35. *Izvestiia*, 30 January 1992.
36. Interfax, 6 August 1992.
37. *Izvestiia*, 10 December 1992; *Krasnaia zvezda*, 21 January 1993.
38. *Liberation*, 8 September 1992.
39. ITAR-TASS, 3 February 1993.
40. Interfax, 24 March 1993.
41. *Nezavisimaia gazeta*, 16 June 1992.
42. Interfax, 22 April 1993.
43. ITAR-TASS, 10 May 1994.
44. For accounts of the civil war in Tajikistan, see Bess Brown, "Tajikistan: The Fall of Nabiev," *RFE/RL Research Report*, 25 September 1992; idem, "Tajikistan: The Conservative Triumph," *RFE/RL Research Report*, 12 February 1993; idem, "Tajik Opposition to Be Banned," *RFE/RL Research Report*, 2 April 1993.

IV

State-Building and Military Power in Context

12

Western Responses to Military Developments in the Former Soviet Union

Craig Nation

The first issue to be confronted in evaluating Western responses to military developments in the former Soviet Union is the phenomenon of transition itself. The disappearance of the USSR and the end of the Cold War are clearly events of world historical importance, but there is still relatively little consensus about their larger meaning, or where the events to which they have given rise are leading.

The "Soviet threat" that preoccupied Western security planners for so long was relatively straightforward. Soviet conventional and nuclear forces in Europe, represented institutionally by the Warsaw Pact, posed a clear and present danger that demanded high levels of readiness on the part of NATO and a steadfast commitment to the defense of Europe by the United States. The Soviet nuclear arsenal was the only existing force capable of wreaking military devastation upon North America and had to be thwarted by a robust deterrence. The post–World War II international system was essentially bipolar, and the United States' Soviet rival was an ideologically driven superpower pledged to shifting the global correlation of forces to its advantage. One might quibble over the Soviets' real intentions, but if for no other reason than the sheer size of their conventional and nuclear arsenal, the logic of the West's identification of Soviet power as its primary security concern appeared to be unchallengeable.

The sudden and unexpected collapse of the Soviet Union and the emergence of fifteen sovereign states upon its ruins have changed the picture almost beyond recognition. Though the Russian Federation inherited the USSR's international status as well as many of its physical assets, and though its armed forces, albeit much reduced, remain impressive on paper, it is clear that the Soviet military threat as traditionally perceived has all but disappeared. Russia has lost the forward positions in the heart of Europe that made its military potential seem so formidable in the Cold War era. It has lost the western borderlands that histori-cally served as a defensive buffer. The non-Russian territories of Eurasia once controlled by the USSR have been torn by a series of armed conflicts claiming tens of thousands of victims. Russia has committed itself to a military build-down along its long common border with China, a region that once absorbed up to 40 percent of Soviet military assets.[1] Its armed forces have been reduced from 4.25 million soldiers at arms in 1989 to fewer than 2 million at present, and the falloff continues. Those forces that remain are riven by major problems, includ-ing a declining base for conscription, a collapse of morale, the loss of important military assets located in the territory of non-Russian former Soviet republics, political division and embitterment within the officer corps, the lack of a clear-cut and compelling mission, and significantly reduced budgets.[2] Although the Russian Federation assumed control of most of the USSR's nuclear assets, its strategic systems and nuclear policy were also seriously disoriented. The rigors of transition have left all the newly independent states of Eurasia significantly weakened, with no hope for short-term redressment. What kind of military and security concerns do these radically altered circumstances pose for the West?

There is of course no self-evident answer to the question. The breakup of the Soviet Union has given rise to layers of instability—within the Russian Federa-tion, among the fifteen nominal Soviet successor states, and among the interna-tional alliances and associations originally drawn together to counter Soviet power—that will take years, if not decades, to resolve themselves. What the West is called upon to respond to is not a discrete event, but an open-ended process that is far from having run its course, and whose very essence is radical discontinuity.

Prevailing uncertainties impose caution. They do not preclude prudent and reasoned policy choices capable of taking advantage of the potential for positive change that is latent in the new geopolitics of Eurasia. How these policy choices will be determined depends to a large extent on how the dynamic of post-Soviet transition is grasped intellectually. How have Western observers sought to inter-pret post-Soviet developments; what assumptions about the motive forces under-lying change have informed policy choices; and what kind of opportunities and risks are perceived to be at stake? These are basic conceptual issues that need to be thought through as a basis for evaluating Western responses to the unprece-dented challenge of post-Soviet transformation.

Western Images of Post-Soviet Instability

The collapse of the USSR in the final months of 1991, culminating the series of events that began with the East European revolutions of 1989, came rapidly and with little forewarning. As the result of an embarrassingly ill-conceived and disastrously unsuccessful coup attempt, almost literally from one day to the next, the Soviet Union disappeared, European communism had been placed into the ash can of history, and power in the Kremlin was transferred to a group of vociferously pro-Western democratic reformers. The suddenness of the transformation and the mysteries that surrounded it made it almost inevitable that the task of coming to terms with its consequences would be a difficult one.

First, reactions were often triumphalistic and euphoric. Though a vestige of the old USSR remained in the hastily assembled Commonwealth of Independent States (CIS), this was widely considered to be a transitional body whose major responsibility was to smooth the way to full independence for the former Soviet republics.[3] Gradual democratization, rapid transition to a market economy, demilitarization, and the consolidation of sovereignty among the newly independent states were presented as a blueprint for the creation of a new Eurasian regional order freed from the weight of the Russian imperial tradition. A democratic Russia would in turn become the key to a new era in international relations marked by the triumph of Western liberalism, with Russian-American partnership as its keystone. "The West naturally welcomed this prospect without reserve," writes Rodric Braithwaite, "in the naive belief that the new Russia would be transformed overnight into a democratic, loyal, and above all unquestioning, supporter of Western policy."[4]

For a fleeting moment the optimistic scenario seemed to be coming true. During the first months of 1992, the post-Soviet republics moved quickly to establish full independence. In Russia, Egor Gaidar's shock therapy reforms were launched with much fanfare, and President Boris Yeltsin and his ambitious young foreign minister, Andrei Kozyrev, went out of their way to adapt their foreign policy to Western tastes. Kozyrev wrote in 1992:

> We resolutely reject a policy of force, and we strive for a qualitative shift in our approach to the problems of humanity. Promotion of political interactions between Russia and the leading countries of the world, the development of partnerships and major progress in disarmament will be the foundation for new global relations characterized by stability and predictability. This will enable us to direct enormous material resources and human potential to raising standards of living and providing social security and health care. It will allow us to undertake significant, urgently needed measures to prevent the imminent environmental crisis; it will pave the way for creative solutions to other global problems—especially those of developing countries: the eradication of mass starvation and poverty, the consequences of overpopulation and natural disasters.[5]

On the strength of such effusive promises, the co-optation of Russia's residual military capacity into the framework of a U.S.-sponsored "new world order" seemed to be a goal that was well within reach.

The rosy picture was of course deceptive, and disappointment was not long in setting in. The breakup of the USSR did not necessarily stimulate democratization. In many of the successor states the structures of Soviet power gave way almost imperceptibly to new forms of authoritarianism. The manipulation of nationalism as an alternative source of political legitimacy also contributed to the eruption of a series of violent regional conflicts along Russia's southern marches. In Russia itself, Gaidar's reform program failed to achieve its most important goals and led quickly to an unprecedented decline in living standards. A swelling sense of disillusionment and national humiliation created a badly polarized political environment, manifested most clearly by a noisy clash between president and parliament. As the confrontation gained momentum from the fall of 1992 onward, the Yeltsin government, perhaps in an effort to co-opt part of its opponents' program, publicly distanced itself from the unambiguously pro-Western stance of its first months in office. Russia began openly to intervene in regional conflicts within the former Soviet territories (now redefined as the "near abroad"), on behalf of an ambiguously defined concept of peacemaking, in what were perceived by many observers as "thinly veiled operations intended to protect or advance Russia's strategic interests."[6] It declared all of the territories of the former USSR to be an area of vital national interest and sought with some success to reanimate the CIS as a vehicle for Russian leadership. Relations between Moscow and Kiev, in particular, became badly agitated over issues such as control over the former Soviet Black Sea fleet, the fate of the Crimea, and the status of the Russian minority inside Ukraine as a whole. In the Balkans, without breaking altogether with the Western peacemaking effort, Moscow responded to nationalist pressures at home by becoming increasingly assertive as an advocate for the new Yugoslavia of its president, Slobodan Milošević. In response to criticism, Foreign Minister Kozyrev and other high-level spokespersons reiterated the determination to pursue a foreign policy defined by an ambitious assertion of Russian state interests.[7]

As a consequence of these developments, Western interpretations of the dynamic of post-Soviet transition moved toward more cautious evaluations emphasizing the threat of a creeping reassertion of Russian imperial prerogatives. Yeltsin's victory of August 1991 was now represented as having been far less than complete. The contest between Yeltsin and his parliamentary antagonists was interpreted as a decisive political struggle pitting democratic reformers against communist restorationists linked to the old Soviet structures of privilege and power. Annoyance with Russian international conduct was not long in making itself felt, and in the United States important members of the foreign policy establishment began to urge action to counter what was now described as Russian "neoimperialism." Zbigniew Brzezinski spoke of the dangers of "premature partnership" and urged a shift of emphasis from relations with the Russian Federation to the non-Russian republics, and particularly Ukraine, as a means for blocking renewed expansionism.[8] Other analysts urged what amounted to a policy of neo-containment designed to coerce Russian compliance with Western norms.[9] In office from January 1993 onward, the Clinton administration sought to maintain the priorities of partnership with Russia and support for the Yeltsin team, but it was an uphill battle against increasingly vocal criticism.

Even the most pessimistic observers were probably surprised by the viciousness of the clash between Yeltsin and the parliamentary opposition, and by its violent resolution in the crisis of 21 September through 4 October 1993. These stormy events, including the dismissal of parliament by fiat in defiance of the constitution and an attempt to launch an armed uprising in the streets of Moscow, culminated with tanks blasting gaping holes in the walls of the building that housed Russia's only democratically chosen parliamentary assembly. Political violence on this scale in the heart of the capital, combined with continuing economic disintegration and rampant criminality, produced a considerable shock to popular consciousness. A reckoning of sorts arrived with the election in December 1993. Originally intended as a plebiscite for the "democratic" forces linked to Yeltsin, the results were disconcerting. Yeltsin's new constitution carried the 50 percent majority of votes cast required for passage, but just barely, and in the best case it was approved by no more than 20 percent of the eligible electorate. Though a fragmented list of reform-oriented parties attracted a respectable share of votes, the real winners in elections by party list to the new State Duma were the communists (12.3 percent), their agrarian allies (7.9 percent), and most of all the aggressively nationalistic Liberal Democratic Party of Vladimir Zhirinovsky (22.7 percent). A worst-case image of the post-Soviet transition was reinforced by the outcome. Analysts now spoke of a "Weimar analogy," with a failed democratic experiment clearing the way for a new authoritarianism, a weakened executive increasingly dependent on the armed forces to ensure his survival, and a humiliated Russia ripe to embrace a fascist demagogue promising redressment through expansion. If such a turn of events was a real possibility, calls for U.S.-Russian partnership were not only premature, they were positively dangerous. The road from the promise of a new era of reconciliation to what almost seemed to be a reincarnation of the Cold War against an eternal Russian enemy, incapable of extricating itself from the demons of authoritarianism and expansionism, threatened to be short indeed.[10]

The Zhirinovsky phenomenon, despite the burlesque elements attached to the comportment of its inspirer, needs to be taken seriously. The possibility that Russia's agonizing transition might lead it into the hands of a radical extremist cannot altogether be discounted, and Zhirinovsky has succeeded in articulating a volatile amalgam of emotive themes drawn from Russia's rich traditions of conservative and Pan-Slavic thought. Zhirinovsky is a flawed personality whose personal prospects are probably limited, but his political discourse, both potent and dangerous, is certain to exercise an important influence on public policy in Russia for some time to come. On balance, however, the Weimar analogy has probably been somewhat overblown. Yeltsin himself helped pave the way for Zhirinovsky's relative electoral success by banning a significant part of the conservative opposition. A portion of the vote was clearly a protest against economic disintegration rather than an expression of positive support for the Zhirinovsky program, and the Russian far right, of which Zhirinovsky was an exemplar, remained a distinct minority despite its impressive gains.

Perhaps the most convincing images of the challenge of post-Soviet transition have been those that seek a middle ground between the unbridled optimism of the partnership agenda and the provocations of neo-containment. Russia has a great-power tradition. It maintains the attributes of great-power status, whether physical, human, or psychological, and it is unlikely to accept subordination as a permanent condition. But Russia is also in the midst of a deep crisis that seriously constrains its capacity to pursue an aggressive or expansionist foreign policy. No one is better aware of these constraints than the Russians themselves, and despite a continuing debate over foreign policy priorities, a kind of consensus appears to have grown up among elites in power concerning long-term national interests and the way to pursue them.[11]

According to that consensus, Russia's essential security interests in the present transitional phase lie in the accomplishment of domestic tasks: economic development, institutional restructuring, and ideological redefinition. Successful fulfillment of these tasks demands cooperative relations with the West and international peace and stability. The role of the Russian armed forces in this kind of security equation would be considerably reduced. Manpower could be reduced to a permanent level well below two million, the premises of minimal defensive sufficiency reinforced as a foundation for military policy, and resources freed for restructuring with an emphasis on more technologically sophisticated, lighter, and mobile components. Russia would seek to retain and reinforce its status as a dominant power in Eurasia but reject any attempt to rival the United States as a global power.

The case for accommodation also has an assertive edge. The most immediate threats to the domestic stability required for the pursuit of reform are perceived to be those that emerge from Russia's immediate periphery. "The greatest security threat to the Russian Federation," according to one evaluation, "is a rapid abandonment of the 'outer' empire, leading to agitation in Russia itself."[12] In view of that threat, both for practical reasons and in order to reinforce the legitimacy of the governing authorities, Moscow is urged to reassert its prerogatives in the "near abroad," either formally through some kind of confederative association under the auspices of the CIS, or informally by imposing something resembling a classic sphere of influence. The unique historical character of the multinational Russian state, it is argued, makes the term neoimperialism inappropriate for characterizing such policies. Furthermore, by providing a new foundation for stability in Eurasia, guaranteed by a Russia pledged to democratization, reassociation under Russian auspices is deemed to work in the West's best interests as well.

These arguments have a certain force, and the calm after the storm that followed Yeltsin's October 1993 crackdown encouraged more moderate evaluations of the dynamic of Russian reform. Though Western confidence in Yeltsin was shaken, he appeared to remain firmly in the saddle. Prime Minister Viktor Chernomyrdin, once portrayed as the embodiment of the conservative Soviet establishment, earned praise for his professional comportment and diligence in presiding over economic restructuring. The Russian armed forces benefited institutionally from the critical role they played in resolving the crisis, but strong historical traditions, it was argued, precluded any risk of Bonapartism. It appeared, in fact, that the armed forces had intervened to restore order on 3–4 October 1993 only with the greatest reluctance and as the result of a direct presidential order.[13] The appointment of Vitalii Radets'kyi as the new Ukrainian defense minister in December 1993, the January 1994 signing of a trilateral accord on nuclear weapons with Russia and the United States, and the July 1994 election of Leonid Kuchma as Ukrainian president on a platform promising conciliation with Moscow also seemed to drain some of the tensions from the Russian-Ukrainian relationship.

In conjunction with these events, a somewhat chastened, less ambitious, but still guardedly hopeful image of the prospects of post-Soviet transition began to assert itself, more prepared to accept occasional disjunctures and setbacks as the inevitable price of far-reaching reform. Taking into account the limits of Western influence as well as the volatility of events, a policy of limited engagement, encouraging positive evolution without insisting on set outcomes, took on clearer contours. The goal was to avoid "choosing" between Russia and its neighbors and to maintain a commitment to support reform by emphasizing practical assistance, but to keep aid tied to reasonable standards of comportment. What was recommended were moderate options that avoided the extremes of naive overconfidence and blind hostility. The situation inside the Soviet successor states was not necessarily conducive to moderation, however, and it was not clear that a policy of limited engagement would be adequate to the task of encouraging change without courting excessive risks.

With due allowance for overgeneralization, the terms partnership, limited engagement, and neo-containment may be used to characterize three distinct Western policy options in regard to the challenge of post-Soviet transition. Each option refers to a relatively coherent set of policy recommendations, and each implies a certain mode of interpretation concerning the dynamics of Russian reform. Hymns of praise to partnership continue to be sung by responsible figures in Washington and Moscow, but the substance of policy on both sides has become considerably more circumspect, and the possibility of a rapid disintegration of East-West relations, under the press of unexpected events or a sudden change in leadership, cannot be ruled out. The challenge for the West should be to tread carefully among these contrasting options, none of which can be presumed to be altogether satisfactory taken by itself, while avoiding alarmist conclusions that foreclose positive outcomes prematurely. These are not just conceptual problems, but also practical ones. Their resolution depends above all on progress in institutionalizing an alternative security order that engages all the states of Eurasia in the effort to confront the unprecedented challenges of the post–Cold War world.

Europe's New Security Architecture

The classic Soviet military threat was focused in Europe, and the centerpiece of Western defense policy during the entire Cold War era was the NATO alliance. NATO always had wide-ranging political functions, but its primary responsibility was to deter aggression by the Soviet Union. With the demise of the Warsaw Pact on 1 July 1991, it could fairly be described as an alliance without a mission. Lacking the Pact to deter, the "scenario which constituted the main frame of reference for NATO's military and political planning" had disappeared.[14] Despite the elimination of its traditional raison d'être, however, NATO demonstrated impressive staying power. The decision to rebuild a new Eurasian security order around the core of a transformed North Atlantic Alliance might be described as the most fundamental of all Western responses to military developments in the former USSR.

Soon after the disassembling of the Soviet Union, U.S. President George Bush announced the intention to reduce gradually the American military presence in Europe from 300,000 to approximately 150,000 active duty personnel. In September 1992, the U.S. Senate voted to deepen these cuts, and Washington fixed the goal of a build-down to about 100,000 (including 75,000 army personnel) by late 1996.[15] Meanwhile, most other NATO members were significantly reducing their military budgets, while Canada opted to withdraw its military forces from Europe altogether. Planned reductions went considerably beyond those demanded by the Conventional Forces in Europe (CFE) Treaty of November 1990 and the CFE 1A follow-up agreement, described by the North Atlantic Council meeting in Copenhagen during June 1991 as "the key-stone for . . . a stable and lasting peace on the continent."[16]

While it accepted the logic of force reductions, Washington made it clear that on the institutional level no alternative to NATO as an anchor for European security was deemed to be acceptable. Survival demanded adaptation, and at its 1991 Copenhagen summit the North Atlantic Council took a first step toward revitalizing the alliance by issuing a statement on "NATO's Core Security Functions in the New Europe," which listed four fundamental tasks:

1. To provide . . . a stable security environment in Europe . . . in which no country would be able to coerce any European nation or to impose hegemony through the threat or use of force.
2. To serve . . . as a transatlantic forum for Allied consultations on any issue that affect[s] their vital interests.
3. To deter and defend against any threat of aggression against the territory of any NATO member state.
4. To preserve the strategic balance within Europe.[17]

The document placed special emphasis on the role of the alliance as a forum for communication and coordination and as an arbiter for Europe's changing balance of power. It also noted the complementary security functions of European institutions such as the European Community (EC), the Western European Union (WEU), and the Council on Security and Cooperation in Europe (CSCE), and supported the creation of a European identity in security and defense to "underline the preparedness of the Europeans to take a greater share of responsibility for their security" and "to reinforce transatlantic solidarity." A strong emphasis was placed on NATO's "peculiar position" as the only organ capable of performing all four core security functions, and the final communiqué stressed the alliance's role as the "essential forum" for European security coordination.[18]

The North Atlantic Council summit in Rome of 7–8 November 1991 culminated a first phase of evolution. The council sought to redefine NATO's military role by publishing a "New Strategic Concept" that underlined the continuing importance of collective defense, called for significant nuclear and conventional force reductions but the maintenance of an "appropriate mix" of same (cuts of up to 50 percent were programmed, though the target date was pushed forward to the year 2000), urged the development of multinational formations within a reinforced integrated command, and placed a new emphasis on mobility, rapid reaction, and conflict management. A centerpiece of the program was the announced creation of a multinational rapid reaction corps of from fifty thousand to seventy thousand men under British command as a potential vehicle for out-of-area interventions. The notion of *interlocking institutions* was coined to characterize a new European security architecture "in which NATO, the CSCE, the European Community, the WEU, and the Council of Europe complement each other." The development of a European security identity and defense function was acknowledged, but strictly as a European pillar of the alliance, whose "enduring value" as the keystone of the European security order was reiterated.[19] Finally, the council sought to address the security vacuum that had appeared in Eastern Europe with the collapse of Soviet power by announcing the creation of a North Atlantic Cooperation Council (NACC) to provide formal linkage between NATO and the countries of the former Warsaw Pact, as well as what would soon become the post-Soviet states.[20]

NATO's new look compared favorably with the extreme caution that characterized the international initiatives of the EC's Maastricht summit one month later.[21] As a foundation for a new European security order it was nonetheless not altogether convincing. The concept of interlocking institutions merely assigned a new name to an existing reality; the latent conflict between NATO, the CSCE, and the EC as forums for security coordination was not resolved. The tasks of peacekeeping and conflict management, as subsequent events painfully demonstrated, were more easily evoked than accomplished. And the NACC, despite the enthusiasm with which it threw itself into its work, was clearly only a first step toward integrating the new Eurasia into a larger security framework. In its own estimation NATO had made the turn toward a post–Cold War security order, but there was some room for skepticism. "NATO will endure," wrote Richard Betts, "because popular organizations can survive for a long time from inertia. The longer peace lasts, however, the more NATO will become a shell . . . bereft of serious strategic activity."[22]

There was more than inertia to NATO's persistence, however. Its capacity for renewal rested on three substantial realities. First, no serious rival to the alliance as a forum for security coordination was in place. Second, the alliance continued to fulfill certain military-technical functions that were relevant to Europe's security needs. Finally, the survival of NATO was perceived in Washington to correspond to the best interests of the United States.

NATO's greatest strength remained the unconvincing nature of possible alternatives. After the fall of the Berlin Wall, the CSCE swelled to encompass no fewer than fifty-six member states. It had become "a small European UN," and by absorbing the Soviet successor states had taken on a burden "that it will not be able to master anytime soon."[23] The November 1990 Charter of Paris gave the CSCE a flexible orientation toward security problems, and it maintains a large network of multilateral negotiating forums. But, required to operate by consensus and without autonomous military forces at its disposal, the CSCE is in no position to confront problems on the ground. The CSCE is certainly more than "an artifact of the Cold War," and it will have a role to play in any European security system built on interlocking institutions.[24] At present, however, it is too weak, dispersed, and divided to offer an attractive forum for real security coordination.

The short-term prospects for a uniquely European defense and security identity are no more promising. These prospects hinge on the further development of the WEU, a process that has only just begun. Though the WEU came into existence in 1954, its revival as a working organ dates only to 1984. Unlike NATO, the WEU's responsibilities are not formally limited to a specific geographic area, but the organization is only partially representative. Its eleven members include most key European powers, but exclude European Union (EU) members Denmark and Ireland and NATO members Norway, Iceland, and Turkey, as well as all of Eastern Europe. It lacks an integrated command structure, has limited operational experience, and is inadequately equipped with the essential tools of communication, intelligence, and command and control. Not least, its leaders assert a self-limiting perception of the organization's responsibilities. According to Secretary General Willem van Eekelin, the WEU aspires to function as "the defense component in the work of European unification and as an instrument for strengthening the European pillar of the Atlantic Alliance."[25] Josef Joffe's characterization of the organization as "a sleeping beauty that continues to resist the rousing kisses of innumerable princes" is cruel, but perhaps not entirely inappropriate.[26]

To point out the limitations of the CSCE and the WEU is not to exclude all possibility of their future growth. The CSCE is potentially as capable of serving as a forum for transatlantic security cooperation as is NATO. The clumsiness produced by consensual decision making could be addressed with the creation of a Security Council–type forum granting key members special prerogatives, or an EC-style troika as a directing organ. In February 1991 Roland Dumas of France and Hans-Dietrich Genscher urged the "progressive development of an organic relationship" between the EC and the WEU that could shift the latter from its present status as a wing of the European Council into something resembling an armed branch of the EU. The plans announced in May 1992 for the creation of a joint Franco-German Eurocorps of thirty-five thousand men (on the basis of the Franco-German joint brigade in existence since 1990), to operate outside the NATO command and with other European nations encouraged to join, lends a certain substance to Europe's aspiration for an autonomous defense capacity. The Eurocorps' tasks are said to include the defense of Western Europe, humanitarian assistance, and peacekeeping operations. They thus overlap with NATO's classic mission, as well as with the mission defined for NATO's rapid reaction corps.[27] One possible scenario foresees the WEU gradually assuming greater operational responsibility as it merges with the EU, the creation of a jointly controlled European nuclear force on the basis of the existing French and British arsenals, and a progressive disengagement by the United States as NATO "withers away," with the CSCE left to assure a stable transatlantic linkage.[28] Such a result would represent a real revolution in European security affairs fully commensurate with the implications of the Soviet collapse. But the scenario presupposes a lengthy period of adaptation as well as what might prove to be an unrealistically high degree of coordination and common purpose among Europeans. In the meantime, only NATO is in a position to respond to the fundamental challenges of Eurasian security.

These challenges are no less significant now than in the past. The alliance keeps the United States engaged in Europe at a time when America's domestic preoccupations have become more compelling. This is perceived to be important precisely because of general uncertainty about what might eventually emerge from the cauldron of instability in the postcommunist East. Both as a "hedge against disasters" and as "our insurance policy against military threats that might emerge in the former Soviet Union," NATO's role as a mechanism for keeping the American balancer committed to Europe is vital.[29] The transatlantic link institutionalized in NATO is also considered to be useful to help calm fears of a potential imbalance of power within Europe in the wake of German unification. Although the extent to which it is legitimate to speak of a German "problem" may be disputed, unification in the context of the ebbing of Russian influence from East-Central Europe has reanimated long-standing concerns over the hegemonic ambitions of the heirs of Bismarck. The United States' role inside NATO, according to Michael Mandelbaum, "is no longer deterrence but reassurance," with the goal of preempting defensive reactions to German "rethinking."[30] The protean notion of "instability" has also been invoked as a new responsibility for the alliance that is directly relevant to the most prominent security challenge of

the post–Cold War era. Collective security based on multilateral peace enforcement has been touted by some as a positive alternative to Cold War bipolarism,
and NATO is uniquely equipped to impose order in regional conflict scenarios
where diplomatic mechanisms fail.[31]

Not least, NATO has striven with some success to engage the former Warsaw
Pact member states and newly independent countries of Eurasia in an open-
ended process of security cooperation. The implementation of an annual NACC
Work Plan beginning in 1992, including consultations on security issues and
extensive military-to-military contacts, was a practical but limited step in that
direction.[32] At its Brussels summit in January 1994, NATO took the effort
further by approving the Framework Document for a Partnership for Peace (PfP)
program, intended, "within the overall framework of the NACC," to move "from
general common activities to individual, tailored programmes of cooperation
between NATO and each of its partners."[33] Invitations were issued to all states
participating in the NACC as well as to other CSCE members. General goals
were said to include transparency in defense planning; democratic control of
armed forces; preparation for cooperative peacekeeping, search and rescue, and
humanitarian missions; and a gradual movement toward interoperability with
NATO forces. A scarcely disguised goal of the PfP was also to forestall insistent
demands from Central European states for full NATO membership. In the words
of NATO's Assistant Secretary General for Political Affairs Gebhardt von
Moltke, "Partnership for Peace restores this question to its proper place, namely
at the end rather than at the beginning of an evolutionary process."[34] An additional goal was to craft a forum that could encompass Russia without destabilizing existing Western institutions. Russia joined the PfP in June 1994 after a
lengthy internal debate, though in his remarks at the ceremonial signing of the
Framework Agreement, Kozyrev reiterated his preference for a new Eurasian
security architecture coordinated not by NATO, but rather by the CSCE.[35]
Moscow's reluctance was disconcerting, but NATO had nonetheless accomplished its basic goal of engaging the East without altering its own internal
dynamics and decision-making procedures.

In the end, and despite the transformation of the European security environment effected by the demise of the USSR, a strong case can be made for maintaining the Atlantic Alliance as the foundation for a new Eurasian security
architecture. Continuity in security policy suits public opinion on both sides of
the Atlantic and can be represented as serving both American and European
interests in an era of chaotic change. Europe itself is unlikely to generate a
convincing alternative any time soon. NATO performs certain kinds of tasks
uniquely well and is still perceived as the best available mechanism for containing a potential threat from the East, constraining the ambitions of the new Germany, enforcing the premise of collective security against rogue states or
revisionist movements, and engaging the former Soviet-bloc countries in new
forms of security cooperation.

Nagging doubts about the future of NATO nonetheless remain. For most of its existence, NATO's legitimacy rested on the ethos of a crusade. With the infidel's camp dispersed, and in the absence of any credible threat on a comparable scale, the alliance's ability to regenerate itself on new foundations can only be problematic.

Skeptics begin by noting that despite the close links of past decades, the dominant U.S. role in Europe remains something of a historical anomaly. Without the cement of an external threat to bind them, it is difficult to see how European and American interests can be prevented from drifting apart. Efforts to define a new military rationale for the alliance also fail entirely to convince. Even in the worst case, defined by some version of the Weimar analogy, the Russian Federation is in no position to re-create the kind of conventional military threat to Europe once posed by the Warsaw Pact. The NACC and PfP programs opened the door to cooperation, but ambiguity concerning their eventual purpose is considerable, and the Kremlin remains hostile to any formal extension of the alliance to the nations of Central Europe if Russia itself is excluded. Peacekeeping operations in Central Europe and the Balkans might seem to offer a convenient set of responsibilities for an alliance in search of new roles to play—"out of area or out of business," as it is put—but there is very little consensus about how such operations should be organized, and the experience of engagement in the Yugoslav crisis has been almost entirely negative. Given its history and general orientation, NATO is not ideally suited for the role of security manager in postcommunist Eastern Europe. Charles Glaser speaks of the need for an "extended transition strategy" for preserving the alliance over "a couple of decades ... in the face of the uncertainties surrounding both Russia and Western Europe."[36] His conclusion is pragmatic, but it may prove to be overly optimistic concerning the capacity of NATO to meet new security challenges effectively, the prospects for a positive alliance role in the East, and the kind of relationship with Europe that the Russian Federation will eventually manage to achieve.

Despite these cautions, on an institutional level Western responses to the Soviet collapse have been both prudent and effective. The huge arsenals accumulated during the Cold War have been reduced, but in the context of programs for modernization and streamlining that allowed for a variety of military contingencies. NATO has weathered the storm as the centerpiece of Western defense policy despite the disappearance of its traditional mission.

In the context of the NACC and the PfP, the former Warsaw Pact member states have been engaged in a positive dialogue over military policy and security issues. The dangerous alternative of broadening NATO in such a way as to draw a new line of demarcation between East and West, whether at the former Soviet or present Russian border, has been for the time being avoided. These are halfway-house solutions, but they do not foreclose more positive alternatives. What these alternatives might be remains to be determined. Moscow's proposal for "upgrading the Conference on Security and Cooperation in Europe into a broader and more universal organization" to which NATO could eventually be subordinated is not particularly convincing.[37] The dilemma of a "security vacuum" in Central Europe has been left unresolved, but given the lack of compelling solutions the current ambiguous status quo may well last for some time.

New Threats, New Opportunities

The substance of Western responses to military developments in the former Soviet Union must be based on an assessment of both threats and opportunities. The old nightmare of a standing-start offensive by the joint forces of the Warsaw Pact has been rendered obsolete. The new threats that emerge from the instabilities associated with transition are perhaps less imposing but no less demanding of attention. They include a proliferation of new national armies and paramilitary forces throughout Eurasia, ongoing regional conflicts along the Russian periphery, a reanimation of the arms trade under much less controlled circumstances than those that prevailed in the past, the possibility of a major war between well-armed adversaries such as Russia and Ukraine, and the implications of a reassertion of Russian prerogative internationally pursued with military means.[38] The worst-case scenario of an accession to power in Moscow by ultranationalist forces determined to use military force as a source of leverage must also be considered. There are also opportunities at hand, however, and it would be regrettable if excessive concern with short-term friction is allowed to sap the initiative required to seize them.

Arms transfer policies provide a case in point. Economic conversion has ravaged the arms production sectors of Russia and other former bloc states, leading to a threat of mass unemployment and the loss of lucrative export markets.[39] Western suppliers, led by the United States, have moved into these markets to their own advantage, with U.S. sales now accounting for more than half of the world total. The resentment that this has created, and the turn back to a more traditional image of foreign policy priorities, have encouraged Russia to reassert an aggressive arms transfer strategy, including the courting of clients such as China, Iran, Syria, and India, that pose special security concerns for the West.[40] Other newly independent states, such as Ukraine, impose virtually no export controls over low-technology weaponry, and the illegal dissemination of materials from the former Soviet arsenal through informal channels is considered by some to be completely out of control.[41] The end of the Cold War contributed to a statistically impressive decline in global military spending and arms transfers, but the opportunity to make use of the Soviet collapse in order to create the kind of cooperative arms transfer regime that might ensure that the situation will be lasting may already have been lost.[42]

Another discrete but important question that poses the issue of Western flexibility in view of new Russian national security requirements concerns the CFE Treaty. This treaty, concluded in November 1990, was negotiated bilaterally in the context of the old NATO–Warsaw Pact standoff. It places limits on the deployment of five categories of offensive weapons (armored combat vehicles, artillery, combat aircraft, attack helicopters, and tanks) within three geographically defined zones reaching across Central Europe from Norway to Greece. In October 1993, Russia requested NATO and those East European states affiliated with the CFE Treaty to lift the regional sublimits that the treaty imposes on its Leningrad and North Caucasus military districts, the only Russian districts affected after the dissolution of the USSR. The North Caucasus district is the nub of the problem. At the time of the conclusion of the treaty the area was in the rear echelon. It now covers a border zone on the front line of an area of turbulence, encompassing Russia's only outlets to the Caspian and Black Seas and common border with Georgia and Azerbaijan, as well as touching on Ukraine and Kazakhstan. Russia is engaged in a military buildup in the North Caucasus, and it wants the CFE Treaty revised in order to allow it to remain in compliance when flank limits go into effect in November 1995. Of the twenty-nine signatories to the treaty, only Russia and Ukraine inherited regional sublimits, but the request has nonetheless encountered strong opposition, spearheaded by Turkey, within NATO (although large parts of southeastern Turkey are not covered by the CFE Treaty). The issue has provided grist for the mill of nationalist elements within the armed forces and the political opposition to the conciliatory policies of Yeltsin and Kozyrev, and if it is not resolved it could threaten the integrity of the entire conventional arms control regime.[43]

Reform of the intelligence services is another area where, for both East and West, the dividends of the end of the Cold War have not yet been realized. The United States and the Russian Federation have each been criticized for maintaining swollen intelligence services and aggressive intelligence functions that are no longer merited by circumstances. The problem is particularly disturbing in the case of the Russian Federation, considering the tradition of arbitrariness inherited from the Soviet experience. Vadim Bakatin, appointed by Gorbachev to reform the Soviet KGB after the failed coup of August 1991, has explained his own inability to reduce the scale of the organization by referring to the need to ensure efficient operations.[44] After December 1991, Yeltsin's new Russian Ministry of Security and Foreign Intelligence Service inherited the bulk of the KGB's assets and a good deal of its prerogative, including responsibility for border protection and professional supervision of nuclear assets.[45] The directors of the Foreign Intelligence Service and the Security Ministry were also made members of the Russian Security Council. On 21 December 1993, allegedly due to lack of support for the government during the October confrontation in Moscow, the Ministry of Security was disbanded and in turn replaced with a Federal Counterintelligence Service. Budget constraints on the organization will doubtless become more severe, but there is no real evidence of major internal transformations. Yeltsin has used the security services in his consolidation of power and prevented them from falling into the hands of his political opponents. The commitment to maintain a powerful, centralized state security apparatus seems to be a part of the new Russia's approach to national security affairs, with substantial reform postponed to the Greek calends.[46] Though there is little that the West can do to reverse this choice, the situation does not contribute to the goal of partnership.

Russian peacemaking in the "near abroad" has probably become the most controversial aspect of the country's international policy. These activities lie at the basis of charges of Russian neoimperialism and are perceived by some to threaten the single greatest strategic gain to result from the end of the Cold War—the shattering of the Russian and Soviet empires and the permanent weakening of the Russian state as a geostrategic competitor.[47] Various kinds of projects for sanctions or behavioral regimes seeking to use a combination of carrots and sticks to induce Russian compliance with international norms have been offered, but none is entirely convincing.[48] Russian spokespersons have become increasingly unapologetic about their prerogatives within the territory of the former USSR, and respect for Russian national interests in these areas is often made a condition for a "partnership of equals" with the West.[49] Russia can make a good case in arguing that its vital national interests are affected by instability on the periphery, and the CIS, perhaps prematurely dismissed as an organization without a future, provides a context within which these interests may be pursued positively and on a basis of mutuality.[50] Most of all, at a moment when multilateral forums for conflict management are already badly overextended, there is really no one else willing to take up the responsibilities of peacemaking throughout the expanse of Eurasia.

In the new geopolitics of Eurasia, military power and the diplomacy of force will remain basic instruments of policy. The idealistic premises of Gorbachev's "new thinking," which echoed the Western interdependence school in invoking the creation of a zone of peace stretching from "Vancouver to Vladivostok," were intended as an antidote to the unbridled rivalries of the Cold War and as a means for reanimating Soviet-American détente. They maintained some relevance in an age of bipolarity, when the Soviet Union and America could still hope to impose peace via condominium arrangements. But these conditions no longer pertain. In all the newly independent states, some more or less virulent form of social, ethnic, or integral nationalism has become an important source of political legitimization.[51] The military problem posed by the CIS is no longer the threat of willful aggression directed outward. But there is a persistent threat of medium-level internal conflicts and of anarchic disorder, including the uncontrolled transfer of military equipment into other world crisis zones. It would be foolish to presume that these conflicts can be managed peacefully. If the role of peacemaker is not to fall to the Russian Federation by default, more effective multilateral mechanisms for exercising that function will have to be developed.

Perhaps the single greatest risk inherent in post-Soviet disorder remains the "loss" of Russia, its exclusion from the dynamic of European cooperation, and its humiliation as a vanquished outsider. The problem would be less severe were

Russia's transition proceeding less traumatically than is actually the case, but the road will probably not become any smoother. At present it appears that the West has abandoned the optimistic premises of partnership and embraced a variant of limited engagement, though perhaps with the essentially negative goal of preventing an uncontrollable nationalist reaction. The shift toward a systematic policy of neo-containment would represent an extreme provocation, likely to conjure up the very ills it seeks to prevent, and has for the time being been set aside. But what are the limits of Western engagement? One limit is almost certainly the integrity of Western institutions. Selective broadening according to relatively demanding criteria may eventually become an option for the EU and NATO, but Russia is too large and distinctive to be incorporated into these institutions without changing their essential nature. Another limit is the centrality of NATO in Western security planning. The Russian option of an expanded role for the CSCE has inherent appeal, but it confronts major practical barriers and directly contradicts the clearly expressed priorities of the United States and its European allies. Some analysts predict the gradual emergence of another "two bloc" system as the basis for a new Eurasian security order, with a NATO zone on one side incorporating the former Warsaw Pact member states of Central Europe, and a CIS zone supervised by Moscow, corresponding to the territory of the former Soviet Union minus the Baltic states, on the other. The scenario is intriguing, but for the moment it is only hypothetical. Much still depends on how the post-Soviet crisis plays itself out.

At the origins of the Cold War, the West reacted to the classic Soviet threat with the policy of containment, which over the years gradually came to take on the contours of a grand strategy. The Soviet collapse was interpreted by many as a vindication for that strategy; by "holding the line" and refusing to give in to blackmail a Western community united behind American leadership bought time during which the inherent contradictions of the Soviet system could catch up with it. The argument is compelling, and the moral would seem to be that in the aftermath of the Soviet apocalypse a new grand strategy of comparable scope is called for, equally prescient, equally compelling, equally capable of unifying the Western security community in a common cause.

The search for a coherent, long-term policy orientation in view of post-Soviet disorder is natural, but almost certainly futile. History is always more lucid when read backward. The containment doctrine did not emerge immediately or without second thoughts and challenges in the postwar era, nor was it maintained with anything like the consistency that some would posit. Though its geostrategic weight was transformed by the outcome of World War II, Stalin's USSR was a familiar and indeed highly stable entity whose rigid fixation upon Soviet state interests held no real surprises. This is not the case for the newly independent states of Eurasia, whose confused transformation can still give rise to any number of alternative outcomes ranging from the benign to the catastrophic. After 1945, with Germany and Japan humbled by defeat and Europe as a whole ravaged by the effects of total war, the stature of the United States as world leader was undisputed. The United States remains the world's dominant power, but its relative weight among the leading industrial democracies has declined, and its ability to impose policies in its own interest has been considerably reduced. The unprecedented nature of the post-Soviet transition, the manifold instabilities to which it has given rise, and the differing priorities that have become manifest among the leading Western powers in reacting to them make it unlikely that anything like a coherent grand strategy comparable to the Cold War's containment doctrine will be crafted anytime soon. There is probably no alternative to ad hoc policies informed by a very approximate vision of long-term aspirations.

Should this sound like an overly pessimistic conclusion, one might reflect upon the true nature of the "stable" geopolitical configuration from which Eurasia is with difficulty emerging, with its ever-growing arsenals and nuclear arms race, periodic Soviet interventions inside the East bloc, and grim ideological posturing. The problem of responding to post-Soviet disorder is frustrating as well as challenging. There are very few fixed points of orientation, and the potential for a slide backward into familiar patterns of hostility is ever present. For the moment, however, worst-case outcomes have been avoided and a momentum of cooperation has been kept alive. The post-Soviet transition will not be peaceful, but it contains a promise of pacification that was sorely lacking in the past.

Notes

1. Michael Specter, "Russia and China Act to Reduce Border Forces," *New York Times,* 4 September 1994, p. 8.

2. "An analysis of the main components of the military power of the armed forces," concludes a contemporary Russian evaluation, "leads to the sad conclusion that not only do they not reach the necessary level, but there is a tendency toward further disintegration." N.P. Klokotov and M.M. Kasenkov, "Voennaia bezopasnost' Rossii: Deklaratsii i realii," *Voennaia mysl'* (August 1993), p. 28. A thorough analysis of these problems from a European perspective is offered by Andreas Heinemann-Grüder, *Das Russische Militär Zwischen Staatszerfall und Nationbildung* (Cologne: Berichte des Bundesinstituts für ostwissenschaftliche und internationale Studien, no. 27, 1993); and Hans-Henning Schröder, *Eine Armee in der Krise: Die Russischen Streitkräfte 1992–93: Risikofaktor oder Garant politischer Stabilität?* (Cologne: Berichte des Bundesinstituts für ostwissenschaftliche und internationale Studien, no. 45, 1993).

3. Paul Goble, "Forget the Soviet Union," *Foreign Policy,* no. 86 (spring 1992), pp. 56–65.

4. Rodric Braithwaite, "Russian Realities and Western Policy," *Survival,* vol. 36, no. 3 (autumn 1994), pp. 11–12.

5. Andrei V. Kozyrev, "Russia and Human Rights," *Slavic Review,* vol. 51, no. 2 (summer 1992), pp. 289–90. This *plaidoyer* for partnership demonstrates the influence of Gorbachev-era "new thinking" on the original foreign policy discourse of the Yeltsin team.

6. Bruce D. Porter and Carol R. Saivetz, "The Once and Future Empire: Russia and the Near Abroad," *Washington Quarterly,* vol. 17, no. 3 (summer 1994), p. 82.

7. See especially Andrei Kozyrev, "The Lagging Partnership," *Foreign Affairs*, vol. 73, no. 3 (May/June 1994), pp. 59–71. Here, Kozyrev asserts that "Russia is predestined to be a great power" and decries "traditional American Sovietologists" who "cannot accept the idea of a strong Russia, whether it be imperial or democratic." Ibid., pp. 60, 62.

8. Zbigniew Brzezinski, "The Premature Partnership," *Foreign Affairs*, vol. 73, no. 2 (March/April 1994), pp. 67–82. In an analysis in the same vein, Paul Goble speaks of the need to display "tough love" toward Russia, including a "balance of power approach in the region . . . backing weaker powers against stronger ones to discourage aggression." Paul Goble, "Russia and Its Neighbors," *Foreign Policy*, no. 90 (spring 1993), pp. 87–88.

9. The analysis in William C. Bodie, "The Threat to America from the Former USSR," *Orbis*, vol. 37, no. 4 (fall 1993), pp. 509–25, tends in this direction.

10. For the acme of fatalistic pessimism, see Yuri N. Afanasyev, "Russian Reform Is Dead," *Foreign Affairs*, vol. 73, no. 2 (March/April 1994), pp. 21–26.

11. For a taste of the debate over priorities and the outline of a more assertive foreign policy posture, see Alexei G. Arbatov, "Russia's Foreign Policy Alternatives," *International Security*, vol. 18, no. 2 (fall 1993), pp. 5–43.

12. Maxim Shashenkov, "Russian Peacekeeping in the 'Near Abroad,' " *Survival*, vol. 36, no. 3 (Autumn 1994), p. 48. The threats in question include the status of the Russian diaspora in the "near abroad," drug trafficking, and uncontrolled immigration into the Russian Federation, as well as more traditional concerns. Russia's new military doctrine emphasizes the importance of stability in regions adjoining Russia's borders. Text in Charles Dick, "The Military Doctrine of the Russian Federation," special section, *Jane's Intelligence Review* (January 1994), pp. 6–12.

13. Brian D. Taylor, "Russian Civil-Military Relations After the October Uprising," *Survival*, vol. 36, no. 1 (spring 1994), pp. 3–29. A discussion of the problem of civil-military relations appearing before the October crisis in the Russian military journal *Voennaia mysl'* leaves open the possibility of military intervention in political affairs in the event of a deep social crisis but concludes that it is the responsibility of "state and society" to prevent events from arriving at such a pass. V.M. Rodachin, "Armiia i politicheskaia vlast'," *Voennaia mysl'*, (May 1993), pp. 12–19.

14. Gianni Bonvicini and Stefano Silvestri, "The New 'Arc of Crisis' and the European Community," *International Spectator* (April–June 1992), p. 32.

15. David Gow, "U.S. to Keep 100,000 Troops in Europe," *Guardian Weekly*, 14 February 1993, p. 9.

16. "Final Communiqué, 6–7 June 1991, North Atlantic Council, Copenhagen," in *NATO Communiqués 1991* (Brussels: NATO Office of Information and Press, 1992), p. 49.

17. "NATO's Core Security Functions in the New Europe: Statement Issued by the North Atlantic Council Meeting in Ministerial Session in Copenhagen on 6 and 7 June 1991," in *NATO Communiqués 1991*, p. 22.

18. Ibid., pp. 22, 49.

19. "Rome Declaration on Peace and Cooperation," in *NATO Communiqués 1991*, pp. 26–27. On the notion of interlocking institutions, see Hans Binnendijk, "The Emerging European Security Order," *Washington Quarterly*, vol. 14, no. 4 (autumn 1991), pp. 71–81.

20. The NACC concept originated in a joint statement by U.S. Secretary of State James Baker and German Foreign Minister Hans-Dietrich Genscher on 10 May 1991. "Partnership with the Countries of Central and Eastern Europe," *NATO Review*, vol. 39, no. 3 (June 1991).

21. Dominique David, "La Communauté entre la paix et la guerre," *Politique étrangère*, vol. 1 (1993), pp. 86–88.

22. Richard K. Betts, "Systems for Peace or Causes of War? Collective Security, Arms Control, and the New Europe," *International Security*, vol. 17, no. 1 (summer

1992), p. 15. An approving summary of the alliance's new look is offered by David M. Abshire, Richard R. Burt, and R. James Woolsey, *The Atlantic Alliance Transformed* (Washington, DC: Center for Strategic and International Studies, 1992).

23. Franz Mendel, "Wo sind die Grenzens Europas?" *Europäische Sicherheit,* vol. 3 (1992), p. 129.

24. Quotation from Gregory F. Treverton, "America's Stakes and Choices in Europe," *Survival,* vol. 34, no. 3 (autumn 1992), p. 123.

25. Willem Frederik van Eekelin, "Die Westeuropäische Union nach Maastricht," *Europäische Sicherheit,* vol. 3 (1992), p. 131.

26. Josef Joffe, "The New Europe: Yesterday's Ghosts," *Foreign Affairs: America and the World 1993,* vol. 72, no. 1 (winter 1993), p. 43.

27. The Eurocorps has been characterized by one team of analysts as "a direct challenge to the NATO Rapid Reaction Corps." Anand Menon, Anthony Fraser, and William Wallace, "A Common European Defense?" *Survival,* vol. 34, no. 3 (autumn 1992), p. 110.

28. A scenario of this kind is developed in Werner Feld, *The Future of European Security and Defense Policy* (Boulder, CO: Lynne Rienner, 1993), pp. 135–49.

29. Treverton, "America's Stakes and Choice in Europe," p. 128; and Richard N. Gardner, "Practical Internationalism: The United States and Collective Security," *SAIS Review,* vol. 12, no. 2 (summer–fall 1992), p. 36.

30. Michael Mandelbaum, "Americans Need to Learn Why America Must Lead," *International Herald Tribune,* 10 June 1993, p. 4. Fred Chernoff elaborates: "The need might someday arise to counterbalance Germany and to keep it working with the West; this could be accomplished much more effectively through NATO by the United States than through the European Community by France, even in combination with the United Kingdom." Fred Chernoff, "Can NATO Outlive the USSR?" *International Relations,* vol. 11, no. 1 (April 1992), p. 5.

31. For statements supportive of and opposed to the concept of collective security as a foundation for a new European security order, see Heinz Gärtner, "Fünf Sicherheitskonzepte für Europa," *Europäische Rundschau,* vol. 1 (1993), pp. 49–51; and Josef Joffe, "Collective Security and the Future of Europe: Failed Dreams and Dead Ends," *Survival,* vol. 34, no. 1 (spring 1992), pp. 36–50.

32. Military-to-military contacts follow in the tradition of a well-established Soviet-American military-to-military relationship, including Incidents at Sea and Dangerous Military Activities agreements, that has been carried over into the post-Soviet period to both sides' satisfaction. John H. McNeill, "Military-to-Military Arrangements for the Prevention of U.S.-Russian Conflict," *Naval War College Review,* vol. 42, no. 2 (spring 1994), pp. 23–29.

33. Gebhardt von Moltke, "Building a Partnership for Peace," *NATO Review,* vol. 42 no. 3 (June 1994), p. 4. The text of the Framework Document appears in *NATO Review,* vol. 42, no. 1 (February 1994), pp. 29–30.

34. von Moltke, "Building a Partnership for Peace," p. 7.

35. Andrei V. Kozyrev, "Russia and NATO: A Partnership for a United and Peaceful Europe," *NATO Review,* vol. 42, no. 4 (August 1994), pp. 3–6. See also Michael Mihalka, "European-Russian Security and NATO's Partnership for Peace," *RFE/RL Research Report,* vol. 3, no. 33 (26 August 1994), pp. 34–45.

36. Charles L. Glaser, "Why NATO Is Still Best: Future Security Arrangements for Europe," *International Security,* vol. 18, no. 1 (summer 1993), p. 7.

37. Cited from Kozyrev, "The Lagging Partnership," p. 65.

38. See Sergei Medvedev, "Security Risks in Russia and the CIS," *International Spectator,* (January–March 1994), pp. 74–79. "The post-Soviet military threat," concludes the author, "is no less substantial than the Soviet military threat" (p. 74).

39. According to Russian sources, the total value of military exports in 1993 was at 35 percent of the 1990 level. Nina Bachkatov, "Impossible reconversion de l'industrie militaire russe," *Monde diplomatique* (July 1994), pp. 12–13.

40. Steven Erlanger, "Moscow Insists It Must Sell the Instruments of War to Pay the Costs of Peace," *New York Times,* 3 February 1993, p. A6.

41. Daniel N. Nelson, "Des armes à profusion: La dissémination des matériels militaires dans des régions instables," *Revue études comparatives Est-Ouest,* vol. 2 (June 1994), pp. 143–60, and Konstantin Sorokin, "Russia's 'New Look' Arms Sales Strategy," *Arms Control Today,* vol. 23, no. 8 (October 1993), pp. 7–12.

42. The regime at stake is outlined by one team of authors as "a genuinely cooperative, security-driven approach, under which they [the great powers] would jointly place tight limits on defense production and arms exports, as well as licensed weapons production and other forms of assistance for emerging arms industries." Jonathan Dean and Randall Watson Forsberg, "CFE and Beyond: The Future of Conventional Arms Control," *International Security,* vol. 17, no. 1 (summer 1992), p. 109.

43. Douglas L. Clarke, "The Russian Military and the CFE Treaty," *RFE/RL Research Report,* vol. 2, no. 12 (22 October 1993), pp. 38–43; and Lee Feinstein, "CFE: Off the Endangered List?" *Arms Control Today,* vol. 23, no. 8 (October 1993), pp. 5–6.

44. Vadim Bakatin, *Izbavlenie ot KGB* (Moscow: Novosti, 1992).

45. Amy Knight, "Russian Security Services Under Yeltsin," *Post-Soviet Affairs,* vol. 9, no. 1 (January–March 1993), pp. 40–65.

46. Alexander Rahr, "Reform of Russia's State Security Apparatus," *RFE/RL Research Report,* vol. 3, no. 8 (25 February 1994), pp. 19–30.

47. See Brzezinski, "The Premature Partnership"; and Porter and Saivetz, "The Once and Future Empire." On 11 May 1994 the Western European Union protested against Russian meddling in crises in peripheral regions, and particularly in Ukraine, in a formal document. *Assemblée de l'Union de l'Europe occidentale, document 1418,* 11 May 1994.

48. Ted Hopf, "Managing Soviet Disintegration: A Demand for Behavioral Regimes," *International Security,* vol. 17, no. 1 (summer 1992), pp. 44–75.

49. Evgenii Ambartsumov, "Rossiia kak velikaia derzhava," *Literaturnaia gazeta,* 28 October 1992, compares Russian prerogative in the "near abroad" with the U.S. prerogative in Latin America.

50. Georgi Arbatov, "Eurasia Letter: A New Cold War?" *Foreign Policy,* no. 95 (summer 1994), pp. 98–100.

51. Social, ethnic, and integral nationalism as categories for analysis are formally defined in Charles F. Furtado Jr., "Nationalism and Foreign Policy in Ukraine," *Political Science Quarterly,* vol. 109, no. 1 (spring 1994), pp. 81–104.

13

State-Building and Post-Soviet Military Affairs

From the Past to the Future

Bruce Parrott

Since 1991 the post-Soviet states have faced the extremely difficult task of devising fundamentally new security concepts and assembling new military forces in the midst of a profound socioeconomic upheaval. As the preceding chapters graphically demonstrate, attempts to fulfill this task have been closely intertwined with efforts to build new states, consolidate nations, and, in varying measures, transform the existing socioeconomic order. Caught up in changes of such sweeping scope, individuals and social groups find it difficult to formulate any stable notion of their own interests, especially when they must weigh short-term against long-term interests.[1] The same is true of military institutions, and indeed of whole national societies. The formulation and effective pursuit of interests, whether individual or collective, presuppose certain fixed realities that permit rational calculation of the costs and benefits of a limited set of alternative courses of action. As a consequence, the conceptualization of national interests and military policies in the post-Soviet states has been fraught with special complexity and confusion.

Drawing on the preceding chapters and other sources, this chapter offers some general propositions about the development of security policy and military affairs in Russia and the other post-Soviet states. Without discussing each national case, it seeks to identify the principal forces impinging on post-Soviet military affairs and to delineate the principal resulting trends. The chapter first treats emerging notions of national interest and perceived security threats in the new states. Next it takes up the problem of formulating national military doctrines and plans, as well as the domestic impediments to linking doctrines and plans with actual national military capabilities. Examining the domestic dimension more broadly, the chapter then discusses the interaction between internal political trends and military affairs in the post-Soviet countries. Turning to the new states' security relations with other countries, the analysis pays special attention to the question of whether Russia has adopted a neoimperialist policy toward its new neighbors. Finally, the chapter briefly discusses the possible consequences of various Western policies toward the post-Soviet states.

National Interests and Threat Perceptions

The surge of national consciousness during the twilight years of the USSR occurred in a setting that provided few political and intellectual guidelines for conceptualizing national interests and ranking their importance.[2] Due to the long-standing ideological legacy of Marxist-Leninist internationalism and Moscow's tight hold on the Soviet republics, those political leaders and thinkers who favored national independence had generally given little thought to any threats to their nation other than those posed by the Soviet regime itself. During the immediate post-Soviet period external policy was sometimes devoted to adopting declaratory postures that served to demonstrate that the country was indeed separate and independent.[3] In countries, such as Ukraine, that were not widely recognized by the international community as having a distinct identity, this quest for "geopolitical name recognition" was an essential task of foreign policy, but it was not always conducive to a balanced assessment of the country's concrete interests. In addition, external policy frequently became a hostage to the internal struggle over the political definition of the nation, rather than a means of promoting and defending the interests of a group whose identity was already reasonably well delimited.

This problem was intensified by the Soviet ideological legacy. In the pre-Gorbachev era, Soviet party oligarchs commonly exaggerated external security threats to the USSR and used these purported dangers to bolster Moscow's dictatorial hold on the country's various national groups. After 1986 Gorbachev, in a move that resonated with the Soviet public's growing skepticism toward Marxist-Leninist ideology, radically deflated these traditional claims by discounting the idea that external dangers to the USSR emanated from the hostile designs of foreign states. Instead his "new political thinking" emphasized the liberal notions that states' divergent interests could be reconciled through negotiation, that the principal external security threat to the USSR was accidental nuclear war due to political miscalculations, and that domestic socioeconomic stagnation posed a grave internal threat to the Soviet system.[4]

Despite the sharp contrast with traditional Marxist-Leninist views, this revamped outlook likewise failed to provide a solid foundation for generating meaningful conceptions of the foreign policy interests of the post-Soviet states. Although an essential corrective, Gorbachev's new political thinking was built on highly optimistic assumptions—not entirely unlike contemporaneous Western beliefs that a harmonious "new world order" was being born. Reinforced by relatively benign international trends and rapidly deteriorating Soviet living conditions during the late Gorbachev era, the new political thinking heavily discounted the notion of traditional security threats emanating from abroad and focused public attention on domestic threats to the well-being of individual citizens. Moreover, these precepts centered on the interests of a semi-reformed Soviet Union, not the diverse interests of the nations that made up the USSR.

Strongly affected by this mixed Soviet legacy, post-Soviet Russia entered the global arena with a national security outlook that possessed a superficial coherence but was not linked with historical Russian security concerns or with any firm public constituency. As pointed out by Tatiana Shakleina, the liberal internationalism espoused by President Yeltsin and Foreign Minister Kozyrev at the start of independence retained a global focus that centered on the United States and other Western countries but neglected countries closer to Russia, including the states that had sprung up in place of the non-Russian Soviet republics. The Yeltsin government's liberal internationalism appears to have stemmed from a genuine affinity for Western political and economic principles, the expectation of a massive infusion of Western economic assistance for Russia, and perhaps a calculation that Russia's great-power status could be maintained by continuing to address a worldwide political agenda. The highly pro-Western approach was also shaped by the lingering effects of the bitter power struggles of 1990–91, when Gorbachev and Yeltsin had vied to strengthen their personal positions by outbidding each other in making concessions to the United States.

After independence, however, the balance of opinion within the Russian political elite soon began to shift from an unqualified pro-Western stance toward an emphasis on discovering and promoting Russia's own interests. Several factors explain this shift.[5] First, the exuberant hopes that accompanied the Soviet breakup were superseded by "empire shock," a dawning recognition that the country had suffered a drastic decline in its international power and that some key successor states, such as Ukraine, were unlikely to follow its political lead. Second, Russia's liberals failed to make a sustained effort to show that their foreign policy objectives were not simply reflexive concessions to the West but genuinely served the interests of Russia.[6] Third, the low level of actual Western financial support for Russian economic reform sharply disappointed the expectations of many Russians. Fourth, many political activists, who regarded the fate of ethnic Russians in other former Soviet republics as an important component of Russia's national interests, concluded that the West had done little to ensure fair treatment for these individuals despite an avowed commitment to human rights. Fifth, centrifugal ethnic and political forces inside the Russian Federation aroused fears that foreign influences could strengthen secessionist forces within Russia and thus destroy its territorial integrity. Together these developments sparked an intense foreign policy debate among politicians and foreign affairs specialists.

The debate has produced a meeting of the minds on some important points. As Mikhail Tsypkin points out, by 1994 Russian officials and security analysts came to a broad philosophical agreement that Russia must remain a great power committed to defending its distinctive interests. Equally significant is the widespread belief that Moscow's circle of vital interests and security concerns no longer spans the globe. In keeping with the new style of geopolitical thinking described by Tsypkin, most Russian commentators and officials have concluded that Russia should aim to be not a global but a continental power, and they have devoted increasing attention to the fate of the other post-Soviet states, which now constitute most of Russia's immediate neighbors. As Shakleina shows, since 1992 the shifting Russian security outlook has also assigned relatively less weight to potential security threats from Europe and has given increased salience to potential threats from the southern region encompassing the Transcaucasus and Central Asia. This shift has resulted partially from mounting concerns about the vulnerability of Russia's southern territories (especially the North Caucasus) to disintegration, and from apprehensions concerning the potential growth of Turkish and Iranian influence in these regions.[7]

Nonetheless, essential disagreements over Russia's national identity and foreign relations have persisted. Entangled in a complex web of intersecting political and cultural issues, these disagreements divide the elite into liberal, centrist, and extreme nationalist tendencies.[8] Exponents of the increasingly influential centrist point of view maintain that Russian national interests should not be subordinated to Western requirements, as they claim has occurred under liberals such as Kozyrev. Nonetheless, centrists also believe that Russia is part of the West in political terms, and that Russian democratization and economic reform depend on the maintenance of good working relations with the Western powers.[9] In contrast, extreme nationalists regard Russia as the core of a unique Eurasian civilization fundamentally different from the West, and they view the United States as a hostile force that engineered the collapse of the USSR.[10] Although the extreme nationalists' outspokenness and impressive gains in the December 1993 parliamentary elections did not precipitate fundamental changes in Russian policy toward the West, they helped spur the Yeltsin government to assert Russia's great-power interests and highlighted the question of Russia's relations with the other post-Soviet states.

As Shakleina demonstrates, the Russian elite has remained divided over how to deal with these states. Despite the fluidity of some individuals' views, the existence of basic differences is clear.[11] Liberals have favored a low-profile confederal approach, fearing the economic costs of heightened involvement in the former Soviet periphery, as well as the destructive political consequences of foreign military intervention for Russian democracy. Centrists, by contrast, have emphasized the need for a more active policy on the grounds that Russia faces serious threats from portions of the "near abroad" and that failure to deal with these threats could itself harm Russian democracy. Extreme nationalists have championed a far more aggressive neoimperialist policy—on the rhetorical level, at least—that rejects the legitimacy of the other new states and wholeheartedly endorses Russian political absorption of major components of the former Soviet empire. Since late 1993 a fourth, "mixed" school has begun to advocate a differentiated approach, depending on the prospective benefits or harm that each of the other new states entails for Russia's national interests.

The rise of the "mixed" school has been stimulated not only by a more discriminating approach to Russia's interests but also by a growing awareness of the limits on Russia's foreign policy means. These limits stem from internal conflict within the political elite, acute pressures on the state's resources, and the public's preoccupation with domestic affairs. As shown by Tsypkin, the level of public concern about outside threats to Russia has remained far below the level of concern about Russia's internal problems. This is especially true of citizens' attitudes toward the West, which have cooled considerably but remain basically nonantagonistic.[12] Moreover, the Russian public generally has remained skeptical about purported threats from the other post-Soviet states and about the desirability of extending Russian control into these territories. Although many members of the public have regarded the collapse of the Soviet empire as a great misfortune, relatively few profess a wish to see the empire restored. Far more share the isolationist mood discussed by Shakleina and Tsypkin.[13] Public attitudes toward individual post-Soviet countries have remained quite positive— with important exceptions such as the Transcaucasian states and Estonia.[14] At least equally as important, most members of the public continue to disapprove of the idea of using coercion to build a new Russian empire.[15]

International concern about a possible recrudescence of Russian neoimperialist attitudes toward the other new states was aroused by the Yeltsin government's sudden military attack in December 1994 on secession-minded Chechnia, a unit of the Russian Federation that had claimed sovereignty ever since the collapse of the USSR. The ultimate consequences of this tragic episode remain unclear at the time of this writing, and the situation could contribute to a more aggressive Russian policy toward other post-Soviet states. However, in the short run the conflict seems more likely to reduce the Russian impulse toward expansionism. Barring an overthrow of Russia's troubled democratic institutions, the conflict in Chechnia will probably increase the political elite's preoccupation with the country's internal vulnerability. It may also breathe new life into the "Afghanistan syndrome"—that is, the public aversion to external military entanglements—and reinforce the Russian military's determination not to be used as a political tool or as a scapegoat for the miscalculations of civilian politicians.

National interests and threat perceptions have proved no easier—and sometimes harder—to define in the other post-Soviet states. In a number of these countries nationalist movements during the late Soviet period provided an initial political foundation for the formulation and pursuit of distinctive national interests. This was true of the Baltic states, the Transcaucasian states, and, to a lesser extent, Ukraine. Virtually all these countries, however, lacked a cadre of officials and policy intellectuals who had thought seriously about long-term national interests and foreign policy issues.[16] What is more, internal political differences, often rooted in ethnic or regional divisions, generated deep disagreements over the definition of the nation and its interests, prompting fears that secessionist movements could destroy the integrity of the new state. In addition, many non-Russians did not initially recognize that national independence might bring a heavy economic burden rather than economic liberation, and they frequently sought to exercise political sovereignty while clinging to large Russian subsidies in the form of monetary credits and low-priced energy supplies.

In Ukraine the political elite has been divided between ardent Ukrainian nationalists and Russophone Ukrainians.[17] Rooted in the divergent historical orientations of the eastern and western portions of the country, these differences have contributed to the dramatic regional disparities in threat perceptions and attitudes toward Russia cited in the chapter by Taras Kuzio. In addition, the Ukrainian public, like the Russian public, has been preoccupied with domestic affairs and relatively unconcerned about external dangers. Near the end of 1993 opinion polls showed a substantial increase in Ukrainian anxiety about the danger of Russian attack, due probably to heightened tensions over the Crimea, the violent confrontation between Yeltsin and the Russian parliament, and the internal Ukrainian debate over the disposition of the Soviet strategic nuclear weapons based in Ukraine. However, these concerns declined sharply during the following year.[18] Instead, internal conditions and centrifugal forces inside Ukraine, especially in the Crimea, were regarded as a much graver threat to Ukraine's national security. Although the internal political conflict generated by the dispute over the Crimea clearly had the potential to provoke a war with Russia, most Ukrainian respondents appeared to believe that Russia does not intend to seek a confrontation over this issue.

In two of the Baltic states, Estonia and Latvia, the inhabitants' conceptions of the "nation" and its interests initially divided sharply along ethnic lines. Ethnic Estonians and ethnic Latvians regarded their countries as intrinsically Western, and they perceived Russia as the major threat, not least because of the large Russian military contingents that remained based in their countries after the Soviet breakup. Nationalist officials were deeply cognizant of their countries' tragic pasts and were passionately determined to protect their countries' territorial integrity. In Estonia, this sense of past grievances led the government to insist on reacquiring a strip of territory legally ceded to independent Estonia by Soviet Russia under a 1920 treaty but forcibly returned to Russia after the 1940 Soviet annexation of the Baltic states. Viewed from this general perspective, the local Russian inhabitants of Estonia and Latvia constituted another potential threat to national independence and a tool that Moscow might manipulate in an attempt to resubordinate these countries to its will. By contrast, Russian residents in the Baltic states, many of whom had voted for the independence of their host country in the referendums of 1991, regarded exclusionary nationalism as the main threat to the country and their place in it.

Among the new states to the west of Russia, Belarus has exhibited the vaguest sense of nationhood and the least pronounced sense of international danger. As a country, Belarus has been the least assertive about the distinctiveness of its national interests, notwithstanding the urgings of the nationalist Belarusian Popular Front.[19] Although the elite was initially polarized by a debate between small groups representing nationalist and pro-Soviet alternatives,[20] most Belarusian citizens have remained undecided about the identity and proper orientation of their country. Many have shared the vague post-Soviet impulse to "join the West," but they also have remained attached to an ill-defined concept of neutrality and have not wished to break politically with Russia.[21] This reluctance was reflected in polls in 1992 in which a large majority of Belarusians expressed a wish to see the USSR resurrected.[22] Due to Belarusian ambivalence about independence, as of mid-1994 the government still had not agreed on general guidelines for Belarusian foreign policy, as Anatolii Rozanov points out.

Moldova graphically illustrates how disagreements about national identity have become entangled with threat perceptions in some post-Soviet states. The modern territories of Moldova were long an object of struggle between Romania and Soviet Russia. The western territories experienced two decades of Romanian control and cultural influence before 1940, whereas the eastern Trans-Dniester region was part of Russia for more than a century and has a large indigenous population of ethnic Russians and Ukrainians. Due partly to this legacy, the Moldovan Popular Front that spurred Moldova's declaration of independence from the USSR in 1990 was eager to reunify Moldova with Romania and was intent on rectifying what it regarded as past Soviet cultural abuses, particularly in the realm of language policy. This prospect, in turn, deeply alarmed many ethnic Russians and Ukrainians in the Trans-Dniester region who viewed independence as a way station on the road to cultural absorption by a much larger Romanian nation well known for its hostile treatment of minorities. The prospect of fusion with Romania also helped draw the Russian Fourteenth Army, based in the Trans-Dniester region, into the domestic violence that escalated during 1992.

In the Transcaucasus national identity and threat perceptions likewise have been affected by political and ethnic conflicts. On the whole, divisions within the individual states of the Transcaucasus—particularly Georgia—and between the states of the region—notably Armenia and Azerbaijan—have been regarded as more dangerous than threats emanating from Russia or other extraregional actors. As Jonathan Aves notes, after 1991 the three states performed very differently in protecting their security from external threats, mostly because of different levels of success in the political process of state-building. Domestic ethnic homogeneity, a history of genocidal tragedy, and skilled political leadership produced an Armenian state that was capable—perhaps too capable—of advancing its security interests vis-à-vis Azerbaijan despite harsh constraints on its economic and human resources. By contrast, in Azerbaijan and Georgia, internal political and ethnic diversity combined with less able leadership to produce divergent threat perceptions and weak responses to external dangers. However, in all three instances, involvement in violent military conflict has increased the need for outside political and military backing, making these countries more vulnerable to Russian intervention or manipulation.

In the new states of Central Asia, the absence of significant anti-Soviet independence movements before 1991 and the political and ethnic heterogeneity of the emerging societies have deeply affected interpretations of the national interest. Distrust of Russia has remained muted, although it may gradually be increasing in some of the Central Asian states, and political and ethnic tensions among these countries have made them wary of one another. Above all, the specter of a violent internal conflict resembling the one in Tajikistan has given all the Central Asian governments (save Turkmenistan) a strong motive to seek Russian political and military support. China also has figured in the thinking of Central Asian elites. Although China's intentions toward the region may be benign and may even complement Central Asian economic needs, it is a tremendously dynamic power with which the Central Asian states, in their earlier guise as Soviet republics, have historically had troubled relations.[23] As Bess Brown notes, these residual apprehensions and concerns about China's expanding economic and demographic influence in the region have pushed some of the Central Asian governments toward a closer relationship with Russia.

Acquiring Military Capabilities and Planning for Their Use

As the USSR disintegrated, the leaders and officials of the new states had to make early decisions about how to treat the military and defense resources situated on their territories. Above all, they had to decide whether to appropriate locally based military forces or press for their removal or dissolution. Broadly speaking, four factors shaped the outcomes in various states: the size of the available military assets, the nature of the role played by Soviet military forces in the country's pre-independence politics, the measure of affinity or hostility toward Russia felt by citizens of the new state, and the presence or absence of an indigenous cadre of trained military professionals. The size and character of such "inherited" professional military forces have had a major impact on the military capabilities of the post-Soviet states and on the missions they can be expected to carry out. The initial decisions about whether to acquire former Soviet forces have also had substantial implications for each country's domestic political affairs.

Several of the new states chose to appropriate the Soviet military units on their territories and transform them into national armed forces. As noted by Raymond Garthoff and Julian Cooper, Russia inherited a very large proportion of the Soviet armed forces, as well as the lion's share of Soviet defense industrial capacity. Ukraine and Belarus likewise appropriated the very substantial Soviet ground forces on their soil, which were among the former USSR's best-equipped and most battle-worthy units—although the fate of the Black Sea fleet became a highly contentious point of dispute between Ukraine and Russia. The political decisions to claim these forces rather than press for their removal stemmed from a desire to have a sizable military establishment both as a symbol of national sovereignty and for substantive national security reasons. Equally important, the Soviet military had not been employed in the late Gorbachev era to suppress independence movements in these republics, diminishing the perceived political risks from locally based Soviet units and increasing the expectation that they could be subordinated to local control. A further contributing factor was a persisting sense of cultural affinity among the three East Slavic peoples, despite the formal commitment of Ukraine and Belarus to achieve independence, as well as the presence of a core cadre of non-Russian professional officers who could help remold the local remnants of the Soviet military into a genuinely national institution.

In the countries of Central Asia, where the impulse to national independence was weakest and the sense of external threat the least pronounced, the new governments generally followed a cautious course of appropriating existing Soviet forces to build national military establishments. Although in several cases the likely size of these forces remains uncertain at the time of this writing, it is clear that in all instances they will be quite small, though not equally so.[24] In the short run, the appropriation of ex-Soviet units was the only workable means of building professional military forces in these countries, due to the minuscule number of trained indigenous officers available, and the Central Asian countries' close alignment with Russia gave no compelling reason not to rely heavily on ethnic Russian officers to command these units.

In the Baltic and Transcaucasian states, the military forces evolved in quite a different fashion. Given the past use of Soviet military formations to intimidate and suppress local independence movements, most of the Baltic and Transcaucasian governments did not attempt to take over the Soviet units on their soil. Save for Azerbaijan, all these governments pressed vigorously for the dissolution or withdrawal of most of those forces to Russia, although a few Russian units were allowed to remain in Armenia and Georgia as a counterweight against a possible expansion of Turkish influence. While demanding the removal of most former Soviet troops, the Transcaucasian governments claimed much of the military equipment and supplies attached to these units, and local irregular units also forcibly seized a substantial share of the weapons stocks. The acquisition of these weapons clearly contributed to the scale and intensity of subsequent fighting in the region.

In the Baltic states the decision to demand a complete withdrawal of Soviet troop formations was more clear-cut. One explanation is that the Baltic countries harbored fewer anxieties about other potential non-Russian regional threats than did the Transcaucasian states. In addition, the Baltic governments were adamantly determined to deny that they had ever been part of the USSR. The presence of a large proportion of local Russian residents in Estonia and Latvia also made the perceived risk of collusion between local Russian troops and local Russian residents look higher than in the Transcaucasus. The result, as Elaine Holoboff notes, was small indigenous Baltic military units and a popular reluctance to make the sacrifices required to maintain larger regular forces. In the Transcaucasus, on the other hand, military forces expanded dramatically under the influence of civil and interstate war, but in the absence of any prior institutional infrastructure they assumed the form of large paramilitary formations and militias rather than professional military establishments.

Although domestic turmoil and intellectual uncertainty have obstructed meaningful military planning in all the post-Soviet states, the development of formal military doctrines and plans has varied substantially from one state to another. The process of doctrinal revision has been carried out most thoroughly in Russia. There the new military doctrine adopted in 1993 bears a significant resemblance to doctrine in the late Gorbachev period. One important similarity noted by Garthoff is a continued stress on war-prevention rather than war-fighting, and on possessing "sufficient" rather than preponderant military means, which in turn has led to further reductions in the projected size of the Russian armed forces. However, as Garthoff also notes, Russian strategists have departed from the Gorbachev legacy in several respects. Prodded by dissatisfied professional officers, the authors of the new doctrine have discarded Gorbachev's exclusive emphasis on defensive military operations, and they have sought to compensate for the weakness of Russia's conventional forces by declaring that Russia might be the first to use nuclear weapons under certain conditions in the event of war. In keeping with the geographic narrowing of threat perceptions, the doctrine lays special emphasis on the risk of local wars resulting from territorial claims on Russia or from the escalation of conflicts in areas adjacent to the Russian border. The military authorities have also taken steps to develop an explicit doctrine of the role of the military forces in peacekeeping operations and have designated several ground and airborne divisions for this purpose.[25] Despite intramilitary controversy over the use of the armed forces to maintain internal order, the doctrine has also attached new weight to the goal of defending Russia against domestic security threats posed by separatist activities or other antistate violence.[26]

Although the new doctrine is intellectually coherent, the actual posture of the Russian military establishment as of late 1994 bears only a tangential resemblance to it. Some correspondences are clear. The Russian government has indeed made sharp reductions in the size of the military establishment, and a substantial number of troops have been redeployed to southern Russia. In other respects, the domestic upheaval in Russia has strongly impeded the full implementation of the new doctrinal principles. As Cooper notes, acute economic pressures have necessitated drastic cuts in military equipment, training, and even in the military research and development needed to create advanced prototypes of weapons that could later be put into mass production once the Russian economy revives. Along with widespread draft evasion and a shortage of volunteers, these economic pressures have led to real Russian military capabilities well below the planned level and have forced the Ministry of Defense to scale back the formation of the new mobile forces it had intended to create. The morale of professional officers has sunk very low, and the institutional cohesion of the armed forces has become dangerously frayed. The result has been what one Russian foreign affairs analyst has called an "absolutely unrealistic and even surrealistic" assessment of Russia's military capabilities and resources by military planners.[27] In other words, post-Soviet Russia has encountered a fundamental contradiction between the political task of maintaining internal order and the military-technical task of preparing for potential wars.

This dilemma has been reflected not only in the tradeoffs among various types of military expenditure, but in the skewed deployment of Russian conventional military forces. Due to the Ukrainian and Belarusian appropriation of Soviet military units in the western USSR, most of Russia's inherited forces were situated east of the Urals. In view of the diagnosis of security threats laid out in the new Russian military doctrine, many of these forces should have been redeployed to guard against potential conflicts with the relatively powerful new states to Russia's west, particularly should these states ally themselves with major outside powers. However, much as the redeployment of Soviet and Russian forces from Eastern Europe and the Baltic countries was slowed by shortages of funds and housing, any sizable westward redeployment of Russia's forces has been blocked by domestic constraints. The redeployments from the Warsaw Pact and Baltic countries were heavily subsidized by Germany and the United States, but no outside material support could be expected for redeployments inside Russia itself.

Ukraine and Belarus have encountered many of the same problems, but in more acute forms. Whereas Russia inherited a large cadre of strategic thinkers and military planners from the Soviet General Staff, Ukraine and Belarus possessed little expertise of this sort, even though their military establishments incorporated many professional officers drawn from lower levels of the military hierarchy. According to Nicholas Krawciw, Ukraine has made special efforts to build up high-level expertise in military strategy, and has made significant progress in this respect. In keeping with a 1992 law that pledged that Ukraine would never be the first to initiate military action, the military doctrine approved in the fall of 1993 emphasizes defensive strategies and conflict prevention, and military officials evidently have begun to think through and plan for various military contingencies.[28] Leading security planners apparently have recognized that their policies must take account of the interests of all Ukraine's citizens, and they have been particularly cognizant of the risk of external involvement in ethnic conflicts inside Ukraine. The development of Belarusian security policy and planning for military contingencies seems to have been much slower and less purposeful. As noted by Rozanov, the published Belarusian military doctrine is exceptionally vague and appears to represent a mechanical repetition of concepts inherited from the Soviet era.

Like Russia, Ukraine and Belarus have experienced a gap between anticipated military missions and available military resources. Both countries have had to accept the necessity of substantial reductions in the conventional military forces inherited from the USSR, and both have had trouble raising the necessary manpower to staff their armed forces at present official levels. Belarus's ability to generate the economic and defense industrial inputs to sustain an independent military establishment is, as Cooper indicates, far inferior to Ukraine's military-industrial capacity, but in the short run neither economy has been able to provide anything approaching reasonable support for its existing military establishment.

This gap between military requirements and economic capacities has produced skewed Ukrainian and Belarusian military deployments that are mirror images of Russia's. For each country the primary potential threat now lies to the east, in Russia, but their main military forces remain based in their western territories. In this respect, the intellectual contradiction is greater in Ukraine, where elites and military planners have attached more significance to a potential military threat from Russia than have their Belarusian counterparts. The causes of the skewed deployments include not only economic constraints but the requirements of diplomacy and domestic politics. Particularly in Ukraine, eastward redeployments would probably alarm Moscow and provoke a dramatic deterioration in bilateral relations. Perhaps equally important, such redeployments would most likely sharpen tensions inside the new military establishments. Especially in Ukraine, such a step would exacerbate political conflicts between ultranationalist officers and Russophone officers, who have espoused conflicting views of the risks and opportunities entailed by relations with Russia.

In Central Asia, the process of doctrinal development appears to have resembled that in Belarus. Although formal doctrinal statements have been promulgated in some countries, such as Kazakhstan, the scope and pace of doctrinal revision have clearly been limited. As Brown notes, military doctrine and planning have followed the lines laid down in Moscow during the late Soviet era, not least because the local military establishments have been so heavily staffed with former Soviet officers of Russian extraction. By comparison with Russia and China, the military forces involved are extremely small, although the differences among the various Central Asian states could conceivably allow some, such as Kazakhstan and Uzbekistan, to exert significant military pressure on the other new states.

In keeping with their desire for the withdrawal of former Soviet military formations, the Baltic and Transcaucasian states have followed different paths. As Holoboff notes, the three Baltic countries have taken steps to develop small professional forces backed by plans for "total defense" based on civilian mobilization and partisan warfare in case of a Russian invasion. In actuality, however, these preparations could succeed in delaying a full-fledged Russian attack only briefly, so that real hopes have been pinned on the quick intervention of Western defenders—an outlook that has made it more difficult to mobilize economic resources and conscripts for the small military contingents that have been planned. In the Transcaucasus, little new appears to have emerged in the way of military doctrine and operations. The conflicts in the region—particularly the war between Armenia and Azerbaijan—have entailed bitter military battles fought with large numbers of troops. However, the forces involved have consisted at best of semiprofessional units, often led by indigenous soldiers who have employed military techniques learned during previous training in the Soviet armed services.

Post-Soviet Domestic Politics and Security Policy

Coming in the wake of the failed August 1991 coup, the Soviet collapse deepened outside observers' uncertainties about the process of security policy making and the role of military forces in postcommunist politics. The fragility of the new states' civilian institutions, the confusion and internal divisions within their military forces, the political competition to define their national interests, and continued domestic turmoil all guaranteed unpredictable twists and turns in security policy and internal political-military affairs.

Two conceptual distinctions can help clarify the twists and turns that have occurred in security policy making during the new states' first four years of existence. One distinction is between elite and mass opinion; another is between security objectives and policy instruments. As shown above, in Russia and some other new states the political elite's attitudes toward national security and national objectives have become more assertive since 1991. However, efforts to achieve more ambitious objectives have frequently been impeded by the weakness of the available policy instruments. One widespread constraint has been the gap between the goals and perceptions of national political elites and those of ordinary citizens. A second constraint has been a crippled national economy. Although elites' ideas about security have been volatile and subject to dramatic swings, the ability to act on these altered conceptions has been encumbered by domestic politics and internal economic pressures. Governments and political groups have found it relatively easy to change security policy when the change has had high symbolic significance but has entailed low domestic political and economic costs. However, major changes demanding large material outlays and popular sacrifices have been far more difficult to implement.

Conceptual distinctions can likewise clarify the role of military forces in post-Soviet domestic politics. To begin with, the role of the military establishment in formulating security policy must be differentiated from its influence over broader policy questions, such as the organization of the economy, and from its potential role in selecting the country's political leadership.[29] In addition, the concept of the military as a unified institutional actor must be distinguished from the notion of fragmented military groups acting at odds with one another or outside the formal chain of command. Third, the expansion of military involvement in politics as a result of military initiative must be differentiated from "demand pull" from civilian groups eager to use the military to settle their political scores with one another. Finally, political-military relations in countries engaged in interstate or internal wars must be distinguished from civil-military relations in countries not involved in these forms of violent conflict.

In Russia, the military has had a central political role in some policy arenas but not in others. As Tsypkin shows, security policy making has remained highly fluid, and professional officers have played a leading part in the formulation of new doctrine and military plans. In this respect, Russian military professionals have reclaimed some of the military-technical authority that the Soviet officer corps lost to civilian defense experts in the heyday of Gorbachev's new political thinking. It is doubtful, however, that the military's influence on strategic planning in a broader sense has increased, since domestic needs and civilian interest groups have impinged much more powerfully on the overall structure and capabilities of the armed forces than was the case under Gorbachev. In 1994 the high command was unable to obtain budgetary allocations that remotely approached its declared requirements. As Cooper notes, even the legislative party factions whose rhetoric favored an expansion of military power refused to support the Defense Ministry's budgetary request. Moreover, once the legislature formally approved the military budget, the high command experienced grave difficulty extracting even these scaled-down resources from a Ministry of Finance besieged by well-organized civilian claimants on the budget.[30]

The military has exerted a much more substantial influence over security policy in specific cases involving marginal resource expenditures and little immediate danger for other aspects of the country's external security. In a number of these instances, the Ministry of Defense has taken a palpably harder line that has been resisted by the Ministry of Foreign Affairs.[31] Russian policy toward the civil conflicts in Moldova and Georgia are cases in point. During the second half of 1992 the newly created Russian Ministry of Defense seized the initiative from the Foreign Ministry in dealing with Moldova, probably because of the Foreign Ministry's preoccupation with relations with the West and its lack of expertise concerning the former republics of the USSR. The Foreign Ministry, however, gradually adjusted its rhetoric to accommodate the pressures from military and civilian critics of Russian policy in the "near abroad." The hardening of Russian civilian attitudes in 1993, together with the Georgian government's paralyzing struggle with internal insurgents and a string of Azerbaijani military defeats in the war with Armenia, allowed the military to press for active Russian involvement in the Transcaucasus and to extract from Tbilisi permanent basing rights for Russian military forces.[32] By 1994, however, the interventionist objectives espoused by some civilian government officials increasingly ran into limits on the capabilities of the Russian armed forces. This in turn prompted some top military officials, who still favored retaining or acquiring military bases in other post-Soviet states, to adopt a more cautious attitude toward new involvements in actual military conflicts on Russia's periphery.[33]

Compared with military influence over security policy, the officer corps appears to have had only a marginal effect on broader issues of socioeconomic policy. For instance, officers opposed to economic reform have thus far been unable to present a united front or to make common cause with their erstwhile industrial allies. The long-standing coalition of military men and defense industrialists that backed high defense spending for decades has been fractured. The officer corps is divided internally over the need for cuts in the defense budget, and several years of plummeting weapons budgets have convinced many defense industrialists not to press for high aggregate expenditures on military procurement.[34] The picture seems broadly similar with respect to industrial privatization, which is an object of disagreement both among uniformed officers and defense producers.[35] As Cooper notes, a number of leading defense enterprises have welcomed privatization, but less flexible defense manufacturers have attempted to remain in the state sector. Whether the privatization of defense enterprises has entailed a genuine adaptation to market conditions or merely the management's personal acquisition of enterprise assets is clearly debatable, but resistance from military officers and manufacturers has not derailed the general process.[36] Some evidence suggests that the advocates of economic reform among the emerging business class have gained considerable ground in the new parliament elected in December 1993.[37]

Although a significant number of military officers have become involved individually in legislative and party politics, most members of the high command have been reluctant to inject the military as an institution into power struggles among the country's civilian politicians.[38] At moments of crisis, such as the October 1993 clash between Yeltsin and the parliament, its influence on the outcome of these conflicts has been critical, but it has entered these disputes more as a result of civilian "demand pull" than as a result of its own initiative. Most Russian military officers have been deeply reluctant to intervene in leadership confrontations because of the high risk that the military would be shattered as an institution and, perhaps even more important, that it might plunge the country into a catastrophic civil war.[39] As Tsypkin notes, historically the Russian military has preferred to pursue its goals by political lobbying designed to play off one civilian politician against another. In the words of another close observer, "as long as the army operates basically as an interest group, rather than as an alternative government, the [military] threat to democracy is limited."[40]

This military reticence could change if extreme nationalist politicians manage to establish a dominant position within the armed forces. However, to date this has not occurred. As Tsypkin notes, the failure to build such a political-military alliance is due in large measure to the fragmentation of the ultranationalist civilian groups themselves. But it may also be due to the residual military aversion to "Bonapartism" that is one of the few positive political benefits of the Soviet military legacy. Although the attitudes of the officer corps toward Russia's democratic institutions remain deeply ambivalent, the military elite does not presently seem disposed to try to bring the system down. As of mid-1994 the officer corps, despite earlier reports of its enthusiastic support for Zhirinovsky's Liberal Democratic Party in the December 1993 parliamentary elections, was highly critical of Zhirinovsky's movement and was as inclined to support a clearly democratic party as an authoritarian one.[41] Perhaps a more serious danger, although one very difficult to gauge, lies in the activities of the paramilitary wing of the Union of Officers and the growth of military-civilian alliances based on local politicians' material support for economically desperate military units. Carried far enough, the fragmentation of the military and the decline of corporate military loyalties could lead to the violent intervention of military factions in civilian politics.

In Ukraine, patterns of security policy making and civil-military relations have borne some resemblance to Russian patterns but have also displayed significant differences. As in Russia, security policy making has been fluid and concentrated largely in the executive branch of government. To the degree that the Ukrainian parliament has played a role, it appears to have focused primarily on nuclear rather than conventional military issues. On the whole, the Ukrainian armed forces appear to have had a less sharply defined view of basic security issues than the Russian high command has exhibited, and the officer corps appears to have made less of an effort to mold security policy to suit its preferences. This relative restraint is probably due partly to the ethnic and attitudinal divisions between ardent Ukrainian nationalists and Russophone officers, which make the articulation of a unified security outlook especially difficult. In addition, the Ukrainian military is a new institution with few prior doctrinal and bureaucratic prerogatives to protect; unlike the Russian military, it does not believe that creation of the state to which it owes allegiance brought grave injury either to itself or to the nation it is pledged to defend.

Although Ukraine has experienced a high level of discord among contending political groups, these conflicts have not reached the same feverish pitch as in Russia, and the military has not been compelled to try to resolve them. Civilian politicians have exerted little "demand pull" for military intervention in politics. Most politicians recognize that this course of action would risk splitting both the military and the state, with potentially catastrophic consequences for Ukraine's security, especially vis-à-vis Russia. It is true, as Kuzio notes, that ardent Ukrainian nationalist officers have engaged in extensive organized political activity within the armed forces. However one appraises the validity of these officers' views on policy, the resulting potential for further polarization inside the military has serious implications. Although comparable political organizations have not sprung up among Russophone officers, such groups would almost certainly crys-

tallize in case of a major military confrontation with Russia. Ukrainian nationalist paramilitary groups have also been set up on a substantial scale in western
Ukraine, although to date they have refrained from any significant acts of political violence inside the country.

Continued insulation of the Ukrainian military from the selection of the
country's leadership depends on the self-restraint of mainline politicians. It also
depends on the government's ability to disabuse armed factions of any notion that
they must seize power to protect the nation against destruction due to misguided
civilian security policies. Writing shortly after the event, Kuzio has underlined
such a risk in connection with Leonid Kuchma's victory in the July 1994 presidential campaign. Although the risk of a future militarization of politics is real, an
alternative interpretation of the election, based on the somewhat longer perspective provided by Kuchma's first six months in office, suggests that his election
may have positive effects on relations with Russia and civil-military relations
inside Ukraine. If Kuchma achieves his goal of reaching a rapprochement with
Moscow without sacrificing the essentials of Ukraine's sovereignty and territorial
integrity, this could calm latent Ukrainian anxieties over relations with Russia,
especially concerning the Crimea.[42] Given the marked weakness of extreme
Ukrainian nationalism among ordinary Ukrainian citizens—not only in the eastern
but in the western regions—a significant easing of relations with Russia would
further reduce the chances of an antigovernment conspiracy between politicians
and ultranationalist military officers suspicious of Russian designs.

Nonetheless, the possibility of Ukrainian nationalist paramilitary violence
cannot be excluded, especially if there were a surge of Russian belligerence and
a pro-Russian Ukrainian government failed to take forceful countermeasures. A
similar ethnically driven resort to military force is less conceivable in Belarus,
despite the approximately even division of the officer corps between ethnic
Belarusians and ethnic Russians noted by Rozanov. The breadth of Russophile
attitudes among the Belarusian public and the low level of societal polarization
around foreign policy issues both weigh against such an outcome.

In the Transcaucasus security policy making has been dominated by the imperatives of waging war. In conjunction with the initial dissolution or removal of
most Soviet military ground formations from the region, these imperatives have
drawn indigenous military forces deeply into the domestic politics of the new
states. As Aves notes, in Georgia and Azerbaijan one of the most salient features
of politics has become warlordism. Based on paramilitary forces and militias
unrestrained by any professional scruples about political intervention, warlords
have become primary political actors in these two countries. The pressures of
war and the urge to assign blame for military defeats have broken down the
barriers to military intrusion into political affairs. In some cases, as Aves indicates, national security has even been sacrificed in order to advance the fortunes
of one or another warlord. The example of Armenia demonstrates that under
such adverse circumstances democracy and tenuous civilian control of military

forces are still possible; but large-scale violence clearly undermines the chances of such an outcome.

In the new states of Central Asia the small military establishments generally appear not to have played an active role in the formation of security policy or in domestic politics. However, their composition would raise a serious obstacle for any Central Asian government that wished to adopt an external policy strongly at odds with Russia's desires. The minuscule number of indigenous professional officers in the Central Asian military forces poses with special sharpness the question of whether these forces are genuinely under the control of the national political authorities. Although these units might reasonably be expected to obey the orders of the national government in case of clashes with regional military opponents, it remains highly uncertain how they would behave were relations with Russia to deteriorate sharply. By the same token, the very high levels of ethnic Central Asian conscripts in the ranks raise some question about whether these forces could be used effectively as part of a Moscow-directed conspiracy to seize direct control in these countries, although this would ultimately depend on the specific circumstances and the level of national consciousness among the conscripts.

This survey of the interplay between domestic politics and security policy has implications for the possible development of future relations among the post-Soviet states. The Transcaucasus apart, few if any of the new states desire war or are even remotely prepared for it. Virtually without exception, the armed forces of the new states have been profoundly disrupted by the USSR's breakup and have not yet been transformed into effective national military establishments. This limitation is especially pronounced in military organizations composed of different ethnic groups that harbor divergent outlooks on the country's interests. On the other hand, in many new states civilian political structures are equally fragile, and they are vulnerable to territorial claims by neighboring countries. Taken together, these considerations suggest that if a new large-scale military conflict breaks out during the next few years, in most cases it is far more likely to begin through a catalytic political clash than through a carefully planned military attack by one country on another. The challenge for the leaders of the new states is to prevent their countries from sliding into wars which are precipitated by the ethnic and political turbulence inside their societies, but for which their societies are profoundly unprepared.

Security Relations with Other States:
The Return of Russian Imperialism?

In theory, the post-Soviet states have had three basic options for safeguarding their security: collective security arrangements with the other new states, alliances with some of these states against others, or alliances with major outside powers. Russia and some like-minded governments have emphasized the idea of collective security within the framework of the Commonwealth of Independent States (CIS). The Treaty on Collective Security concluded in May 1992 among Russia and several other CIS members marked an attempt to move in this direction, although Armenia's unsuccessful effort to invoke the agreement against Azerbaijan, which had not yet joined, demonstrated that Russia intended to interpret the agreement's provisions according to its own lights. In Tajikistan, the one case in which Russia has sought genuine multilateral action by CIS members against a perceived security threat, it has had difficulty eliciting concrete military backing from the Central Asian regimes that wish to prevent a spread of political instability. The Russian push for common CIS security arrangements has led to an expansion of joint military and border control activities with all the other new states save Moldova, and since 1994 Moscow has urged several other post-Soviet states to accept new Russian military bases; but the bases established thus far have been staffed with relatively small garrisons, most already in place, and their scale and number will probably be limited by the high cost of building and maintaining them.[43]

For the new states most determined to protect their sovereignty, one of the most worrisome developments has been the evolution of Russia's stance toward the handling of military conflicts in regions near its border. Since 1993 Russia has become increasingly resistant to proposals for dealing with nearby military conflicts through multilateral peacekeeping efforts that give a major voice to participants from outside the CIS. Instead it has emphasized "peacemaking" operations carried out largely or exclusively by Russian troops, with or without the imprimatur of the international community.[44] Russian military doctrine for the resolution of such conflicts is at best ambiguous about whether to overwhelm the warring parties or mediate between them, and Russian troops have not received the training necessary to perform the military-political role of mediator. In a number of cases, particularly in the Transcaucasus, Moscow's military intervention in third-party military conflicts has shown that Russia is at least as committed to reestablishing its influence in the given states as to settling what are admittedly very complex regional conflicts.

Concern in several non-Russian new states about Russian military behavior has been reinforced by certain trends in Moscow's political line toward other CIS members. During 1994 the Yeltsin government began to press the other former republics to allow dual citizenship for local citizens of ethnic Russian descent. Although Turkmenistan agreed to dual citizenship and Kyrgyzstan considered it as a means of stemming the out-migration of economically essential Russian specialists, the other new states rebuffed this proposal as a threat to their sovereignty. Nonetheless, in the fall of 1994 the Yeltsin government declared its intention to confer Russian citizenship unilaterally on ethnic Russian citizens of other new states that refused to conclude a treaty allowing for this possibility.[45] Although this unresolved issue did not prevent Russia from reaching an agreement on a new treaty of friendship with Ukraine, the dispute over citizenship clearly has the potential to cause an explosive destabilization of Russia's relations with other post-Soviet states.

Taken together, these trends in Russian policy have raised fears of a resurgence of Russian imperialism and strengthened the impulse of several of the new states to find ways to counter Russian influence. Immediately after the USSR's collapse, some of the new governments sought to create regional alignments based primarily on other former Soviet republics. However, regional relationships of this kind have been slow to coalesce, and even where they have crystallized, they have lacked military substance. Ukrainian proposals for a Baltic-to-Black Sea coalition quickly proved unworkable because of the divergent strategic orientations of the participants (especially Belarus), the widespread unwillingness of the citizens in each prospective member-state to fight outside their homeland, and the overriding desire of several countries to establish direct ties with the West. Similarly, proposals for augmented regional alliances between the western new states and neighbors such as Poland have been frustrated by the determination of the latter countries not to encumber their own campaigns to join the West with new eastern ties. In Central Asia as well as the Transcaucasus, local political animosities plus numerous economic and technical constraints have made regional military cooperation against Russia impossible.

Anxieties about Russian behavior have also risen in the West. Struck by the shift in Russian policy after mid-1992, many Western observers have argued that Russia has returned to the imperialist practices of the Soviet Union, or has a high probability of doing so.[46] Russian opinion has indeed swung sharply away from the deferential internationalism of the early 1990s to reaffirm the importance of restoring Russia as a great power in Eurasia. But as Craig Nation points out, this shift of attitude does not by itself amount to a determination to reestablish Russia's imperial domination of the other new states. A critical distinction exists between exercising strong or even preeminent influence over the foreign policies of neighboring countries and exerting the kind of full-fledged imperial control over foreign and domestic policies that the USSR wielded in Eastern Europe after World War II.[47] In this context, it is important to recognize that the epochal nature of the Soviet upheaval has affected the expectations of outside observers almost as profoundly as it has shaped the outlook of the direct participants in the drama. Colored by the high optimism of the late 1980s and early 1990s, Moscow's record of dramatic foreign policy concessions after 1987 has led many Western analysts to equate moderate international behavior with a nearly complete lack of Russian assertiveness. Measured by the yardstick of this exceptionally accommodating period in Soviet and Russian external policy, Russia's recent inclination to spell out and press its own interests has struck some analysts as a direct reversion to old patterns of belligerence.

As we have seen, a significant body of evidence indicates that neoimperialism could become the defining characteristic of Russia's policy toward the other new states. Russia has used military force to expand or defend its security position in several countries—Moldova, Georgia, Azerbaijan, and Tajikistan. Since 1993 it has staked out a declaratory position on the issue of dual citizenship that smacks of imperial thinking and could become profoundly destabilizing. In addition, it has expressed an increasingly assertive desire to have a direct impact on the disposition of the vast energy resources situated in Central Asia. Since 1993 Moscow has exerted heavy pressures on several Central Asian states to obtain a share of the prospective proceeds from massive Western-funded energy extraction projects in which Russia itself has made no significant investments.

Although such behavior signifies Russia's desire for large and perhaps preeminent influence over the external relations of a number of the former Soviet republics, it does not add up to a reversion to Moscow's past patterns of imperial conduct. In Central Asia, Moscow has demanded a share of the proceeds from energy development, but it has not pursued the anti-Western line of the extreme nationalists nor sought to exclude Western influence from the region.[48] Virtually all the cases in which Russia has used military violence to deal with another post-Soviet state have involved prior violent conflict inside that state or between it and a third country. In other instances Moscow has, often reluctantly and despite rhetorical protests to the contrary, accepted a reduction of its influence and refrained from military intervention.

As of the end of 1994, Ukraine, Belarus, and the Baltic states all fitted this generalization. It is worth recalling that on several occasions the Russian government declared its unwillingness to withdraw its forces from the Baltic states without major concessions on the citizenship issue and announced halts in troop withdrawals to underscore the point. Nonetheless, actual withdrawals continued. By 1994 Russia had signed withdrawal agreements with all three Baltic countries, and at the end of the year all Russian ground troops had been removed. Although Russian policy making has been shaped by a spectrum of political forces that includes groups with a clear-cut imperialist agenda, its military actions have frequently also been stimulated by worries concerning potential Russian disintegration and internal disorder. Such behavior is qualitatively different from efforts to seize and conquer stable neighboring polities that present no political or military threat to Russia.[49]

Observers who argue that Russian imperialism has returned frequently cite Russian economic pressures on the other new states to support their case. However, despite Russia's economic preponderance among the new states, there is little reason to believe that Moscow can build anything resembling the old Soviet empire on the basis of economic leverage alone. In a number of cases Russia has attempted to use economic leverage, particularly cut-offs in energy supplies, against other new states. Although Moscow's objective has sometimes been to force payment of large unpaid bills, it has also used economic pressure in an effort to compel other post-Soviet states to make political concessions. However, this economic leverage, painful though it has been for the target countries, has been insufficient to achieve the reabsorption of major post-Soviet states into a new empire, even assuming this to be Moscow's goal. In the case of Ukraine, Moscow has discovered that the disruption of Ukrainian energy supplies can be partially countered by Ukraine and also seriously harms Russia's diplomatic and economic credibility with the major Western countries whose supplies must necessarily be interrupted at the same time as Ukraine's.[50] Moreover, Moscow has shied away from absorbing other post-Soviet countries economically even when they have petitioned for this course of action—as the aborted monetary union with Belarus illustrates. Prompted by the isolationist sentiment described by Shakleina, many Russian citizens and politicians remain deeply reluctant to shoulder the economic burden of efforts to rebuild the empire.

Despite Russia's geopolitical weight, the fate of its future relations with other post-Soviet states depends in significant measure on those countries themselves. One theme of this book is the considerable diversity of the new states and their circumstances. It follows that Russia's relations with these countries may also be characterized by diversity, either because of variations in Russia's objectives or because of differences in its capacity to achieve identical objectives in varying circumstances. Among the qualities required of the non-Russian states are skillful political leadership, a determination to maintain a modicum of domestic political cohesion, especially among different ethnic groups, and a capacity to promote domestic economic and political reforms that over time will strengthen the political and economic foundations of state sovereignty.

Above all, new states that wish to preserve their sovereignty against potential Russian encroachments must maintain domestic peace and avoid war with other neighbors. Involvement in civil or interstate wars has made Tajikistan and the states of the Transcaucasus militarily more vulnerable to Russian intervention by lowering Russia's potential costs in material resources and the number of Russian servicemen who might be killed. It has also made them more vulnerable in a diplomatic sense. Russian spokespersons have been able to depict Moscow's intervention as a prerequisite for the reestablishment of peace, thereby undercutting the target country's grounds for appeal to the international community or to a particular outside protector. Hence the international political cost to Russia of intervening in these situations has also been low.

Considered at the close of 1994, the Ukrainian example suggests that in some instances political reequilibration inside a new state may lead to improved relations with Moscow that fall well short of Russian imperial domination. To the degree that Moscow's policy toward the Baltic states is actually affected by the attitude of the ethnic Russians living there, social trends since 1992 suggest that the prospects for cooperative Baltic relations with Russia may have improved as well—although much will depend on how the Estonian and Latvian governments treat these Russian inhabitants legally and politically.[51] In one of the most recalcitrant cases, Moldova, the Russian and Moldovan governments concluded a November 1994 agreement that, despite political opposition from the local Russian military forces, provided for a substantial measure of internal decentralization to the Trans-Dniester region in exchange for the promised withdrawal of Russian troops.[52]

Western Policy Options and Future Scholarly Research

Given the worrisome Russian trends mentioned above, many post-Soviet states have increasingly turned to major outside powers in the hope of shoring up their security. Like the older states of Eastern Europe, Ukraine and several other new states have entered the U.S.-sponsored Partnership for Peace to strengthen their ties with the West, some in the hope of ultimately becoming members of the North Atlantic Treaty Organization. At the time of this writing the vexing question of the future relationship between Russia and NATO remains unresolved, and it is unlikely that cautious states such as Belarus would consider joining NATO without Russian approval. On the other hand, the Baltic states would quickly seize the opportunity to become NATO members, and possibly even Ukraine would seriously consider the NATO option, which some Ukrainian political groups strongly advocate.

These trends have generated a vigorous Western debate about Western strategy toward Russia. Proponents of expanding NATO to include East European members have argued, inter alia, that this step would help consolidate democratic and economic reform in Eastern Europe and guard against the possibility of a resurgent Russia determined to reestablish its hegemony in the region. Opponents have countered that NATO expansion would alienate Russia politically by excluding it from Europe; some European NATO circles have also suggested that new security threats from the southern Mediterranean should not be complicated by incorporating Eastern Europe's intraregional tensions and rivalries into the alliance.[53] Since 1992 Western reactions to Russia, though diverse, have evinced a palpable disappointment with the travails of Russian democracy and a residual anxiety about security threats from Russia. At the same time, some Western commentators have argued that Russia's present weakness allows NATO to expand into Eastern Europe despite Moscow's protests and that Russian anxieties can be salved with diplomatic gestures demonstrating a continued Western commitment to cooperation with Russia.

In considering this assessment, one signal fact that should be kept in mind is that Russia's conventional military capacities have been slashed, not only quantitatively but especially qualitatively, from what they were in 1991, not to mention what the Soviet Union's were in 1988. Russia today lacks the conventional military capabilities to pose a significant military threat to the former members of the Warsaw Pact. So far as the post-Soviet states are concerned, Russia appears to have the capacity to overwhelm some of them, but by no means all, with a decisive military campaign, and the military debacle in Chechnia calls even this limited capacity into question. Moreover, the domestic political fabric of Russia has become so badly frayed that war with some other post-Soviet states—Ukraine in particular—could easily precipitate civil war inside Russia itself.

STATE-BUILDING AND POST-SOVIET MILITARY AFFAIRS 299

Although Russia's politics remains in a profound state of flux, to date the growth of anti-Western sentiment within elements of the elite has not undermined the Yeltsin government's centrist commitment to cooperation with the West. The government's military weakness, its continuing need for Western economic assistance, and its real though imperfect commitment to democratic principles have all provided an incentive for avoiding a rupture with the West over the NATO issue. Having failed in its efforts to substitute the relatively powerless CSCE for NATO as the principal mechanism for managing security issues in Europe, the Russian government has countered proposals for NATO expansion by voicing its concern and seeking a Western postponement of decisions on the issue, and by demonstratively withholding final action on its previously announced decision to join the Partnership for Peace agreement. It also has floated counterproposals on a limited NATO expansion that are nominally conciliatory but are actually intended to scuttle the proposed expansion by playing on the differences between East European countries and their Western supporters.[54]

An early NATO commitment to eastward expansion carries major risks. Although Russia lacks the military, political, or economic means to block an expansion of NATO into Eastern Europe, an early Western commitment to expansion could contribute to a basic shift in the balance of attitudes toward the West within the Russian political elite. In addition, it could weaken the influence of centrists who advocate a democratic future for Russia. It could even lend political ammunition to the Russian political groups that advocate the subordination of other post-Soviet states, particularly Belarus and Ukraine, to Moscow's full control.[55] To date there has been a tacit, if fragile, understanding between the Yeltsin government and the Western powers that relative Russian restraint in dealing with the western post-Soviet states would be linked with Western delay on the question of NATO expansion.[56] By vitiating this tacit understanding, an early decision to expand NATO would strengthen the hand of politicians and military officers who wish to fasten Moscow's grip on the new states west of Russia in order to eliminate the possibility that those countries might ultimately join NATO and become potential sites for the deployment of NATO military forces.[57] This risk has prompted the Ukrainian minister of defense and some other officials of the western new states to argue against a limited NATO expansion on the grounds that it would make their own country's position less secure.[58]

In the short run the impulse to tighten control over the neighboring post-Soviet states would almost certainly not prompt Moscow to attempt to take over these countries by direct military means, especially given Russia's severe military weakness and the substantial though politically untested military forces at the disposal of Ukraine. However, a political sea-change in Moscow could prompt vigorous Russian attempts to subvert the independence of the western states by exploiting their internal vulnerabilities and could lead to violent confrontations over explosive matters such as the Crimea. Unless managed with exceptional political skill unlikely in the circumstances, such confrontations might escalate into military conflicts that would threaten Russia's political and territorial integrity as well as that of neighboring countries.

Several approaching decision points could bring such fundamental questions of security policy and domestic political development to a head. One is the Russian parliamentary election planned for late 1995. Probably even more important is the presidential election scheduled for mid-1996. If President Yeltsin were to die in office, the requirement to choose a new leader could force a choice on such matters even sooner. Whether an early Western decision to expand NATO would precipitate such negative changes in Russia—or indeed, whether a delay in deciding on expansion would avoid such changes—remains uncertain. Much depends on the fluid distribution of power among Russia's post-Soviet political institutions, including the half-reformed remnants of the KGB, and on whether a newly elected president exploits the dictatorial potential of the Russian presidency's formidable constitutional powers. In any case, the magnitude of the stakes involved and the relative costs and benefits suggest that the risk of an early commitment to NATO expansion is not worth taking.

As of the end of 1994 the Russian state poses no security threat to its former Warsaw Pact allies. In the near to medium term the stability of these countries hinges not on NATO military guarantees but on more generous economic treatment from the West, early membership in the European Union, and inclusion in other international institutions that could strengthen their sense of belonging to Europe. Should Russia turn in a genuinely belligerent and anti-Western direction during the second half of the 1990s, its profound military weakness would still allow the Western powers adequate lead time to take the countermeasures necessary to deter a new Russian military threat to Europe. Among the indicators that might dictate a change in Western policy would be the establishment of an authoritarian political order in Russia, the election of a new president with a clear-cut imperial agenda, successful government-sponsored efforts to reincorporate one or more of the post-Soviet countries into the Russian state, a large-scale reconstruction of Russian conventional military capabilities, or the deployment of large numbers of Russian troops in the western new states.

An effective Western policy toward Russia requires a determination to remain engaged with Russia's troubled political development despite the temptation to focus on Western domestic concerns and other foreign policy issues. It also requires a clearer definition of the national interests of the principal Western countries. To date these powers have been slow to reconceptualize their national strategies, so decisively shaped by nearly a half-century of the Cold War, and to decide in concrete terms where their national interests and purposes now lie. The problems of the post-Soviet states in defining their national identities have been echoed, albeit in far milder form, in the democratic societies of the West. Yet effective Western policies can be devised only if the Western powers have reconceptualized their interests and objectives in concrete, carefully differentiated terms.

One of those interests is surely the democratic and peaceful evolution of

Russia. The consolidation of Russian democracy is desirable not because it will eliminate serious differences between Russia and the advanced democracies but because it will make those differences easier to manage. At least equally important, democratic consolidation in Russia will reduce the chances of escalating interstate violence in Eurasia and large-scale violence inside Russia itself. Large-scale interstate or civil war in Eurasia would raise many perils. One of the gravest is a dramatic increase in the already substantial risks of nuclear proliferation, not only of nuclear weapons but especially of the components and techniques used to make them. The proliferation of nuclear materials could, in turn, multiply the severe threats that nuclear-armed rogue states and terrorists would pose to Western security.[59]

If this diagnosis is correct, it suggests that the greatest immediate contribution the West can make to the prevention of a resurgence of Russian imperialism is to sustain a policy toward Russia that is geared to the long haul. Even if Russia ultimately puts its relations with other post-Soviet states on a solid nonimperial footing, this process will be painful and protracted; under more propitious circumstances, the decolonization of the twentieth-century colonial empires ruled by West European states required decades.[60] The Western powers can encourage the process by engaging the non-Russian new states, especially those in Europe, in strong political and economic relationships that indicate to Russia that the West regards the treatment of these countries as an important index of Russian behavior. Western governments can also firmly condemn and rebuff Russian efforts to impose destabilizing dual citizenship arrangements against the will of other post-Soviet states. In addition to aiding the economic development of these countries, the West can reform and expand its hitherto clumsy efforts to aid the consolidation of democratic institutions and democratic practices in Russia and the other new states.[61]

Not least, the West can strive to help the post-Soviet countries that are currently at peace to avoid the escalation of internal or third-party conflicts into large-scale violence. This is especially important for countries with significant ethnic Russian populations, since, contrary to a common impression, most ethnic violence in the former Soviet Union has been directed against non-Russian victims, and real outbreaks of violence against ethnic Russians would be especially dangerous for political stability in Eurasia. In the longer run, the expansion of Western military guarantees into Eastern Europe may become necessary to block a recrudescence of Russian imperialism. However, taking such a step at a time when it is clearly not necessary, a time of extreme Russian military weakness and unresolved political debate inside Russia, could defeat the goal of enhanced security it was intended to achieve.

Notes

I am grateful to Raymond Garthoff, Ilya Prizel, and Mikhail Tsypkin for their comments on an earlier version of this chapter.

1. For an analysis that lays special emphasis on the pervasiveness of uncertainty in postcommunist transitions, see Valerie Bunce, "Uncertainty in the Transition: Post-Com-

munism in Hungary," *East European Politics and Societies,* vol. 7, no. 2 (spring 1993), pp. 240–75.

2. Karen Dawisha and Bruce Parrott, *Russia and the New States of Eurasia: The Politics of Upheaval* (Cambridge: Cambridge University Press, 1994), chaps. 1–2; and *The Making of Foreign Policy in Russia and the New States of Eurasia,* ed. Karen Dawisha and Adeed Dawisha, (Armonk, NY: M.E. Sharpe, 1995). For an unusually thorough and nuanced analysis of these matters in Russia and Ukraine, see Ilya Prizel, *National Identity and Foreign Policy in Russia, Poland, and Ukraine* (forthcoming). I am indebted to Professor Prizel for allowing me to read his book in manuscript and cite it in this chapter.

3. Ilya Prizel, "Nation Building and Foreign Policy: The Diplomacy of Ukraine," in *Ukraine in the Post-Soviet World: Building a State,* ed. Sharon Wolchik (Budapest: Central European University, forthcoming).

4. Bruce Parrott, "Soviet National Security Under Gorbachev," *Problems of Communism,* vol. 37, no. 4 (November–December 1988), pp. 1–36.

5. A number of the points in this paragraph are drawn from Prizel, *National Identity and Foreign Policy.*

6. Alexei Arbatov, "Russia's Foreign Policy Alternatives," *International Security,* vol. 18, no. 2 (fall 1993), pp. 15–19; Stephen Sestanovich, "Russia Turns the Corner," *Foreign Affairs,* vol. 73, no. 1 (January–February 1994), p. 93.

7. The real scope of such potential influence is a separate question. For analyses of Turkey's and Iran's objectives toward Russia and the states of the southern tier—and the constraints on those objectives—see the chapters by Kemal Karpat and Mohiaddin Mesbahi in Dawisha and Dawisha, eds. *The Making of Foreign Policy.*

8. The multifaceted debate summarized below actually encompasses at least five overlapping issues: (1) whether Russia has national interests distinct from those of other states, particularly in the West; (2) whether Russia belongs or should belong to the West in the political sense of having a domestic democratic order and adopting Western methods of resolving interstate disputes; (3) whether Russia's geographical location between Europe and Asia requires a foreign policy strategy oriented eastward as well as westward; (4) whether Russia's "Eurasian" popular culture is significantly different from the cultures of Europe and North America and deserves to be protected; and (5) whether that culture is or is not compatible with democratic principles. An especially informative and nuanced discussion of differing national attitudes within the Russian elite is provided by Prizel, *National Identity and Foreign Policy,* from which I have adopted the three categories used in this analysis. Readers should note that these are not hard-and-fast groups. Some Russians have combined ideas from each school of thought, and many individuals have shifted from one school to another over time. Compare Arbatov, "Russia's Foreign Policy Alternatives," pp. 9–14.

9. Prizel, *National Identity and Foreign Policy*; S. Neil MacFarlane, "Russian Conceptions of Europe," and Robert Legvold, "Observations on International Order: A Comment on MacFarlane and Adomeit," *Post-Soviet Affairs,* vol. 10, no. 3 (July–September 1994), pp. 249–50, 266–67, 275.

10. Prizel, *National Identity and Foreign Policy.*

11. The fluidity accounts for the fact that the categories I have used in this discussion differ slightly from those delineated by Shakleina.

12. As late as the summer of 1994, a large majority (69 percent) of respondents in the Russian Federation believed that it was in Russia's interest to work closely with the United States and other Western powers. Only 16 percent disagreed with this proposition, although much larger percentages entertained suspicions that the Western powers were not genuinely seeking to aid the revitalization of the Russian economy. "Russians Want to

Work with West, But Suspect Its Motives," *Briefing Paper* (U.S. Information Agency, Washington, DC), 13 September 1994.

13. A poll conducted in the summer of 1994 showed that although half the respondents endorsed the concept of a strong Russian state, only a fifth (21 percent) ranked the restoration of the USSR as one of the country's most important tasks. Almost twice as many respondents (55 percent) preferred a leader who would develop Russia within its present boundaries to a leader committed to building a new empire encompassing territories from other former Soviet republics (29 percent). *Briefing Paper* (U.S. Information Agency, Washington, DC), 13 September 1994.

14. In a survey conducted during October and November 1994, the respondents characterized a selection of the other new states as follows: Ukraine, 58 percent as friendly and 19 percent as unfriendly; Kazakhstan, 59 percent as friendly and 11 percent as unfriendly; Belarus, 75 percent as friendly and 6 percent as unfriendly; Armenia, 20 percent as friendly and 39 percent as unfriendly; Azerbaijan, 17 percent as friendly and 43 percent as unfriendly; and Estonia, 7 percent as friendly and 67 percent as unfriendly. For most of these countries, more than half of the other responses ranked the country as "neutral"; the remaining answers were "don't know." *Opinion Analysis* (U.S. Information Agency, Washington, DC), 17 January 1995.

15. By a margin of slightly greater than two to one, respondents said in the summer of 1994 that Moscow should never exert pressures on regions outside Russia to reunite with Russia; of the 28 percent minority favoring Russian expansion, only 6 percent were willing to countenance military pressure, whereas 11 percent favored diplomatic pressure and another 11 percent thought economic pressure acceptable as well. *Briefing Paper* (U.S. Information Agency, Washington, DC), 13 September 1994.

16. See, for example, the chapters by Nikolai Kulinich, Peeter Vares, and Oleg Kasenov in Dawisha and Dawisha, eds. *The Making of Foreign Policy.*

17. For an especially sophisticated analysis of the linguistic dimension of national identity in Ukraine, see Dominique Arel, "Ukraine: The Temptation of the Nationalizing State," Russian Littoral Project Working Paper, no. 77, draft, October–November 1994.

18. By the fall of 1994 only one in four respondents foresaw a significant possibility of a military attack on Ukraine by any other country during the next five years, and only one in ten respondents identified Russia as the "biggest threat" among the countries that might launch such an attack. *Opinion Analysis* (U.S. Information Agency, Washington, DC), 17 January 1995.

19. In the Belarusian presidential elections of July 1994, the candidate of the Belarusian Popular Front received 13 percent of the votes cast.

20. Vyacheslau E. Paznyak, "Belarus's Foreign Policy Priorities and the Decision-Making Process," in Dawisha and Dawisha, *The Making of Foreign Policy,* pp. 141–156.

21. Dawisha and Parrott, eds. *Russia and the New States of Eurasia,* pp. 74–76; Paznyak, "Belarus's Foreign Policy Priorities," pp. 141–156.

22. *Opinion Research Memorandum* (U.S. Information Agency, Washington, DC), 18 March 1993.

23. For relevant discussions of current Chinese policy, see Ross H. Munro, "Central Asia and China," in *Central Asia and the World*, Michael Mandelbaum ed. (New York: Council on Foreign Relations, 1994), pp. 225–38; and Michael D. Swaine, "The Modernization of the Chinese People's Liberation Army: Prospects and Implications for Northeast Asia," *National Bureau of Asian Research Analysis,* vol. 5, no. 3 (October 1994).

24. One Western estimate in 1994 set the possible future number of regular troops in Kazakhstan at upwards of fifty thousand, in Turkmenistan somewhere in the range of twenty thousand, and in Kyrgyzstan at around five thousand to seven thousand. Roy

Allison, *Military Forces in the Soviet Successor States,* Adelphi Paper 280 (London: International Institute for Strategic Studies, 1993), pp. 60–62.

25. In addition to Raymond Garthoff's chapter in this volume, see Roy Allison, *Peacekeeping in the Soviet Successor States* (Paris: WEU Institute for Security Studies, 1995).

26. On the reluctance among officers to assume responsibility in the realm of domestic security, see James H. Brusstar and Ellen Jones, *The Russian Military's Role in Politics,* McNair Paper No. 34, Institute for National Strategic Studies, National Defense University, January 1995, pp. 5, 40.

27. Pavel K. Baev, "Russia's Experiments and Experience in Conflict Management and Peacemaking," *International Peacekeeping,* vol. 1, no. 3 (1994), p. 255. See p. 256 on the postponement of the creation of mobile forces.

28. See also Taras Kuzio, "Nuclear Weapons and Military Policy in Independent Ukraine," *The Harriman Institute Forum,* vol. 6, no. 9 (May 1993), p. 7.

29. Timothy J. Colton, *Commissars and Commanders: The Structure of Soviet Military Politics* (Cambridge, MA: Harvard University Press, 1979).

30. Due to such resistance, during the first nine months of 1994 the Ministry of Defense reportedly obtained only 14.6 trillion rubles, rather than the 27.2 trillion to which the state budget formally entitled it for that period. Vitaly V. Shlykov, "Economic Reform and the Military in Russia," paper presented at the Conference on National Security Decision-Making in Russia, Naval Postgraduate School, Monterey, CA, 14–17 November 1994, pp. 17–19. I am grateful to Mikhail Tsypkin for calling this paper to my attention.

31. In the spring of 1992, for example, Foreign Minister Kozyrev continued to emphasize Russia's commitment to nonintervention in the other new states and emphasized the importance of neutrality on the part of the armed forces. A few months later he lamented the Russian intelligentsia's shift toward nationalist views and called for "deep reforms" in the military establishment on the grounds that it was arming separatists in Moldova and the Transcaucasus (presumably Georgia and Azerbaijan). Janel Lardizabal, "Shaping Russia's Policy in the 'Near Abroad,'" unpublished paper, Georgetown University Russian Area Studies Program, November 1994; *RFE/RL Daily Report,* 2 July 1992. On Kozyrev's complaints about military "warmongering," see also Baev, "Russia's Experiments and Experience in Conflict Management and Peacemaking," p. 246.

32. Baev, "Russia's Experiments and Experience in Conflict Management and Peacemaking," p. 257.

33. Ibid., p. 252; Allison, *Peacekeeping in the Soviet Successor States,* pp. 21, 25–28, 52–55.

34. According to a 1994 survey, a substantial minority of officers accepted the need for cuts in the defense budget. See *Militäreliten in Russland 1994* (Munich and Moscow: Moscow SINUS and Gesellschaft für Sozialforschung und Marktforschung, 1994), p. 17. The survey was conducted for the Moscow office of the Friedrich-Ebert Stiftung.

35. In the same survey, slightly less than a third of the military respondents stated that the economy should be based on state planning and distribution, but almost half favored shifting to a market economy, and nearly as many favored full or partial privatization of the defense industries. Ibid., p. 17.

36. On this complex subject, see Keith Bush, "Converting Russia's Defense Industry," *RFE/RL Research Report,* vol. 3, no. 17 (29 April 1994); and Michael McFaul, "Privatization at Four Enterprises," in *Defense Industry Restructuring in Russia: Case Studies and Analysis,* ed. David Bernstein, (Stanford, CA: Center for International Security and Arms Control, 1994), pp. 111–36.

37. According to one analysis, "in 1992 the 'industrial lobby' had shaky democratic credentials." However, "in 1993 the leading parties of business were unimpeachably

the parties of reform. There were almost three times as many candidates for parliament from privatized businesses as from state-owned enterprises." Sestanovich, "Russia Turns the Corner," p. 90.

38. Since 1987 the former Soviet distinction between professional military and civilian political matters—a line never precisely delineated—has been increasingly blurred. In post-Soviet Russia intermittent efforts to prohibit individual officers from participating in civilian politics have been undercut by the personal plight of many military servicemen and by the desire of some professed advocates of a professional military (such as Minister of Defense Grachev) to hold the armed forces in reserve as an instrument of coercion to decide fundamental conflicts against opposition politicians. See Robert Arnett, "Russia After the Crisis: Can Civilians Control the Military?" *Orbis,* vol. 38, no. 1 (winter 1994), pp. 41–57; and Thomas Nichols, *The Sacred Cause: Civil-Military Conflict Over Soviet National Security, 1917–1992* (Ithaca, NY: Cornell University Press, 1993).

39. Sestanovich, "Russia Turns the Corner," pp. 86–87.

40. Ibid., p. 88.

41. For a discussion of the limited evidence on how servicemen voted in the December 1993 elections and the party affiliations of military candidates, see Thomas M. Nichols, "The Impact of the Russian Elections on Civil-Military Relations," in *Does Russian Democracy Have a Future?* ed. Stephen J. Blank and Earl H. Tilford, Jr., (Carlisle Barracks, PA: Strategic Studies Institute, U.S. Army War College, 1994) pp. 84–88. In the summer of 1994 a poll of 615 military officers in six military regions showed that only about 15 percent of the respondents would vote for the Liberal Democratic Party, compared with about 40 percent who would vote for the democratic "Yabloko" coalition and a similar share who would vote for the Communist Party of Russia. In answering this question, respondents were free to identify more than one party for which they might vote. *Militäreliten in Russland,* pp. 21, 23.

42. For two analyses that lend some support to this interpretation, see Prizel, "Nation Building and Foreign Policy"; and Zenovia Sochor, "Political Culture and Foreign Policy: Elections in Ukraine 1994," Russian Littoral Project, Working Paper no. 79, draft, October–November 1994.

43. Allison, *Peacekeeping in the Soviet Successor States,* pp. 31, 37. According to Allison, in 1994 the General Staff aspired to establish thirty such bases, but the feasibility of the plan remained uncertain. Ibid., pp. 19, 53–55.

44. Ibid., pp. 3, 11–12, 51–55.

45. *RFE/RL Daily Report,* 30 March 1994, 28 April 1994, 10 June 1994, 28 November 1994, 29 November 1994. This policy was embodied in a presidential decree in the fall of 1994. Reportedly the practice had already begun in Moldova (where Romania was also reported to have secretly granted citizenship to some local citizens in contravention of Moldovan law).

46. Fiona Hill and Pamela Jewett, *"Back in the USSR": Russia's Intervention in the Internal Affairs of the Former Soviet Republics and the Implications for United States Policy Toward Russia* (Cambridge, MA: Kennedy School of Government, Harvard University, 1994); Zbigniew Brzezinski, "The Premature Partnership," *Foreign Affairs,* vol. 73, no. 2 (March–April 1994), pp. 67–82.

47. Michael Doyle, *Empires* (Ithaca, NY: Cornell University Press, 1986).

48. Elizabeth Valkenier, "Russian Politics in Central Asia," *SAIS Review,* vol. 14, no. 2 (summer/fall 1994), pp. 15–28.

49. As one observer has put it, Russian behavior "is definitely not a traditional imperialism coming from a position of strength, but a quasi-imperialism from a position of weakness." Baev, "Russia's Experiments and Experience in Conflict Management and Peacekeeping," vol. 1, no. 3 (1994), p. 246.

50. John Clapp, "Ukrainian-Russian Energy Relations," SAIS Occasional Papers in Russian Area and East European Studies, September 1994, pp. 18, 20, 27.

51. Toivo Raun, "Post-Soviet Estonia, 1991–1993," *Journal of Baltic Studies,* vol. 35, no. 1 (spring 1994), p. 79; Andrus Park, "Ethnicity and Independence: The Case of Estonia in Comparative Perspective," *Europe-Asia Studies,* vol. 46, no. 1 (1994), p. 69; Richard Rose and William Maley, "Conflict or Compromise in the Baltic States?" *RFE/RL Research Report,* vol. 3, no. 28 (15 July 1994), pp. 26–35; Martin Klatt, "Russians in the 'Near Abroad,'" *RFE/RL Research Report,* vol. 3, no. 32 (19 August 1994), p. 36.

52. See William Crowther, "Moldova After Independence," *Current History* (October 1994), pp. 345–47. See also *RFE/RL Daily Report,* 13 October 1994, 25 October 1994, and 15 November 1994.

53. For two early expositions of the pro- and anti-expansion arguments, see Ronald D. Asmus, Richard L. Kugler, and F. Stephen Larrabee, "Building a New NATO," and Owen Harries, "The Collapse of 'The West,' " *Foreign Affairs,* vol. 72, no. 4 (September–October 1993), pp. 28–54. See also Zbigniew Brzezinski, "A Plan for Europe," *Foreign Affairs,* vol. 74, no. 1 (January–February 1995), pp. 26–42.

54. In particular, the idea of accepting an expansion that includes only countries that do not border on Russian territory would exclude the crucial country, Poland, because of its border with the Russian exclave of Kaliningrad. See *Irish Times,* 5 December 1994.

55. Ilya Prizel, "The United States and a Resurgent Russia: A New Cold War or a Balance of Power Recast?" in Blank and Tilford, eds., *Does Russian Democracy Have a Future?* pp. 135–60.

56. This linkage was spelled out by German Chancellor Helmut Kohl in February 1994. See Baev, "Russia's Experiments and Experience in Conflict Management and Peacekeeping," pp. 253, 260.

57. Prizel, "The United States and a Resurgent Russia."

58. See the comments of Ukrainian Defense Mininster Valerii Shmarov to a visiting NATO delegation, quoted in *OMRI Daily Digest,* no. 32, part II, 14 February 1995.

59. On this issue, see especially Oleg Bukharin, "Technical Aspects of Proliferation and Nonproliferation," and George Quester, "Introduction" and "Conclusion," in *The Nuclear Challenge in Russia and the New States of Eurasia,* ed. George Quester (Armonk, NY: M.E. Sharpe, forthcoming).

60. Karen Dawisha, "Imperialism, Dependence, and Interdependence in the Eurasian Space," in Dawisha and Dawisha, eds., *The Making of Foreign Policy.*

61. Michael McFaul, "Russia's Political Key," *Foreign Affairs,* vol. 74, no. 1 (January/February 1995), pp. 87–99.

Appendix: Project Participants

List of Workshop Participants, July 11–15, 1994
State-Building and Military Power in Russia and the New States of Eurasia

Olga Alexandrova, Federal Institute for Russian, East European
    and International Studies
Roy Allison, Royal Institute of International Affairs
Jonathan Aves, Centre for Defence Studies, King's College
Bess Brown, Radio Free Europe/Radio Liberty Research Institute
Oleg Bukharin, Moscow Institute of Physics and Technology
Julian Cooper, University of Birmingham
Roland Dannreuther, International Institute for Strategic Studies
Christopher Davis, Oxford University
Karen Dawisha, University of Maryland
Renee de Nevers, International Institute for Strategic Studies
    and Hoover Institution
Lawrence Freedman, Department of War Studies, King's College
Sherman Garnett, Carnegie Endowment for International Peace
Raymond Garthoff, The Brookings Institution
Elaine Holoboff, Department of War Studies, King's College
Major General Nicholas Krawciw, U.S. Army, Ret.
Taras Kuzio, School of Slavonic and East European Studies,
    University of London
Murat Laumulin, Ministry of Foreign Affairs, Kazakhstan
John Lepingwell, Radio Free Europe/Radio Liberty Research Institute
Janine Ludlam, Russian Littoral Project
Michael MccGwire, Cambridge University
Steven Miller, Harvard University
David Mussington, International Institute for Strategic Studies

Michael Nacht, University of Maryland
Craig Nation, The Johns Hopkins University Bologna Center
Piotr Ogrodzinski, Department of Strategic Research, Ministry
  of Foreign Affairs, Poland
Bruce Parrott, The Johns Hopkins University School of Advanced
  International Studies
Fiona Paton, Department of War Studies, King's College
Vyacheslau Paznyak, Centre for Strategic Initiatives, Minsk
Wolfgang Pfeiler, Ernst Moritz Arndt University
William Potter, Monterey Institute of International Studies
Alex Pravda, Oxford University
Aline Quester, Center for Naval Analyses
George Quester, University of Maryland
Kjetil Ribe, Department of War Studies, King's College
Anatolii Rozanov, Belarusian State University
Anna Scherbakova, Monterey Institute of International Studies
Tatiana Shakleina, Institute of USA and Canada Studies, Moscow
Maxim Shashenkov, Oxford University
Mikhail Tsypkin, Naval Postgraduate School, Monterey

Index

Abashidze, Aslan, 214
Abiev, Safar, 219
Abkhazia, 94–96, 213–17, 221, 226–27
Achalov, General, 27
Afghanistan, 47, 235, 237, 246, 248, 249–50
Afghanistan syndrome, 99, 280
Agdam (Azerbaijan), 220
Ajaria, 214
Akaev, Askar, 243, 244
Aliev, Gaidar, 218, 219–20, 221, 227, 229
Allison, Roy, 195, 220
All-Ukrainian Cossack Union (VUKS), 173–74
All-Ukrainian UPA Brotherhood, 173
Almaty agreements, 89
ANA. *See* Armenian National Army
Anti-Imperialist—Anti-Communist Front, 171
Anti-Mafia, 171
Antonov, Viktor, 74
APF. *See* Azerbaijani Popular Front
APNM. *See* Armenian Pan-National Movement
Arbatov, Aleksei, 86, 104
Armenia, 229, 282, 294
 and Azerbaijan, 103–4, 222, 282
 foreign policy of, 230–31
 genocide in, 211
 and Georgia, 215, 230
 isolation of, 222
 Lachin "corridor", 218
 military victories, 219–20

Armenia *(continued)*
 national army in, 223, 284
 national security in, 211–12, 292–93
 state building in, 221–24
Armenian National Army (ANA), 223
Armenian Pan-National Movement (APNM), 222–23, 230, 231
Arms market, 67–68, 72, 80*n.10*, 268
 export controls, 29
Ashurov, M., 248
Asia. *See* Central Asia
Aspin, Les, 203
Association of Independent Ukrainian Youth (SNUM), 160
Association of Manufacturers Engaged in the Sphere of National Security, 173
Austro-Hungarian Empire, 135
Authoritarianism, 257
Aviation industry, 67, 80*n.8*
Azerbaijan, 51, 89, 282–83, 294
 administrative structures, 220
 and Armenia, 104–5, 222, 282
 army of, 218–19, 284
 conscription in, 220
 foreign policy of, 227–29
 and Georgia, 215
 national security in, 211–12, 292
 political leadership changes in, 218
 resources of, 217–18
 and Russia, 227–28, 229
 state building in, 217–21
Azerbaijani Popular Front (APF), 218, 219, 228